Wild in the City

Wild in the City

A Guide to
Portland's Natural Areas

Edited by
Michael C. Houck and M.J. Cody

Oregon Historical Society Press
Portland, Oregon

The Audubon Society of Portland has given generous permission to use material originally published in the *Urban Naturalist* from 1982 to 1996. William Stafford's poem on page 78 is published with permission of the Confluence Press.

Cover illustration by Evelyn Hicks
Designed and produced by the Oregon Historical Society Press

© 2000 Oregon Historical Society
Oregon Historical Society Press
1200 S.W. Park Ave.
Portland, OR 97205-2483
www.ohs.org

Third printing, revised
Printed in the United States of America

Library of Congress Cataloging-in-Publication Data
Wild in the city: A guide to Portland's natural areas / edited by Michael C. Houck and M.J. Cody
p.   cm.
Includes bibliographical references.
ISBN 0-87595-273-9
1. Natural history—Oregon—Portland Region—Guidebooks.   2. Portland Region (Or.)—Guidebooks.   I. Houck, Michael C., 1947–   II. Cody, M.J. (Mary Jane)   III. Oregon Historical Society.
QH105.O7 W56 2000
508.795′49—dc21   00-038504

The paper used in this publication meets the minimum requirements of American National Standard for Information Sciences—Permanence of Paper for Printed Library Materials, ANZI Z39.48–1992.

Acknowledgements

To

The Audubon Society of Portland for agreeing in the early 1980s, long before it was popular to do so, to focus on protecting urban wildlife in the Portland area and for recognizing that, as Robert Michael Pyle so aptly writes, "What is the extinction of the condor to a child who has never known a wren?"

And to

All the splendid volunteer writers and illustrators who are dedicated to preserving, restoring, and celebrating nature in a singular place. And without whom this book would not exist.

Thanks to Mike Uhtoff, who as the first Director of the Audubon Society of Portland in the early 1980s, was inspired by *The Curious Naturalist* and insisted we produce our own "curious naturalist" that evolved into *The Urban Naturalist.*

The Urban Naturalist core group: Elayne Barclay, Diana Bradshaw, Laurie Causgrove, Virginia Church, Eric Eaton, Kris Elkin, Richard B. Forbes, Martha Gannett, Tom Hanrahan, Mike Houck, Lynn Kitigawa, Connie Levesque, Harry Nehls, Florence Riddle, Ralph Thomas Rogers, Bob Wilson, Dawn Wilson.

What began as *The Urban Naturalist* cadre grew to include professional and amateur naturalists from across the metropolitan region as we added sites and essays. We are indebted to the citizens; park professionals; federal, state, and local natural resource agency professionals; university professors; and professional writers, all of whom volunteered their talents and time to this project.

Special thanks to Dave Drescher, U.S. Fish and Wildlife Service; Ann Elquist, J.O. Price, and Mark Bosworth, Metro's Data Resource Center; and David Ausherman for assistance with aerial photographs and mapping database. And to Rafael Gutierrez, Martha Gannett, Connie Levesque, and Bob Wilson for transforming hand-scrawled notes and marked-up aerial photos into useful maps. And to J.M. Warner for his support.

*The publication of this volume is made possible
by a generous gift from the*

Margaret Thiele Petti Foundation

and with the support of the

*Audubon Society of Portland
Metro Data Resource Center and
Urban Greenspaces Institute*

Contents

Clark County Watersheds

Preface

"In wildness is the preservation of the world." —Henry David Thoreau

As we strive to protect the wilderness that Thoreau, Aldo Leopold, and successive waves of conservationists have urged us to guard, we need a new mantra. Ironically, it should be "In livable cities is preservation of the wild" if we want to protect the wild places "out there" beyond the urban fringe. For it will only be through the creation of humane, wildlife-rich cities—urban areas where people actually want to live—that we will staunch the flow of an ever-increasing population across the rural landscape and wild lands.

We face significant challenges to creating livable cities. They have been demonized as ecological deserts and undesirable places to live, often by conservationists who would concentrate on protecting only the pristine places. But until we integrate nature with the built environment by protecting and restoring urban streams, wetlands, and woodlands—the "greenfrastructure" of our cities—we will not succeed in producing cities that draw people to urban living rather than pursuing the so-called "American Dream" of escaping to a faux rural lifestyle in the large-lot, sprawl-inducing suburbs.

Wild in the City celebrates the city as a unique, vibrant ecosystem that is worthy of environmental stewardship on its own terms. It is also an invitation and guide to exploring the Portland-Vancouver metropolitan region's urban Greenspaces.

Wild in the City is a product of serendipity and hard work. It began with the publication of *The Urban Naturalist* in the summer of 1982. This seasonal journal, sponsored by the Audubon Society of Portland, was a labor of love written, illustrated, and designed by a cadre of dedicated volunteers from across the metropolitan region—the only publication dedicated exclusively to exploring the natural history of indigenous and exotic plants and animals of the metropolitan region. Our home-grown journal had won numerous awards, but after nearly two decades of quarterly deadlines it was time to take a break.

That's when serendipity interceded. While a larger project, perhaps even a book, was always in the back of our minds, inertia ruled. The energy would have to come from elsewhere. And, that it did—from a totally unsuspected source, an old high school chum, Mary Jane Cody.

—*Mike Houck*

If this project started anywhere, it started on the Clackamas River nearly 30 years ago. Mike and I were teenagers rambling the shores, not observing particularly, but absorbing. Tramping the hidden paths under Douglas fir, up and down the river—berries here, fish there. Birds and beaver, salamanders, crawdads, snakes. Licorice root in the maples, Oregon grape, salal, and poison oak. Spiders and slugs. Freshwater springs trickling down the steep lush mossy maidenhair-ferned banks, spectacular in the tiniest way, green upon green upon green. It was a magic realm teeming with life before we thought about habitat, environment, conservation. We lived in a logging community on the edge of the wild and didn't fathom a time when we would worry about how to keep a beautiful, tender place.

Of course, Mike will say he didn't notice, was more concerned with the next track meet or football game, but he is not considering osmosis. The place just gets you.

On my voyages home from Los Angeles, I'd often tell Houck that we needed to do a book, something on the Steens, or Malheur, places he'd explored and that we had visited on my return visits, but I could never win these discussions. When I moved back to Oregon, I took up the cause in earnest and Mike said what really should be done was a comprehensive naturalist guide to Portland. I agreed. Good. Let's do it. Then, the flash of realization: *The Urban Naturalist*. Would the old crew be willing to update the material? Would others join the cause? Would a publisher take the project on? They would. They did. Here, then, is that effort.

—*M.J. Cody*

Wild In The City is a compilation of nearly one hundred site guides to Greenspaces in the Portland-Vancouver metropolitan region; updated essays from *The Urban Naturalist*; new essays; and several introductory pieces that set the stage for exploring both the natural landscape and the green interstices that have become interwoven with the built environment. The book is organized by watershed since nature does not adhere to political boundaries.

Sites were selected because of each writer's passion for their special spot. As Metro and local park providers add more than 6,000 acres and hundreds of miles to the regional trail network there is no question that *Wild in the City* will be an ongoing project. In the meantime, climb into your boat, kayak, or canoe, mount your bike, or pull on your boots and get wild in the city.

—*Mike Houck & M.J. Cody, Co-Editors*

A Sense of Place

River City

I poke around Portland by boat, catching the sights and smells here at the confluence of two great rivers. At water level I get a new angle on the city. Familiar arrangements can appear to be marvelous.

One summer Saturday I headed up the Columbia and into the Willamette, where the natural and the human gave every sign of getting along. Herons and kingfishers worked the water near the growl and diesel whiff of a working tug. Men in small boats, fishing for steelhead, were catching and tossing back shad. Ocean-going ships took on lumber, gave up Toyotas. In the foreground, an osprey lifted a wide-eyed shad to a nest atop pilings. Behind that, a crane lifted buckets of gravel from a barge.

In the background, Forest Park.

Spring chinook already had passed, but a great sustaining notion of this place is that salmon and steelhead still surge through the heart of a metro area of 1.6 million people. One of America's great fishing holes lies within view of a Merrill Lynch office. Here is a heron rookery within paddling distance of NBA basketball. I can dock the boat and stroll to the world's best bookstore.

Where else on the continent—on the planet—do the great intentions of nature and people come braided so closely together?

It's what sets us apart, and always has. Captain John Couch, a city founder, had his eye on commerce. Seafaring ships could probe this far, and no farther, into the Willamette. But what really got Couch—what he wrote east about—was that he could shoot ducks from his front porch.

Although Portlanders are now a fully urbanized people, the rivers still make us who we are. Never too deeply buried in the urban ethos is an imaginative truth, that not so long ago we emerged to a riverside clearing, the sons and daughters of pioneers, self-selected for rugged individuality.

Oddly, the view from a boat suggests how we insulate ourselves, with bridges and sea walls, from the river. In a darker mood I think we might be as estranged from natural rhythms as any other urban folk. We wrap ourselves in the River City myth but measure our well-being in economic terms. The danger of a working river rises to consciousness only occasionally, when we have to break out the sandbags. Or ludicrously, when a gravel barge runs over a dozen rugged individualists from Nike rowing an unlit dragon boat at night.

As a people we Euro-Americans came here busting woods and taming rivers. Now that we've mostly done that, our sense of identity hinges on what we have left of woods and rivers. We could easily lose what is unique and beautiful about this place. Or we could learn to coexist with the creatures and features of the wild.

The encouraging thing is that we got here too late to have completely screwed things up. And in the last couple of decades, the notion of responsibility toward the habitat has begun to penetrate city life. Kids these days are alert to the connectedness of things—of woods to salmon, and of rivers to our sense of spirit and well-being.

We're getting wiser.

Will we be wise enough in time?

More and more people are coming. As my species crowds the river, the threat is more subtle, more quietly insidious, than toxic outflow from a paper plant. It's the threat of losing in small increments the surrounding greenspaces to asphalt and condos, of leaching small poisons from driveways and lawns. From a boat the river looks and smells clean to me, but I am haunted by warnings: Do not eat the bottom-fish. In the paper I read sickening reports of one-eyed fish with crooked spines, and of river otters with withered penises, shrunken testicles.

Another time, on another outing, I anchored overnight near the edge of city limits. When the morning sun rose high enough to catch the bank, a small river otter emerged from willow roots and slid down into the water. Then another slid the mud bank. And another. Five, in all, liquid black and glossy, climbed up the bank and went skidding down again, nosing into the water without a splash.

The otters started wrestling in the water. They made of themselves an otterball. Heads over tails over heads over tails, the otterball went churning along the surface, throwing up spray. When that got old, they dived and surfaced separately. One little show-off came up near the boat with a crawdad between his teeth. He cracked and ate the crawdad.

When I glanced up, I saw the otters' parents. They had come out to watch, and to watch me watching.

I felt, for my own crowding species, on the spot.

This collection of essays, *Wild in the City*, puts the reader on the spot. Written by people with mud on their boots and a consciousness of place. Locals and visitors will find here a guide book to the wild places. And drama, too. You don't have to live here to wonder—to take heart or to find despair—at whether or not America's greenest big city can save what makes it unique.

By Robin Cody

Life on the Edge

E cologists tell us that things are a little livelier at the edge where two ecosystems come together. Usually more wildlife can be found in this *ecotone* than in either one of the adjacent ecosystems. Moderns find it convenient to see the edge between country and city as a sharp one. To us, it is less a meeting place than a radical disjunction. Still, I think there is value in seeing how indistinct this edge can be.

Portland is blessed with many such beautiful edges—places where the wild and the city are joined. Take Mt. Tabor for example, an oasis of green that is deeply connected to the human environment. On it are playgrounds, picnic areas and old orchards, not to mention a couple of city reservoirs; houses creep up on every flank; and from its summit, Portland's skyscrapers seem closer than their four-mile distance.

Still, the wild has been deliberately retained. The Olmsted brothers, recognizing the old volcano's potential early in the century, made recommendations to preserve its pastoral qualities, and remarkably a good bit of Mt. Tabor's wild character remains. The result is that a spring sunrise can evoke the songs of 20 different songbirds, while nightfall can call forth the low whistle of a screech-owl, or bats winging over one of the reservoirs. And in the grove that stands near the summit there can even be found winter wrens and other deep-woods species.

According to the prevalent twentieth century view, humanity and nature are polar opposites, each an affront to the other. But places like Mt. Tabor reveal a nature that includes people and point toward a way that people can include nature in their plans. If we let them, they can change how we see our place in the natural world.

Such places also suggest another small change in how we look at things. Five hundred years ago, restless explorers—chafing under old-world constraints—brought their dissatisfactions to a new world. With the great voyages of exploration as models, we continue to look at other countries, other cultures, other landscapes as far more attractive than our own. However, Portland's "urban wildernesses" help to moderate that prejudice and remind us of the innate fascination of the near-at-hand.

Wild in the City attends to these local "greenspaces" and to that edge between nature and human culture. Our hope is that it will help to formulate new ways of looking at the natural world. But this place between the urban and the natural isn't always an easy place to be. It is in fact a hard edge, placing great stress on both nature and culture. It calls on nature for tremendous adaptability and on culture for tremendous restraint. But as urban naturalists know, it is also a place of surpassing creativity, suggesting new possibilities for nature and for culture. It's a wonderful place to call home. It's wild. It's where the action is.

By Bob Wilson

Hometown

Wildness is as much perception as reality. As we enter the twenty-first century in this City of Portland, its 510,000 inhabitants (1,363,100 in the tri-county area) think of places like Forest Park, Oaks Bottom Wildlife Refuge, Tryon Creek State Park, or Elk Rock Island as wild. Surely these are undeveloped havens for wild creatures and for people seeking the natural world.

But these places are not the "howling wilderness" described by the pioneer settlers. All is altered since the first developers, Francis Pettygrove and Asa Lovejoy, in 1845 platted 16 blocks near today's Tom McCall Waterfront Park and cleared four streets of Douglas fir and western red cedar from two to six feet through. They whitewashed the stumps because they were traffic hazards. They picked the town name on a coin toss between Portland, Maine, and Boston, Massachusetts.

In 1850, Charles and Sarah Talbot took up 640 acres of Donation Land Claim in the West Hills. It took them three days to pack their possessions from the Willamette River bank upward through the primal forest onto Council Crest. Here, they built their cabin, burned and hewed forest into pasture, garden, and orchard, and raised their family.

The Talbots, now recalled by SW Talbot Road and Talbot Terrace, knew the howl of timber wolves on Portland Heights. They used the beaten trails of Roosevelt elk, lost some of their sheep to black bear and cougar (they called them panther), and hunted black-tailed deer and blue and ruffed grouse in what's now an upscale residential district.

A daughter, Ella, was among the first 50 pupils at St. Helens Hall. She sped down the hill path three miles to school on her black pacing pony. Her parents sent their shepherd dog to discourage any panther.

That was wild in the city like we will never know, and it's one reason the nation sets aside national parks, wildlife refuges, seashores, wild rivers, and wilderness areas.

But those places are distant. We also want to celebrate the mysteries of the natural world, the passage of the seasons, and that sense of participation in an ancient ritual of renewal near our doorstep.

These experiences, in modified form, await in all those special places described in this book. They can even take place over the downtown high-rises where adaptable red-tailed hawks and peregrine falcons hunt the rock pigeon brought here from the Old World.

As boys growing up before World War II in a Portland that was more overgrown hometown than city, we had unlimited freedom to roam on our bicycles. The one parental admonition was, "Be sure you're home by dinnertime."

Our passion was birding. The connection began for David through his family and for Tom in the Portland Public Schools when Nature Study was part of the curriculum. There were terrariums, aquariums, plant presses, and small animal cages for the specimens we collected for study and display.

Mineral, agate, and fossil specimens were big swap items in our varied collections. We used aromatic cigar boxes for our insect collections. It was a hands-on period for young naturalists.

Oregon Audubon Society (now Audubon Society of Portland) supplied the schools with nickel leaflets about each bird, including glorious color prints matched by an outline page that could be hand-colored.

David went to Glencoe Grade School and Tom to Laurelhurst Grade School, but we connected at Multnomah County Library lecture hall, where Audubon members heard from noted area naturalists like William L. Finley, Stanley G. Jewett, Leo Simon, and Alex Walker. They were keen to encourage youthful interests and set the course for our careers.

In 1936 David could walk to school listening to western meadowlarks in the old pasture between 49th and 53rd Avenues on SE Belmont. David's earliest field trips were after school into Mt. Tabor Park. It was fine habitat for California quail, Cassin's and Hutton's vireos, and orange-crowned, yellow-rumped, black-throated gray, and Wilson's warblers.

David showed Tom his first MacGillivray's warbler and lazuli bunting on the brushy west slope of Mt. Tabor. The city reservoirs were a stopover for perky bufflehead ducks. In later years, removal of the natural understory made the park less attractive to a variety of birds.

During spring lunch breaks at Laurelhurst, Tom walked into the old apple orchard and pasture between Glisan Street and Sullivan Gulch (an ice-age flood channel that now holds Interstate 84).

Rooster pheasants crowed, house wrens scolded, and his first western bluebird was there on a fence post. It was as sky blue as in the Audubon pamphlet. Another exciting first in that orchard was a migrant northern shrike. We called it "butcher bird" because it impaled its prey on thorns. The background was there from Nature Study class. As youngsters, this was adventure first hand—pre television or Internet. Providence Portland Medical Center now covers that area.

Birding was not sophisticated in the 1930s. Keyed field guides, powerful binoculars, spotting scopes, and tape-recorded bird calls were all to come. Tom had 4X field glasses, and David scored when his dad bought him 6 x 30 World War I surplus artillery binoculars with solid brass frames.

Our guides were *Birds of the Pacific States* by Ralph Hoffman and *Birds of the Pacific Coast* by Willard Ayres Eliot, the latter illustrated with the Bruce Horsfall paintings now displayed at Audubon headquarters on NW Cornell Road. Eliot and Horsfall were Portland Audubon members.

Tom received the two-volume *National Geographic Book of Birds* for his 12th birthday, and the challenge was to match as many birds as possible with those in the color plates.

From left to right:
Albert W. Marshall,
William H. (Bill) Telfer,
Tom McAllister, and
David B. Marshall
circa 1940

Our territory expanded with narrow-tired Columbia bicycles and New Departure two-speed gearshifts. All the other kids had balloon-tired bikes. We were going the distance. There were no bike lanes, but traffic wasn't a problem.

We were joined through Audubon by another lad, Bill Telfer, from the Garthwick District. As a trio we camped and birded around Portland, the Pacific beaches, and the Cascade Mountains on our bikes. This continued until we went our separate ways in the Army, Navy, and Air Force in World War II.

The edge of town was 82nd Avenue. Beyond were cultivated fields and extinct volcanic buttes. Short-eared owls that resembled giant bouncing moths and harriers swept the fields for voles. Vesper and savannah sparrows nested in the grass, and seasonal flocks of horned lark and pipit rose from underfoot.

In the tall timber and margins of hazelnut, alder, and dogwood on Kelly and Powell Buttes and Mt. Scott, the blue grouse hooted and ruffed grouse drummed when the red flowering currant bloomed.

The bluffs under N Willamette Boulevard overlooked Mocks Bottom, now supplanted with Swan Island Industrial Park. We scrambled down a slope of Oregon white oak and Pacific madrone, avoiding poison oak en route, to get to this back bay of the Willamette River.

Mocks Bottom drew an array of wintering waterfowl. Showy hooded mergansers gathered here for courtship display. The southwest-facing bluff gets the winter sun, and it attracted flocks of yellow-rumped warblers and sometimes a Townsend's warbler. The oak woodland was a perfect niche for white-breasted nuthatches.

If there was one wildest spot for us in that boyhood interlude, it was the Columbia lowlands drained by Columbia Slough, and especially North Portland Peninsula, converging at Kelley Point where the Willamette and Columbia Rivers meet. Lakes, sloughs, seasonal ponds, Oregon ash and black cottonwood forest, sedge meadows, and willow and red-osier thickets intertwined and confused a sense of direction.

After ditching the bikes, we hiked and waded through a holdover of what the naturalist John Kirk Townsend experienced while collecting out of Fort Vancouver in the 1830s. Western painted turtles lined floater logs to absorb the solar heat. A blue heron rookery that filled the cottonwoods was a cacophony of clacking, clicking, and squawking. We called it the "heron factory." Deer, raccoon, mink, otter, and beaver left fine track impressions along silty margins. Wood duck pairs squealed and twisted upward through the hardwoods. Green heron crouched in the bank shadows.

Bullock's orioles brought a splash of tropical color to the green mansions. We focused on a new bird song of rising and falling phrases, as if in conversation, and got our first red-eyed vireo.

Bill recorded one of the last yellow-billed cuckoos in this region.

The once-common cuckoo summered in the understory willow thickets and dined on tent caterpillars. The cuckoo's willow habitat, which tolerated prolonged deep flooding, faded with the taming of the Columbia and Willamette Rivers and an invasion of hybrid reed canarygrass and Himalayan blackberry.

In June, prior to its harnessing, the Columbia River, fresh and swollen from melting snowpack far in the Rocky, Teton, Bitterroot, and Wallowa Mountains, shut us briefly out of our lowland haunts.

Young ears are tuned to sound in all registers. We had a game of running down every natural sound and attaching it to bird, amphibian, or other animal call. We could camp and make a breeding bird list by lying in our sleeping bags and listening to the morning chorus. Night ended with screech and pygmy owl calls and the dawn song of violet-green swallows and purple martins.

David's brother Albert, who later played in the Portland Symphony, brought his flute and called pygmy owls when we camped in Audubon's Pittock Bird Sanctuary.

By August the lowland lakes shrank and exposed mud flats and beds of smartweed and wapato. The best was Ramsey Lake for its assembly of shorebirds en route from tundra nesting grounds. Pectoral sandpipers spread through the sedges to pick insects. Flocks of long-billed dowitcher, least and western sandpiper, and dunlin probed the lake bed before it dried into polygon patterns.

Watchful yellowlegs waded belly deep. The sound of their downscale whistle alarm took the smaller shorebirds with them.

To catch the shorebird show on Ramsey meant an early arrival. By the time the sun burned off the morning cloud cover, the flocks were away, the pectoral sandpipers to the pampas of Argentina. Ramsey Lake is now part of the Port of Portland's South Rivergate industrial area. But adjoining Smith and Bybee Lakes have been encompassed into nearly 2,000 acres of protected urban wetland.

What are the most notable changes in 60 years of city birding? Certainly there's the loss of nighthawks that hunted insects in the neon-lit sky over SW Broadway when we came out of the movie theaters. The wing rush and boom as the male nighthawk dove toward a rooftop where the female laid her two eggs was part of a downtown Portland June or July night.

David's Grandmother Marshall, who lived in a big family home with numerous aunts and an uncle on SW Summit Drive, lamented the disappearance of the western bluebirds that used her birdhouses and the mountain quail that ran through her yard. She also remembered the blue and ruffed grouse, but they can still be found in Forest Park.

The yellow warbler's incisive songs from the tops of the elms lining our residential streets were pure summer music. Did the invasion of cowbirds that might parasitize their nests, the zealous use of insecticide spray, or the steady attrition of tropical forest on the wintering grounds affect the yellow warbler? Those waves of migrating warblers we anticipated each spring are sadly diminished.

The largest of our warblers, the yellow breasted-chat, hid in the tightest cover and was common in the hazel and spirea thickets west of Rocky Butte. Its staccato burst of chucks, chortles, and hews could be heard any time night or day, and especially on moonlit nights. That cover is gone, and so is the chat.

When we ranged the city on our bikes the "sip three beers" call of the olive-sided flycatcher rang from the tallest fir tops, native brush rabbits grazed at wooded road margins, and Swainson's thrushes filled the summer twilight with song. House finches extended their range north and within a few years displaced one of our finest songsters, the purple finch. David found the first house finch nest in 1939. In a few years they frequented every bird feeder in town. The starling invasion followed.

One of our trio's best days was the discovery of a spring-fed marsh off SE Linwood Avenue. It held nesting sora and Virginia rails, pied-billed grebes, and an eastern kingbird that was feasting on dragonflies. Don't look for that marsh; it's filled and gone.

Birds now regularly seen along the Willamette and Columbia that we considered a rarity are Caspian tern, bald eagle, and osprey.

Another range extender, now found citywide, is the western scrub-jay. We found it only in an isolated northern colony on Sauvie Island around the stately oaks.

Anna's hummingbird was not on our Oregon bird list as boys. In the 1970s it was nesting and residing year-round in Portland following a rapid range extension north from California, where it lived on chaparral slopes.

Today, expect itinerant cattle egrets and great egrets in West Delta Park or Sauvie Island. Nesting Canada geese are all along the waterways where none used to reside year-round in western Oregon. Adaptable raccoon and coyote have found city sanctuary (no hunting) and food sources from direct handouts to fruiting ornamentals, unsecured garbage, and dog food.

Nature is dynamic and the flora and fauna change, too often with finality, in response to building, filling, paving, and draining. Climate fluctuates, food sources alter, and distribution patterns advance and shrink. The introduction of exotic species had a dramatic impact on natives. Examples in Portland are English ivy, carp, fox squirrels, starlings, and bullfrogs.

Bringing the wild into our city life, whether through yard plantings, recreating stream corridors and wetlands, or setting aside tracts of natural parkland and trail corridors will continue those pleasures of discovery and connection with nature that we knew in our home town.

By Tom McAllister and David B. Marshall

What Makes A Place?

We come to places individually. We bring with us memories and expectations. Things happen, and new memories are created. What was once a solitary pursuit soon becomes a collective achievement. In its simplest form, making a place involves the interaction of people with and in a specific location. Places are both a cultural phenomenon and a physical fact. In the truest sense, they are intersections.

Sights: mountains, water, clouds, great blue herons, hawks on a pole, salmon in the Sandy River in October, misty fog dragging through trees, fir and maple, trillium, green all the time

The Portland-Vancouver metropolitan area has been an intersection for a long time. It is one of the oldest continuously inhabited places in North America. It is also one of this nation's younger places. It lies at the confluence of two great rivers, the Willamette and the Columbia, and is cradled within valleys that possess some of the best agricultural soils in the world. This has been an abundant landscape. The challenge here has been to cut things back fast enough, not willing them to grow.

Tastes: strawberries, marionberries, raspberries, blackberries, beer, pinot noir, hazelnuts, coffee, crab, clams, salmon

Abundance drew Native Americans to the banks of the region's rivers and, later, settlers across a wide continent. Abundance resulted in a patchwork of small land holdings, the largest owned by the federal government. From an early point, this has been a place with a very fine grain. Rich and poor live in close proximity, and it's not far to go to find green or a job or a store. We don't do development 10,000 acres at a crack. For the most part, the fine grain has reproduced itself. We are still a land of towering trees, sweeping landscapes, and small things.

Touch: moss, snow, sand, bark, sun

This metropolitan area is Oregon's most urban place. It's a home-grown urbanity, however. Our cities have grown historically in service to the timber and agricultural economies of the entire Columbia Basin. Our suburbs have grown incrementally from historic town centers. Yet, we find ourselves in the midst of a profound transition. The growth that we've experienced in the 1990s is occurring for reasons not rooted in the productive capacity of the landscape. Make no mistake: agriculture is still an important and vital component of this metropolitan region. Washington, Clackamas, and even populous Multnomah Counties are all major contributors to Oregon's annual agricultural take. Nonetheless, the fundamental shift in our economy stands as a watershed in our history, and a harbinger of cultural change.

Sounds: geese calling, wind, rain, waves, bird songs, winter silence

Furthermore, despite being "the City," it's still possible to take a day trip to the wilderness. Put a compass point on Pioneer Square in Downtown Portland, and then draw a circle with one edge on the Pacific shore and the other close to the Deschutes River. Consider everything that lies within that circle, the diversity of landscapes, resources, communities, and experiences. This is a rich legacy. Few cities in the nation can boast putting oceans, mountains, fresh strawberries, spawning salmon, and spectacular waterfalls in the same sentence, much less in the same day.

Smells: ocean, damp soil, flowers, smoke, Camas paper mill

In a similar sense, consider that this is a place where close to 90 percent of the school-age children attend the public schools. Here, civic participation, whether through neighborhoods or simply sitting down with the mayor, is a popular pursuit. We read more, subscribe in lower numbers to cable TV, and spend less time at theme parks than residents of other metropolitan areas.

We are known for seeking our own solutions, even when they make us look different from other places. The Bottle Bill made our roadsides look different. Our Beach Bill preserves public access for all of us to what is arguably one of North America's most stunning landscapes. Both of these acts, and more, stand as testament to our interest in getting it right even if it's not the way they do it in other cities or in textbooks.

Simply put, this is an intentional place. Our ability to be intentional rests squarely on our belief in the validity of what citizens have to think. This isn't easy work, and it isn't always fun. Still, citizens expect to share in the task of getting arms around problems and formulating solutions. Perhaps our willingness to connect with each other in ways that others haven't has something to do with the overwhelming sense that we share a common fate in an incomparable landscape.

Places: Mt. Tabor, Sauvie Island, Saturday Market, Pioneer Square, the Oregon City Elevator, Jackson Bottom, Block A, Waterfront Park, Tualatin Commons, Officer's Row, the Gorge, Elk Rock Island, Oaks Bottom/Oaks Amusement Park, the Grotto

Still, not all is well or done. Places are never done. Each person, each exchange, each interaction adds to what we have and what we are. We can't shake our history, and we're constantly in the process of becoming a different place. You can view this as paradoxical or as simply a fact of life. Change is a fact of life for places. Caring makes a difference. In the coming years we have some critical questions to address. No matter how many people come here, and no matter when they get here, what ought to be true about this place? How can the change that comes from both growth and decline help to improve the fit between people and the landscape? What would our civic conversation look like if instead of addressing what we'll be adding to this place, we begin to think about what it will mean for this place to mature?

What we've lost: the tip of Mt. St. Helens, the taste of wild spring chinook, stars through the night glow of cities, the sense that no one knows we're here...

By Ethan Seltzer

The Emerald Compass

The Portland area enjoys a Pacific Maritime climate: year-round mild temperatures, frequent but moderate precipitation for eight or nine months, and a pronounced dry period during the three or four warmest months. The hospitable growing conditions within the densely populated Portland urban area help create a situation where trees are an important landscape element. Within cities and towns the pattern of trees and associated vegetation is known as the "urban forest," and its distinguishing characteristic is that its composition and pattern is a product of the physical environment and the people. Most urban forestry specialists would agree that the urban forest is as much about people as about trees.

How does the urban forest differ from the pre-urban forest that existed here only a little more than 150 years ago? One answer can be framed in terms of three d's— density, diversity, and deadwood.

Density

Over large areas forest density may be described by how much of the area is in continuous canopy. Historical evidence indicates that at the time of the Oregon Trail migration, the majority of the Portland region was in a continuous canopy. Except for some remnant patches, most of that original forest is gone, replaced by an increasingly dense pattern of development. While there are trees along roads and interspersed between buildings, there are few locales where the canopy of trees is nearly as continuous as in the pre-urban forest.

The major exceptions to the pattern of continuous forest were large segments of the Willamette and Tualatin Valleys, where records indicate Indians used fire to suppress the forest and to maintain localized areas of grassland with widely-scattered and discontinuous canopy of oaks, creating an oak-savanna prairie. Most of the former prairie areas are also gone. And in some former prairies the amount of continuous canopy may be much greater today than before urbanization. Overall, however, the density of continuous canopy today over the Portland region is significantly lower than in pre-urban times.

Diversity

Approximately 29 species of trees are identified as native to the pre-urban Portland area (Jensen et al.). Most prominent in the mix were Douglas fir, western hemlock, grand fir, big-leaf maple, vine maple, Oregon white oak, red alder, Oregon ash, and black cottonwood. In contrast, a recent survey of trees (Reynolds and Dimon) describes 132 species of trees in the yards, parks, public spaces, and roadsides of the greater Portland urban forest. The current figure represents a 450 percent increase over the pre-urban forest. While all the native trees remain, their numbers are greatly reduced, and many are largely confined to remnant strips along streams, in wetlands, and on hillsides. More than three-fourths of the current species come from places other than Oregon, primarily the eastern United States, Europe, and Asia. Particularly numerous are species of maples, cherries, and plums.

The dominant influence in the composition of the urban forest is not a slowly-evolving natural selection process, but human preference based on such factors as size, shape, color, texture, showy flowers, maintenance demands, and emotional attachment. The result of this process of human selection is a much greater diversity of plants in the Portland area today than there has been at any time in the past.

Deadwood

In any forest, tree limbs die due to shade, disease, or physical injury. A dead limb stays, decaying and weakening until it falls to the ground, where it is attacked by insects, fungi, and other organisms. Likewise, when a tree dies in the pre-urban forest it remains standing as a snag, perhaps for many years, though eventually it too comes down and becomes more compost.

In the urban forest, this pattern is disrupted. Dead limbs and dead trees are assumed to be a hazard to people or property. Only in rare instances—such as in a remnant forest patch, away from frequent human traffic—is deadwood left to stand or lie on the ground. Frequently it becomes firewood or is chipped, mulched, and moved off-site. Nutrients and organic matter are lost, resulting in a nutrient-poor soil.

Trees and Wildlife

If we consider the forest as habitat, the three d's of density, diversity, and deadwood also help to describe changes in wildlife within the urban forest.

A continuous forest canopy means there are naturally large areas of "interior forest," that is, environments dominated by shade/speckled sunlight, cooler temperatures, reduced wind, and more moist conditions. By contrast, the discontinuous character of the urban canopy provides more sunlight and air movement, creating a habitat that tends to be warmer, breezier, and drier. Urban forest trees tend to be adjacent to open areas, creating more edge and less interior forest. Wildlife preferring an open, edge-like woodland, consisting of a simple structure of canopy and ground cover and having generally widely-spaced trees, will be favored. Thus, the reduced density of trees in the urban forest means some species lack critical habitat and are excluded from the urban forest. Others preferring edge habitat will increase in number.

The greater diversity of tree species in the urban forest is not simply a quantitative difference in terms of number of species, but also represents a qualitative difference with regard to the characteristics of the species. The urban forest has a higher proportion and variety of flowering trees than the pre-urban forest and it contains a greater variety of fruiting trees, such as the naturalized mountain ash (*Sorbus* sp.), plums/cherries (*Prunus* sp.), and crabapples (*Malus* sp.). The result of these qualitative differences is that wildlife species—primarily a variety of insects—

associated with flowers will have enhanced food sources. They in turn may serve to attract other wildlife that feed on them. In addition, species that prefer fruit and berries will find more variety in the urban forest, though not necessarily greater numbers of fruit-bearing trees.

A second aspect of diversity relates to the organization of the vegetation. In the natural forest there are a series of vertical zones, identifiable as an upper canopy, middle canopy, shrub layer, and ground cover. This stratification of the vegetation represents a variety of nesting, feeding, and cover habitats. The structural character of the urban forest often consists of canopy and ground cover, more closely resembling a savanna. The many species of wildlife that depend on the middle layers of the forest for their habitat are thus not accommodated.

Deadwood, both standing and down, provides habitat for a variety of wildlife, including insects, birds, reptiles, and small mammals. In some cases, such as cavity nesting birds and insect-eating species like woodpeckers, deadwood may be more important than a live tree. These species may occur only infrequently, or not at all, in the urban forest.

Threats to the Urban Forest

The urban forest is susceptible to typical threats that face the pre-urban forest: diseases, insects, storm damage, and competition from other plants. Additionally, in the urban environment tree losses are magnified by a number of other stresses: poor soils, reduced air quality, increased heat and dryness due to the urban heat island, and physical damage. Other stresses come from competition with non-native plants such as English ivy (*Hedera helix*); improper maintenance, such as tree topping, that can cut short the life of a tree; or failure to water non-native trees that lack resistance to the late-summer drought. More direct human action may also affect the urban forest, such as premature tree removal due to perceived maintenance demands, a change in what species are "fashionable," or simply the desire to "open up the view."

Portland's Emerald Compass

The issue of views and trees is an extremely important long-term challenge for the greater Portland area. As impressive as the vegetation of the immediate urban landscape may be, the most lasting impression comes when looking beyond the immediate surroundings. From almost any location in the Portland region, in every direction as far as the eye can see, is a surrounding green rim of tree-covered mountains, buttes, and hills. To identify this surrounding rim of green landscape, I use the term "Emerald Compass."

The "emerald" portion of the term captures the color of the landscape, and, in its precious-gem denotation, reflects the natural resource wealth that the forest represents. For most people the "compass" portion of the term conjures the image of an instrument for determining direction—an appropriate association, given the important role that the forest has had in setting the course for a major portion of Portland's evolution. But a stronger association is offered by another meaning of the term "compass," that of an encircling rim or edge, as in the word "encompass." This second meaning captures the physical presence and enveloping character of the forest that defines the circumference of the urban landscape. In this second meaning, the term also reflects a subtle historical connection, being reminiscent of the *Emerald Necklace*, the name of the renowned park system surrounding Boston—the city which, but for the chance flip of a coin, would have been Portland's namesake. A major difference, of course, is that Boston required the genius of Frederick Law Olmsted to design the Emerald Necklace, while Portland's Emerald Compass is an undeniable fact of our geography.

A number of studies have demonstrated the role that a view of green vegetation can play in relieving human stress and helping regenerate people emotionally and psychologically. A key part of the much-mentioned "quality of life" that Portlanders enjoy stems from the psychological amenity that the Emerald Compass provides. Such areas as the buttes of east Multnomah County, Forest Park in the northern center of the region, and the Tualatin Mountains/Skyline Drive in the west are key defining elements of the region. As these areas come under increasing pressure for development, we are incrementally losing one of the most valuable heritages of the local landscape. More than any other element of the landscape, the highly visible Emerald Compass serves as a symbol of the past, present, and future of the region.

By Joseph Poracsky

References

Jensen, Edward C., and Charles R. Ross. *Trees to Know in Oregon.* Extension Circular 1450. Corvallis: Oregon State University Extension Service and Oregon Department of Forestry, 1994.

Reynolds, Phyllis C., and Elizabeth F. Dimon. *Trees of Greater Portland.* Portland: Timber Press, 1993.

Oceans, Volcanoes, and Cataclysms

Portland's diverse landscapes are due, in large part, to a long and varied geologic history, including ocean and river sediment deposition, volcanic eruptions, river erosion, and floods of unimaginable proportions.

Oceans, Volcanoes, and Mountain-Building: The Early Days

The oldest rocks exposed in the metropolitan area consist of shale and sandstone, indicating that what is now western Oregon was part of a shallow ocean tens of millions of years ago. These sedimentary rocks, which exceed 8,000 feet in thickness, are exposed in places along the base of the Tualatin Mountains (locally referred to as the Portland Hills) and in the coastal foothills west of the Tualatin Valley. Excellent exposures of these rocks can be seen in road cuts along Highway 26 as it climbs into the Coast Range. About 16 million years ago, stresses in the earth's crust caused regional uplift, raising western Oregon above sea level. This upheaval ended deposition of marine sediments, and ushered in development of the Coast Range.

At the time western Oregon was a shallow ocean, the volcanic Cascade Range was forming to the east. Basalt and andesite lava flows of the early Cascade Range compose much of the landscape in eastern Clark County, Washington north of Washougal, Washington.

About 16 million years ago, the marine sedimentary rocks in the Portland area were covered with several hundred feet of Columbia River Basalt, lava which originated from tremendous eruptions in eastern Oregon and Washington. These massive lava flows covered much of central Washington and north-central Oregon, continued through the ancestral Cascade Range into what is now the northern Willamette Valley, and on through the Coast Range to the ocean. The flows now underlie much of the Portland metropolitan area and can be seen in many places in and around Portland, including the Portland Hills, along the Willamette River south of Oregon City, and, of course, east of Portland in the spectacular Columbia River Gorge.

Following the emplacement of the Columbia River Basalt, stresses in the earth's crust warped and faulted the once-flat basalt into a series of basins, including the Portland Basin, the Tualatin Basin, and the central Willamette Valley. The Portland Basin comprises the Portland-Vancouver area and extends east to the Sandy River. The Tualatin Basin encompasses Beaverton, Hillsboro, and Forest Grove, and the central Willamette Valley extends from Salem to Canby. The remnant basalt uplands separating the basins are known to us today as the Portland Hills, Pete's Mountain, the Chehalem Mountains, and Cooper and Bull Mountains, some of the most prominent landforms in the Portland Metropolitan area.

Generalized Geologic Map of the Portland Metropolitan Area

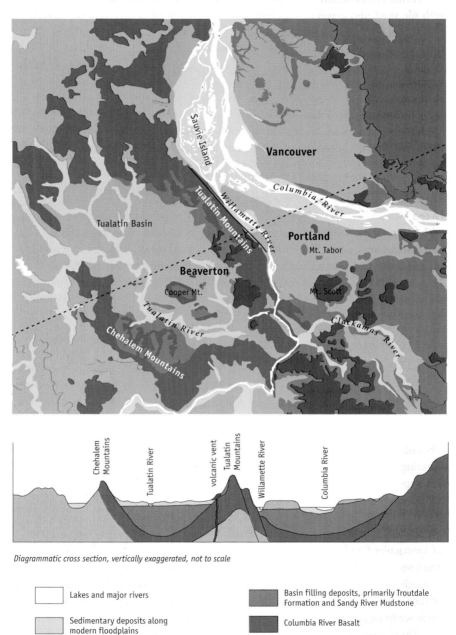

Diagrammatic cross section, vertically exaggerated, not to scale

☐ Lakes and major rivers	▨ Basin filling deposits, primarily Troutdale Formation and Sandy River Mudstone
▨ Sedimentary deposits along modern floodplains	▨ Columbia River Basalt
▨ Glacial flood deposits and older stream deposits	▨ Volcanic rocks of the Cascade Range
▨ Boring Volcanics (basaltic lava)	▨ Marine sedimentary and volcanic rocks
- - - - Approximate line of cross section	╲ Portland Hills fault

Geology modified from the Geologic Map of Oregon *by G.W. Walker and N.S. MacLeod, 1991, U.S. Geological Survey*

As the Portland and Tualatin Basins were developing, they were continually filled with silt, sand, and gravel transported by the Columbia River and by Cascade and Coast Range streams. These basin-filling sedimentary deposits are over 1,400 feet thick in the center of the basins. The coarser-grained sand and gravel deposits, which occur mostly in the Portland Basin, are now generally known as the Troutdale Formation. The finer-grained deposits, which occur in both the Tualatin and Portland Basins, are generally referred to as the Sandy River Mudstone.

During and after deposition of the basin-filling sediments, between approximately two million and 500,000 years ago, numerous volcanic eruptions occurred. The lava flows and vent deposits from these eruptions are known as the Boring Volcanics, because they were first described near the town of Boring. Small volcanic eruptive centers can be found in Portland at Rocky Butte, Mt. Tabor, Kelly Butte, and Powell Butte. Eruptive centers occur in Clark County, Washington at Green Mountain, Brunner Hill, and near Battle Ground. Larger eruptive centers with more extensive lava flows include Mt. Scott, the uplands around Damascus and Boring, and Swede Hill and Mt. Sylvania in the Tualatin Basin. The entire upland south of Oregon City is capped by lava flows of the Boring Volcanics.

Wearing It Down
No sooner had volcanism and sedimentation built up hills and filled basins than streams began to erode the landscape. The volcanic rocks, being resistant to erosion, protected the underlying basin-filling sediments from erosion in some places. Several East Portland hills that are composed of basin-filling gravel and protected from erosion by overlying lava include Mt. Tabor, Kelly Butte, Powell Butte, and Mt. Scott.

Catastrophic Floods
The last major geologic event in the Portland Metropolitan area is perhaps the most amazing and unique of all: floods of gigantic proportions. Between 15,000 and 12,000 years ago, during the last Ice Age, glacial ice dammed the Clark Fork River in western Montana, impounding a tremendous volume of water estimated to be about half the volume of Lake Michigan. This ice-dammed reservoir is known as glacial Lake Missoula. The ice dam formed and failed, probably multiple times, sending a series of spectacular floods across eastern Washington, down the Columbia River Gorge, and into the Willamette Valley. Peak flood discharge is estimated to have been approximately 386 million cubic feet per second. For comparison, the average discharge of the Columbia River at The Dalles is about 192,000 cubic feet per second. There is evidence to suggest that there may have been as many as 80 individual floods.

Flood water reached an elevation of about 400 feet above sea level in the Portland area, and spilled into the Tualatin Basin through the gaps now occupied by Lake Oswego and the Tualatin River. Water flooded into the central Willamette Valley through the Willamette River gap south of Oregon City. Water also rushed from the Tualatin Basin into the central Willamette Valley through a low spot in the divide between Sherwood and Wilsonville, creating a region of scoured, bare basalt bedrock known as the Tonquin Scablands. The rushing water deposited a large amount of silt, sand, and gravel in the Portland area, and its erosive force sculpted much of the landscape, creating some prominent landforms. For example, next time you struggle up the Alameda ridge on your bicycle or whiz down its steep south slope, think about the fact that it is a gigantic gravel bar formed by floodwater downstream of Rocky Butte. Sullivans Gulch, the dry canyon now occupied by the Banfield Freeway (I-84) and the MAX line, was scoured by floodwater channeled between Rocky Butte and Mt. Tabor.

Since the Ice Age Floods, sea level has risen, causing the Columbia and Willamette Rivers to deposit sediment and meander on their floodplains. These processes have given rise to the numerous lakes, sloughs, and side channels common in areas such as North Portland and Sauvie Island.

The geologic history of the Portland metropolitan area is a continuing story. Geologic processes such as volcanic eruptions, earthquakes, floods, and landslides are continually affecting the landscape. Human activities can influence some of these geologic processes. Our understanding of the geology of the Portland area is still evolving, and geologists continue to work to understand how the geologic history and geologic processes affect our environment and our lives.

By Marshall Gannett

References

Beeson, Marvin H., Terry L. Tolan, and Ian P. Madin. *Geologic map of the Lake Oswego Quadrangle, Clackamas, Multnomah, and Washington Counties, Oregon.* Oregon Department of Geology and Mineral Industries, Geological Map Series GMS-59, 1989.

——. *Geologic map of the Portland Quadrangle, Multnomah, and Washington Counties, Oregon, and Clark County, Washington.* Oregon Department of Geology and Mineral Industries, Geological Map Series GMS-75, 1991.

Madin, Ian P. *Geologic map of the Damascus Quadrangle, Clackamas and Multnomah Counties, Oregon.* Oregon Department of Geology and Mineral Industries, Geological Map Series GMS-60, 1994.

Trimble, D. E. *Geology of Portland, Oregon and adjacent areas.* U.S. Geological Survey Bulletin 1119, Washington, D.C.: U.S. Government Printing Office, 1963.

No Vacancy

In nature, the "No Vacancy" sign is always out. Biology tends to fill its niches. Ecologists speak in terms such as "species packing" and "carrying capacity" to describe how a piece of habitat enrolls as many species, and as many individuals of those species, as its resources can support. Of course disequilibria may occur, through extinction or overpopulation. But adjustments may be expected, with invasive aliens or native generalists moving into the vacated habitat, and busts will follow booms. The resulting biota may well be simplified and less stable than the old, but it is rare for habitat to remain vacant—unless the habitat itself is replaced by something else, like strip malls.

"Vacancy," however, possesses another meaning entirely—one imbued with charm, fascination, and the invitation to discovery. I refer to my favorite oxymoron: the blessed Vacant Lot. What, after all, is less empty than a vacant lot to a curious kid? On a recent trip to the Southeast, I was entranced by the many species of trilliums, violets, and swallowtails, if saddened by the proliferation of strip malls and "palace projects"—one- to five-acre subdivisions clotted with enormities thrown up by developers for people with too much money and an edifice complex. One of the best things I saw was a wooded branch stream with the wonderful name Thicketty Creek, which was still just that.

Fortunate is the child who grows up close to a thicket, a good ditch or "crick" or watercourse of any kind, or an unbuilt, undeveloped field. These are the kinds of humble places where most people make their first deep connection with nature, if they ever do at all. Once, folks lived near great mountains, meadows, forests—and some still do. But with most of the bloated population now huddled in the cities and suburbs, the vacant lot takes on heroic proportions. It becomes the job of the overlooked rough, the fragments of secondhand lands, and all such hand-me-down habitats to provide initiation for kids who would know more of the world than walls and malls afford.

A woman told me recently how lucky she was to grow up on a family lot of five acres surrounded by farms in Minnesota. She could walk out and find grouse bursting from the dust, and sometimes even spy the rare lady's-slipper orchid. Lucky, indeed. For me, it was an old irrigation ditch on the Colorado plains that furnished my escape hatch from the grid, and that of countless other Denver kids over the ages. I worry that fewer and fewer kids grow up with even a back lot or an uncut alley to explore. And when they have some rough ground nearby, it is often off limits. After a reading I gave in Denver, concentrating on this topic, I was approached by a person who handed me a clipping from the morning paper. It seemed two boys were arrested and booked—not for stealing cars or trashing buildings, but for digging a foot-deep hole in Jefferson County Open Space. Somehow they thought that, on land with such a name, they could make a fort. Whither the culture whose kids no longer go forth to make forts?

In *Having Everything Right*, hands down the best book of Northwest essays, Kim Stafford wrote of his "Separate Hearth:"

> Two blocks from home the human world dwindled to a path threading through nettle and alder. A spider web across the path meant no one was there before me. I crawled under its fragile gate to solitude and was gone.
>
> ...The Woods was a wild tract developers had somehow missed in their swathe through old Oregon. It probably stretched about three miles long by two miles wide, and was surrounded by the city of Portland and its suburbs. Raccoon, beaver, salmon, deer, awesome pileated woodpeckers, and exotic newts were among the secret lives of the place...
>
> A huge tree had fallen, and where the root-mass tore out from the earth a hollow was left that no one could see, roofed over with the arched limbs of fir, woven with sword fern and moss, with leaf litter, until the roof became a knob of the earth itself. Like Ishi, I approached by a different way each time, so as not to wear a path, and I covered the entrance to my den with boughs broken, not cut in a human way.

In his "separate hearth," Kim spent much of his boyhood, finding almost everything that was important. Often, speaking to groups, I ask them how many had such a place. Almost all the hands go up. Not that many embraced their cricks and trees and forts with the fervor and completeness that Stafford devoted to his secret spot, but I find most people can remember an outdoors-place that made a difference to how they view the world. Yet when I ask how many could return and find that place substantially unchanged, few hands rise and faces drop. It seems most folks know the betrayal of special places ruined. So what difference does it make?

I have written (in *The Thunder Tree: Lessons from an Urban Wildland*, Lyons Press, 1998) about a phenomenon I call the extinction of experience. By this scenario, people become increasingly disaffected from nature the more that common species and elements are lost from their immediate vicinities. When experience of nature dries up within one's radius of reach—which is smaller for the very old, young, poor, and disabled—one tends to see less, know less, thus care less. And when caring flees, conservation heads out the back door, and further local extinctions ensue. I am convinced that this is one of the most insidious cycles driving the environmental crisis.

Now there is a timely corollary that worries me almost as much as the extinction of experience itself. Cities are beginning to address growth management in a meaningful way, and this is unquestionably a good thing. If urban growth boundaries can be maintained, sprawl can be contained. But the UGB has a dark flip side, called infilling. When growth is contained but not stemmed, pressure increases to fill in the last blank spots on the developers' maps. Infilling is touted as one of the remedies for more livable cities. Maybe so, when densities are increased in poorly used zones to the benefit of community structure as well as outlying lands. But saving the rural should not be the only goal of growth management. Every time infilling takes a vacant lot, either through direct development or conversion to formal parkland, something precious is lost in the heart of the living city.

Portland, and every city, needs to maintain a generous ration of what British nature writer Richard Mabey calls the "unofficial countryside"—undedicated, unmanaged, undeveloped ground where unplanned, unsupervised, and unexpected discovery can take place. Realtors tend to refer to such places as "raw land," and others call it "waste ground." But in my view, nothing is less wasted than ground where the hand of man has held back and the minds of boys and girls can engage with plants and animals and dirt; nothing more sacred than land that is yet raw, and ripe with surprise.

The big urban wilds—the Tryon and Forest Parks, the Oaks Bottoms, the rivers and islands—are extraordinarily important. But the little places, the corners and crannies and ravines, the urban greenspaces writ small, claim their own significance. In England, the ancient Commons may still be found, benisons among the urban landscape. But we have no such commons. If we are to remain a people who love the land, we must champion the scraps of wild land within the reach of the children as well as the wilderness, the remnants along with the whole bolts. When kids actually put down the mouse and go outdoors, they must find more than a No Vacancy sign where once their parents played.

By Robert Michael Pyle

Coyote in the Field

L ast week I was driving past a field in town when a big yellow sign staked in tall grass caught my eye: "Mary's Woods." In the background, inexorable bulldozers were peeling back the sod to begin construction of the new retirement center. I mourned the field, and in the same moment I wondered, Will I live there someday? Stakes with fluttering orange flags marked the bulldozers' path across the wavering grass. I stopped the car then to watch them work, and as I gazed, I remembered.

I remembered the Sunday some years ago when an odd patch of gray in that same field had stopped me. Cruising home from church, I had pulled the car over, and stared. Was it a hay bale I saw? A dog, alert at the center of the field? No, it was coyote there, electric with attention, hunting mice. Broad daylight modern times, a busy suburban place, and there was the wild, the old, the native, and the free— coyote. It seemed to be standing on its toes, with a kind of suspended spring that defied gravity even when it was still. I had never witnessed such vivid attention, in animal or human being. The coyote turned—danced—prayed passionate in the grass with a devotion to what was underfoot beyond anything I had seen in my home country.

In that field then, as I watched the bulldozers lumber across the same ground, it struck me what the next age will be like. The ponderous and the powerful— the bulldozers among us—by old habit will do their work. But the wild and the inventive will dart among them, and prevail. For in the new age, the master will not be the one who knows, but the one who can learn quickly, can listen without bias, can respond to the slightest signal. The leader will be the one with that power the poet John Keats called "negative capability"—the capability to be utterly sensitive to what is possible, open to instinct, available to an idea that is utterly new. The happy citizen of this place will be the one with access to the wild in the city—in the marshes, the stream margins, the forests, and the self.

And this insight brought clear to me what an artist does in our time. A writer, a musician, a painter, a child—any being eager as a wild coyote—will find a place of freedom among the tame, and work there in the spirit of our oldest ways. A computer, for all its lightning capabilities, will lumber along with predictable results, unless the coyote spirit of the inventor takes hold. And the great machine of our money will grind through peoples' lives, unless some creative spirit finds a way to turn dollars into alert human expression.

They say that in the world of drama whenever an animal or a child appears on stage, the audience comes suddenly alive. For we have no idea what is about to happen. A child might howl, or jump off the stage; a cat might climb the curtain. No famous actor can match that wild being. On stage, it is that way. And in the city, it is that way: whenever we see the heron fly over, or hear the winter wren sing, or glimpse the peregrine falcon dive. To the extent the wild spirit prevails, we citizens will dwell in a possible future.

As I looked out over the field that would soon be a retirement center, my gaze bored through the dust scared up by the bulldozers. There beyond them, in a wild thicket of blackberry, our future crouched, unafraid.

By Kim Stafford

How to Use This Book

Wild in the City is a general introduction to the natural history of the Portland-Vancouver metropolitan region and compilation of Greenspace sites, including an overview of local and regional Greenspace efforts. The sites were selected to ensure the best sampling of Greenspaces within the metropolitan area. Since new sites are constantly being acquired and developed throughout the region, we hope to include these in subsequent editions.

Sites are organized by watershed. Although this may at first appear confusing, this approach is consistent with a growing awareness of the importance of streams, rivers, and their watersheds to the protection and restoration of Greenspaces. Natural areas do not respect artificial jurisdictional boundaries any more than the plants or animals that use them. Progressing down a stream or river provides a more realistic understanding of how natural areas develop and interact with one another.

Because of the nature of nature in the Pacific Northwest, we cannot guarantee that you will find the sites exactly as described in this book. Please be aware that adverse weather, development, or maintenance may lead to closures or restrictions, or make areas impassable or even dangerous. In our climate you may encounter mudslides, high water, fallen trees, or overgrown paths. Although care is taken to maintain many of the paths or trails, these Greenspaces are not manicured parks, but wild places where nature prevails. It is recommended that you bring any necessary gear for your excursion and attempt only hikes, bike trips, or boating for which you have adequate knowledge, skill, and physical conditioning.

Rules and regulations of some sites may change without notice, so please check with the appropriate site managers and owners for current information, which you can find at the back of this book.

Our primary responsibility is to be good stewards of these natural areas. Take only pictures and memories; leave only footprints. Please be considerate of private property as well.

In preparing site guides, the authors and editors relied on the following map references: *The Thomas Guide, Portland Metro Area 2000*, published by Thomas Bros. Maps, 1999. *Road Atlas, Clark County, Washington*, published by Clark County Department of Assessment and GIS, 1998. These are abbreviated in the text as "Thomas Guide" and "Clark County Road Atlas," respectively. Readers are encouraged to use these or other reliable maps and atlases to plan excursions.

Specific styles and standards for naming animals and plants varies from reference to reference. The following references provided the citation standards used in *Wild in the City*. *Flora of the Pacific Northwest: An Illustrated Manual* by C. Leo Hitchcock, and Arthur Cronquist. *Familiar Birds of the Northwest* by Harry B. Nehls.

.... Existing Trail

----- Future Trail

(40) Part of the 40-Mile Loop

P Parking

R Restrooms

B Boat/Canoe Launch

Maps are oriented with North at the top unless otherwise indicated.

About the Trails

Local and regional trail locations may change over time. Future trail alignments are generalized, based on long-range planning maps. They will likely change as they are constructed. The most current information was used for the Wild In The City *maps. If in doubt about any trail locations contact the local park provider and/or Metro's Regional Trail Program.*

Regional Watersheds and Site Locations

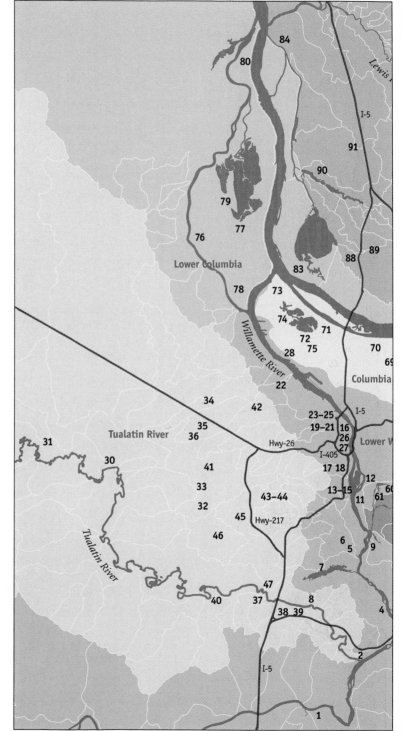

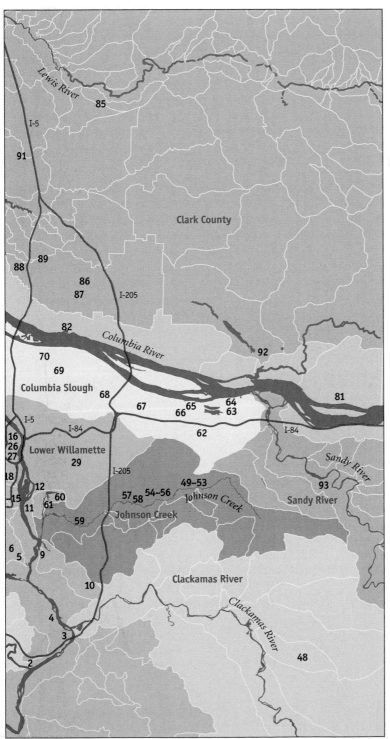

48 Eagle Fern Park
49 Gresham Main City Park
50 Gresham Butte
51 Gresham Pioneer Cemeteries
52 Jenne Butte
53 Butler Creek Greenway and
   Johnson Creek
54 Powell Butte Nature Park
55 Bundy Park
56 Leach Botanical Garden
57 Beggars-Tick Wildlife Refuge
58 Zenger Farm
59 Tideman Johnson Park
60 Reed College Canyon
61 Crystal Springs
   Rhododendron Gardens
62 Gresham-Fairview Trail
63 Blue Lake Regional Park
64 Chinook Landing Marine Park
65 Big Four Corners Wetlands
   and 40-Mile Loop Access
66 40-Mile Loop Trailhead and
   Canoe Launch
67 Little Four Corners and
   Prison Pond
68 Johnson Lake and Woodlands
69 Whitaker Ponds
70 Children's Arboretum
71 Heron Lakes Golf Course
72 Smith and Bybee Lakes
73 Kelley Point Park
74 St. Johns Landfill Canoe
   Launch
75 Peninsula Crossing Trail
76 Wapato Access Greenway
77 Coon Point Viewpoint
78 Howell Territorial Park
79 Oak Island Trail
80 Warrior Rock Lighthouse Trail
81 Columbia River Gorge
   National Wildlife Refuges
82 Clark County Marine Park
   Wetlands
83 Vancouver Lake Lowlands
84 Ridgefield National Wildlife
   Refuge
85 La Center Bottoms
86 Beaver Marsh Nature Preserve
87 Meadowbrook Marsh and
   North Meadowbrook Marsh
88 Discovery Trail
89 Ellen Davis Trail
90 Salmon Creek Greenway
91 Whipple Creek Park
92 Lacamas Lake Park
93 Oxbow Regional Park

Regional Trails and Greenways

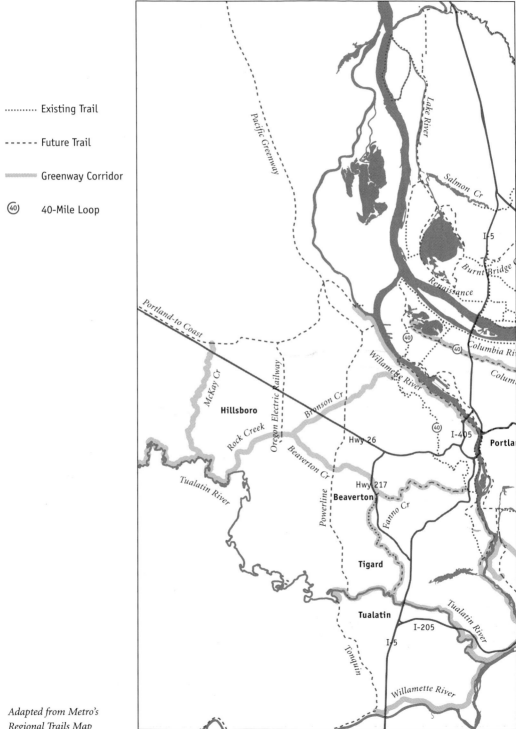

- .... Existing Trail
- ----- Future Trail
- ▧▧▧▧ Greenway Corridor
- ⓐ 40-Mile Loop

*Adapted from Metro's
Regional Trails Map*

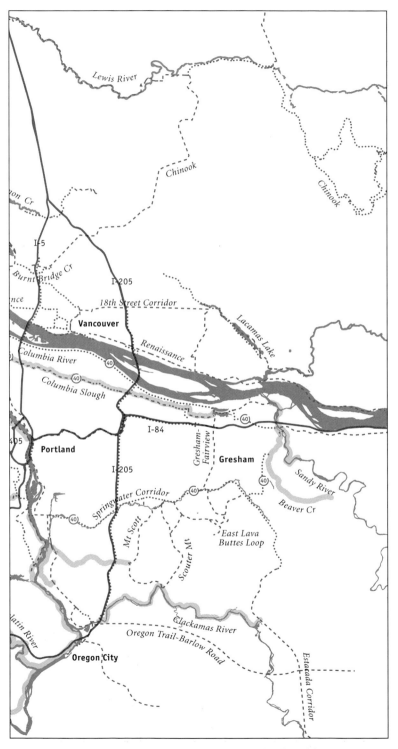

Lewis River

Chinook

Chinook

Chinook

on Cr

I-5

Burnt Bridge Cr

nce

18th Street Corridor

Vancouver

Renaissance

Lacamas Lake

Columbia River

Columbia Slough

I-84

405

Portland

I-205

Gresham-Fairview

Gresham

Sandy River

Springwater Corridor

Beaver Cr

Mt Scott

East Lava Buttes Loop

Scouter Mt

latin River

Clackamas River

Oregon Trail-Barlow Road

Estacada Corridor

Oregon City

Lower Willamette River Watershed

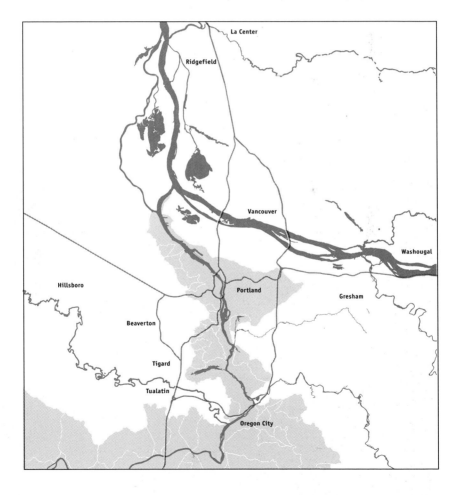

La Center

Ridgefield

Vancouver

Washougal

Hillsboro

Portland

Gresham

Beaverton

Tigard

Tualatin

Oregon City

The Changing Fortunes of the
Lower Willamette River

The lower Willamette River is now only a ghost of what it was when Lewis and Clark first saw it in the spring of 1806. However, there are still those alive today who can remember when Swan Island was truly an island, when Mocks Bottom was a haven for waterfowl, and when Guilds Lake was a 50-acre pond in the Willamette floodplain where you could go ice-skating by moonlight of a winter night away from the sights and sounds of the city.

Lewis and Clark passed the entrance to the Willamette twice without noticing it. A cluster of bushy green islands screened it from their view as they canoed down the north shore of the Columbia in the fall of 1805 and back upriver the same way the next spring. After some Indians told them of its existence, Clark backtracked to see for himself the entrance to the great river which the Indians called Multnomah (meaning "down the river") below the Falls where Oregon City is now and Willampth (meaning "green water") above the Falls. Clark, who served President Jefferson's dream of making the United States span the continent, admired its width and depth and wishfully imagined that it linked the Columbia with central California.

Up from the mouth, the Willamette wound through rolling meadows and woodlands rooted in rich, black alluvial soil and was watered with many clear, swiftly running streams. Its banks, lined with groves of fir and cedar, were mostly well above flood levels, but occasionally spread out in bottomlands clothed in thickets of alder, cottonwood, and willow.

In the eyes of the new arrivals who saw it in its natural state, the Willamette Valley was like paradise regained. On a tour of the Oregon Trail in 1832, Captain Bonneville recognized it as a bounty of prime agricultural land. Joel Palmer, in a handbook for immigrants based on his own journey over the Trail in 1845, saw it as the site of a great industrial city surrounded by farmlands to support it: stone and timber for buildings would be ready at hand; surpluses could be carried abroad and raw materials brought in along the navigable, ocean-going river. He imagined tremendous power being generated by the water that thundered over the Willamette Falls and majestic homes on the heights above them.

For the Indians of the valley, the Willamette was a paradise lost. By 1849, they had nearly all died of diseases brought by white explorers. Thus it was that by 1851, when Portland had become a city, and the United States Congress had entitled settlers to a square mile of free land per couple, Portland's founding fathers seemed to accept the Willamette as a wholly unencumbered gift from God and briskly set about adapting it to their purposes.

Timber was cleared from the shelf of land at the foot of the west hills to make way for buildings laid out on a rectangular grid. The harbor front was crammed solid with warehouse-backed wharves to receive cargo ships bound for the Orient, California, or Alaska. River traffic was crowded with ferries carrying passengers back and forth to the east and west banks, and river steamers taking sightseers on excursions up the Willamette to the "Niagara of the West," up the Columbia to the Gorge, or downriver to the ocean. Logs were rafted in to whining sawmills that occupied the banks north and south of the harbor, next to flour mills, grain elevators, and rail yards.

Sand bars were scooped away to clear a 25-foot channel from Portland to the Columbia. Frog ponds and cattail marshes were filled to support rail lines and rail yards along both banks. Bridges were built to link the west bank to the east. These initial steps in the development of Portland's waterfront were uncoordinated in the faith that individual liberty served the common good. However, since Portland's existence depended on its functioning as a commercial seaport, it was natural that commercial interests would control its development. Well before 1900, railroad companies owned 50% of the waterfront. Shortly after 1900, a railroad company began the chain of events that did away with Guilds Lake, Swan Island, and Mocks Bottom.

The world-famous Olmsted Brothers, who designed the Guilds Lake site for the Lewis and Clark Exposition of 1905, had recommended that it be preserved as the centerpiece of a city park system. The year after the fair, however, United Railways bought up the site, lake and all, for commercial development. Guilds Lake was first used as an unofficial dump, then filled with earth sluiced off one of the west hills.

Around the same time, the Port of Portland Commission, formed in 1891 to dredge the harbor, had become increasingly interested in acquiring land to hold dredge spoils to be developed for industrial use. So it was that in 1921, acting on the recommendation of a planning commission appointed by the mayor, the Port proceeded to fill Mocks Bottom, join Swan Island to the east bank, deepen the river channel west of Swan Island, and extend the Guilds Lake fill into an industrial acreage that now sells for up to 50 times its original price.

However, the disadvantages of unregulated use of the river were beginning to be noticed. In 1910, the Public Dock Commission was formed to stop the waterfront blight that was running rampant because of the railroads' hold on the Port. Two years later there was a call for a merger of the Dock Commission and the Port so that they might cooperate in this task, but this did not come about until 1970. By the 1920s, the river had become so polluted as to be unusable for swimming, boating, or fishing. The wharves disappeared. The harbor moved down river. A seawall was built.

A study of the river in 1934 revealed that in a three-mile stretch through the city center there was not enough oxygen to support a single gasping fish. The river whose name once meant "green water" had turned a murky brown. At sewer outfalls, sludge banks formed and solid debris floated on the surface of the river. In spite of such dire need for pollution control, it was six years before sludge treatment began and ten more before the city's present interceptor sewer system was installed.

In the long run, however, awareness of the city's impact on its environment has led to an era of cleanup and restoration. By 1970, as a result of concerted statewide efforts to control pollution, the Willamette was once again clean enough for fish to live in. Since the late 1980s, Portland has been working toward elimination of the combined-sewer overflows which, until recently, dumped as much as nine billion gallons of untreated sewage-laden stormwater into the Willamette and Columbia Slough. The overall plan is to replace all sewers that combine sewage and stormwater with a separated sewer system, first in the Columbia Slough and eventually on the Willamette, along with restoration of tributary streams that contribute pollutants to the river.

Concurrently, there has been renewed interest in greening of the waterfront. The proposed OMSI-Springwater Trail will provide the kind of river-side experience formerly reserved for the west side, and there are hopes for having it linked to greenspaces as far downstream as Willamette Cove and Cathedral Park in the St. Johns area. This Willamette Greenway renaissance could add a "loop-within-a-loop" to the already more than 150-mile-long "40-Mile-Loop" trail system.

By Florence Riddle

Molalla River State Park

Molalla River State Park is unique in that it encompasses the confluence of the Pudding, Molalla, and Willamette Rivers. These three rivers have created broad floodplains with many sloughs and old channels.

Most of the 566-acre park is in the floodplain of those rivers, and has a large riparian forest and wetland complex in the lowlands. These areas are highly productive habitat for many species of wildlife. The park is noted for its large great blue heron colony, but is home to many other species, including wading birds, waterfowl, neo-tropical migratory songbirds, grassland birds, amphibians, reptiles, deer, and other mammals. Bald eagles are occasionally seen perched along the riverbanks or soaring overhead.

Watch for mammal and wading bird tracks in wet areas as you travel through the park. Nutria (introduced) can be seen near the ponds.

Numerous waterfowl (including wood ducks), an occasional bald eagle, double-crested cormorants, and several species of woodpeckers and songbirds inhabit this site. As you follow the pond loop trail, look for sapsucker holes in straight horizontal rows on the trunks of pines at the far west end of the pond trail.

The great blue heron rookery dates back to 1910. At one time more than 80 heron nests could be seen in this large rookery before the cottonwoods leafed out. The heron rookery was located on the Molalla, close to its confluence with the Willamette, until 1996 when the flood took out the nesting trees. The birds moved to an inaccessible location out of view, but can be observed flying back and forth from feeding areas to the new rookery location along the Molalla River bordering the park.

Vegetation in the floodplain forest is dominated by cottonwoods, ash, and alder, with an understory of willow, dogwood, and snowberry. Ferns and other native herbaceous plants are found throughout the forest, but non-native reed canarygrass has become a monoculture in less shaded areas.

The park also has an upland component, comprised of large open fields that in the past have been leased for agricultural use and wildlife forage areas. In the early spring, watch for flocks of meadowlarks, an occasional lazuli bunting, and other grassland birds. Adjacent to the fields, in the east corner of the park, are ponds and a mixture of native and ornamental trees and shrubs. The ponds support wetland vegetation and the trail around the ponds provides good viewing opportunities for wildlife.

The riverbank of the Willamette has a canopy of large Douglas fir, big-leaf maple, vine maple, and Oregon white oak. Non-native shrubs are well-established in the riparian area, especially Himalayan

Location
On the south bank of the Willamette River and straddling the Pudding and Molalla Rivers, at the Canby Ferry just downstream from Wilsonville and north of Canby.

Highlights
The park is at the confluence of the Molalla, Pudding, and Willamette Rivers. Although access to the Molalla and Pudding is limited, the area encompasses a variety of habitats including upland coniferous forest, small ponds near the entrance, open fields, riparian areas, and dynamic floodplain areas. The pond near the wooden bridge provides a spectacular display of yellow iris in the spring.

Public Transit
Take Tri-Met #79 to the corner of Territorial Rd. and Holly St. Walk approx. 1.4 miles north on Holly St. to the park. A designated bike lane is planned along Territorial Rd. and Holly St. and will be completed in 2000.

Thomas Guide 745/746

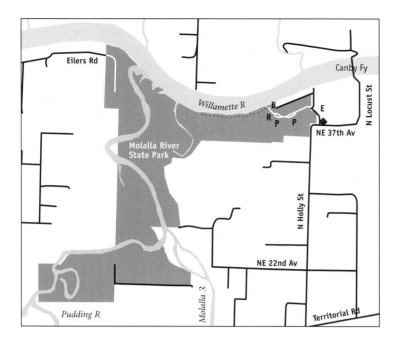

Eilers Rd

Canby Fy

Willamette R

B

R P P

E

N Locust St

NE 37th Av

Molalla River
State Park

N Holly St

NE 22nd Av

Molalla R

Pudding R

Territorial Rd

blackberry and Scot's broom. Grapevines are entwined around many large trees.

The park site was once a cottonwood plantation for the paper industry. In 1896, 420 acres were planted and those acres were thinned many times before harvest in 1964. The heron rookery was protected from harvest. The site was acquired by Oregon State Parks in 1971. Today, large cottonwoods have re-established on the site, and the floodplain has returned to a more natural system.

Look for sapsucker holes in straight horizontal rows on the trunks of pines at the far west end of the pond trail.

Access
The park has a paved entry road and parking lot allowing access to the boat ramp on the Willamette River and to the 3/4-mile paved trail around the pond area. A wheelchair accessible restroom is near the boat ramp. During periods of high water, some of these areas are inaccessible. A well-maintained gravel trail leads from the boat ramp along the upper banks of the Willamette for approximately 3/4 mile with some views of the river. A dirt section then descends into a riparian area with several side trails. The main trail generally follows the banks of the Willamette upriver for a short way and meanders near backwater sloughs, which are inaccessible during high water.

Access to the Willamette by boat provides opportunities to travel up or down river to explore riparian areas and observe wildlife. This section of the river runs west to east. Boaters can put in here heading downstream, round the bend at Peach Cove, pass Rock Island, and take out at Willamette Park in West Linn. The Canby Ferry just beyond the park entrance carries cars and bicyclists across the river for travel to and from Wilsonville, Stafford, or the West Linn area for a small fee.

How to Get There
From Oregon City, the park is approximately 10 miles. Take Hwy. 99E south. After passing through New Era, continue approximately 1 mile to a sign on the right for Territorial Rd., Molalla River State Park, and the Canby Ferry. Turn right onto Territorial Rd. and continue about 1.5 miles to Holly St. Turn right on Holly and travel 1.4 miles to the park entrance on the left.

From Portland, take I-5 south to the Canby exit just south of Wilsonville. Turn left at the first stop light onto Arndt Rd. At the 4-way stop, continue straight down a long straight stretch of road. After crossing the Pudding River Bridge, the road curves left and becomes Knights Bridge Rd. Continue on Knights Bridge Rd., crossing the Molalla River, and into Canby. At Holly St. (a "T" intersection at the stop sign), go left onto Holly. Continue on Holly, crossing Territorial Rd. From this point, the park is about 1.4 miles down Holly. The park entrance is on the left.

(Note: the Canby Ferry is .4 mile beyond the park entrance.)

By Holly Michael and Kathy Shinn

For more information: Oregon State Parks and Recreation 503-678-1251. No park headquarters on site, but a volunteer park host is usually present.

Upper Willamette Narrows Paddle

Willamette Park is set up for family and group picnics and similar activities. The only two things that recommend it for wildlife enthusiasts are a small wetland area and access to the Willamette River above the Oregon City falls. Motorized boating activity is given priority, so you may not want to use this site on crowded sunny days.

Once you're on the river you can poke around at the mouth of the Tualatin River. This lower reach of the Tualatin is generally not accessible to canoes or kayaks. The river is full of rocks and the river level is generally too low to negotiate this reach of the river, which is far different in character from the slow-moving, meandering river as it flows past Cook Park and other upstream put-in points.

As you paddle upstream in the Willamette's main channel I have found it's much more pleasant to hug the west bank, both to avoid wakes from passing motorized craft and to be closer to the adjacent forests that are alive with bird calls and songs in spring and early summer. You may want to avert your eyes as you pass the ostentatious "McMansions" on the west bank. Once you paddle upstream, however, the stark, rock riprap gives way to a well-vegetated, shady riparian forest.

The highlight of a paddle upstream from Bernet Landing is picking your way behind basalt islands that create the "narrows." My favorite route is to stay right in the narrow, shady channel as you approach the first island, just over a mile upstream from Willamette Park. This is also the quietest part of the trip, even on hot summer days when the motorized traffic can be heavy. The basalt islands, with their thin soils, are reminiscent of the Camassia Preserve and Elk Rock Island downstream. The thin soils dry out quickly and support dry-site species like Oregon white oak and Pacific madrone. In spring the islands are festooned with wildflowers. A variety of saxifrages, *Lomatium*, white *Delphinium*, buckwheats, *Brodiaea*, sedum, and yellow composites grow on the small island's steep faces. As testament to the ecological importance of the Willamette Narrows portion of the Willamette Greenway, Metro Regional Parks and Greenspaces has purchased 140 acres, and both The Nature Conservancy and Oregon State Parks own land here as well.

The birding in this stretch of the river is particularly rewarding, owing to the narrow channel and relatively pristine forest habitat that literally surrounds you. I let my kayak drift a bit and sit for minutes at a time listening for pileated woodpeckers, flickers, Wilson's warblers, purple finches, Swainson's thrush, and waxwings. Once out on the main channel, turkey vultures, red-tailed hawks, and osprey soar overhead while spotted sandpipers flutter up and down stream in front of your craft.

At the upstream end of the island, keep to the right bank, which is also covered with sedum, yellow sunflowers, and other wildflowers.

Location
West Linn, Historic Willamette Area, Rivermile 28.

Activities
Canoeing, Boating Fishing

Facilities
Toilets
Wheelchair accessible
Trail unpaved
Parking
Picnic area
Dock, canoe launch

Fees and Regulations
None

Highlights
The best canoe put-in to explore the Rock Island area, an island complex of basalt covered with wildflowers in the late spring and early summer and one of Metro's target areas for Greenspace acquisitions.

Thomas Guide 716

When you see buoys in the middle of the river at about river mile 30 (Rock Island Landing on the west bank and Coalca Landing on the east bank), cross the river to the east bank and you can return downstream through narrow back-channels. There is a very narrow channel to negotiate at the start of this downstream leg. You need to thread your canoe or kayak between rocks at this point, but once inside the quiet backwater, it's smooth sailing. I prefer to cut back across the river and return to Willamette Park along the west bank to avoid motorized traffic in the main channel.

If you decide to paddle downstream of Willamette Park, be careful not to go near or over the Willamette Falls. You will have to stay to the left of the channel and should call ahead to the U.S. Army Corps of Engineers (503-656-3381) if you wish to continue downstream below the Oregon City Falls via the locks.

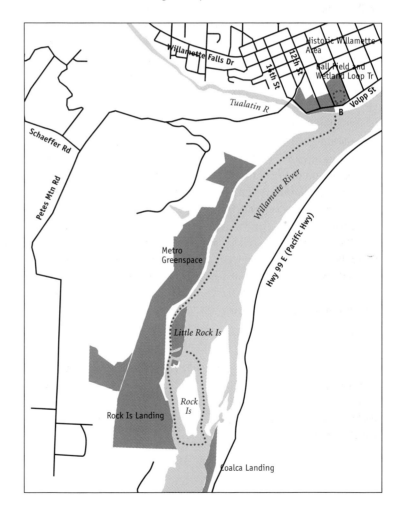

Access

Boat docks are located just downstream (north) of the main Willamette Park. There are two launch sites. The preferable one, if it is not a hot, busy weekend, is to the left at the end of 12th St. There is another informal ramp at the foot of 14th St., which is one-way back up the hill at the west end of the park. You can park along the road and carry your canoe or kayak down a short embankment to a crumbling ramp at the mouth of the Tualatin River.

The formal boat ramp is located east of the main park. This is a fully-developed facility with restrooms and two docks. One of the launch areas has a gangplank down to a floating dock, which is better to use if there is a lot of motorized boat activity. A second dock is adjacent to a concrete boat ramp. There is very limited car parking here, as almost all of the spaces are dedicated to vehicles with boat trailers. The local constabulary will issue citations if you use the spaces designated for vehicles with trailers. If you decide to use the primary ramp and parking is limited, you can park just west of the ramp in an unpaved area across from the park. Alternatively, if there are no parking spaces and the ramp is busy you can drive to the other end of the park at the foot of or along 14th.

How to Get There

From I-205, go west of Oregon City; take West Linn's Historic Willamette Area exit off I-205. Head south on 10th St., get into the right lane, and turn right (west) onto Willamette Falls Dr. and then immediately left on 12th St. Keep straight at the stop sign at Tualatin Ave. and head down the hill on 12th, which is one-way at this point. The park is on your right and the formal boat ramp is to the left.

It's also possible to take a scenic route paralleling the Tualatin River. Take the Stafford Rd. exit off I-205. Head north on Stafford Rd. to Wankers Corner and turn right onto SW Borland Rd. Follow Borland southeast until it becomes Willamette Falls Dr. and turn right on 12th into Willamette Park.

By Mike Houck

If you have some time to kill, there is a boardwalk and loop trail through a marsh across the street from the primary boat ramp. If you walk clockwise the trail runs along the edge of the baseball field, adjacent to some homes, and then cuts back through the marsh via a wooden boardwalk. It's really quite a nice walk. I flushed a Virginia rail on my first walk through the marsh.

For more information: West Linn Parks Department, see Resources. Excellent resources for paddling the Willamette are the Willamette River Recreation Guide, Oregon State Marine Board, and Oregon Parks. Also consult Philip N. Jones, *Canoe and Kayak Routes of Northwest Oregon*, Seattle: The Mountaineers, 1997.

Camassia Preserve

The Pacific Northwest is all about dark forests and Douglas fir, right? Well, not entirely. There are also river bottoms and marshlands, ash swales, oak groves, and prairies. One of the strangest and most enticing un-forests in the Portland area is The Nature Conservancy's Camassia Natural Area near West Linn High School. Setting foot in this delicate preserve is like stepping into another world.

Certainly that is how naturalist Murray Miller must have felt when he explored this area in the 1950s. Impressed by Camassia's unique values, he persuaded The Nature Conservancy to acquire the property, and in 1962 it became the Conservancy's first Oregon preserve and remains one of the loveliest spots in the region.

The approach to Camassia is through a Douglas fir forest, and although it features a number of uncommon wildflowers—Oregon fawn lily, for example, and sessile trillium—it doesn't prepare the visitor for what lies ahead. For after a short distance, the ground rises and the trail opens into Camassia proper, a tangled bluff-top landscape of oak trees and madrone, ash swales, wet meadows, and rocks.

The rocky appearance of Camassia can be credited to the great Missoula, or Bretz, floods of 15,000 years ago. At that time glacial ice dammed many of the northwest rivers, creating huge glacial lakes such as Lake Missoula, which lay along the Idaho-Montana border.

When Lake Missoula's ice dam broke, as it did periodically (some think as many as 40 times, as John Eliot Allen notes in *Cataclysms on the Columbia*), a vast volume of water came cascading down the Columbia, pouring through the Willamette Valley and scouring the existing landscape down to bare rock. At the same time, huge boulders floated in on ice rafts. As the ice melted, these "erratics"—many from hundreds of miles away—were deposited throughout northwest Oregon. At Camassia both the gray of the native basalt and the "salt and pepper" of the erratics are readily visible.

Another dominant feature of the Camassia Natural Area is an oak and madrone woodland. This chaparral-like landscape was once a common feature of the Willamette Valley, but it seems to have required regular burning (something the native inhabitants did frequently to preserve the characteristics of this habitat). When European settlers displaced the Indian population the burning stopped, permitting encroachment from the coniferous forest. Now it is unusual to find this habitat in northwestern Oregon.

The woodland is dominated by two trees. Oregon white (Garry) oak is the most important commercial oak in the west, but as a tree it cannot compare to its arresting companion, Pacific madrone. Madrone is a native tree—the only native broadleaf evergreen tree in this part of the world—but its coppery bark, peeling to reveal a cinnamon, satin-smooth interior, gives it an exotic look. And in April

Location
End of Walnut St. in West Linn.

Activities
Hiking
Botany

Facilities
None

Fees and Regulations
Permission to enter must be granted by The Nature Conservancy
No pets
No bikes
Do not pick flowers; leave them for others to enjoy.
Vibram-soled boots discouraged
Stay on trails!

Highlights
In mid-to-late April, the grassy plateaus are awash with the color of blooming camas, large-flowered collinsia, and rosy plectritis. The diversity of plant communities and habitats provides for a wide variety of wildlife on the preserve.

it bears spectacular clusters of creamy-white flowers. April is also the season for an even more extraordinary flower display which takes place in the wet meadows interspersed between the oak groves.

Perhaps the most important food plant of Native Americans of the northwest was the camas, a beautiful blue six-petaled lily. Camas prairies were major meeting grounds for the various tribes, and wars over the rights to these prairies were common. But the sight of a wet meadow turned blue with the springtime camas bloom has become an uncommon sight.

Over 300 flowering plants can be found at Camassia, many of which are rare in the Willamette Valley.

Camas—namesake of the Camassia Natural Area—can still be found here in abundance, reaching its peak bloom in mid-to-late April. And at the same time, the meadows of Camassia are also carpeted with the purple-blue blossoms of large collinsia and the pink of rosy plectritis—an unforgettable sight.

As if that weren't enough, over 300 other flowering plants can be found at Camassia, many of which are rare in the Willamette Valley. Birds and other animals find a haven here too, and visitors can see such unusual species as western bluebirds, ringneck snakes, and lazuli buntings.

A visit to Camassia is not a hike in the ordinary sense. The natural area is small and the trails are meandering and sometimes hard to make out. Wet places abound and the rocky nature of the place requires frequent stepping up and down. And poison oak is present in abundance.

But hiking isn't the main point anyway. A visit to Camassia is a visit to a wildflower garden, beautiful but fragile. Staying on the trails is essential and vibram-soled boots are discouraged in order to protect this delicate jewel.

How to Get There

The Nature Conservancy, the owner of this private property, requests that anyone visiting this site contact them for permission and for information about their work parties and tours of the site. Please respect this request.

By Bob Wilson

For more information: The Nature Conservancy of Oregon, see Resources.

Mary S. Young State Park

These 133 acres offer something for everyone. The open fields provide space for soccer games and an off-leash dog exercise area. A kitchen shelter and picnic tables scattered throughout the forest allow for large gatherings or a more intimate rendevous. Although these activities don't necessarily coincide with wildlife viewing, the diverse nature of the park creates a rich natural environment that is home to songbirds, osprey, deer, and coyote.

An open field, mixed woodlands, ponds, riparian areas, and access to the Willamette River make Mary S. Young a mecca for bird watching, especially in the spring migratory season. The osprey nests are easy to spot from the dog exercise area by looking toward the river for a few old snags with huge nests on top. There is also a pair of pileated woodpeckers that you can count on hearing if you quietly walk the trails long enough. The paved trail toward the river brings you to a meadow with stone walls on the far side. This is a great viewpoint of the Willamette River as well as of the forest canopy below. Warblers, vireos, tanagers, and other canopy bird species can be easily observed from this vista. Continuing down toward the river, typical riparian bird species such as Pacific-slope flycatchers, black-headed grosbeaks, and Swainson's thrush can usually be heard. With binoculars or a spotting scope you can actually see great blue heron nests high in the cottonwoods across from Clackamette Park, far upstream.

These same environs create conditions for a variety of native plant species, although there is an incredible problem with English ivy that threatens much of this diversity. The mixed conifer-deciduous forest of Douglas fir, western red cedar, and big-leaf maple provides a canopy for Indian plum, salmonberry, and vine maple. More sensitive species such as trillium and snowberry exist but are harder to find amidst the sea of ivy.

The land was originally owned by Mary Scarsborough Young, who donated it to the state of Oregon with the provision that it be kept a natural area and not further developed beyond the ball fields. Mary S. Young had plans to build a house there with tennis courts and an equestrian trail. Although the house was never built, Mary did fence in the property, build many trails, and create extensive gardens. Remnants of familiar garden plants can be seen along portions of the trail, such as skimmia, Pieris, rhododendron, Portugal laurel, and St. John's-wort.

Once you work your way through the reed canarygrass, the banks of the Willamette offer opportunities to dip your toes or a fishing pole into the water. When the river level is low enough, a small footbridge offers access to Cedar Island, which is part of the Willamette River Greenway along with Mary S. Young State Park.

Location
On Hwy. 43 in West Linn, 1.5 miles south of Marylhurst University.

Activities
Hiking
Biking
Fishing

Facilities
Toilets
Wheelchair accessibility
Trail paved
Parking
Picnic areas
Sports fields

Fees and Regulations
No fees
Pets on leash on trails
Pet exercise area where pets can be off leash

Highlights
The Horsetail Trail leads through a variety of park environs, making it a botanically rich site to visit. Viewpoints of the Willamette River offer peaceful settings for birdwatching.

Public Transit
Tri-Met #35 can be taken from Portland or Oregon City directly to Mary S. Young State Park.

Thomas Guide 686/687

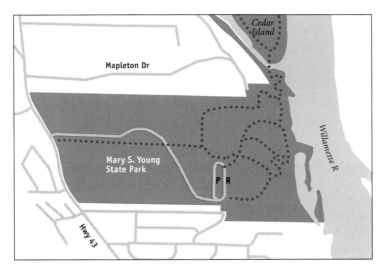

Access

An extensive network of trails begins on the east side of the main parking lot and goes down to the Willamette River. A bike path begins at the entrance to the park on Hwy. 43, passes by the soccer fields, and connects to the park's trail system. Bikes are required to stay on designated bike paths, so as not to interfere with hikers. A brochure titled "Horsetail Trail" leads a hiker through a descriptive one-mile hike through a variety of environments.

Part of the trail system is paved and wheelchair accessible. While sections leading down to the river are unpaved and a bit steep, it is still an easy trail to navigate. Another portion of the trail system is made of various boardwalks and stairs, leading the hiker through a sensitive wetland environment.

How to Get There

From Portland, take Hwy. 43 through Lake Oswego into West Linn. Mary S. Young State Park is well signed on the left-hand side of the road, about 1.5 miles south of Marylhurst University.

By Mary Rose Navarro and Ron Carley

For more information: Oregon State Parks owns and manages Mary S. Young State Park. For more information or trail maps, contact park managers at Tryon Creek State Park Headquarters, see Resources.

Tryon Creek and Lake Oswego Area

William H. Whyte wrote in his book, *The Last Landscape*, "Where water flows, the positive benefits of open space are the clearest . . . If we follow [its path] we are at once securing the prime lands and the lands which give linkage and continuity."

Whyte knew in the late 1960s what we have only recently begun to act on—acquiring and managing open spaces along urban waterways.

Tryon Creek flows approximately seven miles, collecting water from Falling Creek and Arnold Creek before it flows through Tryon Creek State Park and empties into the Willamette River more than 1,000 feet below its highest point in the watershed in Portland's west hills. Most of its almost 5,000-acre watershed is within Portland, about 20% being in Lake Oswego and unincorporated Multnomah and Clackamas Counties.

If anything characterizes Tryon, it is its steeply sloped watershed, almost three-quarters of which exceeds 30% in grade and much of which is steeper than 50%. The steep slopes are one of the greatest threats to the creek itself and wild fish that spawn there.

Portland's Bureau of Environmental Services estimates the current impervious surfaces in Tryon are about 26%. The watershed is dominated by typical west side plant communities, having been logged in the late 1800s like the rest of the metropolitan region. Dominant plants are red alder, big-leaf maple, Douglas fir, western red cedar, and western hemlock. The Friends of Tryon Creek State Park have catalogued 80 species of birds and mammals in the park, and both steelhead and coho salmon have been recorded spawning in the creek.

Around Lake Oswego

From 973-foot Mt. Sylvania, water flows in several directions: west to Ball or Carter Creeks, then into Fanno Creek; northeast to Arnold and Tryon Creeks; or south to Springbrook Creek. South of Oswego Lake, surface waters run to Pecan Creek, Blue Heron Canal, or Lost Dog Creek, depending on which flank of 717-foot Cooks Butte they fall. To the east of 60-acre Luscher Farm, water flows to Wilson Creek.

Springbrook Creek drains an area from west of the Oswego Country Club northwest as far as Mountain Park, where walking paths access the creek's privately owned headwaters. Even fully developed, Mountain Park retains important forested stream corridors and wildlife habitat. Farther southeast and downstream, nature trails wind through alder forests in 52-acre Springbrook Park, whence the creek then flows southeast under Brookside Road and plunges through a forested ravine into Oswego Lake.

By Mike Houck

Tryon Creek State Park

Socrates Tryon was not a philosopher, but a physician who moved to Oregon from Hawaii in 1849. The park that bears the good doctor's name was then a virgin forest of towering Douglas fir laced with cedar and hemlock. The forest remains, though logged historically, 645 wooded acres bordering Nettle, Park, and Tryon Creeks.

This small but important watershed feeds the Willamette River and typifies the protection efforts underway to protect the salmon and steelhead that still spawn in our urban streams. Additional lands purchased through Metro's Regional Parks and Greenspaces Department link Tryon Creek State Park to city-owned Marshall Park just upstream and protect remnants of Tryon Creek's headwaters from impending development.

Try to take in Tryon Creek in early spring when the trilliums are in bloom. The triangular-shaped trillium is more than a tongue-twisting alliteration. Trilliums personify spring at Tryon Creek, and are honored at the park's annual Trillium Festival. The creamy white blossoms sprouting among the sword-fern are sure to brighten the

Location
11321 SW Terwilliger Blvd.

Activities
Hiking
Biking
Jogging
Horseback riding

Facilities
Toilets
Wheelchair accessible
Parking
Nature Center
Covered shelter
Drinking water

Fees and Regulations
Pets on leash

Highlights
All-abilities interpretive trail. Annual Trillium Festival and native plant sale in early spring. Forest, canyon, stream.

Public Transit
Tri-Met #39 serves the Lewis and Clark Campus at the north end of Tryon Creek State Park and the #38 runs along SW Boones Ferry Road, which borders the west side of the park. There is no service to the park's main entrance on SW Terwilliger.

Thomas Guide 656

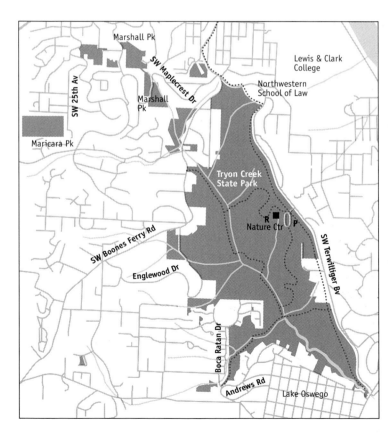

gloom of Oregon's early spring and are followed by fringecup, waterleaf, and over 90 other species of wildflower.

The five bridges that cross Tryon Creek offer great vantage points for budding naturalists. You can look for tracks of raccoon or deer (and the occasional troll) along the muddy banks. Observe, too, how fallen logs and woody debris change the course and character of the creek, providing habitat for aquatic animals.

Be sure to watch for water striders dimpling the creek's surface. Water striders may sound like the latest craze in aerobic exercise, but they are fascinating, often overlooked invertebrates, and are plentiful in Tryon Creek's pools and backwaters.

Visit the Tryon Creek Nature Center for information on hikes, classes, and concerts sponsored by the Friends of Tryon Creek, an active community group whose efforts were instrumental in establishing the park in 1970.

Access
Fourteen miles of trails including paved all-abilities trail, paved bike path, and equestrian trail. Hiking and jogging trails are of variable difficulty; often muddy in winter and spring.

How to Get There
Take the Terwilliger Blvd. exit off I-5 and head south on Terwilliger Blvd. toward Lewis and Clark College. Continue on Terwilliger about 1 mile past the Northwestern School of Law heading toward Lake Oswego. Additional access off Boones Ferry Rd., Engelwood Dr. (no parking), and Iron Mountain Rd.

By Connie Levesque

For more information: Tryon Creek State Park and Friends of Tryon Creek State Park, see Resources.

Trillium, the Little Western Flower

What could be a more certain herald of spring than the blooming of a wildflower known as wake-robin? Or as one Portland wag puts it, "The appearance of trillium in the city is the first sure sign that only four more months of rain lie ahead."

Trilliums derive their name from the root words "tri" and "lily," which indicates their affinity to the lily family and to having all their parts in threes—three leaves, sepals, petals, and stigma, and two times three stamens.

A wide variety of colors are found in the 20 or so species of trillium native to North America. Their petals can range from white to greenish-yellow and pink to dark violet. In Portland most of the trilliums that begin blooming toward the end of winter will be snowy white. But as the plants mature, their petals will gradually turn pink and finally wine-purple by the end of spring. Shakespeare describes this transformation poetically in *A Midsummer Night's Dream*:

> Yet mark'd I where the bolt of Cupid fell:
> It fell upon a little western flower,
> Before milk-white, now purple with love's wound . . .
> Act ll, Scene i.

Trilliums grow in moist, steady, undisturbed woods, and in Portland they are most likely to be found in Forest Park and Tryon Creek State Park. According to Bill Gifford, a wildflower enthusiast with the Sierra Club, trilliums quickly disappear from areas with high levels of human activity. The plants are easily damaged and slow to recover, taking several years to flower again if their leaves are lost.

So vulnerable are trilliums, in fact, that Beth Horn of the Forest Service stresses, "People need to be informed that picking a trillium's leaves and flower can destroy the plant forever." Being part of the lily family, the trillium has a bulb and depends on its leaves for nourishment to support growth and development.

Trilliums typically bloom from late February to June, and of the two species commonly found in Portland, the mottled or sessile trillium (*Trillium chloropetalum*) usually precedes the western trillium (*Trillium ovatum*) by a couple of weeks each year.

Mottled Trillium

Also known as the giant trillium, the mottled or sessile trillium is easily recognized by the lack of a stem between its flower and leaves. Its petals are narrow and often green-tinted, as the flower's Latin name, *chloropetalum*, implies. Its leaves are broad and mottled with reddish-brown splotches.

Western Trillium

The western trillium, sometimes called western wake-robin, is by far the most common trillium in Portland. Its flower is fuller than the mottled's, and sits on a long pedicel or stem above the plant's leaves. The western trillium's flower begins the season white, but becomes tinged with pink and purple before finally turning very dark.

The trillium may hardly be a robin-waker in a climate as mild as Portland's, but with its promise of spring and hint of blossoms and buds to come, the little western flower is just the ticket to brighten a wet and dreary day.

By Thomas E. Hanrahan

Marshall Park

The temperature drops noticeably as you descend into Marshall Park, a wooded canyon along Tryon Creek upstream from the state park. Formerly the site of an abandoned quarry, Marshall Park honors the restoration efforts of F. C. and Addie Marshall, whose summer home has been replaced by a small playground and picnic site.

Tryon Creek is a boulder-strewn brook here, its banks lined with maidenhair and sword-fern. Water-tolerant western red cedars lend their graceful shade to the surrounding forest. The fibrous bark of the cedar was used extensively by Native Americans for clothing and shelter. The trees now shelter the raucous Steller's jay, whose crested head of sooty black and preference for coniferous forests sets it apart from the more common scrub jay.

A network of trails suitable for dry-weather hiking crisscrosses the canyon. However, beyond Maplecrest Drive, the trail dwindles to an unimproved path bisected by creeks, fallen logs, and thickets of blackberry. Recent land acquisitions by Metro will link Marshall Park with Tryon Creek State Park downstream, providing an important greenspace corridor for wildlife and visitors alike.

Late summer is a good time to visit Marshall Park when trails are packed hard and the shady canyon offers a welcome reprieve from the heat. This is also prime spider season and tiny orb weavers abound. Their gossamer webs are strung unerringly across the trail. It is best to visit Marshall Park with friends, preferably tall ones, and let them walk first.

Location
SW 18th Pl.

Activities
Hiking
Jogging

Facilities
Picnic
Playground

Fees and Regulations
None

Highlights
Forest; stream; western red cedar

Thomas Guide 626/656

Access
Some steep trails into and out of canyon; muddy in winter and spring; trail unimproved beyond Maplecrest Dr.

How to Get There
Take Taylor's Ferry Rd. to SW 12th Dr. or SW 18th Pl.

By Connie Levesque

For more information:
Portland Bureau of Parks and Recreation, see Resources.

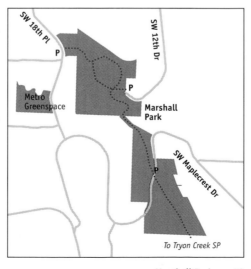

Under the Sweet Gum Tree

Each fall under the sweet gum tree, where the moss is thick and the soil moist and a carpet of red and gold leaves lies ready for raking, there sprouts a ring of tiny translucent mushrooms.

It is as if my small piece of Portland had been transported on a wonderful flight to Eleanor Cameron's Mushroom Planet, where the dome-headed Basidiumites hold their pale, somber council. But it will take more than two adventuresome boys and a pet chicken to save these seemingly alien life forms. Crisp fall days turn quickly to rain in the Northwest. Raking days must be not be squandered. And so the mushrooms are minced, caps severed from stems, and stirred into a pungent stew of leaves, moss, fir cones, and half-rotted apples that will make its way to the steaming heart of the compost pile.

If the thought of steamed mushrooms made your mouth water, you are one of many Oregonians who share a fondness for fungi. Perhaps you go each fall in search of chanterelles, or wax poetic on the merits of morels. I neither search, nor wax. What I know about edible mushrooms could fit in the cap of a *Marisimus*, which is quite a small mushroom indeed. So if you've come to this essay to learn about mushroom hunting, turn back now. Find a good field guide. Take a good class. The only advice I can offer is to eat what you know.

Similar advice is often given to writers. Write what you know. I know the thick, crusty, shoulder-pad-like growth on the sides of trees and stumps is a shelf fungus, *Phellinus chrysoloma*, to be exact. What I did not know was that this fungus is parasitic and will kill the

tree on which it feeds. So, too, will the pleasant-sounding honey mushroom (*Armillariella mellea*), whose alias—black shoestring root-rot—underscores its true nature.

Most mushrooms are more benign. They are the fruits of a much larger fungal body, the mycelium, that grows in a vast network of tubules called hyphae, spreading through soil and under leaves and inside trees, both living and dead. These tubules can both draw nourishment from decaying plant and animal matter and give nourishment to living plants through close association with their root fibers.

Neither plant nor animal, mushrooms are part a large family of fungi that do well in Oregon's moist, temperate climate. Look for them on rotting logs or spongy beds of moss. Note their delicate gills, from which spores are loosed on the wind. Note, too, their colors—brown, white, beige, cream, red, orange. Fungi lack chlorophyll, the stuff that gives the plant kingdom its trademark green and helps convert sunlight to energy. They are decomposers. Saprophytes. Pale omens of death and decay. Do you still want to eat them? Then happy hunting.

Mushrooms common to the Portland area include the delicate, pure-white angel wing (*Pleurocybella porrigens*) which grows on alder, and the garish orange chicken of the woods (*Laetiporus sulphurus*) which prefers conifers such as hemlock and Douglas fir. Wooded areas such as Tryon Creek State Park are great places to check for these and other fall mushrooms. Over 240 species of fungi have been identified in Tryon Creek alone.

Perhaps what we can all share about mushrooms, foragers and abstainers alike, is an appreciation for the vital role these queer, quizzical organisms play in the health of our forests and our gardens. Watch for them in your yard come fall as I will in mine, where the fairies dance to the harvest moon, under the sweet gum tree.

By Connie Levesque

Beth Ryan Nature Reserve

This 2.3-acre natural area was donated to the Three Rivers Land Conservancy in December of 1991. Owned by the Oregon Iron and Steel Company during the 1800s, Beth Ryan Nature Reserve was mined for iron ore prior to residential development in the 1930s. Today, Beth Ryan Nature Reserve is nestled in a neighborhood just north of Oswego Lake. A forested wetland covers a substantial portion of the Reserve with wooded slopes and rocky outcroppings surrounding the site. The property is bordered by the Southern Pacific Railroad to the north, Summit Drive to the east, Ridgewood Road to the west, and a rocky bluff to the south. Despite its small size and proximity to residential development, the Reserve continues to support a diverse community of plants and wildlife.

A variety of trees and shrubs are scattered throughout the wetland and surrounding area. The canopy, dominated by Pacific willow and Oregon ash, also contains black cottonwood and Douglas fir. A shrub understory supporting vine maple, red-osier dogwood, spirea, hazelnut, and snowberry is present. Abundant emergent vegetation in the wetland includes bur-reed, mannagrass, bulrush, smartweed, water-parsley, bittersweet nightshade, and duckweed.

Multi-layered vegetation and varied terrain provide a unique habitat for birds and small wildlife species. Along the short trail there are excellent opportunities to observe the many species of birds frequenting the Reserve. Be on the lookout for migrants such as Wilson's and orange-crowned warblers, warbling vireos, western wood-pewees, and olive-sided flycatchers. Walk quietly as you

Location
Summit Dr. and Village Dr. in Lake Oswego. Near intersection of Summit Dr. and Iron Mountain Blvd.

Activities
Birding
Limited hiking

Fees and Regulations
None

Highlights
Varied terrain provides a unique habitat for a variety of birds and small wildlife hidden in the midst of a residential neighborhood. Wooded slopes and rocky outcroppings surround the site.

Public Transit
Tri-Met #37

Thomas Guide 656

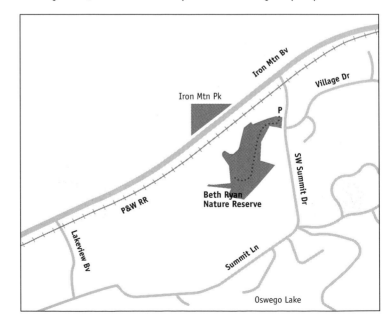

approach the viewing platform overlooking the wetland and you might catch a glimpse of a resident pair of wood ducks or a green heron. The wetland also provides a breeding area for frogs and salamanders, including the red-legged frog.

Beth Ryan Nature Reserve is a haven for wildlife and people in a dense residential community. Visitors to the Reserve are reminded of the importance that natural habitat plays in preserving wildlife and water quality. Beth Ryan serves as a link between busy suburban lifestyles and concern for natural area conservation.

Access
A trail less than 1/4 mile long traverses the outer edge of the forested wetland with two benches and a viewing platform.

How to Get There
From downtown Lake Oswego, take Iron Mountain Blvd. to Summit Dr. Turn left, immediately passing over the Southern Pacific Railroad tracks. Look for a sign on the right after crossing the railroad overpass.

By Jayne Cronlund

For more information: Three Rivers Land Conservancy, see Resources.

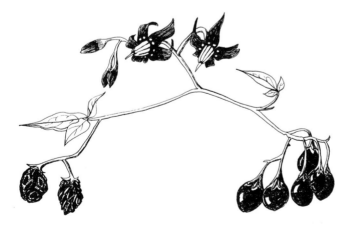

Bryant Woods Nature Park/Canal Acres Natural Area

Five habitat types in a 25-acre park in Lake Oswego? You'll find it at Bryant Woods Nature Park on the Oswego Canal. Oregon ash and Oregon white oak ring a wet meadow edged with camas and dotted with seasonal ponds where red-legged frogs thrive. A larger excavated pond, fed by natural springs, has been partially filled in with sediment and grasses but still provides homes for wood ducks and mallards. Douglas fir and big-leaf maple dominate in the upland forest.

From the small parking area, the main trail follows the route of the former Canal Road along the edge of the meadow. This graveled road bed is passable all year. Oswego Canal, a short cut between the Tualatin and Willamette Rivers, parallels the trail. A side trail crosses the wetlands on a wooden bridge and loops through the upland forest to return to the main trail. This one-half mile loop can be flooded and muddy in the winter.

Less traveled and less disturbed, Canal Acres Natural Area is just across Childs Road. A trail through the Natural Area begins on Canal Road about 100 feet from Childs Road. Look for the bollard posts that mark the trailhead. There is no parking at the trailhead; leave your car at the Bryant Woods lot or use the small pullover a short way beyond the trail on Canal Road. The trail keeps to the high ground above the wooded wetlands where deer forage and the call of the winter wren floats from beneath the dense tree canopy. Just a few steps into the trail, you feel as though you are far from the city. Traffic noise is replaced by bird song, and native plants dominate. Spring provides a succession of native blooms, with trillium, inside-out-flower, or snowberry peeking out from the dense thicket of ferns. Watch out for the three-leafed poison oak, also common along the edges of the trail. So remote does Canal Acres feel that the sight of houses near the trail's end is jarring. The trail comes out of the park between two houses on Dogwood Drive. Please stay on the trail and be respectful of the private property on either side.

To view the Canal, walk along Canal Road past the trailhead. Walk around the gate marked "Emergency Access Road"; pedestrians only are allowed beyond the gate. Past the headgate dam which controls the flow of water from the Tualatin into the Canal is a Tualatin River overlook. The little clearing is a great spot to eat lunch or just sit and contemplate the history of the region.

Waluga to Sucker to Oswego

This area is as rich in cultural history as it is in natural history. The wetlands of Bryant Woods and Canal Acres historically fed Waluga (white swan) Lake, as the Indians called it. These waters flowed to the Willamette and were not connected to the Tualatin River, as they

Location
Childs Rd. at Oswego Canal, between Bryant and Pilkington

Activities
Hiking (walking)

Facilities
Parking
Interpretive information
Picnic area (picnic table)

Fees and Regulations
Restricted hours
Pets on leash (poop scooping required)

Highlights
Five habitat types on one site. Natural springs, wetland forest, wood ducks, red-legged frogs.

Public Transit
Tri-Met #36, closest stop at Childs and Pilkington.

Thomas Guide 685/686

are today, although the short portage may well have been used by
local Indians.

Waluga Lake became known as Sucker Lake by the early settlers
for its resident fish. The name was changed to Oswego Lake in 1913.
*Oregon's Iron Dream: A Story of Old Oswego and the Proposed Iron
Empire of the West*, by Mary Goodall (Binfords and Mort, 1958), tells
the story of commercial development of the Lake Oswego area.
Goodall recounts the shipping of goods in the 1860s from the fertile
Tualatin Valley by Tualatin River steamer, transferring to horse-drawn
tram for the journey to Sucker Lake where loads were carried by
another steamer, with a final portage to the Willamette. In 1871
construction began on a canal to carry steamers directly from the
Tualatin to an enlarged Sucker Lake. Chinese laborers dug the canal
by hand in 18 months. A narrow-gauge railroad began operation in

*In 1871 construction
began on a canal to carry
steamers directly from the
Tualatin to an enlarged
Sucker Lake. Chinese
laborers dug the canal
by hand in 18 months.*

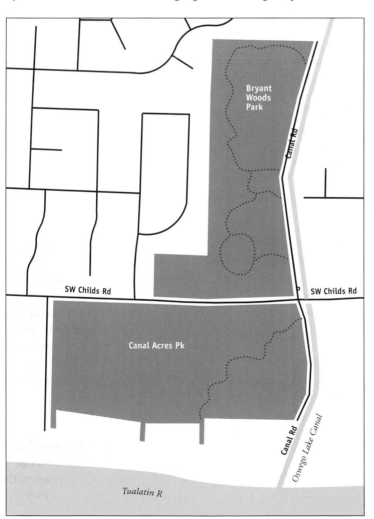

1887, ending the canal's use for shipping. A second planned canal between the Lake and the Willamette River was never built.

After a period of neglect, the canal was widened beginning in 1939 but not completed until after World War II. Today the canal and Oswego Lake are owned by the private Oswego Lake Corporation and maintained for hydropower and recreation. Oswego Creek flows through George Rogers Park from the dam at the end of Oswego Lake to the Willamette near downtown Lake Oswego. A pedestrian bridge next to the lower parking lot at George Rogers Park (entrance from State Street) offers a good view of the mouth of Oswego Creek, where it's common to see great blue herons fishing in the shallows and families of ducks heading up the Creek.

A local Friends group worked tirelessly throughout the 1970s to preserve and protect Bryant Woods Park in the face of attempts to develop the property. Their efforts were rewarded in 1979 with the purchase of the original park land by the City of Lake Oswego. The Canal Acres tract was purchased by the City in 1994. The Friends of Bryant Woods are still active in stewardship of these resource areas.

Access

Bryant Woods trail begins at the small parking area on the north side of SW Childs Rd., just west of Oswego Canal. The main trail follows the closed Canal Rd. along the edge of the meadow. This graveled roadbed is passable all year. There is a side loop through the upland forest across the creek. The Canal Acres trail begins at bollards off of Canal Rd. south of SW Childs Rd. Trails are unpaved and may be muddy in winter.

How to Get There

From Lake Oswego drive south on State St. (Hwy. 43) to the south end of Oswego Lake and take McVey Ave. west. McVey turns into SW Stafford Rd. Follow Stafford Road south, and just south of SW Rosemont, turn right (west) onto SW Childs. Bryant Woods Park is on the right just past SW Bryant Ave. From the south take I-205 to Stafford exit (Exit #3), drive north on Stafford Rd., and turn west on SW Childs Rd.

By Deborah Lev

For more information: City of Lake Oswego, see Resources.

Elk Rock Island and Spring Park

Elk Rock Island offers a wilderness adventure a mere six miles south of downtown Portland. You can hop the boulders across the river channel to this untamed spot (when the water is low enough), claim an ascent of a 15,000-foot extinct volcano (the tip of which is now the island), and gaze upon a historic Native American hunting ground on the west side of the Willamette—the rocky cliff called Elk Rock. How's that for an urban adventure?

The trail system covers the perimeter as well as the wooded interior of the island. On the west side of the island there is a secluded beach within an inlet suitable for boat landing. You can take a leisurely stroll among the trees and along the beach areas, or scramble up and over rocks. Although there are several "unofficial" trails branching off from the main path, use of these is strongly discouraged in order to protect existing native vegetation and exposed rock outcroppings. Some of the regulation trails are rough, but there is very little chance you would get lost with the exception of losing oneself in the rugged beauty of this uncommon place.

The island is commonly known as Elk Rock Island, even though it was donated to the City of Portland in 1940 by the Peter Kerr family with the condition that the property "shall be used solely as a public park . . . and that (it) shall be known as 'Peter Kerr Park.'" The island and the cliff opposite were named, so the story goes, from a time when Native American hunters would herd elk from the Tualatin Valley to the river's edge, and force them over the cliff into the water to slaughter them.

The formation of Elk Rock Island began over 40 million years ago as a sea-floor eruption. The resulting dense, mountain-sized mass of lava is made up of Waverly Heights Basalt. Older than the more

Location
Willamette River, near SE 19th and SE Sparrow in Milwaukie.

Activities
Hiking
Canoeing, boating
Fishing

Facilities
None

Fees and Regulations
No entrance fees
No pets
No bikes

Highlights
Directly opposite the island you'll see the high, rocky cliff called Elk Rock (at Bishop's Close), where indigenous Native American hunters once drove game animals over the edge to slaughter them, much like neolithic hunters in Europe. There is also an active great blue heron rookery on the island, best viewed before the spring foliage returns.

Public Transit
Take Tri-Met #33 to the north end of Milwaukie, near the River Rd. stop. Walk approximately 1/4 mile to the trailhead.

Thomas Guide 656

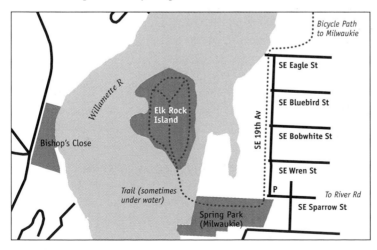

common Columbia River Basalt, Waverly Heights Basalt is also harder and therefore impervious to the erosion that afflicts its softer, younger cousin. The fact that much of this unique lava flow is exposed on the island should be a draw to budding geologists.

Several endemic and uncommon plant species are known to grow on the island including snowberry, salal, tall Oregon grape, Columbia lily, trillium, false Solomon's-seal, black cottonwood, Oregon white oak, Pacific madrone, Pacific yew, tiger lily, cluster lily, and rattlesnake plantain.

Over 60 species of birds have been observed on the island. A highlight is the active heron rookery best viewed before the spring foliage returns. You may also spot osprey, downy woodpeckers, great egrets, and northern shrike. An island bird list is available through Portland Parks and Recreation.

Elk Rock Island is that wild place we all wanted in our backyard when we were kids. Here's your chance to be a kid again.

Access

On foot, Elk Rock Island can be reached most of the summer and fall via the trail through Spring Park and across the dry rocky channel that connects this "island" to the east bank of the Willamette River. Seasonal freshets raise the river's water level and fill the connecting channel, typically cutting off trail access in November, December, and sometimes January through April or May. The trails through Spring Park are a bit overgrown, unpaved, and fraught with blackberries (in summer bring a bucket!). There is a slight slope leading down to the channel crossing that can get muddy in the spring. Tennis shoes or light hiking boots are appropriate.

Elk Rock Island can be reached by canoe or kayak year-round. The nearest boat ramp is just north of the island at the Jefferson Boat Ramp in Milwaukie.

How to Get There

From the Ross Island Bridge, take SE McLoughlin Blvd. south 4 miles; veer right onto SE River Rd. and go approximately 1/4 mile. Turn right (west) on SE Sparrow St. and proceed 3 blocks to the trailhead at SE 19th St. The trailhead is to the left, just past the overhead railroad trestle. There is limited parking on SE 19th and SE 20th.

By Ron Carley and Mary Rose Navarro

For more information: Portland Bureau of Parks and Recreation or Friends of Elk Rock Island, see Resources.

Mt. Scott and Kellogg Creek Watershed

Mt. Scott and Kellogg Creeks flow for more than 24 miles, at times snaking through residential backyards and at other times buried in underground culverts. Where allowed to course in their natural channels, they provide open space, fish and wildlife habitat, scenic views, and enhanced water quality for more than 36,000 residents of their combined 16-square-mile watershed.

Springs at the base of Scouter's Mountain form the headwaters of Mt. Scott Creek. From pastoral Happy Valley the stream flows through rural, residential, and commercial lands as it meanders through remnant greenspaces. The headwaters near Happy Valley Park were once owned by the stream's namesake, Harvey Scott, The *Oregonian's* editor from 1865 to 1910.

From Happy Valley the stream flows through a deep, western red cedar-canopied canyon before it dives under Sunnyside Road, flows between Mt. Talbert and Mt. Scott, and cascades over a waterfall into the Clackamas River's prehistoric channel.

Between Precision Castparts' corporate park and North Clackamas Regional Park, Mt. Scott is joined by Phillips and Deer Creeks, both of which have been channelized. Once through culverts under Hwy. 224, the stream flows freely again among alder thickets and camas lily wetlands, meandering at the northern edge of North Clackamas Park and joining Kellogg Creek in the park's southwest corner.

Adapted from "Kellogg Creek, Mt. Scott Creek: Wetlands, Wildlife, Water Quality;" The Wetlands Conservancy, Urban Streams Council

North Clackamas District Park

Location
Between SE 82nd and
Linwood Ave., south of
SE Harmony Rd. and
north of the Southern
Pacific/Burlington
Northern railroad tracks.
South of the North
Clackamas Aquatic Park
and the Oregon Institute
of Technology campus.

Activities
Hiking

Facilities
None

Fees and Regulations
Restricted hours
Pets on leash

Highlights
Mature Oregon white oak
and an oak-ash-camas
community that is rare in
north Clackamas County.

Public Transit
Tri-Met #29, #72, and #79
stop at SE 82nd and
Harmony/Sunnyside.
Tri-Met #28 stops at
Harmony Rd. and Price
Fuller across from the
Oregon Institute of
Technology campus and
Aquatic Park access road.

Thomas Guide 657

The as-yet unnamed and undeveloped North Clackamas District Park occupies approximately 85 acres of upland and wetland forest and meadow on the floodplain of Mt. Scott Creek, and upland forest on the slope north of the creek. The area has recovered nicely from severe overgrazing by horses when it was "Slim's Warbonnet Stables" in the 1980s. This is one of the few remaining areas in developing north Clackamas County where mature Oregon white oaks are common. A community of Oregon white oak and Oregon ash with an understory of camas can be found near the Southern Pacific/Burlington Northern railroad tracks that form the southern boundary of the park. There is a large central meadow which is ringed by forest and provides a marvelous natural vista. The east end of this meadow can be accessed from the parking lot of the North Clackamas Aquatic Park. Nesting red-tailed hawks and barn owls feed on the abundant mice and cottontails. The nightly late winter-early spring din of Pacific chorus frogs can be heard for quite a distance. Wintering varied thrushes are common, and accipiters are year-round residents.

Forest vegetation is being replanted along Mt. Scott Creek by volunteers, and stream improvements are also planned to improve fish habitat. Development of park amenities, such as trails, was delayed by an ongoing cleanup of soil and groundwater contamination at the eastern end, and recently-completed construction of a stormwater detention facility near the western end by Clackamas County. The master plan was designed to be compatible with the stormwater detention function, and the first phase, trail development, will be implemented in 2001. Park facilities will likely emphasize the natural values of the site and focus on recreational trails and environmental education. The plan also calls for an active recreation component, including sports fields.

Clackamas County and the Clackamas County Development Agency own the land. The Inter-governmental Agreement between Clackamas County, the Clackamas County Development Agency, Water and Environment Services, and North Clackamas Parks and Recreation District includes a designated transportation corridor through the site which could be developed for expansion of Harmony Road, an extension of Sunnybrook Road, and/or light rail along the slope south of Harmony Road, and in the vicinity of OIT and the North Clackamas Aquatic Park.

Access

There is no formal access and trails are being planned as *Wild in the City* goes to press. Contact the Park District Office at 503-794-8002 for information about access.

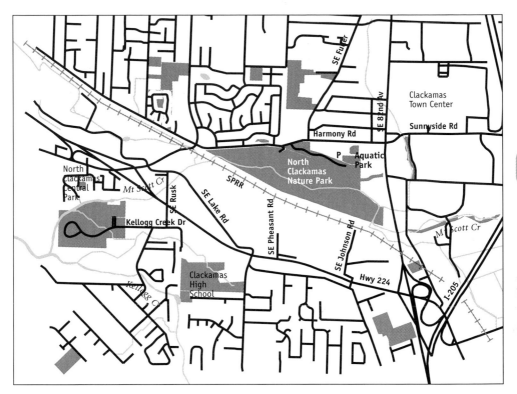

How to Get There

From I-205 take the Clackamas Town Center exit and go west on Sunnyside Rd. past SE 82nd Ave. (where Sunnyside becomes Harmony Rd.). Turn left at the second light by the North Clackamas Park District Aquatic Park sign. Follow the entrance and park in the Aquatic Park lot.

By Lynn Sharp

For more information: North Clackamas Parks and Recreation District, see Resources.

Sellwood Riverfront Park

Location
SE Spokane and Oaks Park Way

Activities
Hiking
Biking
Canoeing, boating

Facilities
Toilets
Wheelchair accessible
Paved and unpaved trail
Parking
Picnic area
Dock, canoe launch

Fees and Regulations
Pets on leash

Highlights
The best access to the Willamette on the east side of the river. Small created wetland next to cottonwood forest in the northeast portion of the park. Dock and canoe/kayak launch. Great views of the Macadam Bay Club across the river and downtown Portland skyline juxtaposed with the west side of Ross Island.

It may look a little "skanky" but the tiny wetland created at the north end of the park is a great place for kids to look at dragonflies and catch tadpoles.

Be sure to check out the historic Sellwood Pioneer Church en route to Sellwood Riverfront Park. The church (corner of SE Grand and SE Spokane), formerly St John's Episcopal Church of Milwaukie, Oregon, was dedicated in 1851. It was moved to its present location in June 1961 by barge by the Lang Syne Society of Portland. The church is now maintained by the Sellwood-Moreland Improvement League (SMILE) and is rented out for weddings, funerals, and other special events. This is a major money-maker for the neighborhood association.

Sellwood Riverfront Park was acquired in the 1960s but wasn't developed until the late 1980s. Prior to development it was a Himalayan blackberry and sawdust patch and former mill site. The Portland Park Bureau, working with Carol Mayer Reed, a local landscape architect, created this much-needed access to the Willamette for the Sellwood-Moreland neighborhood.

One of the conditions for development of the park was the installation of a native plant wetland and riparian area in the north portion of the park, adjacent to the cottonwood forest. Unfortunately, the wetland has been invaded by the voracious, introduced bullfrog that preys on our native frogs. On the positive side, stealthy green herons, which I've seen several times plying the shallow, dirty-looking water, prey on bullfrogs, and the small demonstration wetland which was created with native emergent marsh plants and the adjacent willow and other riparian vegetation continues to thrive.

Purple iris now dominate the open water, where wapato used to flourish. The easily accessible path curves around the wetland and leads to the boat ramp and parking area through the more formal, grassy areas that are home to boom boxes and frisbees.

A rough, informal trail runs along the bank of the Willamette toward Oaks Amusement Park. The trail passes through what used to be Portland General Electric (Enron) property and is now one of Metro's newest Greenspace acquisitions. In fact, Metro not only acquired the five-acre forest that lies between Sellwood Riverfront Park and Oaks Amusement Park but they also acquired an additional 39 acres along the railroad right of way between the park and OMSI. This is the land that will be the OMSI to Springwater Greenway Trail, which is scheduled to open in summer of 2001. The five-acre forest will be integrated into Portland's park holdings and managed as an extension of the wetland feature and Oaks Bottom Wildlife Refuge, which is a short walk to the north on the OMSI-Springwater Trail.

There are great views of the Macadam Bay Club across the river and downtown Portland skyline to the west side of Ross Island. The former owner of the Sellwood Riverfront property was given the right to a long-term lease at Macadam Bay Club moorage as the quid pro quo for the city receiving development rights to Sellwood Riverfront

Park. Two great Portland parks were created in the process: Sellwood Riverfront and Willamette Butterfly Park. With the addition of the cottonwood forest, known for years as Willamettte Crossing, and the existing Oaks Bottom Wildlife Refuge, you can explore the natural history of the Willamette River for days.

Access

Via SE Spokane on the east end of the Sellwood Bridge on Oaks Park Way en route to Oaks Pioneer Amusement Park. You can walk here easily from Oaks Bottom Wildlife Refuge or Sellwood Park.

In the park, there is an easily accessible path that curves around the wetland. A sturdy, wheelchair-accessible boardwalk crosses over the open water area of this wetland.

Another very rough, informal trail runs along the bank of the Willamette toward Oaks Amusement Park.

There are two good canoe and kayak put-ins at the park. The first is a fully wheelchair-accessible public dock and the second is two sets of steps just past the boat ramp, both of which allow direct access to the Willamette River.

How to Get There

From the west side of the Willamette, take the Sellwood Bridge. Take a left on SE 6th and turn immediately west (left) on SE Spokane; cross the railroad tracks and turn right onto Oaks Park Way and then left into the park. You can also walk from Oaks Bottom Wildlife Refuge or Sellwood Park. *See Map on Page 69.*

By Mike Houck

For more information: Portland Bureau of Parks and Recreation, see Resources.

Public Transit
Tri-Met #40 on SE Spokane or #70 on SE 13th.

Thomas Guide 626

Oaks Bottom Wildlife Refuge

While Forest Park garners most of the attention for being Portland's largest park and a major element of Olmsted's vision for Portland's park system, it was Oaks Bottom that became the city's first official urban wildlife refuge. It is both Portland's premier Willamette River natural area and where I first got my feet wet in city politics.

A walk around Oaks Bottom

When visiting Oaks Bottom, plan two to three hours for a leisurely stroll which should begin on SE Sellwood Boulevard at the north end of Sellwood Park for a general overview of the Bottoms. It's from the bluff overlooking the Bottoms that you get an appreciation for how precious, and unique, Oaks Bottom is in the Portland landscape. The 163-acre refuge spreads before you, creating a greensward between the historic Sellwood neighborhood and Ross Island. It is the juxtaposition of this Willamette River floodplain with the downtown skyline that epitomizes "wild in the city."

From the bluff walk back to Sellwood Park and take the dirt path down to the bottoms, stopping briefly to scan the south fill's now-grassy habitat for ring-necked pheasant and California quail. The trail down the bluff can be muddy if it has been raining, so be prepared for wet, muddy shoes. The most popular route is to walk counter-clockwise, east along the base of the bluff. The entire loop is two miles. Here, song sparrows, Bewick's wrens, black-capped chickadees, bushtits, and spotted towhees vie for your attention. If you look north across the open water you'll see as many as 50 or sometimes 100 herons feeding, resting, or flying about, depending on the time of year. Great egrets can often be seen feeding with the herons. Common and hooded mergansers, double-crested cormorants, northern shovelers, mallards, green-winged teal, and wood ducks are usually quite abundant. More than 100 species of birds have been seen in the bottoms. A few rarities have also been spotted in the bottoms, including magpie, red-shouldered hawk, raven, swamp sparrow, and nesting Anna's hummingbird. Jimbo Beckmann got the first state record for an Anna's nest in the thick willows near the mausoleum in the mid-1980s.

The rest of the walk to the north fill is along an undulating, usually muddy path that constitutes about two-thirds of the hike. This is where you're most likely to see green herons. It can be either thick with birds or almost dead, depending on time of year and day. This is the place to look for downy woodpeckers and northern flickers, both the yellow-shafted and red-shafted races. More bushtit nests, penduline sock-like affairs made of muted green and gray moss and lichens, hanging low from ash trees or shrubs, are seen here than anywhere in the metro area.

Location
East of the OMSI-Springwater Trail, north of Sellwood Park in the Willamette River floodplain

Activities
Hiking

Facilities
Trail unpaved

Fees and Regulations
Pets on leash

Highlights
Portland's first official urban wildlife refuge. A 163-acre wetland system within view of downtown Portland. Home to more than a hundred species of birds. The adjacent Sellwood Park, in addition to having restrooms, has a grove of Douglas fir that add to Oaks Bottom's habitat diversity. Rustic and wild. One of the region's best-known and most popular greenspaces.

Public Transit
Tri-Met #19 on SE Milwaukie Ave. or #70 on SE 13th

Thomas Guide 626

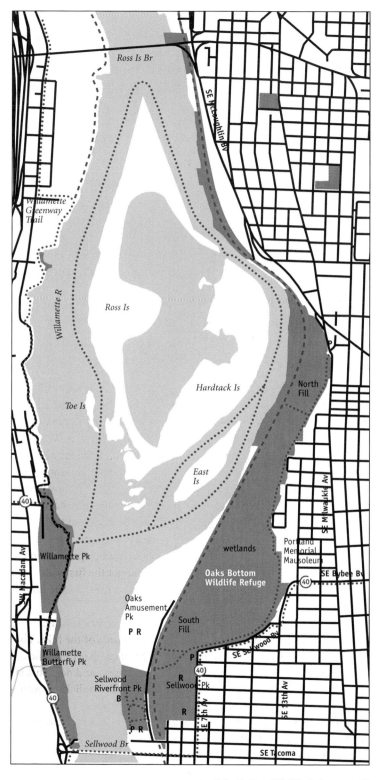

Ross Is Br

SE McLoughlin Bv

Willamette
Greenway
Trail

Willamette R

Ross Is

Toe Is

Hardtack Is

North
Fill

40

SE Milwaukie Av

East
Is

SW Macadan Av

Willamette Pk

wetlands

Portland
Memorial
Mausoleum

SE Bybee Bv

40

Oaks Bottom
Wildlife Refuge

Oaks
Amusement
Pk

P R

South
Fill

P

SE Sellwood Bv

Willamette
Butterfly Pk

40

R

40

SE 13th Av

Sellwood
Riverfront Pk

B

Sellwood Pk

R

SE 7th Av

R

P R

Sellwood Br

SE Tacoma

After walking directly under the mausoleum and crematorium, which is reputed to have a fantastic art collection inside (as well as the oversized great blue heron mural), it's another mile or so to the north fill. See if you can observe the subtle vegetation changes along the way. As you walk north, the trail trends slightly toward a southwest aspect. The combination of this southerly exposure and apparently well-drained soil yields a slightly more xeric plant community than you start out with at Sellwood Park. Where there were no oak trees at all at the trip's start, both Oregon white oak and Pacific madrone grow here. And anytime you see oak, look for poison oak, which does grow along the trail. For some reason there is one purple patch of *Collinsia* growing amidst the snowberry and sword-fern understory.

Oregon white oak and Pacific madrone grow here. And any time you see oak, look for poison oak.

After crossing a short wooden bridge and a brief walk through a cottonwood and black locust forest, you break out into the open of the north fill. From here you can continue up the vacated road that serves as a trail back to the north parking area on SE Milwaukie Avenue. If you plan to complete the two-mile loop, bear left toward the Willamette River across the North Fill. (A pedestrian underpass is planned to allow for passage under the railroad tracks to the Greenway Trail.) Walk back south along the OMSI-Springwater Trail. (The OMSI-Springwater Trail is scheduled to open the summer of 2001. Until then, there may be restricted access by the rail line owner.) Along the exposed, well-drained railroad berm, the vegetation is decidedly more dry-site species like Scot's broom, dogbane, Oregon grape, and poison oak. You can either walk north and explore the riparian forest along the OMSI-Springwater Trail or head south to complete your two-mile loop. As you walk south, there are great views of East and Hardtack Islands and the Willamette's main channel from the elevated railroad berm.

Just downstream of the Oregon Yacht Club's houseboats, look for the culvert that allows water into and out of Oaks Bottom. On the east side of the tracks you can see the water control structure, or small dam, that allows the water level in the Bottoms to be controlled. This is an area where it's good to have a spotting scope. You can scan the Willamette's shallow water upstream from East Island for gulls and the Bottoms for waterfowl and great blue heron. I've counted over 100 herons in the Bottoms during nesting season, when they cram the open water to catch carp to feed their young on nearby Ross Island.

As you reach the south fill you can either cross immediately back to the east (through a second underpass) and the point at which the trail descends from the bluff or continue another 200 feet south along the tracks and head up the bluff next to the Park Bureau composting and storage area. Or, if you are ambitious, continue south along the tracks or Oaks Park Way to Sellwood Park and access to the Willamette River.

Saving the Bottoms

In the early 1970s, the city envisioned museums, possibly a motocross course, and a gondola that would transport people into the Bottoms from the adjacent Sellwood neighborhood. Oaks Bottom became an instant *cause celebre* and the city's first serious foray into debates about the future management of the Portland Park system, and the larger question of the city's responsibility for retaining wildlife and wildlife habitat in the urban core. It was also the training ground for urban Greenspace activists.

The Audubon Society of Portland, led by Al Miller, had joined forces with the Sellwood-Moreland Improvement League (SMILE), The Nature Conservancy, and others to fight the ill-conceived scheme to fill the bottoms. The entire episode was captured in the film "Riparian," by Diana Cvitanovich for Jim Blashfield's PSU film studio. "Riparian," available on tape through Portland Parks and Bureau of Environmental Services, explores the history of the Willamette River in downtown Portland. Through extensive interviews, Cvitanovich set up the first real discussion regarding the role of natural areas like Oaks Bottom in an urban park system.

The Bottoms was already well on its way to conversion from wetland to upland by the mid-1970s. The stadium (I-405) freeway rubble had been deposited in the north end of the wetlands, forming what we now call the north fill. The south end of the bottoms, now the south fill, had been used for years as a garbage dump. And, much earlier, the bottoms had been cut off from the Willamette by the railroad fill for the Portland Traction rail line.

Due to intense public pressure, a changing Park Bureau, and emerging political support for urban Greenspaces, the city dropped its plans to fill the Bottoms. Even so, the Park Bureau was reluctant to designate the Bottoms as an "official" wildlife refuge. Some bureaucrats still had visions of soccer and baseball fields. Sporadic guerrilla activism became common. Brilliant yellow "wildlife refuge" signs, fashioned from standard Oregon Department of Fish and Wildlife signs, with "city park" stenciled on them, mysteriously appeared around the Bottoms in the early '80s. Shortly thereafter The *Oregonian*, the *Sellwood Bee* and other media were referring to "Oaks Bottom Wildlife Refuge." But it wasn't until 1988 that Portland City Council formally adopted a management plan that established Oaks Bottom as Portland's first urban wildlife refuge.

During this period the Park Bureau also underwent a metamorphosis under the leadership of then-city commissioner Mike Lindberg and through sustained work of Jim Sjulin, Steve Bricker, and Fred Nilsen, all with the bureau's nascent natural resource program. Charles Jordan, who was once City Commissioner, was brought back to Portland from Austin, Texas, as Portland Park Commissioner.

Oaks Bottom became an instant cause celebre *and the city's first serious foray into debates about the future management of the Portland Park system, and the larger question of the city's responsibility for retaining wildlife and wildlife habitat in the urban core.*

Jordan returned a nationally prominent parks and greenways advocate, which helped pave the way for a renaissance in natural area management in Portland. Oaks Bottom, formerly the catalyst for change, is now one of Portland's urban greenspace flagships.

Swamped by Eager Beavers

Many people ask why the Bottoms seems to have more standing water year-round than it did, say, ten or fifteen years ago. While the management team decided a water control structure was needed to regulate water into and from the Willamette River, it was the original Corps of Engineers—pesky beavers —that beat us to the punch by damming up the meandering channel that connects the Bottoms with the Willamette. The Oaks Bottom management team then had to figure out a way to lower the water after virtually all of the willow had been eliminated, drowning after years of high water. Ralph Rogers, wetland ecologist for the Environmental Protection Agency, put a drain pipe through the beaver dam. The beaver promptly backed up to the pipe and crammed mud into the downstream end. It was only after a perforated pipe was inserted through the dam that the water control structure could be used.

Slow Recovery

Rogers then did a vegetation survey of the Bottoms and devised a water level control scheme. The Portland Park Bureau can now remove or replace "stop logs" in the small dam that is adjacent to the railroad berm to control water level throughout the year, the objective being to mimic the natural fluctuations in water level that would occur in Oaks Bottom were it still part of the Willamette River. A walk around the Bottoms today will demonstrate that unwanted invasive, non-native plants like reed canarygrass and purple loosestrife have, indeed, begun to be replaced by native species like wapato, rushes, and sedges. It's likely, however, that some physical removal, especially of purple loosestrife, will also be an ongoing aspect of a long-term management plan for Oaks Bottom.

The south fill is now being managed as a meadow habitat and has even been burned to discourage woody plant growth. Himalayan blackberry, ivy, and clematis are being removed and replaced with native trees and shrubs; and the very rough trail that runs along the base of the bluff continues to be maintained in its rustic state.

Access

From the north via parking area off SE Milwaukie Ave.; from the south from Sellwood Park via a switchback trail at the north end of Sellwood Park; from the OMSI-Springwater Trail along the

Willamette River. The entire loop is two miles, although there are alternative routes. Trails can be rough and muddy.

The walk to the north fill is along an undulating, usually partially muddy path that constitutes about two-thirds of the hike.

How to Get There

From the west side of the Willamette take the Sellwood Bridge and turn left (north) onto SE 7th. Park in the parking lot at the north end of Sellwood Park (where SE 7th curves east as SE Sellwood Blvd.). A few feet from the parking lot is a trailhead that winds down the bluff (keep right) to the bottoms. From the north take the SE Milwaukie exit off SE McLoughlin and turn immediately right into the parking lot that overlooks Oaks Bottom's north fill area.

You can also access the bottoms by foot or bicycle from the OMSI-Springwater Greenway Trail.

By Mike Houck

For more information: Portland Bureau of Parks and Recreation, see Resources.

Fall: A Berry Special Season

Yet when the Autumn sun
  Colours the trees,
Should you come seeking me,
  Know me by these:
Bronze leaves and crimson leaves,
  Soon to be shed;
Dark little berries,
  On stalks turning red.
From "Song of the Dogwood Fairy," by Cicely Mary Barker

By late summer and early fall, the glut of juicy blackberries, raspberries, and strawberries has all been jellied and jammed, and most berry pickers have retired to mend their scratched and stained hands. But when these conventional fruits have withered from the vine, there are still berries to be had.

Black and Blue All Over

The berries of the red-osier dogwood (*Cornus stolonifera*), a shrub of moist stream bottoms such as are found along the Columbia Slough, are typical of the fruits of the autumn season. In early fall, the dogwood bears small, greenish-blue berries on the red stems that are the hallmark of this species. These berries usually persist well into the season.

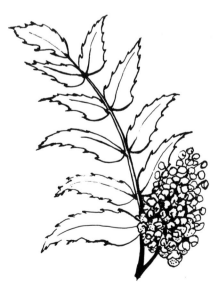

Most of the fall fruits of our native shrubs fall into this category—small and black or blue—often a dull, dusty blue, such as Oregon grape (*Berberis nervosa*). Salal berries are also a case in point. The dull, dark blue berries of the salal (*Gaultheria shallon*) often go unnoticed, as they grow hidden beneath the leathery leaves. The berries are somewhat seedy and lack the luster of the more popular blackberries, but they are certainly tasty. Salal figured prominently in the diet of Northwest Indians.

Oranges and Reds

Many of the fall berries in the metro area are the orange and red fruits of ornamentals. These small, pulpy berries, like those of the introduced English holly (*Ilex aquifolium*), seem to herald the fast-approaching season of yuletide cheer. However, eating these fruits is not such a cheery experience; these berries are strictly for show!

Native, berry-laden trees are often used in urban landscapes where their bright red or orange fruits blend with the colors of the fall canopy. Sitka mountain ash (*Sorbus sitchensis*) is normally a tree of the Cascades. Its orange berries, borne in clusters, are dulled somewhat by a dusty bloom. This is a smaller tree than the European mountain ash often found in urban areas. Birds seem to find the fermented berries of our native ash and hawthorn quite a treat, but to human tastes, the berries of Sitka ash are apparently quite sour.

Winter White

A list of fall berries would not be complete without the snowberry (*Symphoricarpus albus*). Also called waxberry, for its white, waxy fruits, the snowberry is an unmistakable and fairly common component of our fall landscape. Its berries persist well into winter on the bare shrub stalk. Northwest Indians reportedly rubbed the berries on burns and rashes, but considered them unfit for consumption.

The fruits of fall may not be as plump and juicy as the summer fare; they may not even be edible, but to an ardent urban naturalist, they are the aesthetic (and sometimes tasty) rewards of diligent observation.

By Connie Levesque

Mosquitoes: What's The Buzz?

Portlanders take every opportunity on summer evenings to break out the barbecues, play softball, enjoy their favorite music, and play in our parks. A whining cloud of hungry mosquitoes, however, can put a damper on even the driest and most pleasant of evenings.

To most people the mosquito is a pest to be avoided or at best tolerated. Despite their bad rep and irritating manner, they are a fascinating part of the local insect scene, and knowing something of their natural history may help make those itchy lumps on your shoulder easier to take.

There have been 17 species found since Multnomah County began collecting mosquitoes in the 1930s. As one might suspect, they occur most often near water and can be separated in part by the habitat they live in: floodwater species, rainwater dwellers, and those mosquitoes that inhabit still waters of ditches, old tires, ponds, and swamps.

Floodwater Mosquitoes

Mosquitoes of the genus *Aedes* are our floodwater species, which lay their eggs in exposed soil that is susceptible to seasonal flooding. Their larvae develop in temporary water and generally only produce one generation yearly. *Aedes vexans* (guess how it got its name!) and *A. sticticus* are two flood species. *Vexans* is our most common pest and makes its home in riverine floodplains. Spring freshets flood the areas between eight and 20 feet along these watercourses and eggs hatch in response to warming springtime temperatures (45° to 50° F). Cottonwood and willow wetlands in places such as Smith and Bybee Lakes and Oaks Bottom Wildlife Refuge are good floodwater habitat. The young develop quite rapidly, sometimes within a week of flooding. The adults remain in the vicinity to mate. Females will fly as far as 20 miles in search of a blood meal for their eggs.

Rainwater Mosquitoes

Three other species of *Aedes* breed in areas where winter rainwater collects. I have sampled their larvae in December and January and there are reports of *Aedes* under frozen pools of water! March is the time of greatest larval activity for these species. The most persistent pest from this trio is *Aedes increpitus*, which is found in wooded areas.

Permanent Water Mosquitoes

The Portland area hosts five species of *Culex* that are found in ditches, ponds, buckets, tires, catch basins, and swamps. *Culex pipiens* is the common house mosquito and is our most frequent residential pest. This is probably the culprit at your Sunday evening barbecue. They lay eggs in masses or rafts in polluted areas such as septic water, remain near their breeding area, and are generally active from dusk 'til dawn. *Culex* mosquitoes can be told by their blunt abdomen or stomach, which contrasts with the acute posterior of *Aedes*.

Anopheline Mosquitoes

Anopheline mosquitoes are uncommon in the city and lay their eggs singly on the edges of open, shaded water such as sloughs, slow streams, and ponds. They like unpolluted water, and their larvae must lie flat on the water's surface since they lack the typical breathing siphon found in other species. Female *Anopheles* can easily be recognized because they hold their body in a vertical position when they rest and bite. All other species sit and bite in a more horizontal position. Columbia Slough, Sauvie Island, and Multnomah Channel are good places to meet Anopheline mosquitoes.

Eggs

Up to 200 eggs are laid and some *Aedes* eggs remain viable for ten years!

Blood Sucking

Only female mosquitoes bite for blood and all Northwest species have this habit. There is one tropical genus, *Toxorhynchites*, which has a curved proboscis that it uses to feed on nectar, that does not require a blood meal for egg development. The larvae of this genus also feed on other mosquito larvae. You should be advised that to the maximum extent practicable, mosquito bites should be avoided, given one recent West Nile virus outbreak in New York and the northward progression of tropical diseases.

Crane flies

Crane flies resemble large, long-legged mosquitoes. They are often mistaken for their biting cousins but are in a totally different family of flies and feed as adults on vegetable matter. If handled, their legs fall off easily. They are also known as mosquito hawks, although there is no evidence they feed on mosquitoes. In fact, little is known about their adult feeding habits.

Portland Mosquito History

In 1924 D. C. Mote, chair of Oregon State University's entomology department, advised a group of Portland's leading citizens on a major impediment to economic development—the local mosquito population! It was Mote who introduced the first mosquito-eating fish Gambusia (*Gambusia affinis*) from California in 1926. Mr. H. H. Riddel of Skamania County, Washington, started a mosquito control program and led field operations for the Portland Chamber of Commerce's Mosquito Control Committee from 1930 to 1940. The Chamber provided funds for mosquito control.

By Peter DeChant

Portland, City of Herons

Spirit of Place:
Great Blue Heron

Out of their loneliness for each other

two reeds, or maybe two shadows, lurch

forward and become suddenly a life

lifted from the dawn to the rain. It is

the wilderness come back again, a lagoon

with our city reflected in its eye.

We live by faith in such presences.

It is a test for us, that thin

but real, undulating figure that promises,

"if you keep faith I will exist

at the edge, where your vision joins

the sunlight and the rain: heads in the light,

feet that go down in the mud where the truth is."

—William Stafford

It took me several minutes to catch up with him as he hurried from the Hilton ballroom, but I finally caught up with Mayor Bud Clark, arguably Portland's most colorful—and accessible—mayor. Clark had just welcomed several hundred fish and wildlife managers from around the United States to Portland, regaling them with stories about poling his canoe on the backwaters of Scappoose bottoms and the Willamette River. He waxed poetic about watching great blue herons coursing across Portland's skyline, eye-level with diners at Atwater's, and recounted repeated heron sightings as he plied the Willamette. Here was a major city mayor who drags his canoe on a bicycle-drawn trailer down to the Willamette every chance he gets. The wildlife managers were dumbstruck! Clark went on, enthusing about how important it was for him to see herons glide by downtown skyscrapers as they cruised between their nesting colony on Ross Island and feeding grounds at Smith and Bybee Lakes.

This presented an opportunity too good to pass up. After collaring him before he managed to exit on SW Sixth, I asked why Portland didn't establish "old cranky" as our official city bird?

In his inimitable style, Mayor Clark emitted a "Whoop, whoop," and said, "Hell, why not? Go see Lindberg," referring to City Commissioner Mike Lindberg, who was then Commissioner of Parks. Ethan Seltzer, Lindberg's staffer, arranged for a formal proclamation, initiating the official city process. Within a week or two, Portland City Council had adopted the great blue heron as nature's emissary to Portland.

To ensure an air of respectability for this auspicious occasion, we asked Oregon's then-poet laureate, William Stafford, if he would write a poem to commemorate the adoption of the heron as our city bird. Stafford penned his "Spirit of Place" in 1987 for the annual Great Blue Heron week, which falls in late May or early June each year, and captured our intent marvelously.

Blue Heron, An Activist's Ale

As with most good things in Portland, one thing led to another, which in turn led to the nearest brew pub. BridgePort was at the time the first among a small flock of microbreweries that became the watering holes for hatching greenspace schemes. The afternoon that Portland formally adopted the heron, Ralph Rogers and I were quaffing a stout when pubster and single-malt visionary Stuart Ramsey approached our table. "How're things at Audubon?" he queried. After I recounted our success at adopting the heron as our official city bird, Stuart disappeared and re-materialized with brewmeister Karl Ockert, who had just concocted a great, as-yet-unnamed, ale. A few sips later, and BridgePort's newest brew was christened Blue Heron Ale.

Blue Heron became BridgePort's flagship brew, although there was one brief hiatus during the mid-1980s, until a devout group of heron and ale supporters pestered owners Dick and Nancy Ponzi to continue its production. The Ponzis moved on, having sold the brewery, but Ockert is still brewmaster; Blue Heron Ale lives on, its logo having morphed to a stylized dark-blue silhouette.

Art of the Deal: Bringing Herons Downtown

Before Dick Ponzi became a Northwest vintner, he engineered amusement rides in southern California. He and his wife Nancy were chums with Portland artists Ray and Jere

Grimm.

Again, one thing led to another and the heron raised its ungainly head to be celebrated in Pioneer Square. The Ponzis and their comrades-in-arts had decided to install a "weather machine" at the square, having settled on three semiotic designs for the sculpture's apex—a sun, a dragon, and a pelican. "A pelican?!" I bellowed to Dick. "Pelicans don't live in Portland," I insisted. "You've got to do a heron—a great blue heron." I wasn't at all sure he really took me seriously, but a few months later, when the now-famous, whimsical Weather Machine was dedicated, it was a tall, stately-looking heron that popped out of the machine's penultimate silver globe. The brilliant, gold sun portends an all-too-infrequent sunny day, and the dragon presages storms. The heron's role is to foretell rain, which means most days the heron's steel-blue visage sits atop the weather machine.

Going To the Wall for Herons

The final chapter, thus far, in establishing the preeminence of herons in River City came as serendipitously as Blue Heron Ale. Walking up West Burnside, I noted a wall mural, a 30-foot likeness of a bottle of Henry Weinhard's Ale being applied to a heretofore shabby-looking brick wall. I checked to see who was responsible and, finding no one in the office, left a cryptic note: "Love your beer mural, willing to do a heron in Southeast Portland?" By the time I had walked back to my Northwest Portland apartment, my message machine was flashing. "Sure, I'd love to do a heron. My name is Mark Bennett; give me a call." A short while later we had established that Bennett lived directly across the Willamette from Oaks Bottom Wildlife Refuge, and would love nothing more than to beautify what we both thought to be the ugliest blank wall in Portland—the Portland Memorial, which presented its drab, gray fortress-like wall over the Bottoms' wetlands.

Lynn Kitagawa, long-time Audubon volunteer and artist, supplied the heron watercolor; Miller Paint donated the paint; Don Bolton, who lives on the bluff overlooking Oaks Bottom, provided the scaffolding; and by May of 1991 Bennett had installed a 70-by-50-foot stately heron looking out over Oaks Bottom and the Willamette floodplain. Portland Memorial's manager received so many rave reviews for the newly adorned wall that there may one day be a wapato, wood duck, and wetlands motif covering the entire structure.

By Mike Houck

Willamette Park

No place on the Willamette combines as many pleasurable activities as along the Greenway near Willamette Park. You can walk or bike to the park and rent a canoe or kayak at Ebb and Flow Paddlesports, just up the street on SW Nebraska. It's a short walk from there with your craft, which you have the option of pulling behind you on foot with a small trailer to the boat ramp, for a paddle on the Willamette River. You could start the day at Café Du Berry just across the street, and at the end of a long hot paddle take in a brew at the Fulton Pub, which is immediately adjacent to Ebb and Flow.

Willamette Park itself is one of the best wildlife viewing areas on the river. From near the boat ramp you can see great blue heron and bald eagle nests on Ross Island. If you have a pair of binoculars or, better yet, a spotting scope, you can see osprey and Canada goose nests atop the electrical transmission towers at Oaks Bottom Wildlife Refuge across the Willamette. After they return from sunnier southern climes, purple martins can be seen nesting or feeding their young that poke their heads out of the large white gourds just north of the boat ramp. Dave Fouts, local martin advocate, has established hanging gourds that attract martins and repel starlings. The gourds swing in the wind, high on an artificial nesting pole that looks more like a mobile sculpture than nesting site.

Martins were nearly eliminated by starlings and house sparrows, which usurped all available nest sites in this region and elsewhere in the west. It is only through efforts of martin lovers like Fouts, and before him Hugh Prescott, that martins still ply the Willamette and lower Columbia. Unlike the Eastern martin, ours abhor the condominium lifestyle, nesting only in single-family structures like the five white teardrop-shaped gourds at Willamette Park.

Adjacent to the martin nesting pole is one of the few exposed mud flats on the Willamette in the Portland harbor. This is a good place to look for least, western, and spotted sandpipers and gulls. Other species commonly seen along this segment of the Greenway include beaver, double-crested cormorants, Canada geese, and belted kingfisher. Osprey and bald eagles often catch fish within a few hundred feet of the dock. Come early on a Sunday morning if you're looking for peace and quiet, before the testosterone-powered jet skis and boats take to the Willamette.

There are also incredible views of Ross, Hardtack, East, and Toe Islands. The huge grass recreation area attracts low-flying barn, violet-green, and tree swallows that dart among soccer players and walkers. At the south end of the park a memorial plaque honors a huge, stately Oregon white oak which the International Society of Arborculture and the National Arborist Association jointly recognized during the United States Bicentennial as having "lived during the American Revolution."

Location
SW Macadam and Nebraska

Activities
Hiking
Biking
Canoeing, boating
Fishing
Tennis
Soccer

Facilities
Toilets, lots of restrooms, both next to the boat ramp and at the south end of the park
Wheelchair accessible
Trail paved
Parking
Picnic area
Dock, canoe launch

Fees and Regulations
Parking fees
Restricted hours
Pets on leash

Highlights
Willamette River views, including bald eagle and heron nests on Ross Island. Large grassy areas for lollygagging, watching spirited volleyball matches, or pick-up frisbee tossing. Easy access boat ramps and docks. Purple martin nests.

Public Transit
Tri-Met #35, #36, and #40

Thomas Guide 626

Whether it was alive then or not, it is certainly one of the largest oaks now residing along the Willamette River Greenway.

Access
Willamette Greenway Trail by foot or bicycle. Via SW Macadam at SW Nebraska. Floating docks make getting in and out of boats, canoes, and kayaks easy.

How to Get There
SW Macadam Blvd. to SW Nebraska.

By Mike Houck

For more information: Portland Bureau of Parks and Recreation, see Resources.

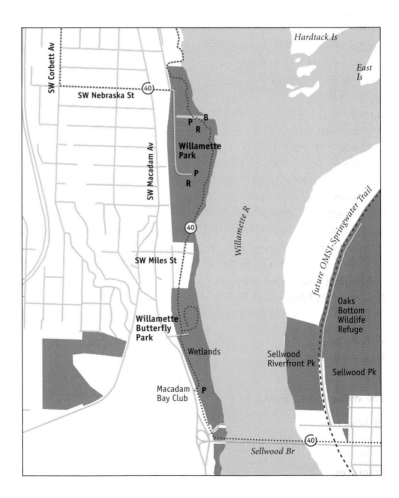

Willamette Butterfly Park

The local neighborhood feels a lot like you've somehow been transported to Sausalito's houseboat community and, given their proximity to the river and the heights of the 1996 flood, that might not be much exaggerated. This is the only place I know in Portland that has a row of six garages for sale, none of them associated with a house. Here, "garage sale" takes on a whole new meaning.

The entrance to the Butterfly Park is a spectacular floral display in a rock garden that was imported to the site by the park's designers. In early summer, orange columbines, blue *Penstemon*, yellow *Potentilla*, red fireweed, and white *Saxifraga* bloom in profusion among the nooks and crannies of the basalt pile that marks the park's entrance. At only slightly more than one acre, this is one of the region's smallest, but most biologically productive, Greenspaces. Next to the basalt rock garden is an attractive interpretive sign, describing the butterflies common to Portland, their life cycles, defensive mechanisms, and favorite food plants.

There is no better example of the importance of persistence than the Willamette Butterfly Park. Although the Portland Park Bureau required the owners of the Macadam Bay Club to create a park at this site, it took five years of concerted, vocal effort by the Corbett-Terwilliger-Lair Hill neighborhood association, in particular Jeanne Galick and Jerry Ward, to get the Park Bureau to enforce the agreement. It then took another five years for nearby residents, working with the Park Bureau's natural resource group and a native plant and landscape specialist, to complete the park in May 1996.

Today, you can sit next to a colorful floral display and listen to cedar waxwings, the "pumpkin eeeeater" of red-winged blackbirds, song sparrows, killdeer, northern orioles, brown-headed cowbirds, house finches, black-capped chickadees, and pewees. What was once a derelict patch of land overrun by Himalayan blackberries is now surrounded by a border of wild rose, red-osier dogwood, and a central core area of native grasses and wildflowers.

From a bench overlooking the Willamette you can contemplate Ross and East Islands, watch boats move up and down the river.

Access
Willamette River Greenway Trail—a straight shot from Willamette Park along the Greenway Trail and SW Miles Pl.

How to Get There
The Willamette Greenway Trail south from Willamette Park.

By Mike Houck

For more information: Portland Bureau of Parks and Recreation, see Resources.

Location
1/4 mile north of Macadam Bay Club (7720 SW Macadam Ave.) and 1/2 mile south of Willamette Park on the Willamette River Greenway Trail.

Activities
Wildflower identification, butterfly viewing and views of the Willamette River.

Facilities
None

Highlights
An enchanting view of the Willamette River. One of Portland's most romantic and serene haunts. Wildflower and butterfly viewing in spring and summer.

Public Transit
Tri-Met #35, #36, and #40

Thomas Guide 626

Bright Butterflies, Big City

The City of Roses is not exactly the City of Butterflies. More species of butterflies may be found in Manhattan than in Portland. For a city of undisputed natural charm and extensive undeveloped habitat, Portland supports a relatively poor butterfly fauna. This sad fact relates less to the city itself than to its position on the continent. Ecotopia as a whole—wet, cool, cloudy, forested, and off in a biogeographical backwater—is less a butterfly utopia than a mollusk metropolis. Of the qualities that butterflies like best in a setting, we have no shortage of nectar or larval host plants; but sunshine is nearly a *sine qua non* for butterflies. Whether shaded by heavy coniferous forest or heavy cloud cover, habitat unsunny much of the time means habitat less than optimal for butterflies. Then too, I call my expanding theory of Northwest butterfly poverty the "Rot Factor": the idea that winter rot (of eggs, larvae, pupae, adults, whatever stage hibernates) limits both abundance and diversity of butterflies in western Oregon and Washington. This can be seen in reverse by the large number of mourning cloaks that survived relatively dry and mild winters such as 1982–83.

That reservation duly lodged, we can go on to say this: While we may enjoy far fewer species and individuals of butterflies than Los Angeles, Laramie, or Lynchburg, nonetheless we can boast of several very beautiful and interesting types, easy to spot, watch, and enjoy.

Winter Butterflies

Since butterflies emerge sequentially over the long flight season, we may mention a few of the more prominent species in the order we might find them on the wing through the year. Butterfly watching, and this is a surprise for many, actually begins with the New Year (or winter solstice, as you prefer). Any sunny, relatively warm day in winter offers the prospect of butterflies on the wing. Species that overwinter as adults, in hollow trees or sheds or other shelters, commonly awaken to fly about on unseasonal midwinter days. Too, these are the first to be seen in spring, often in rather tatty condition following their winter rigors. (From these a fresh, colorful brood will be spawned in summertime.) The winter hibernators here are all brush-footed butterflies (Nymphalidae). The mourning cloak (*Nymphalis antiopa*), with its cream-edged, blue-spotted, chocolate-maroon wings, may be the most conspicuous among them. Two close relatives, the orange-and-brown Milbert's and California tortoiseshells (*N. milberti, N. californica*), show up in Portland in greatly fluctuating numbers. During years when California tortoiseshells erupt by the many thousands in the Cascades, they also become common in the city. And of the russet-and-bark colored anglewings, the satyr (*Polygonia satyrus*) is most likely to be encountered in Forest Park and other sylvan city spots where nettles, their larval host plants, occur. Watch for spiny black caterpillars with skunk-like bands down their backs among the nettles and for a golden flash in a forest glade. The rustier faun (*P. faunus*), though less an urban habitué, may also be seen. All these butterflies are successful woodland species.

Spring Butterflies

Of the butterflies emerging freshly from their chrysalides in spring, two species predominate here. They may be expected in almost any clearing or woodland roadside and become more abundant as the city is left behind. Showing up on sunny days in April and carrying an additional generation or two through the summer, both may be truly common in years with warm, early springs. They are the margined white (*Pieris marginalis*) and the spring azure (*Celastrina argiolus*). The former is indigenous, feeding as a larva on wild crucifers such as toothwort (mustard family), unlike the garden-chomping European cabbage butterfly (*P. rapae*), which also appears early. While the cabbage bears round black spots and gray tips on white, *P. marginalis*' linen wings have olive scaling to the veins below and a lemony cast to the females, especially in the spring brood. Whites are quite lovely in their simplicity, nectaring on spring beauty or cardamine. Their companion, the spring azure, is one of our brightest blues—a clear lilac-blue above and pale silvery-gray beneath, with gray chevrons. Its larvae feed on an array of shrub- and tree-borne flowers and buds, including dogwoods and viburnums. Oaks Bottom is a fine place to seek both the spring and later broods of azures. Nearly all city blues belong to this species, while several other kinds occur in the mountains and deserts.

Not far behind the margined whites emerges another member of the family Pieridae, the Sara orangetip (*Anthocharis sara*). Surely one of our most attractive butterflies, Sara flashes brilliant orange wingtips on white wings that bear grass-green mottling below. The female is buttery yellow. She will lay her eggs on a variety of mustard plants. Just at lilac-time, Sara may be seen but seldom expected dancing through many of the city's green sunny spots, including smaller parks and less disturbed residential areas. If you see two bits of orange flitting through the air, connected by a scrap of bright white, it will be the Sara orangetip—a springtime beauty well worth watching for and getting to know.

Summer Butterflies

Late May and June bring on the swallowtails. We are blessed with three species of city swallowtails and an odd but very pretty relative. The anise swallowtail (*Papilio zelicaon*), black with broad yellow bands, uses dill, fennel, cow parsnip, and other umbels (parsley family) as its larval hosts. Males like to fly around hilltops, where they joust and seek unmated females flying up to meet them. The two tigers feed on broad-leafed trees and wander everywhere in town. While the black-banded, creamy pale tiger swallowtail (*P. eurymedon*) feeds on alder and probably cascara, the lemon-yellow western tiger swallowtail (*P. rutulus*) browses big-leaf maple, willows, and several other broad-leafed trees and shrubs, making it the more common. The western tiger is probably our most conspicuous city butterfly all through the summer, as it soars and glides down city streets and through park glades, pausing to nectar on bramble or phlox. Washington Park is good for it, but your garden will do as well.

The swallowtail relative I spoke of is the Clodius parnassian (*Parnassius clodius*). Though untailed and very unlike the other swallowtails in Oregon except one mountain relative, it nonetheless belongs to the Papilionidae. Ruby and coal spots set off the milky white, waxy wings, largely transparent in the female. Seek it around patches of bleeding heart, its larval hostplant, in the Forest Park area or other outlying woods.

High summer belongs to bright butterflies mostly of the brush-footed family (Nymphalidae). Lorquin's admiral, a willow feeder as a caterpillar, hang-glides all over Portland for much of the summer. *Limenitis lorquini* is unmistakable: big, jet black with creamy bands and apricot wingtips. The larvae and pupae camouflage themselves as bird droppings, while the adults are as dramatic as any bird; males sometimes defend their territories against birds or mistake them for females. Not a close relative, the red admiral (*Vanessa atalanta*) actually allies with the painted lady (*V. cardui*) and west coast lady (*V. annabella*). While the west coast lady is resident, painted ladies and red admirals immigrate annually and die off in the fall, unable to withstand the winter. Their numbers fluctuate radically according to parasites, rain and nectar in Mexico, and other factors. The shabby, drab arrivals of early summer yield big, brilliant individuals in the next generations, from July to October. Your chances of seeing them well and in good numbers will be best if you plant purple butterfly bushes (*Buddleia*) in your garden and let some nettles grow for red admirals to breed on, thistles for painted ladies. Or watch for them in open areas, wood edges, or hilltops near sunset, such as the summit of Rocky Butte.

Another thistle-feeding nymphalid is the little mylitta crescent (*Phyciodes mylitta*). Clear orange with sharp black markings, and only an inch across, mylitta patrols roadsides or paths through vacant lots and meadows, gliding with an occasional flap. Similar in size, the ochre-colored common ringlet (*Coenonympha tullia*) haunts grassy spots since its caterpillars, like those of related wood nymphs and satyrs, eat grasses exclusively. Ringlets cavort in Oaks Bottom meadows.

As summer progresses, the bright yellow flags of tansy ragwort, that persistent alien weed, make themselves apparent and provide fodder for cinnabar moths (*Tyria jacobaeae*), a European species introduced to fight tansy. So brilliant are the day-flying cinnabars—scarlet and gun-barrel blue-black—that most people take them for butterflies. See how differently they fold their wings, and note that they lack knobs on their antennae such as butterflies possess. Children call the striped larvae "tansy tigers."

Tansy ragwort does at least furnish a prolific nectar source for butterflies in late summer. Nearly every patch—along with every garden stand of lavender—supports a cluster of woodland skippers in August. *Ochlodes sylvanoides* is our commonest skipper by far. The skippers, family Hesperiidae, have hooked knobs on their antennae, stout bodies, short wings and speedy, skipping flight. This one is tawny-gold with black dashes and pale patches. Another grass-feeder, it can turn up nearly anywhere, including unsprayed lawns where it does no real damage, but provides excellent company. With it on goldenrod might be nectaring a purplish copper (*Lycaena helloides*), which along with the spring azure is a member of the gossamer wings (Lycaenidae). Otherwise brown, males of this butterfly flash brilliant metallic purple when the sun catches the wings right; you may spot them courting the bright orange, black-spotted females. Coppers hang about dock and pink knotweed, and I find the Multnomah Slough and the Delta Park area good for them.

Fall Butterflies

Early autumn is the time of the pine white, veined with red and black on white. Pale sailors around the crowns of Douglas firs will be this species, *Neophasia menapia*. Now is the time also to watch for orange and clouded sulphurs (*Colias eurytheme, C. philodice*) streaking and spiraling together in courtship over alfalfa or red clover fields on Sauvie Island or in the Tualatin Valley. Then as nights begin to chill, the tortoiseshells and anglewings again seek winter shelter, yet come out to nectar and bask as long as autumn remains mild and sunny.

Did I say we have a poor butterfly fauna? It doesn't sound so bad in review. They may not compare so well to the prolific assemblage of Cascade meadows and canyons, yet Portland butterflies offer variety, beauty, and fascination enough to recommend them to our notice. I urge you to go forth with wide-open eyes into the parks, gardens, greenspaces, and vacant lots and become a butterfly-loving lepidopterist. If you do, you'll find the city a richer place for it, and your days brighter than ever before.

By Robert Michael Pyle

Paddling: Ross Island Loop

In early April, before the black cottonwoods leaf out, you can get fantastic views of courtship behavior and nest refurbishing of great blue herons.

As far back as 1903, when John Charles Olmsted identified it as an important element of Portland's natural landscape, it has simply been assumed that Ross Island and its companion islands, Hardtack, East, and Toe, would one day come into the Portland park system. With the listings of steelhead and salmon as "Threatened" under the Endangered Species Act, increased scrutiny on Willamette River gravel extraction, and renewed commitments to clean up the Willamette River, public ownership may finally be close at hand. In late 1999, Ross Island Sand and Gravel announced that it would cease dredging of Ross Island and the lagoon between Ross and Hardtack Islands by 2005.

In the meantime, the best way to explore the islands is by canoe or kayak. The best time of year to view the great blue heron nesting colony or nesting bald eagles is mid-February through June, and Sunday is by far the best day of the week. On Sundays, preferably early in the morning, you'll miss both the heavy boat and jet-ski traffic on the Willamette and the noisy machinery in the lagoon.

Both herons and eagles resume nesting activity in February. It's between the onset of nest rebuilding and egg-laying in early April, before the black cottonwoods leaf out, that you can get fantastic views of courtship behavior and refurbishing of their loose-knit stick nests that are reused each year.

The herons had nested in the same place for over 20 years, where the 50 to 60 nests could easily be seen from the Willamette River Greenway. In fact, they had begun nesting as usual in February 2000 when, inexplicably, the bald eagles decided to move from their former location to nearer the heronry. Apparently, this was a bit too close for comfort and as of early March 2000, the entire heron colony had moved, lock, stock, and barrel, to East Island, with a few nests across the narrow channel on Hardtack Island.

Whether the herons will move back to the original Ross Island site once things have settled down remains to be seen. The eagles are relatively recent arrivals, having nested for four years beginning in 1996. There is also a red-tailed hawk nest on the island, and an osprey nest on artificial platforms in nearby Oaks Bottom Wildlife Refuge.

Willamette Park To Ross Island Lagoon

My favorite put-in is the floating boat dock at Willamette Park, just upstream from the islands, although Sellwood Riverfront Park on the east side of the Willamette is an equally convenient launch site. From Willamette Park, paddle straight across the Willamette past the upstream end of Ross and Hardtack Islands, being careful not to run aground during low summer and fall flows. The first thing you'll notice is the low, artificial-looking berm that joins Ross to

Hardtack Island. In 1926 the U.S. Army Corps of Engineers constructed a levee between Hardtack and Ross Islands to facilitate Ross Island Sand and Gravel's dredging activities. The berm also diverted the Willamette west of the islands, which has scoured a deeper channel for river traffic.

If the water is high, I prefer to paddle downstream through the narrow, shallow channel between East and Hardtack Island. The newly established great blue heron colony is on the west side of East Island near the downstream tip where the narrow waterway joins Holgate Channel. A few newly constructed nests can also be spotted across the channel on Hardtack Island. Early in the nesting season—mid-February into March—you can easily see the nests as you enter the narrow channel. Later, after the cottonwoods have leafed out, the nests will not be visible until you are further down the channel. If the water is low, the always-deep Holgate Channel between East Island and the Willamette's east shore is the best route. Either way most of your downstream paddle will be on Holgate Channel.

If you visit the heronry in mid-to-late June, after the young have reached near-adult size, you will see them vigorously flapping their wings, preparing for their first forays out of the nest.

A half-mile downstream Ross Island Lagoon, which is marked with huge "Danger: Do Not Enter" signs, will be on your left. The signs relieve Ross Island Sand and Gravel of responsibility for any mishaps that occur in the lagoon. The river, including the lagoon, is in the public domain, however, and accessible to the public. As a matter of safety as well as easier canoeing, it's best to plan your trip on a Sunday when the operation is shut down.

To get to the "old" heron colony and the newly established eagle nest, paddle southwest across the lagoon toward the upstream end of Ross Island. There are buoys anchored in the lagoon several hundred feet out from the heron nests that delimit where dredging may occur during nesting season. This is also a safe distance from which you can see the nests, which are high in the tops of the cottonwoods. If the herons have reestablished their nests, you will be able to hear and see the young, and still be far enough away to avoid disturbing the herons.

While the new bald eagle nest on the lagoon side of Ross Island is easy to see, after the leaves are on the cottonwoods, you'll have to jockey your boat so that you are looking due west or toward the northwest to get the best views of the heron nests. Look for partially denuded cottonwoods where the limbs and leaves have been beaten down from years of nesting activity. If you visit the heronry in mid-to-late June, after the young have reached near-adult size, you will see them vigorously flapping their wings, preparing for their first forays out of the nest. It's at this time that the colony is also the loudest. However, it's also when the cottonwood canopy is leafed out, so you'll have to catch glimpses of the young and adult herons through the leaves. Each time an adult returns to its nest with a crop full of carp the cacophony of young is reminiscent of a fully loaded train rolling through a freight yard.

From the new bald eagle nest and the abandoned heronry, it's a short paddle a bit farther south through the lagoon to the now unoccupied former bald eagle nest. As with the herons, buoys mark the distance beyond which Ross Island Sand and Gravel is prohibited from extracting gravel during nesting season (February to July). This should also mark your closest approach to the nest to avoid disturbing either the herons, if they have returned, or the eagles. Although both the herons and eagles are used to mining activity and boat traffic, kayakers and canoeists should be mindful of disturbing the birds at all times of the year. New research on eagle-human interaction indicates that you should keep a distance of at least 800 feet away from any perch or nesting area to avoid disturbing them.

New research on eagle-human interaction indicates that you should keep a distance of at least 800 feet away from any perch or nesting area to avoid disturbing them.

Back to Willamette Park

If you prefer loops to straight out-and-backs, paddle back out of the lagoon and head left, downstream, to the tip of Ross Island to complete your trip around the island. To avoid boat wakes and see more wildlife, hug the island's shore. Once you've rounded the downstream tip of Ross Island, continue upstream, hugging the shore or staying between the island and log rafts that sometimes are tied up to the island. The log rafts reduce the wake from motor boats and jet-skis and are favorite perches for wood ducks, spotted sandpipers, and herons. Tree, violet-green, and northern rough-winged swallows also nest in the pilings. There is a red-tailed hawk nest just opposite the heronry, and belted kingfishers nest in the steep banks near Toe Island. While there are many cavities in the bank, some of which are beaver dens, the telltale sign of a kingfisher nest is two parallel grooves on the bottom rim of the hole. This is where the kingfisher grabs on with its feet as it enters the nest. Once past the red-tailed hawk and kingfisher nests, you'll come to Toe Island, where the old bald eagle nest should be clearly visible.

The best route back to the Willamette Park boat ramp is to paddle east of Toe Island, which now is owned by Portland Parks, back to Willamette or Sellwood Riverfront Park.

What You'll See

The islands' remnant riparian habitat is dominated by towering black cottonwoods and scattered Oregon white ash. A few Oregon white oak and Pacific madrone also grow on Ross Island. Willow and red-osier dogwood, along with stinging nettle, Himalayan blackberry, elderberry, Douglas spirea, and snowberry form a dense understory. In winter, the dogwood provides a brilliant red band around the islands' periphery, especially on East Island.

Birding is good any time of year. In winter there are year-round residents such as double-crested cormorants, common merganser, Canada geese, and lots of gulls, including glaucous-winged, herring, and ring-billed. Although most Portland-area wintering bald eagles concentrate at an old growth forest roost west of Sauvie Island, the pair that began nesting on Ross Island in 1996 seem to have chosen to over-winter regularly at Ross Island, where they have access to abundant prey at Oaks Bottom Wildlife Refuge.

Other birds that hang out in the brushy understory are song, fox, and golden-crowned sparrows, Bewick's wrens, and spotted towhees. If you watch the ash-cottonwood canopy you'll see and hear black-capped chickadee, ruby-crowned kinglet, western scrub jay, American

The Willamette River may at times look docile, but the current can be strong and sudden winds may crop up. Check seasonally for dangerous flood conditions (generally November through April) where dead-head logs and other debris may be hazardous to crossing.

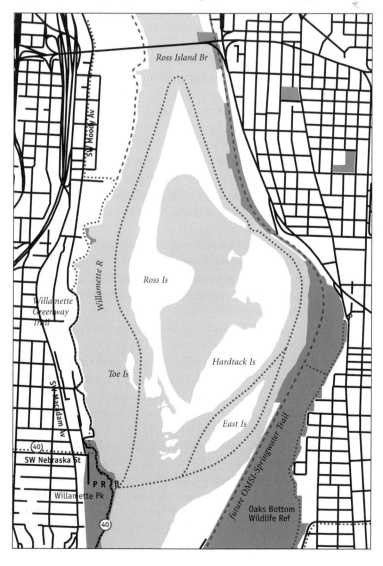

robin, bushtit, and house finch. Northern flickers and downy woodpeckers are also common. Watch at the water's edge and on log rafts if they are present for mallards, wood ducks, and killdeer.

While winter birding can be productive, it's during the spring migration when the warblers are on the move and early summer when the grosbeaks and thrushes are singing that the islands come alive. The herons start nesting in February so you can observe adults making their pilgrimage from Ross Island to Oaks Bottom to refuel in between nuptial goings-on. The islands resonate with the calls and songs of Pacific-slope, willow, and olive-sided flycatchers, western wood-pewees, warbling vireo, purple finch, and cedar waxwing. Fresh in from sunnier climes are a host of warblers: Wilson's, yellow, black-throated gray, MacGillivray's, and Townsend's. The brilliant yellow-and-orange western tanager can be seen hanging out in the upper tree canopy. The mourning dove's cooing sounds vaguely like a great horned owl. Black-headed grosbeaks, whose song is superficially robin-like but more of a rolling staccato, are abundant during the summer, as is the ascending flute-like Swainson's thrush.

By the time you've circumnavigated all four islands, you will not only have gotten a good workout, but on a late spring or mid-summer paddle you'll also have seen or heard 50 or more species of birds.

Spotted sandpipers, easily the noisiest bird you'll encounter on the water, often fly with their signature rapid, fluttering wing beat, just in front of your boat or back and forth across the channel, all the while emitting their repetitive call, which sounds as if someone is whistling for a dog. They can also be seen walking along a log boom or raft or on the shore poking about for insects. Look for their trademark tail bobbing, from which they acquired the more informal moniker, "teeter butt."

Also look for osprey that nest atop the metal power poles along the railroad tracks at Oaks Bottom, that is, if they haven't been displaced by Canada geese that have appropriated these high-placed nesting platforms before the osprey return from Mexico and South America.

By the time you've circumnavigated all four islands, which usually takes about two and a half hours—three, if the birding's really hot or you want to loaf about in Holgate Channel—you will not only have gotten a good workout, but on a late spring or mid-summer paddle you'll also have seen or heard 50 or more species of birds.

If you park at Willamette Park, be sure not to park in the larger trailer-only parking spaces or you will be ticketed. There are car-only parking spaces along the margins of the parking lot. If you do not own a canoe or kayak you can rent them from Ebb and Flow Paddlesports, just across SW Macadam. They have small hand-pulled trailers that can be used to pull a canoe or kayak to the boat ramp at Willamette Park.

By Mike Houck

South Park Blocks

In the heart of downtown lies one of Portland's gems of nature, the South Park Blocks. Though it was envisioned in the late 1840s by Portland's founders as a continuous strip of green running the length of the city, subsequent events conspired to remove eight blocks from the center of the strip, separating it into two sections and leaving the North and South Park Blocks as two islands of green to be engulfed by the rapidly-growing city.

By the late 1870s the perimeter of the South Park Blocks had become an area of large, elegant homes and one of the two most fashionable neighborhoods in the city. The single-family homes have long since been removed, replaced by an array of apartment buildings, historic churches, the Portland State University campus, the Oregon History Center, the Portland Art Museum, and the Performing Arts Center. The aggregation of all these functions around a unique green core makes the South Park Blocks not only the cultural and educational heart of Portland, but a symbol of the importance of greenspaces to Portlanders.

The most prominent feature of the area is the trees. Interspersed throughout the stand are maples, oaks, sycamores, lindens, and several other species. But the predominant trees of the South Park Blocks are American elms and it is these large, graceful sentinels that do most to create the special character of the area. This human-designed arbor-scape of the South Park Blocks proper creates the special atmosphere that dominates the whole area. Like a rough-hewn colonnade, five rows of trees stretch the length of the twelve blocks, creating a high canopy that shelters the grass, walkways, and benches below. From the center, looking either to the north or the south between any two rows of trees, you have a vista down a long, green, arched tunnel narrowing into an indistinct vanishing point blocks away.

Throughout the year the trees are home to a number of native birds, including downy woodpeckers, American crows, black-capped chickadees, American robins, and house finches. Well-established exotic species include European starlings, house sparrows, and rock doves, the latter being a favorite food of the occasional native Cooper's hawk. The trees also support several mammals, the most common being fox squirrels, expatriates of the Mid-Western deciduous forest. Occasionally raccoons will find a comfortable limb to snooze on while in the area in search of food. At night, bats fly among the trees hunting for insects.

While the character of the South Park Blocks is shaped by its trees, that grandeur is magnified by the contrast of the serene and majestic sensibility of the trees with the bustle of traffic and urban activity just a few blocks away. The proximity of the city's noise, the restful songs of birds, and the cool, refreshing taste of the air of the

Location
A 12-block strip of trees and grass within the heart of downtown Portland. Strictly speaking, the area running from SW Salmon on the north to I-405 on the south, and what would be SW 8th and 9th, though these two numbered streets are both called SW Park in this area.

Activites
Strolling, lounging, bird-watching, tree-watching, and people-watching.

Facilities
Lots of benches, water fountains, several stone chessboard tables adjacent to Portland State University. Numerous coffee shops either on or within a block of the area. No public restrooms.

Highlights
Besides the Park Blocks proper, the greatest concentration of cultural, educational and historic landmarks in the city fronts on the area. In summer, luxurious shade. In fall, a spectacular, colorful display of autumn leaves.

Thomas Guide 596

Blocks are distinctive. Just one visit helps you understand what Frederick Law Olmsted and other nineteenth century urban greenspace advocates meant when they referred to urban parks as the "lungs of the city." But to fully understand the allure of the South Park Blocks, you need to observe its changes throughout the four seasons.

In summer the high-arching trees offer a cooling and peaceful shade that beckons a variety of people to stroll, sit on one of the many benches, or lounge on the grass. Groups of small children from the several nearby day-care centers may be seen playing or walking through the park. Kept in line by their tight grasps on a rope tether, they follow their adult leader like a line of ducklings. Teenagers and young twenty-somethings laze about, talking, sunning, or engaging in an intense session of hacky-sack. Joggers rhythmically grind through the area, winding their way along the tree-lined walks, chattering to each other as they dodge groups of strolling people and pets. Groups of rock doves strut around on their never-ending pigeon-quest to sweep the walkways clean of popcorn and assorted crumbs. Parts of

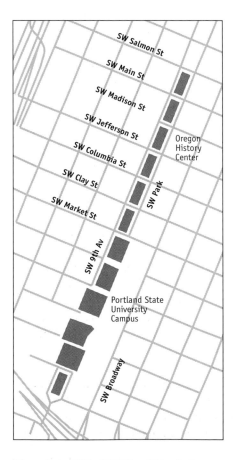

the scene are highlighted by bright shafts of sunlight breaking through the deep shadows of the lush canopy. The overwhelming sense of summer on the Blocks is one of sensory overload and intense but relaxed activity.

As the summer ends, the days get noticeably shorter and the air acquires a dry, almost dusty flavor. Fall slips in and the visual senses are bombarded. The green canopy of leaves becomes transformed into a bright yellow that over the course of a week or two slowly drifts down, creating a dense yellow carpet. Fall breezes drag across this carpet and create swirling eddies of yellow and brown, filling the air with the dusty smell and sound of crackling leaves. But not for long, for the rustle of leaves is inevitably replaced by the rains of autumn, creating a sticky and sometimes slippery brown mass of decaying leaves underfoot. A corps of rakers appears to gather the leaves up in bags and trucks and deliver them to continue their cycle of life as compost. The now-barren trees combine with the sunless weather and the rapidly declining hours of daylight to produce the twilight of grayness that replaces the bright contrasts that marked the beginning of the season.

Just as the weight of the relentless repetition of grayness seems to become unbearable, spring arrives.

Winter arrives, not as an event, but as a simple deepening and continuation of the gray end of fall. People still venture out, though less often, and, seemingly, more often alone. Several species of gulls regularly descend on the park, warily strutting about the muddy ground in small flocks as they systematically scavenge unrecognizable but apparently edible tidbits of food scraps, worms, and other invertebrates. Overhead, the noticeably shortened days of winter offer a new treat, as the graceful tangle of naked tree limbs outlined against the blue-gray sky dominates the scene. One of the most interesting views this time of year is from the balcony on the fourth floor of PSU's Cramer Hall. Looking out at eye level, you see the maze of limbs floating above the surface and may get a view of a Townsend's warbler, sweeping the branches for morsels of overwintering insects. The trees invite you to extend your hand to touch them, but remain tantalizingly out of reach. In its gray solitude, the park is mute beneath a seemingly unending background rhythm of rain, drizzle, showers, or whatever flavor of precipitation the weather service chooses to assign to the day's wetness.

Just as the weight of the relentless repetition of grayness seems to become unbearable, spring arrives. At first, the swelling buds lend a limey tint to the trees. But soon the buds burst open, painting the stark gray branches a refreshing green. Colorful flowers begin popping out of the brown earth, or appear full-grown as the former corps-of-rakers returns, armed this time with a new crop of annuals to brighten the many flower beds. People suddenly return to enjoy the newly-minted sunshine and the smell of spring. To celebrate the spring and

the return of people (or perhaps, to help entice them back?) a choir
of birds comes suddenly to life, adding an auditory element to the
visual. Drawn by the burst of elm seeds, hordes of pine siskins,
American goldfinches, and occasional evening grosbeaks descend on
the Blocks. Migrating warblers feed on insects they find among the
leaf buds and flowers. This burst of energy continues and intensifies
as spring advances, rehearsing a performance that will run throughout
the summer on the special urban stage of nature that is the South
Park Blocks.

What of the North Park Blocks, the other half of the vision of a
continuous green strip for downtown Portland? The smaller northern
patch covers only five blocks and has not developed in the same way as
its sister area in the south. Physically, the landscape of the North Park
Blocks is similar to that of the South. It too has large trees over a
swath of grass and sidewalks. But surrounded by warehouses and
industrial neighbors, it historically has not been as inviting, and has
a feel that is very different from the South Park Blocks. But that is
changing. The Pearl District, in which the North Park Blocks lie,
is undergoing a major redevelopment effort. Former warehouses
are being converted to loft apartments, new buildings are being
constructed, and street-level stores, restaurants, and art galleries are
proliferating. In short, people are beginning to reside and recreate in
the surrounding area. As this district continues to become more
densely populated, the importance of the North Park Blocks will
increase and they will begin to develop their own unique character.

Someday there will be two distinctive and extensive arborscapes
in downtown Portland. Both will be full of people and the sights,
sounds, and smells of nature in the four seasons, and they will provide
two islands of green to testify that Nature thrives in the central city.

Access
A walk westward up any cross street from Broadway (SW "7th") in
downtown Portland will lead you right into the area.

How to Get There
Parking is very scarce, so best to walk, bike, or bus (several bus routes
cross or pass within a few blocks, including the transit mall on 5th and
6th Aves.).

By Joseph Poracsky

Willamette Greenway Connection To 40-Mile Loop

If this one doesn't jog childhood memories of tree forts and hidden places, you've lost your sense of adventure. In addition to your willingness to explore, you'll need a good nose for direction to find this entryway to Portland's west hills.

Situated next to a private home, what appears to be a private driveway is your gateway to adventure. Don't let the fact that you have to walk through what appears to be a driveway deter you. Simply amble up the driveway onto railroad tie steps that rise up from the surrounding Corbett-Terwilliger neighborhood into the netherworld of the I-5 Freeway and Barbur Boulevard, both of which loom and boom overhead, and cast dark shadows even on a bright summer day.

The uphill trek is a bit surreal as the repetitive thump, thump, rumble, rumble of semis and cars roars overhead, mixed with muted songs of chickadees, sparrows, and western tanagers from the forest understory. While the noise might be maddening at first, the trail's seclusion and ambience cannot help but take you back to childhood

Location
Willamette Park to SW Iowa and Viewpoint Terr.

Activities
Hiking

Facilities
None

Fees and Regulations
None

Highlights
The only access to Terwilliger Blvd. and 40-Mile Loop Trail directly from the Willamette River Greenway. One of the region's most secret of public paths. Once at George Himes Park, spectacular views into the Ross Island lagoon and Oaks Bottom Wildlife Refuge.

Public Transit
Tri-Met #35, #36, and #40

Thomas Guide 626

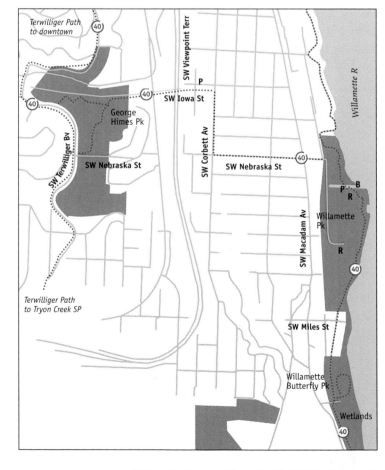

forays as you sneaked off to explore forbidden neighborhood haunts. There are even twin swings slung beneath the girders of the Barbur Boulevard bridge.

The extremely informal, rustic trail winds through fields of *Geum*, bedstraw, lady-fern, and waterleaf, under a canopy of big-leaf maple and Douglas fir. The steep but short route winds up and under both bridges, and eventually bifurcates to provide two points of access to Portland's George Himes Park and the SW Terwilliger Parkway. If you are a frequent habitué of the Terwilliger running path, you have probably passed the entrance to George Himes many times without noting it.

Access
Connector trailhead at SW Iowa and Viewpoint Terr. Situated adjacent to a private home, what at first glance appears to be a private driveway is your gateway to adventure. A challenging but short climb on a very informal dirt trail.

How to Get There
From Willamette Park, walk, bicycle, or drive back out of the park and continue west on SW Nebraska. Turn right onto SW Corbett and go north to SW Iowa. Turn left and park at SW Viewpoint Terr.

By Mike Houck

For more information: Portland Bureau of Parks and Recreation, see Resources.

Portland's Greenway Movement:
From Olmsted and the 40-Mile Loop
To Metropolitan Greenspaces

Portland is divided by the Willamette River, with more than seventy percent of the population living east of the river. Having grown up on the west side of Portland, I have a distinct bias. The west side of the city is lush, green, hilly, and perfect, whereas the east side is flat, monotonous, and devoid of trees, I tell myself. So when I began to read about the 40-Mile Loop it was hard for me to believe that a trail on the east side of town would appeal to me at all. "You really must see the Springwater Corridor," people told me. "And take a bike—it's the best way." Still holding onto my unwarranted bias after all these years, I hesitantly made the eastward trek.

At first the ride along the converted rail corridor fed my expectations—fairly boring, I thought, through an industrial part of town. After a few miles I needed to rest, aching from a bike that was no longer the right size, and from being out of shape despite the flat terrain. I figured I should push a few more miles to Powell Butte, a massive green square on my map.

At one point I looked up and was rewarded with a spectacular view of Mt. Hood—it seemed that if I pedaled for just a few more miles I'd run straight into the snow-covered peak. At once more aware of my surroundings, I realized I was in thick forest, breezing past farms and cows. When I reached the park I veered off, directly up the dirt trails. Indeed, the view from the top was breathtaking, all the more so after the hilly climb. I could see for miles—every hill and every wrinkle of green throughout the city. On the way back, my view of the east side changed. I was more observant and wasn't just pushing to get somewhere. I still love the west side, but know from experience the east side has its own splendid riches.

Often cities are viewed in the same manner I used to see east Portland, as vast urban expanses with little to offer in the way of natural areas. To see nature one must travel away from the city, we think. However, if we are going to prevent the urban sprawl that has characterized so many American cities, there must be a reason for people to stay in the city, and creating and protecting natural areas is part of the answer. An integral element of Portland's efforts to ensure we all have immediate access to nature is the 40-Mile Loop, an extensive network of trails and parks linked throughout the city.

The 40-Mile Loop circles the city of Portland, extends to Gresham, Troutdale, and Boring, and serves a multitude of functions. The primary purpose of this greenway is to link several parks together, while serving as a means for recreation. In many places, though, it also supports important ecological functions and connects densely populated areas to urban wilderness.

Forest Park, Tryon Creek, and Marquam: The Three Anchors

The cornerstone of the 40-Mile Loop, and also the foundation of the Olmsted report, was Forest Park. Often when one brings up the loop, most people immediately think of the broad network of urban trails in Forest Park, unaware of the more than one hundred additional miles of trail that exist outside of the park.

While much has been written about Forest Park, relatively little is known by the general public about Tryon and Marquam. Forest Park is by far the largest of the three anchors, but Tryon Creek State Park, at 640 acres, was the region's first urban State Park. And it was with the creation of Marquam Nature Park that the 40-Mile Loop really took shape. In 1968, a massive housing development was being planned for an area in Portland's West Hills. Similar to the Tryon Creek movement, neighbors joined together, not content to merely combine with the opposition to development. Instead, they wanted to determine the feasibility of saving some of the ravines as a park. The neighbors founded the group Friends of Marquam Nature Park.

40-Mile Loop Land Trust

In other parts of the city, as momentum for the completion of the loop grew, the need for an overall managing body became clear. As a result, the 40-Mile Loop Land Trust was formed. Its goal, according to the 1983 Master Plan, is "the protection of lands, including timber lands, natural and wilderness areas, waterways, lakes, and streams in the Portland metropolitan area, as well as to set aside other lands for present and future generations for recreation, exercise, education, research, sustenance, and preservation."

The long-term goal is to link the trails in the 40-Mile Loop to other state and regional trail systems, such as the Willamette River Greenway Trail, the Sandy River Gorge Trail, and the Pacific Crest Trail, which runs the entire length of the western United States from Canada to Mexico.

Movement forward

Another key player was Metro, the only directly elected regional government in the United States. Metro was created in 1979 as part of the development of a region-wide Urban Growth Boundary. Its jurisdiction includes all 24 cities and unincorporated Washington, Multnomah, and Clackamas Counties. More than 1.3 million people live within Metro's authority.

But before Metro there was the Columbia Region Association of Governments (CRAG), which encompassed five counties and two states. In 1971, CRAG developed a report on the "urban outdoors," which called for "preserving and enhancing these environmental features (the rivers, streams, floodplains, high points and historical sites) that have already stamped the region with their unique form and character, which make it a very special place to live" (as quoted in the Metro Greenspaces Master Plan 1992). Unfortunately, the CRAG report promptly went to the shelves, where it gathered dust until 1988.

In 1988 Mike Houck, the Audubon Society of Portland's Urban Naturalist, proposed the establishment of a metropolitan wildlife system. His inspiration came directly from the 40-Mile Loop and Olmsted's master plan for Portland parks. Houck had earlier met Barbara Walker of The Friends of Marquam Nature Park, and realized that most of the Loop traveled through the types of resources he was promoting for conservation purposes.

London and East Bay Regional Park District: Urban Greenspace Models

Houck's plan was also inspired by two other successful urban Greenspace models. He invited Dr. David Goode, Director of the London Ecology Unit, to speak to the City Club of Portland and to participate in several "country in the city" symposia that were hosted by Portland State University. Dr. Goode's City Club address was a key point in securing the support of civic leaders in promoting a regional Greenspaces initiative. The San Francisco area's East Bay Regional Park District had just passed a $225 million bond in the late 1980s. Houck collaborated with Dr. Joe Poracsky of PSU's Geography Department, and Esther Lev and Lynn Sharp, both wildlife consultants, to organize two tours of East Bay's system for Metro officials and local park providers. Janet Cobb, now Executive Director of the California Oak Foundation in Oakland, arranged for bus tours of the District's 60,000 acres of natural areas and for meetings with their staff to discuss acquisition and management strategies. These trips convinced both park planners and elected officials that the creation and maintenance of a similar natural areas system in the Portland region was possible.

In the fall of 1992, the Metro Council managed to get a Greenspace bond measure on the election ballot. The ballot measure called for $200 million to acquire land for a regional system of open space, trails, river access, and wildlife habitat. The measure failed, but in 1995 a new $135.6 million measure passed easily with 62% approval.

As we make choices between urban sprawl or smarter growth, the Portland region is making a concerted effort to avoid sprawl-oriented development experienced elsewhere in the country. The 40-Mile Loop is a harbinger of better city planning and serves as a key means of preserving a livable city.

Picturing a snowball rolling down a hill provides a useful analogy to put the process of Portland planning into perspective. The initial snowball was packed in 1903 by the Olmsteds, who rested it neatly on top of a hill. The ball was packed a little more with the creation of Forest Park in the 1950s, and still further with the creation of Tryon Creek State Park in the 1970s. Barbara Walker and the Friends of Marquam Nature Park campaign to protect Marquam Hill packed a lot more snow on, which started it rolling down the hill. In the 1980s the snowball expanded, collecting more speed, with the 40-Mile Loop Land Trust and Master Plan, Springwater Corridor, Powell Butte, Houck's Urban Wildlife Refuge System, Metro, the Regional Park Study, the Region 2040 Project, and the Metropolitan Greenspaces Master Plan. In the late 1980s, by the time Walker and Houck got together and the regional Greenspaces plan gathered momentum, the snowball had become an avalanche of enthusiasm for greenspace planning. The fact that the Portland region has citizens willing to become directly engaged in creating their own livable future and progressive, visionary leadership to institutionalize these efforts at the regional level, through Metro as well as local agencies, makes this city unique. The future prospects of Portland urban planning look bright, thanks in no small part to the efforts in creating the 40-Mile Loop and the additional programs that stemmed from the loop.

By Karen Murray

40-Mile Loop: Terwilliger Parkway through Forest Park

The 40-Mile Loop is a much more grandiose, and lengthy, proposition than the limited, auto-oriented parkway and boulevard system envisaged by John Charles Olmsted in his 1903 report to the Portland Park Board. While, by definition, a loop can start anywhere along its course, most people pick Kelley Point Park as the logical place to start a Loop tour, possibly because it sits at the confluence of the Willamette and Columbia Rivers and acts as a geographic point of reference. For bicycling or hiking adventure, the now 150-mile long Loop extends from Kelley Point Park, east to Troutdale and to the Sandy and Columbia River Gorges, and then wanders through Gresham and a bit farther east to Boring before snaking its way along the sinuosities of Johnson Creek, west along what is popularly known as the Springwater Corridor Trail to the Willamette River. The Loop then crosses the river and climbs over the West Hills, and eventually comes full circle, back to Kelley Point Park.

The Willamette River Greenway, which is designed for bicycles and pedestrians, serves as a second, although still discontinuous, north-south loop-within-a-loop on both sides of the Willamette River. After crossing the Willamette on the Sellwood Bridge the 40-Mile-Loop is coincident with the Greenway as far downstream as Willamette Park; from there, it sneaks up and over the West Hills to George Himes Park and the Terwilliger Parkway. It then shares a common route with the Terwilliger Parkway just downhill from the Chart House before diverging on its own path back uphill, past Marquam Nature Park, to Council Crest.

Bicycle alternative

The entire route over the west hills and through Forest Park is for foot traffic only, so if you're bicycling continue along Terwilliger to downtown and the Willamette River Greenway or Portland's ever-growing system of on-street bike paths. Although you can ride out Hwy. 30 towards St. Helens and cross the St. Johns bridge, the more scenic route is to cross to the east side to Willamette Blvd. and ride north, past the University of Portland; from here you can jump on the Peninsula Crossing Trail at N Carey and Princeton or continue back to Kelley Point Park via the Rivergate Industrial District on N Lombard.

Continuing the 40-Mile Loop, on Foot Through the West Hills

If you have a philosophical aversion to losing elevation once gained, or you have creaky knees, be prepared for a lot of up and down from where the 40-Mile Loop leaves Terwilliger to Council Crest on out through Forest Park. On the other hand, if you're into conditioning, nothing could be better than the 40-Mile Loop as it descends from Council Crest to the Oregon Zoo, and from W Burnside, the Zoo, and the Vietnam Memorial, see-saws up to the Hoyt Arboretum. Then, it's back up to 1,000-foot-high Pittock Mansion and switchbacks down into moss-clad Balch Creek Canyon and Lower Macleay Park. From the Lower Macleay's stone shelter, Wildwood Trail continues to undulate through Forest Park all the way to the St. Johns Bridge. From the St. Johns Bridge, it's dead-flat through Pier Park to the Columbia Slough and 2,000-acre Smith and Bybee Lakes and Kelley Point Park.

The Regional Trail System

Of course, the 40-Mile Loop isn't the only way to connect with nature. There's the Willamette River Greenway, Gresham-to-Fairview Trail, Peninsula Crossing Trail, Fanno Creek Greenway, Terwilliger Parkway, Clark County's Chinook Trail, and numerous local trail systems, all of which add up to an ever-growing regional trail system.

Metro's 1992 Greenspaces Master Plan calls for an "interconnected system of open spaces, parks, natural areas, trails and greenways, for wildlife and people in the Portland metropolitan region." While most of the well-deserved public hoopla has focused on the acquisition of Greenspaces with the $135.6 million bond measure, it's the greenway and trail system that connects people to local and regional Greenspaces.

The Greenspaces Master Plan identified 34 trail and greenway corridor projects, encompassing more than 350 miles of trails and natural area linkages that follow the natural landscape, focusing on ridge lines, abandoned railways, and stream corridors.

The 40-Mile Loop, once the only game in town, is now a hub around which spokes are rapidly forming. One day, an anastomosing trail network will spread throughout Clark County in Washington State along the Chinook Trail, Burnt Bridge Creek, Salmon Creek, and the Renaissance Trail. On the Oregon side of the Columbia River, Gresham, Lake Oswego, and the Tualatin Hills Park and Recreation District are all adding their own spokes. There are proposed greenway corridors along the Tualatin and Sandy Rivers as well as Beaverton, Fanno, Johnson, and Rock-Bronson-Willow Creeks.

Not all of these trails follow waterways. Metro and Gresham are working on a cooperative effort to purchase as much of the scenic and wildlife-rich East Lava Domes as possible and create an internal East Buttes Loop Trail that will connect the Springwater Corridor Trail with several extinct volcanic buttes on the south edge of Gresham. A Mt. Scott-Scouter Mountain trail loop will eventually connect the Springwater Trail with the Clackamas River to the south and North Clackamas Greenway, west to the Willamette Greenway. And Beaver Creek Canyon trail is being planned by Metro and Troutdale to develop a crescent-shaped trail that will run from near the mouth of the Sandy River through Troutdale and back to the Sandy River at Oxbow Regional Park.

A non-governmental initiative has caught on in Southwest Portland as well. Never content to sit back and be told what their priorities should be, a group of Southwest Portland residents, under the leadership of Don Baack, has initiated its own "connectivity" drive by expanding walking options beyond sidewalks and formal trails to include rights-of-way through private property, in addition to the more traditional trail, street, and sidewalk options. These neighborhood trail advocates have produced a map that identifies two north-south and five east-west routes that lead from the downtown core and the Willamette River throughout Southwest Portland (see below for information).

There are also more long-term, equally ambitious projects being planned to connect the Portland region with the coast via the Portland-to-Coast Trail. To the southeast the Oregon Trail-Barlow Road trail will head east from Oregon City, and the Estacada Corridor Trail will continue from the current Springwater Trail terminus in Boring all the way to Estacada on the abandoned rail line. In Clark County, the Chinook Trail is evolving to connect Vancouver Lake and Burnt Bridge and Salmon Creeks to the Columbia Gorge Scenic Area. Many of these projects will be either rails-to-trails projects or involve a shared right-of-way in rails-with-trails efforts, like the OMSI-Springwater Trail.

By Mike Houck

For more information: For Metro's bicycle route guide/map and Multnomah County's East Multnomah County Bikeways map, call 503-248-5050; for Washington County's "Getting There by Bike," call 503-644-5555. Or contact 40-Mile Loop Land Trust, see Resources.

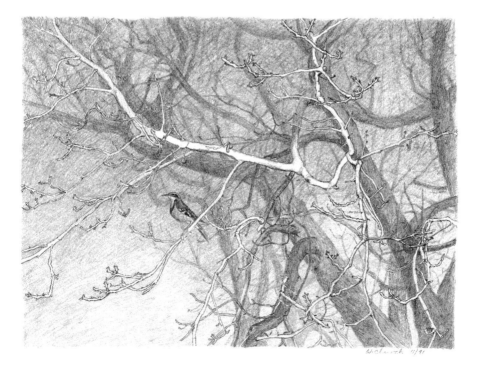

George Himes Nature Park

This park could not be more obscure. One would be hard-pressed to recognize this as a park, much less as a critical link in the 40-Mile Loop trail system, save for a large rock and adjacent purple-flowered rhododendron shrub at the corner of SW Nebraska and Terwilliger Boulevard, and a plaque that reads:

Location
SW Nebraska and SW Terwilliger, south of Beaverton-Hillsdale Hwy.

Activities
Hiking

Facilities
Trail unpaved
Picnic area

Fees and Regulations
Pets on leash

Highlights
A 35-acre natural park on the Terwilliger Parkway, with fantastic views of Ross Island Lagoon and Oaks Bottom Wildlife Refuge, just downhill from the park on SW Parkhill Way.

Public Transit
Tri-Met #8, #1, #38, and #12

Thomas Guide 626

Honoring the work of George H. Himes, pioneer of 1853, who throughout his life has devotedly searched out and recorded early history of the Oregon country; and who is here present on his 91st birthday, May 18, 1935 to witness for himself the naming of this park, and the placing therein of this marker for a perpetual commemoration. Oregon State Chapter, National Society, Daughters of Founders and Patriots of America.

The park itself falls off sharply from SW Terwilliger, so its highest value to the surrounding neighborhoods is as scenic green relief from surrounding developments and as wildlife habitat that extends to I-5. The 40-Mile Loop connector trail is an unassuming, almost hidden feature in the southwest corner of the park just behind the George Himes memorial plaque. There are a few picnic tables along the southern border of the park along SW Nebraska.

In late May, the Douglas fir, western red cedar, and maple forest canopy is alive with pine siskins, while the inside-out-flower, elderberry, waterleaf, and Oregon grape understory resounds with

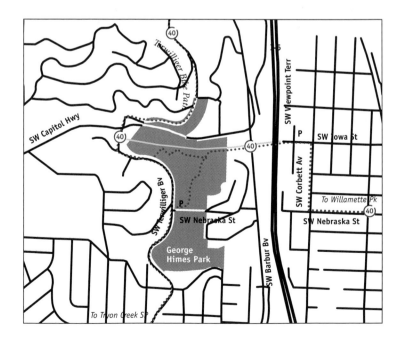

spotted towhee trills, flycatchers, black-throated gray warbler, song sparrows, and house finches. In contrast with the rough-and-ready link at SW Iowa, the trail at George Himes is of the same relatively high quality as Forest Park's Wildwood Trail.

On the southern border of George Himes at SW Nebraska and SW Parkhill Way is one of the city's most breathtaking views of the Willamette River. The perspective and height provide unparalleled opportunities to look down into the Oaks Bottom wetlands and the Ross Island Lagoon. For the best views you have to walk downhill from Himes Park along SW Parkhill Drive and around the corner. With binoculars or a spotting scope you can see the great blue heron nests and bald eagle nests on Ross Island, even when the black cottonwoods are leafed-out.

You can also clearly see the great blue heron mural on the west-facing wall of the Portland Memorial building which stands guard over Oaks Bottom. There are also stunning views of the now-extinct volcanoes starting with Mt. Tabor and extending to Gresham's lava domes area and Mt. Scott.

George Himes came across the Oregon Trail with his family in 1853. He was in the printing business and it is said that he set the type telling the news of Lincoln's assasination. He was the first secretary/ director of the Oregon Historical Society in 1898. The legacy of his interest in printing and publication is indirectly responsible for this book's publication with OHS Press.

Access
Off SW Terwilliger at SW Nebraska

How to Get There
Take SW Terwilliger south from Beaverton-Hillsdale Hwy. to SW Nebraska and park on Nebraska. From the south take SW Terwilliger from SW Barbur Blvd. and drive to SW Nebraska. From the east walk up the trail from the Corbett area via the trailhead on SW Iowa and SW Viewpoint Terr.

By Mike Houck

For more information: Portland Bureau of Parks and Recreation, see Resources.

Marquam Nature Trail

Marquam Hill, alias "Pill Hill," sprouts more than high-rise hospitals and medical schools. Douglas fir and big-leaf maple vie to be the tallest tree along the Marquam Nature Trail, named for Portland pioneer and legal eagle Philip Marquam. Sheltered beneath these arboreal giants is an understory lush with vine maple, elderberry, Oregon grape, ferns, and wildflowers.

The Marquam Trail is part of Portland's 40-Mile Loop; this section is unpaved and designated for foot traffic only. You can walk or jog the entire five miles from Terwilliger Boulevard to Washington Park; take a three-mile jaunt up to Council Crest for excellent views of Portland, Mt. Hood, and points west; or visit the Marquam Shelter for a less strenuous nature walk.

Fall is a great time to take in the Marquam Trail when maple and alder cloak the canyons in glowing gold and carpet the trail with crackling leaves. Look, too, for the bright red or purple accents of elderberry, huckleberry, and Oregon grape, replenishing summer's fading bounty of tasty but invasive blackberry.

Like the blackberry, English ivy is an introduced, invasive plant, whose tough tendrils smother shrubs and wildflowers and clamber up the trunks of trees. Efforts to remove this plant pest are evident along portions of the Marquam Trail. Watch for dry, brown vines stranded high on the trunks of trees; volunteers have severed connections with the ground to prevent the ivy from flowering and going to seed. Compare the variety and abundance of plants that can grow where ivy is still rampant with those where native species thrive, and you will appreciate the battle being waged in many of Portland's natural areas.

Take a moment on your uphill climb to catch your breath and examine the fallen trees and stumps along the Marquam Trail. Note the gigantic but shallow root system of a toppled Douglas fir. Logs and stumps are great places to look at mosses and lichens. Banana slugs hang out in these moist reserves, as well as the spindly invertebrates like the harvestmen, also called daddy-long-legs, a close cousin to spiders. Seedlings of trees and shrubs often sprout in the nutrient-rich decaying wood, and ferns such as licorice root are plentiful here.

Whether you seek sweeping views of distant mountains, including Mounts Hood, Jefferson, Adams, St. Helens, and Rainier, or a close-up look at nature's small and obscure, the Marquam Trail generously offers it all.

Location
SW Marquam and Sam Jackson Park Rd.

Activities
Hiking
Jogging
Wildlife Viewing

Facilities
None

Fees and Regulations
None

Highlights
Part of 40-Mile Loop Trail with panoramic views from Council Crest, Portland's highest point, and access to Washington Park. An interpretive kiosk provides information on local wildflowers.

Public Transit
Tri-Met #8, which serves Oregon Health Sciences University, will take you to within a short walking distance of the trail.

Thomas Guide 626

Access
An uphill 3.2 mile walk on unpaved trails to Council Crest including sections with stairs; trail crosses several roads and can be muddy in

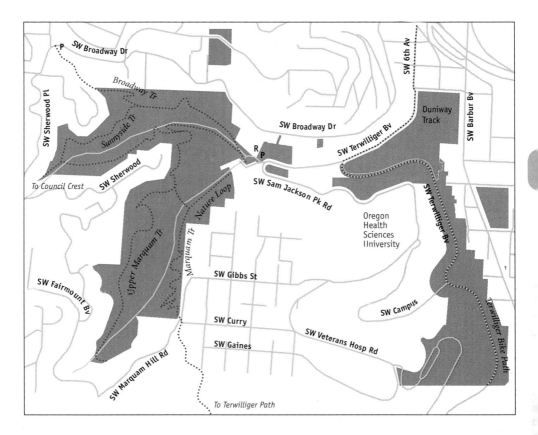

winter and spring. (See SW Terwilliger, George Himes site entries for other access on SW Terwilliger.)

How to Get There

From Capitol Hwy., take Terwilliger Blvd. north approximately 1 mile, or proceed to Sam Jackson Park Rd. near Duniway Track and go west to the sharp curve in the road at SW Marquam. Trail is also accessible from Council Crest Park.

By Connie Levesque

For more information: Portland Bureau of Parks and Recreation or Friends of Marquam Nature Park, see Resources.

The Lands of the Wildwood Trail

The Wildwood Trail runs for 30 miles along the ridge of forested hills that, seen from Portland's east side, stands as a backdrop to the city center. Running roughly northwest, it begins near the Zoo entrance on the Sunset Highway (US 26) and ends at Newberry Road, nine miles as the crow flies from its point of origin. It is the longest section of the 40-Mile Loop, which is actually a 150-mile loop trail following riverways around the circumference of the Portland metropolitan area. It is the backbone of a network of about 100 additional miles of connecting and interconnecting trails through the remnants or successors of aboriginal forestlands, with trail names posted at junctions and mileage markers on blue-blazed trees at quarter-mile intervals. It links together two of Portland's oldest, largest, and most remarkable parks, Washington Park and Forest Park.

By Florence Riddle

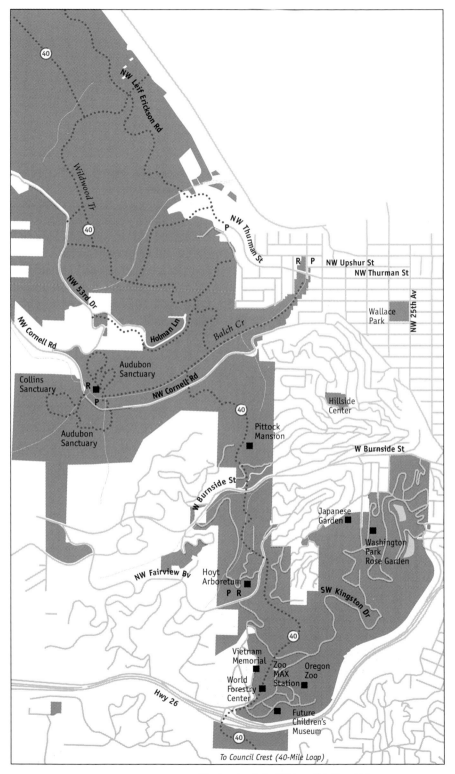

Washington Park

Washington Park is a 332-acre mosaic of recreational areas and facilities sprawled over the many-faceted ridge that extends from the Sunset Highway to West Burnside, between SW Vista Avenue on the east and an imaginary north/south line near Skyline Boulevard on the west. From an aerial view, it is shaped roughly like a chunky horseshoe magnet with its open end pointing due north and its western arm directly in line with the Pittock Mansion, which stands on top of the hill just across Burnside from its northern border.

It began as Portland's one, central city park on 40.78 acres of land purchased from a private owner in 1871, when Portland was a town of 8,000 at a bend in the Willamette surrounded by the forest primeval. This nucleus of what is now Washington Park was soon developed, in accordance with the same way of thinking which had inspired the creation of Central Park in New York City about ten years before, with rose gardens, lawns, a fountain, statuary, and patterned drives and walkways. After the turn of the century, its boundaries were gradually expanded to include adjacent lands which had proved unsuitable for agricultural or residential development until 1922, when incorporation of the land now dedicated to the Hoyt Arboretum brought the park to its present dimensions.

A native Portlander's mental image of Washington Park is usually composed of the features along its city-side edge: the Lewis and Clark circle, the Sacajawea statue, the reservoirs, the rose gardens and tennis courts with picnic grounds in between, the amphitheater, the archery field, and the Forestry Center. It also may well include the Japanese Gardens, the Zoo, and OMSI, although officially they're not part of it, the Japanese Gardens being privately owned, the Zoo now belonging to Metro rather than the City of Portland, and most of OMSI having moved away. What is not so well known is that within this rim of developments, most of Washington Park is a forest.

Essentially the same trees and undergrowth of the native forest that are showcased in the Cascade Nature Trail at the Zoo are to be seen growing wild around the borders of the park and its subdivisions, and interspersed with the plantings in the arboretum throughout the western half of the park. Those who ride the Zoo railway on its two-mile loop through the southeastern quadrant of the park or walk through the park on the Wildwood Trail are immersed in it, so that they may see the city as bordering on the forest rather than the other way around.

The Wildwood Trail Corridor

If you approach Washington Park by way of the 40-Mile Loop trail section that comes over Council Crest and down to the Sunset Highway canyon, you will come into the park at the southern tip of

Location
Sunset Hwy. to W Burnside, between SW Vista Ave. on the east and an imaginary north/south line near Skyline Blvd. on the west.

Activities
Hiking
Biking

Facilities
Toilets
Wheelchair accessible
Paved and unpaved trail
Parking
Interpretive information (brochures/maps)
Picnic area

Fees and Regulations
Pets on leash

Highlights
Washington Park contains some of Portland's most well-known tourist sites, including the Japanese Gardens, Oregon Zoo, and Hoyt Arboretum. Both groomed and natural parkland and stunning views of the city and Cascades.

the arboretum on a trail that leads you for half a mile, through a dogwood grove and past the Vietnam memorial, to the beginning of the Wildwood Trail.

From there, another half mile of comfortably graded switchbacks will take you to the top of the ridge through a deciduous forest which is a blaze of color in the fall and a festival of bloom in the spring. At the summit, just south of the Hoyt Arboretum Visitor Center and Picnic Shelter, is a viewpoint with a directional marker identifying the peaks of the Cascades that can be seen on the horizon. The trail then winds toward the older, eastern side of the park, alongside the forested ravines traveled by the Zoo railway, until it reaches the cliff above the Japanese Gardens. A spur trail that climbs a steep half-mile up from the Japanese Gardens joins the main trail at this point. A little farther on, there is another spur trail coming in from the northeast corner of the park. The Wildwood Trail then winds back to the west around a peninsula of residential development in the center of the park, past the Arboretum's Winter Garden, and up through its oak collection. It crosses the summit of the ridge just north of the Visitor Center, before winding down through the conifers on the western slope of the ridge, crossing the creek that runs along the western bottom land, and leaving the park through a wilderness preserve bordering on Burnside in its northwest corner.

Access
Multiple access points as described in text.

How to Get There
From Hwy. 26 west take the Oregon Zoo exit; from W Burnside take SW Vista Ave. at NW 23rd Ave., head south on Vista to SW Park Pl., and turn right (west). Proceed around the roundabout that circles counterclockwise around the Oregon Column and flower beds. Drive past Sacajawea and you can either park along the roadway here or continue, following the signs to your destination. From SW Skyline take SW Fairview Blvd. downhill to SW Kingston, turn right, and park near the Japanese Gardens and tennis courts. From the Oregon Zoo, wind your way down SW Kingston Blvd. to the tennis courts and train stop.

There is a spur trail from the 23-mile-long Wildwood Trail that zigzags downhill from SW Kingston between the Oregon Zoo and Hoyt Arboretum to the Big Meadow. It then passes through the children's play area and between SW Sherwood Blvd. and the Rose Garden service road. The Oregon Zoo runs a train from the Zoo to the picnic shelter next to the Rose Garden. *See map on page 114.*

By Florence Riddle

For more information: Portland Bureau of Parks and Recreation, see Resources.

Public Transit
Multiple services including: Tri-Met #63 stops near the Oregon Column on SW Park Pl.; at the restrooms near Sacajawea; at the base of SW Sherwood; at the restrooms in the Rose Garden; and at the foot of SW Fairview Blvd. where it meets SW Kingston. Tri-Met #20 runs along W Burnside. Tri-Met #63 runs to the Oregon Zoo once an hour, and Tri-Met also runs a shuttle bus every 15 minutes between the Zoo and the Rose Gardens, but only during the summer.

West-side MAX light rail stops at the Oregon Zoo. To get to street level you have to take a 400-foot elevator ride. The interpretive materials on local geology, flora, and fauna are worth the ride.

Thomas Guide 596

Hoyt Arboretum

The Hoyt Arboretum is a lovingly maintained tree museum where 4,300 trees and shrubs of over 800 species from all over the world are exhibited on 214 acres of the hilly terrain in the western arm of the park, in amongst native Douglas fir, western hemlock, western red cedar, and big-leaf maple. Nearly every tree is labeled with a four-by-six-inch metal sign stating its family, genus, species, variety, common name, native location, and age or time of planting (if known). Portland's tree-friendly climate and the mini-climates within the arboretum which result from the many and varied furrowings, tiltings, drainage patterns, and exposures of its terrain make this tree collection one of the largest, most varied, and most interesting of its kind. It contains the largest collection of conifers anywhere in the world, including the dawn redwood, a species thought to have been long extinct until a few specimens were discovered in a remote area of China, one of which was brought to the Arboretum.

Plantings are grouped according to families in the terrain where they seem most at home. Oaks are to be found in a drier area, flowering trees and hardwoods on a south-facing slope, with

Location
4000 SW Fairview Blvd.

Activities
Hiking

Facilities
Toilets
Wheelchair accessible
Paved and unpaved trail
Parking
Interpretive center
Interpretive information
    (brochures/maps)
Picnic area

Fees and Regulations
None

Highlights
Largest collection of conifers anywhere in the world, including the dawn redwood, discovered in China, a species thought to have been long extinct.

Public Transit
Tri-Met #63; MAX light rail station at the Zoo.

Thomas Guide 596

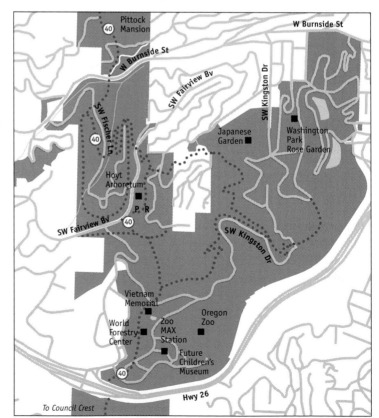

evergreens on the western side of the ridge. In a sheltered pocket below the oak collection is a winter garden where colorful and fragrant flowers bloom in December. There is a wedding meadow fringed with white-flowering trees and shrubs, to which road access can be opened on occasion.

Winding through the various collections, there are ten miles of trails, never far from a road though seldom in sight of one, so that immersion in the peace, beauty, and endless fascination of the arboretum is quickly come by. Two of the trails are wheelchair-accessible, one along the creekside bottomland at the western edge of the arboretum and one leading from the canyon of the Sunset Highway to the spacious views of the summit.

Booklets in support of self-guided tours to various collections—the conifers, the oaks, the flowering trees, etc.—and identifying the wildlife attracted to specific areas are available in the Visitors' Center. Guided tours are conducted year-round, and there are many opportunities for volunteers to participate in the care of the park

Access
On SW Fairview Blvd. or via the Wildwood Trail, 40-Mile Loop

How to Get There
From the Rose Gardens of Washington Park drive up the very steep and curvy SW Fairview Blvd. From Hwy. 26 take the Sylvan exit and drive on SW Skyline Blvd. to SW Fairview Blvd., and take a right on Fairview Blvd. just past the Zoo turnoff. The Arboretum headquarters is on the right; parking for the picnic shelter is on the left. From W Burnside you can enter the Arboretum's "back door" by driving west on Burnside, past the Pittock Mansion, and turning left on SW Fischer Ln. Fischer Ln. winds through the Arboretum, where you can park several places, or it will take you to SW Fairview Blvd. and the Arboretum headquarters and picnic shelter.

By Florence Riddle

For more information: Hoyt Arboretum or Hoyt Arboretum Friends Foundation, see Resources.

Pittock Mansion Acres Park

When early *Oregonian* publisher Henry L. Pittock built his house on a large West Hills promontory overlooking the Willamette River, he certainly knew what he was doing. On a clear day he could see all the Cascades snowcaps from his back yard. No doubt there is more smog now than there was in 1914, and Portland has certainly crept closer to Pittock's promontory, but the snowcaps are still there along with stunning city views. Portland Parks acquired the 46-acre site in 1964.

Less obviously, this location—which is situated 1,000 feet above the surrounding valley floor and acts something like a headland on the coast—makes Pittock Mansion Acres a natural stop for migrating birds. Consequently, it is among the best spots to view songbirds during April and May. In addition to its situation on the "Willamette Flyway," Pittock Mansion is also blessed with a diversity of habitat, which enhances its bird list. From the scattered trees and lawn of the mansion's back yard to the tangle of vegetation below the promontory to the warbler-laden maples around the parking lot and the deep woods just beyond, a circuit of the grounds can easily turn up 25 species on a spring morning. Because of the elevation of the mansion grounds, rare views *down* into the treetops of the surrounding forest are possible, and a glance overhead will frequently afford good looks at swifts, swallows, and raptors. This is a particularly good location for warbling and Cassin's vireo, pine siskin, red crossbills, black-headed grosbeaks, and purple finches. In wintertime the patch of Himalayan blackberries below the Mansion to the north is an excellent site for comparing fox and song sparrows and winter and Bewick's wrens.

Although Pittock Mansion Acres can be birded in an hour, a visit can be extended by a tour of the mansion or a picnic. And it's an easy stopping place or jumping off point for a more extended tour of Forest Park.

Access

Pittock Mansion Acres Park comprises the house and grounds of the Pittock Mansion. There is a short trail that loops around the edge of the promontory on which the mansion sits. The park is also a stop on the Wildwood Trail.

How to Get There

Follow W Burnside about 1.2 miles west of NW 23rd and turn right onto NW Barnes Rd. Follow the well-marked signs through the neighborhood for another .7 mile to the park.

By Bob Wilson

For more information: Portland Bureau of Parks and Recreation, Pittock Mansion Acres, see Resources.

Location
Pittock Mansion Acres is located at 3229 NW Pittock Dr., just north of W Burnside, about 1.2 miles west of NW 23rd.

Activities
Hiking
Birding
Viewpoint
Historic home tour

Facilities
Picnic
Toilets
Wheelchair access
Parking

Fees and Regulations
Entrance fees: None for grounds, $4.50 for mansion (children $2.00, seniors $4.00)
Restricted hours
Pets on leash

Highlights
In addition to offering a spectacular view of Portland's cityscape and Cascade Mountains, Pittock Mansion Acres is one of the city's premier locations for observing the spring songbird migration.

Public Transit
Take Tri-Met #20 and get off at the Wildwood Trail. The eastbound stop is at Barnes Rd. The closest westbound stop is at NW Hermosa.

Thomas Guide 596

Forest Park

Forest Park is a 5,000-acre wilderness preserve which owes its existence to a curious geological formation known to the native Indians as Tuality Mountain—an upfolding of basalt overlaid with silt, which rises abruptly from the west bank of the Willamette to a height of 1,200 feet and extends from the river valley now occupied by West Burnside to where the Willamette forks around the southern tip of Sauvie Island. Forested uplands that fan out from the northern end of this ridge merge with the forests of the Oregon Coast Range.

When early explorers first saw Tuality Mountain in 1805, it had been covered with a Douglas fir forest from time immemorial. By 1851, its acreage had all been parceled out to white settlers in Donation Land Claims. However, it was not long before the claims on its eastern face defaulted, or were donated, to the city after attempts to develop them for residential or commercial use had been defeated by the landslides which routinely scoured the silt off the basalt foundation of these steep slopes during the first rainy season after they had been cleared of trees. In 1897, the 30-acre parcel around Balch Creek Canyon, now known as Macleay Park, was donated to the city as a nature park. In 1948, about 3,000 acres of adjacent land were incorporated with it as Forest Park, and a concerted effort to add the remaining forest lands of this hillside to the park was begun.

Today, Forest Park covers the whole east face of the ridge, bounded by Skyline Boulevard on the west, Newberry Road on the north, St. Helens Road (US 30) on the east, and West Burnside on the south. It is furrowed crosswise by streams running swiftly toward the Willamette, including two major waterways: Balch Creek, which leaves the park at the end of NW Upshur, under the Thurman Street Bridge; and Miller Creek, which drains into the wetlands across from Sauvie Island.

Because it is a peninsula of the coastal forest, it is accessible even to the large mammals whose survival depends on a wide range and diversity of old-growth forest habitat, such as mountain lions, bobcats, coyotes, foxes, bear, elk, and deer. It is also home to hundreds of species of birds and smaller animals. Fish and amphibians inhabit its streams; and although beavers seem to have found that dams in the waterways of the park silt over too rapidly to be worth their while, they enjoy the bottomlands at the end of Miller Creek.

There are now 60 miles of trails and firelanes within Forest Park, including the Wildwood Trail, which runs the length of the park near the summit, through the full range of successional stages of the aboriginal forest, and intersects the roads which began as Indian trails or white settlers' market roads over the ridge (Burnside, Cornell, Saltzman, Springville, Germantown, and Newberry), as well as easements for an oil line, a gas line, and BPA electric-power

Location
Portland's West Hills or Tualatin Mountains, stretching from W Burnside to where the Willamette forks around the southern tip of Sauvie Island.

Activities
Hiking
Biking (bicycling is restricted to specific trails and Leif Erikson Road)

Facilities
Toilets
Trail unpaved
Parking
Interpretive information (brochures/maps)
Picnic area

Fees and Regulations
Pets on leash

Highlights
The region's largest publicly owned park and a 5,000-acre Greenspace in the heart of the metropolitan region.

Public Transit
Tri-Met #17, #15, #77, and #18. MAX west-side light rail to Oregon Zoo. Wildwood Trail and 40-Mile Loop Trail.

Thomas Guide 535/565/ 595/596

transmitters. Leif Erikson Drive, a roadway closed to motor vehicles, runs alongside the Wildwood Trail a little lower on the ridge for 11 miles, from the end of NW Thurman to NW Germantown Rd.

Forest Park offers a unique opportunity for people of an urbanized world to see creatures of the wild in their native environment and to study an ecosystem still extensive enough to support the aboriginal flora and fauna of the Pacific Northwest in all

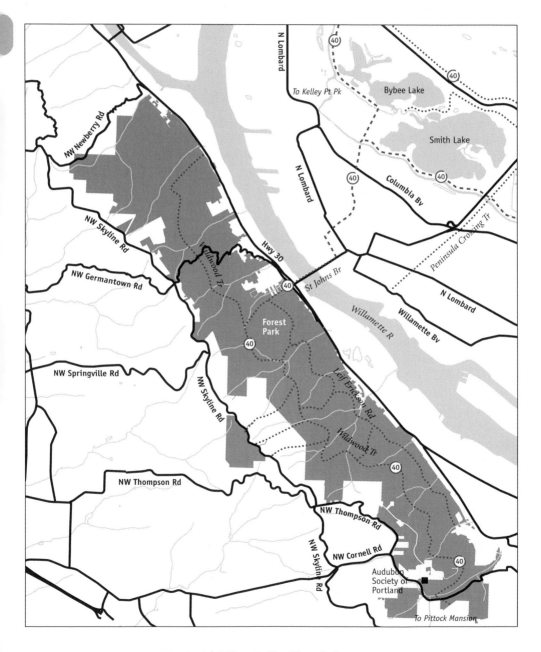

their diversity. The present plan for management of the park aims at restoration of the self-sustaining old-growth forest that was here before we were, and identifies special needs and values of the parklands within three management units.

The Near End of Forest Park

The South Management Unit extends from Burnside to Firelane One and includes lands which were the earliest to come under protection as natural areas: Pittock Acres, Macleay Park, and Holman Park. Although this part of the park is the most vulnerable to overuse and ivy invasion, on the whole it is the best preserved. To enter the park through the Balch Canyon is to pass from a city street into the heart of an ancient forest with a single step, as if walking through a doorway into a theme park whose theme is Nature.

To enter the park through the Balch Canyon is to pass from a city street into the heart of an ancient forest with a single step, as if walking through a doorway into a theme park whose theme is Nature.

The largest tree in the park is very near this entryway, and the abundant waters of Balch Creek are a reminder that streams once ran where West Burnside and the Sunset Highway are now and still tunnel under city pavement into the Willamette. Guided tours, interpretive literature, and opportunities to join an ivy-removal army are available to all through the field headquarters of the park located at this entry point.

The Central Management Unit, which extends from Firelane 1 to Germantown Road, is an ideal place for hiking, jogging, or biking, for long or short distances. The Wildwood Trail and Leif Erikson Drive meander along the ridge through dappled shade, with hardly any ups and downs, through this section of the park to the sounds of rushing streams, wind in treetops, industrious bees, bird songs, and the chatter of squirrels, with a panorama of the city endlessly in view.

There are no stopping places to speak of along this stretch, but many spur trails give quick access to clearings along Leif Erikson Drive, the firelanes, and the edges of the park.

And the Far Reaches

The North Management Unit, which extends from Germantown to Newberry, offers the most powerful experience of the otherness of the ancient forest from urban civilization. There are striking contrasts between the cleared areas of the power-line easements in this section and the enormous firs and deeply textured understory, which are to be found here in remnants of the old-growth forest. The trail system here is minimal, much of it a recent arrival into areas previously unknown and bordering on areas where it seems that people may never have been—and never should be, since they are the homes of other species. It is a place to see glimpses and traces of forest inhabitants in their own territory and to experience the forest as a sanctuary.

Access

A variety of access points, including the 23-mile long Wildwood Trail and the 40-Mile Loop. Primary access is at Macleay Park on NW Cornell Rd., just east of the Audubon Society of Portland headquarters; from the western end of NW Upshur at Lower Macleay Park; from the end of NW Thurman which dead-ends at Leif Erikson Rd.; and along NW 53rd. A new access is planned from Hwy. 30. The northernmost reach of the park is accessible via Newberry Rd. via Wildwood Trail. Wildwood crosses NW Newton Rd. about midway between Hwy. 30 and NW Skyline Blvd., and crosses Germantown Rd. east of Skyline. NW 53rd Dr. provides access to feeder trails that link up with Wildwood. Going from south to north they are Birch, Dogwood, and Alder.

A series of firelanes provides access from the park's perimeter, including Firelane 3 directly off NW Skyline, Firelane 5 off Saltzman Rd. just east of Skyline, and Firelane 1 off NW 53rd Dr. and Leif Erikson Rd.

How to Get There

See Access, above.

By Florence Riddle

For more information: Portland Bureau of Parks and Recreation, see Resources.

An excellent source for Forest Park exploration is Marcy C. Houle's *One City's Wilderness: Portland's Forest Park* (Oregon Historical Society Press, 1995).

Slip Slidin' Away

All an animal really needs for human acceptance is to be warm, fuzzy, and preferably small. As a critter moves along or, more accurately, down the furry-warm blooded/slimy-cold blooded continuum, its human appeal, even to naturalists, diminishes. It is hard to slip any farther than a creature that produces a slimy trail as it glides through our forests and gardens. I refer, of course, to that cold-blooded, molluscan herbivore, that destroyer of gardens—the slug.

One species in particular, the banana slug, has received a lot of bad press over the years. Not only is it a native Oregonian, a status which should assure it respect, it is only infrequently the real culprit of our lost heads of lettuce, chewed chard, or mutilated mums. It's the exotic immigrants that wreak havoc on our gardens, not the benign "king of slugs" which prefers decaying forest debris and mushrooms to radishes and parsley. In fact, by eating fallen leaves, fungus, and animal wastes found on the forest floor, banana slugs help other decomposers perform a Herculean janitorial service by recycling organic debris and returning nutrients to the soil.

Occasionally you will find the banana slug (*Ariolimax columbianus*) in a northwest garden, but the gastropod eating the lettuce is more likely the black slug (*Arion ater*) or common little gray garden slug (*Ariolimax reticulatus*), both imports from abroad. These and several other northwest species appear to have hitchhiked in bulbs or containerized plants from Europe.

Not only does the banana slug suffer persecution from human assailants, but the exotic interlopers, being both prolific and aggressive, have forced the Oregonian out of its native habitat and pushed it into what forested refuges remain in Portland.

Banana slugs range in color from a solid bright yellow to yellow-green with spots. In those with spots, the mantle, a region just behind the head, never seems to have more than one large spot. This slug is our largest species, sometimes weighing as much as a McDonald's Quarter Pounder and measuring up to twelve inches from the tip of its tail to its all-consuming snout. Size can be highly variable due to the slug's elasticity. Some species have been observed crawling into glass tubes until they have stretched 11 times their usual length!

The banana slug shares many physical and behavioral characteristics with its non-native competitors. First of all, slugs appear to have arisen from a snail-like ancestor and lost their external shell in the process. Some slugs have retained vestigial shells within their mantle tissue.

Sluggish Movement

All slugs and snails are grouped together in one class of animals, the gastropods, which translates literally to "stomach-foot." Aside from its garden-destroying tendencies, it is the slug's ability to produce the copious amounts of slime essential for locomotion on its stomach-foot that evokes our repulsion and fascination with slugs. Rick Gauger's article "The Lives of a Slug" (*Pacific Northwest* May 1983) contains a detailed description of how a researcher at the University of British Columbia solved the mystery of slug movement in 1979 by freezing them in "midripple," then dissecting and examining their "foot." Scientist Mark Denny found that slugs move from back to front. The feat of slug movement is accomplished by their amazing ability to convert the slime from a sticky, solid substance, which gives it grip, into a slippery fluid which allows the foot to glide. Gauger reports that slugs have been observed zipping along at speeds in excess of 0.007 miles per hour!

Predator Aversion

Fortunately for the slug, its slime is not only disgusting to humans but also repulsive to many predators. Although garter snakes and Pacific giant salamanders do consume slugs, other slug eaters are thwarted by molluscan slime and body contortions. Scott Forslund, in his article "On Death and Dying: Why Killing a Slug Isn't Easy," describes in gory detail how a slug "curls into a tight ball and rocks from side to side, sometimes lodging itself into the duck's throat so securely that the duck chokes and dies. [The slug] can then crawl out of the duck's throat and go on its way."

The Eyes Have It

Slugs have two sets of tentacles or antennae, which allow them to "see" and smell. Close-up smelling and tasting are done by the shorter pair, the longer pair sniffing out tasty morsels from 30 feet away. The tips of the antennae contain black specks which act as the slug's eyes. With these rudimentary "eyes" slugs can distinguish light and dark and possibly vague shapes. On a sunny day, the shadow of a hand passing over these rudimentary eyes will cause the slug to retract into its mantle.

A Toothsome Smile

The radula, or business end of a slug, is equipped with over 27,000 "teeth." The organ acts like a file and allows the slug to rasp away at its food much as sandpaper removes paint from a surface. These "teeth" are worn away and constantly replaced. Next time you get the nerve to pick up a nice large banana slug, let it crawl along your outstretched hand. If you can inspire its confidence, the slug will resume its rasping, feeding activity and you can actually feel the tiny teeth working away at your skin.

The Outside Connections

On the right side of the slug is an opening which serves as a breathing hole that meets 50 percent of the slug's oxygen needs. The other 50 percent comes via diffusion through the moist skin. Another orifice in front of the pneumostome is the site for sexual reproduction.

Slug sex is a bit off the beaten path. To begin with, each slug possesses both male and female sexual organs, making them hermaphrodites. However, two individuals are still necessary for reproduction, which in some species can last 72 hours. There is a scintillating account of slug sex in Scott Forslund's "The Sex Life of Slugs: Elaborate Rituals and Prolific Reproduction." His article includes passages that would be blocked on most school Internets. After the sexual act, eggs develop in both slugs. Delay of egg-laying occurs if the soil moisture is less than 10 percent. Clutches of eggs range in number, but 50–100 is the average. Some species cover their eggs with slime to keep moisture in. When hatched, slugs are about three-eighths of an inch long and can grow to two inches in the first month. Lifespans of slugs vary, but two years is the maximum a slug can expect to strike terror into the hearts of northwest gardeners and hikers.

On your next walk in the woods, watch your step and stop for a moment to examine this maligned and misunderstood animal. If you are looking for the most likely places to make a slug's acquaintance, start in Tryon Creek State Park , Forest Park, Hoyt Arboretum, Eagle Fern Park, and other similar banana slug refuges.

By Mike Houck

Bibliography

Forslund, Scott. "The Sex Life of Slugs: Elaborate Rituals and Prolific Reproduction." *Pacific Northwest*, May 1983, 32.

Gauger, Rick. "On Death and Dying: Why Killing a Slug Isn't Easy." *Pacific Northwest*, May 1983, 49.

——. "The Lives of a Slug." *Pacific Northwest*, May 1983, 30-49.

Thanks are also due Dr. H. H. Crowell, Oregon State University, and the late Sallie Jacobsen, Oregon State Parks.

Macleay Park and Balch Creek Canyon

Hardly a summer weekend goes by without picnickers using Macleay Park. It has a small parking lot—eight slots—plus bathrooms, and enough space to throw a frisbee around. A few hundred yards down a trail is the Audubon Society of Portland's facility, with a Nature Store, Interpretive Room, Wildlife Care Center, and more parking. The Upper Macleay Trail leads through old growth Douglas fir, big-leaf maples, hemlock, and red alder. You can either take the loop back to Macleay Park or take the trail spur that leads up to Pittock Mansion.

The Lower Macleay Trail coincides with the Wildwood Trail along Balch Creek and leads through one of the richest riparian ecosystems in Forest Park, where one can find roughskin newts or the Pacific giant salamander. Dippers hunt for insects and small fish under rocks and woody debris. Other birds are attracted to Balch Creek Canyon habitat: pileated woodpecker, brown creeper, chickadee, band-tailed pigeon, olive-sided flycatchers, and winter wren. Resident native cutthroat trout live in the creek from the Upshur conduit up through the Audubon property.

This is a trail to take on those hot summer days when you haven't either the time or transportation to get out to the gorge or mountain trails. The trails here are always shaded, with cooling breezes off the creek.

Location
5151 NW Cornell Rd., Portland. The closest cross street is 53rd Ave. and Cornell Rd.

Activities
Hiking

Facilities
Picnic area
Toilets
Wheelchair access
Parking

Fees and Regulations
Pets on leash

Highlights
This is one of the oldest parks in Portland. Over 100 acres were donated by Donald Macleay as a city park in 1897. The Lower Macleay Trail coincides with the Wildwood Trail along Balch Creek and leads through one of the richest riparian ecosystems in Forest Park. Amphibians like the roughskin newt and Pacific giant salamander roam here.

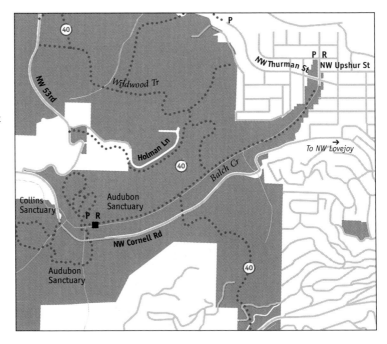

Access

Both the upper and lower trails are easily accessible from the Macleay Park parking lot. The lower trail that leads down into Balch Creek Canyon and runs along Balch Creek can be very wet in winter.

How to Get There

From the east side of the Willamette River, take I-5 south and take the Hwy. 30 exit across the Fremont Bridge. Stay right onto Vaughn Street, heading west, to NW 25th and turn left. Head south on 25th to NW Lovejoy and turn right. Lovejoy winds up the hill and turns into Cornell Rd. after the "right turn without stopping" stop sign. Head west on NW Cornell Rd., passing through two tunnels, and Macleay Park is on the right a couple hundred yards past the second tunnel. It's approximately 1.6 miles from 25th and Lovejoy.

By Mitch Luckett

For more information: Portland Bureau of Parks and Recreation, see Resources.

Public Transit

The primary bus is Tri-Met #15, which runs frequently during the day from the downtown transit mall to the corner of NW Lovejoy and 23rd. The most direct route from the east side is Tri-Met #77, which runs on NW Lovejoy and north on NW 25th. The closest bus is Tri-Met #18, which only runs in a loop at the corner of Cornell and Westover. Tri-Met #18 only runs during rush hour.

Thomas Guide 595/596

Audubon Society of Portland Sanctuaries

Pittock Sanctuary

The forest surrounding the Audubon Society of Portland's Nature Store, Wildlife Care Center, and offices is a wildlife sanctuary. No bikes or pets are allowed on the trails. The Pittock Trail crosses Balch Creek and runs beside a pond, one of the few still-water habitats in Balch Creek Canyon. In the spring, roughskin newts float lazily in the still waters. Great blue herons, mallards, and wood ducks occasionally stop by for a quick flirtation or meal. One winter, two river otters took up residence on the little island in the middle of the pond; they stayed for a couple of weeks, dining on non-native fish released into the pond by careless people. On a spur called Woodpecker Trail is a stand of old-growth Douglas fir that survived the big cut of the west hills at the turn of the century. Benches sit beneath the tall trees as rest and reflection stops for passersby.

Founders Trail Sanctuary

Across Cornell Road from Pittock Sanctuary, the Founders Trail begins. Established in 1976, it is the newest Audubon Sanctuary. This is a narrow trail and was the victim of many landslides during the excessive rains of 1996. The hiker has an opportunity to examine many retaining walls constructed out of native materials. This 3/4 mile trail has many near-old growth groves of western hemlock, Douglas fir, and western red cedar. About halfway through the trail, the hiker will notice a relatively clear corridor approximately 60 feet wide with many dead tree snags all in a downsloping pattern. This pattern is a result of a massive landslide ripping through Founders Sanctuary in 1986. The slide was caused by illegal dumping on Skyline Boulevard. While devastating at the time, the massive slide is a good study in how nature repairs catastrophe. The slide area is also a good spot to catch a glimpse of pileated woodpeckers.

The Collins Sanctuary

Founders Trail runs into the east branch of Collins Trail. Collins Sanctuary is 86 acres and is owned by Oregon Parks Foundation, Inc., but managed by Audubon Society of Portland. Turn right at the junction of Founders and Collins and get back down to Cornell Road in a few minutes, or turn left and take the whole one-mile loop. Unlike the narrow Founders Trail, Collins Trail is wide and spacious. It was originally constructed as a wagon road. In the winter, it is easy to see the outline of the old road, but in summertime native vegetation—elderberry, salmonberry, sword-fern, and stinging nettles—obscures the ancient highway. Speaking of stinging nettles, wear long pants and long-sleeved shirts on Collins Trail in the spring and summer.

Location
5151 NW Cornell Rd., Portland. The closest cross street is 53rd Ave. and Cornell Rd.

Activities
Hiking

Facilities
Toilets
Wheelchair access
Parking

Fees and Regulations
Restricted hours
Interpretive center
Interpretive information (brochures, signs available at site)
No pets

Highlights
The trailhead of this site is the Audubon Society of Portland's campus. Audubon has a Nature Bookstore, Interpretive Center, Community Meeting Rooms, Administration Offices, Trail Maintenance Shop and Wildlife Care Center. Audubon has been feeding birds at this site for over 50 years, so depending on the season, several species of birds can be seen.

Access

The Audubon complex at Cornell Rd. consists of three interconnected Sanctuaries: Pittock, Founders, and Collins. Pittock and Founders trails begin from the main parking lot. Collins Trail starts a few hundred yards west on Cornell Rd. There is also a small parking lot at Collins Trail. All three trails are slippery when wet, and have many small bridges to cross and stairs to climb. It is advisable to wear long pants and long-sleeved shirts on Collins Trail in the spring and summer due to stinging nettles.

How to Get There

Coming from either north or south on I-5, take the US 30 exit. You'll go over the Fremont Bridge (watch for peregrines) and take the Vaughn St. exit off the bridge. Go to 25th and Vaughn. Turn left on 25th and go to Lovejoy, then turn right. Lovejoy becomes Cornell Rd. Continue on Cornell through 2 tunnels, past Macleay Park. On your right, 100 yards past Macleay Park, is the Audubon Society of Portland's main campus, approx. 1-1/2 mile from 25th.

From the west, find Cornell Rd. and follow it east until you come to the Audubon campus on the left. *See map on page 124.*

By Mitch Luckett

For more information: Audubon Society of Portland. Audubon's monthly newsletter, *The Warbler*, has information on the Sanctuary, see Resources.

Public Transit

The primary bus is Tri-Met #15, which runs frequently during the day from the downtown transit mall to the corner of NW Lovejoy and 23rd. The most direct route from the east side is Tri-Met #77, which runs west on NW Lovejoy and north on NW 25th. The closest bus is Tri-Met #18, which only runs in a loop at corner of Cornell and Westover, an uphill walk along Cornell to the Sanctuary. Tri-Met #18 only runs during rush hour.

Thomas Guide 595/596

Portland, City of Mosses

What could possibly create a sense of anticipation for another wet Northwest winter? In a word, moss. While the prospect of another long, soggy, and gray winter seldom fails to depress recent immigrants and, at times, even some native-born, if you learn to appreciate the multitude of non-flowering, spore-producing "lower plants" that abound in our forests, doorsteps, and lawns, you might also learn to embrace the wet in which they thrive.

After most flowering plants have shed their seeds, deciduous trees have dropped their leaves, and the faint of heart have fled to Baja, most of the non-flowering, so-called "primitive" plants come into their own—thanks to the long, dark, and moist days of winter. One group in particular, the mosses, busily soaks up the moisture, creating tufts of emerald green on our forests, reservoirs, and front steps, and dense mats of green in our lawns.

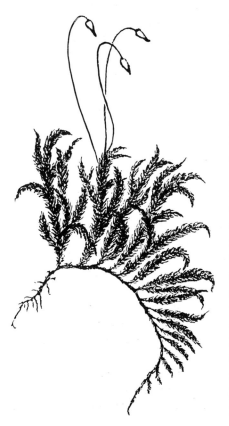

The mosses, evolutionarily juxtaposed between the algae and fungi and the "higher" club mosses, horsetails, and ferns, are a diverse group of spore-bearing plants that lack the veins and vessels of ferns and the more advanced flowering plants but are further along in their ability to colonize new turf than the algae. They're the botanical equivalent of amphibians, still needing lots of water to reproduce, but having developed the ability to strike out onto a drier *terra firma* as well.

Get down on your knees and peer at the ground, a rotting log, or a moss-clad rock, or poke around on the trunk of a big-leaf maple or red alder. You'll find Lilliputian mossy forests, fascinating microcosms of the real forests that tower overhead. Moss forays are especially well-suited to the sedentary naturalist. One need travel no farther than a few feet on any forest path for two or three hours of intense bryology. Mosses and their slightly less "advanced" cousins, the liverworts, are lumped together as Bryophytes, from the green "bryos," which in a rather circular manner means—moss. As with other green plants, mosses produce their own food through photosynthesis. Like ferns, they reproduce via spores, but mosses also have the ability to spread by simply breaking off bits of their leaves which allow them to spread vegetatively. The main reason they are relegated to wet or at least periodically moist habitats is they have no true leaves or roots, which means they have to extract water and nutrients from the surface they grow on, through diffusion and osmosis.

One aid to the identification of mosses is their substrate fealty. That is, if you learn which species grow on one big-leaf maple, it is a certainty that the next maple you examine will harbor the same species. The same is true for the rich, loamy duff of Forest Park or the Sandy River gorge. If it's a moist, nutrient-rich soil you know you'll find Menzie's tree moss (*Leucolepsis menziesii*) or stair-step moss (*Hylocomium splendens*) and Badge Mnium. If you check out the reservoirs at Mt. Tabor or other calcium-rich structures around town, you'll find the white hair-tipped *Tortulas* and *Grimmias*. The hoary-white, silvery-colored *Bryum argenteum* grows just as well on the calcareous front steps of homes from Gresham to Forest Grove.

How to go about learning to recognize at least a handful of the over 400 species that call the Pacific Northwest home? It's really not that hard. Get yourself a 10-power hand lens. Inverting binoculars and looking through the "wrong end" works well if you don't happen to have a hand lens with you. The only trick with using binoculars is you need to hold the specimen *really* close to the lens. You'll also need a copy of Dan Mathews' *Cascade-Olympic Natural History, A Trailside Reference; Common Mosses of the Pacific Coast*, by Marion Harthill and Irene O'Connor; or *Some Common Mosses of British Columbia*, by W. B. Schofield. There are other guides, but these are my favorites. Mathews' is a general natural history guide but has described many of the species you will encounter in the metro region, and has the most up-to-date scientific nomenclature. Mathews, like O'Connor and Harthill, provides both common and scientific names.

Best Place to Stay if You're Moss

Where are the best moss haunts? Virtually anywhere there is a surface that stays moist long enough to support them. My favorites are along Lower Macleay Trail in Forest Park. A walk from Audubon House down to Balch Creek and back will net you 30 or 40 species of mosses and several liverworts, with a bonus of numerous lichens. The Sandy River Gorge, in particular Metro's Oxbow Regional Park, and The Nature Conservancy's Diack Tract are outstanding moss, liverwort, and lichen haunts, more closely resembling the verdant Olympic Peninsula than any other place I've been. The Sandy gorge is the only place I have seen extensive carpets of my favorite moss, the feathery, lace-like stair-step moss (*Hylocomium splendens*).

Look on the maples for Balsam-Tree Moss (*Dendroalsia abietina*), which rolls up like a fiddle neck or parchment scroll when dry and stands out like a miniature tree when moist. It carries its spore-producing capsules on the underside of the frond-like collection of "leaves." Other mosses that are commonly epiphytic to big-leaf maple and other deciduous trees are the flat-growing, wavy-leaved Douglas' and Menzie's (*Metaneckeras*); beaked moss (*Stokesiella oregana*); the tuft-forming straight-haired moss (*Orthotrichum lyelii*); and Cardot's or icicle moss (*Isothecium spiculiferum*), which hangs from smaller twigs on alder and salmonberry in a manner that's reminiscent of hanging tinsel on the Christmas tree.

Get down on the ground and you'll see palm tree-like Menzies' tree moss (*Leucolepis menziesii*); the lettuce-like, large-leaved badge Mnium (*Plagiomnium insigne* or in older books referred to as *Mnium insigne*); and the hairy-looking, big shaggy or fox tail moss (*Rhytidiadelphus triquetrus*). On a nearby rotting log, the wetter and more decayed the better, the smaller, blunt-leaved cousin to badge Mnium, early Mnium (*Mnium glabrescens*), sends large spore capsules up from a small, moist-looking clump of obtuse, big-veined leaves. I have never seen this moss growing on anything other than damp logs and stumps. If you see it growing on bare dirt, a little prodding will turn up decayed wood underneath. Invariably, sharing the downed tree with early or smooth Mnium will be a cascading layer of snake-like, flattened sheet of *Plagiothecium undulatum* or wavy Plagiothecium.

If you don't have time for going far afield, look on your front steps, or even downtown walls, especially those made of old ballast like the dark rock wall at SW 5th and Mill that used to be the foundation for St. Mary's Academy. In addition to harboring some beautiful floral displays, these artificial surfaces provide a home to desiccation-tolerant mosses like silver-tipped moss (*Bryum argentum*); Tortula princeps or twisted moss; and the low, tuft-forming *Grimmias*, with their small, nodding spore capsules.

Finally, don't overlook fence posts and the drier, less hospitable Douglas fir and other conifers. A closer look at a Doug fir's furrowed bark never fails to turn up the sickle-shaped leaves of *Dicranum scoparium* (broom moss) or the brittle-tipped, ramrod-straight leaves of broken tipped moss (*Dicranum strictum*). You'll not see nearly as many mosses and virtually never a liverwort growing on conifers because their year-round needles prevent the trunk from ever getting wet enough to support water-dependent bryophytes. Where the tree leans, or incoming weather soaks, enough water does moisten the bark to support the *Dicranums* and a few other more drought-tolerant species. In other words, moss does not always grow on the north side of a tree. It grows where it's wettest. Broken tipped moss grows on virtually every split-rail fence and fence post in the area, along with the gray-colored red-tipped lichen, British soldier (*Cladonia*).

By Mike Houck

Vaux's Swifts of Chapman School

The only significant reason to come to Wallace Park to view wildlife is the gathering of Vaux's swifts that begin to swarm about and dive into Chapman Elementary School's chimney every September.

The best viewing is from the sloped lawn on the west edge of the school. You may have to park several blocks away, since on some warm fall evenings most of Portland seems to come out to view the awesome swirling masses of as many as 40,000 or more tiny "flying cigars" as they form a dark vortex above the chimney. The swifts pulse back and forth, sometimes directly above the chimney, sometimes darting away.

Plan to arrive 45 minutes or more before sunset. At first you'll wonder if this isn't Portland's version of a "snipe hunt," as only a very few birds are on the scene that early. Before long, however, new flights continue to bring additional swifts, sometimes dozens at a time and sometimes several hundred in a new wave as they swirl and dive, a tornado of swifts, into the chimney.

Access
Off NW 25th and Pettygrove or NW Raleigh

How to Get There
From the north take I-5 south and go west over the Fremont Bridge. Stay in the right-hand lane and take the NW Portland exit, staying right. Continue on NW Vaughn to NW 25th. Turn left (south) onto NW 25th and proceed to NW Pettygrove, and turn right. *By Mike Houck*

For more information: Audubon Society of Portland, see Resources.

Location
1445 NW 25th Ave., Portland (corner of NW 25th and Pettygrove)

Activities
Wildlife viewing

Facilities
Toilets (in the park)
Wheelchair accessible (on the north)
Parking (on street around the park)
Picnic area

Fees and Regulations
None

Highlights
As many as 30,000 Vaux's swifts gather in mid-September, before migrating to Central and South America, and fly into the large chimney at Chapman Elementary School. Also great people-watching, as up to 300 people gather with picnic baskets and blankets to take in the amazing spectacle of swifts wheeling over the chimney in a huge black vortex just before sunset.

Public Transit
Tri-Met #77 and #15

Thomas Guide 596

Portland Bridge Walks

> . . . one must leap into one's own scene before uncovering the
> unity and continuity that lie half hidden in everyday
> happenings and workaday views.
>
> Grady Clay, *Close-up: How to Read the American City*
> (New York: Praeger, 1973)

Research is never predictable when one's scene is ever-changing
Portland and the subject is the Willamette River and its bridges, one
of the finest movable bridge collections in the world. Opened in 1910,
Hawthorne Bridge is the oldest operating vertical lift bridge in the
United States. With Portland's draw-style Morrison, Burnside, and
Broadway Bridges, and the swing railroad bridges located in the St.
Johns "cut," Portland has all three main movable bridge types.

Hawthorne Bridge is the oldest operating vertical lift bridge in the United States.

City blocks only 200 feet long, and five mid-town bridges one
third of a mile apart make Portland extraordinarily accessible. The
trick for noticing downtown's nature is to concentrate, despite the
urban uproar. I have found that binoculars help as well.

To see urban wildlife, to get nearer the Willamette River and
walk across bridges legal for pedestrians and bicyclists, I suggest the
following 1.5- to 3-mile walk, depending on which option you choose.
The basic route, which can be expanded upon or shortened, provides a
look at eight Willamette River bridges and a short, free ride on MAX.

Because 80% of Portland's population lives on the east side, we
begin beneath the east end of Hawthorne Bridge, the oldest operating
vertical lift bridge in the United States. When walking across
Hawthorne Bridge's west end, notice the public bathroom in Tom
McCall Waterfront Park, located adjacent to the bridge's north end.
The concrete building's roof is covered with growing plants—perhaps
the smallest rooftop garden in the world.

Hawthorne Bridge
Start at the east end, at the intersection of SE Water and Madison
Streets.

Re-opened March 31, 1999 after a one-year closure for extensive
rehabilitation, this urban caterpillar-turned-butterfly now has two red
counterweights. Each weighs 440 tons. While Hawthorne was closed to
traffic, a raccoon had free roam; she was fed and cared for by
construction workers who have since moved on. All the movable
bridges across the Willamette River are owned by Multnomah County,
except the Steel Bridge. An operator is on duty on Hawthorne Bridge
24 hours a day. Hawthorne opens about 300 times a month during the
summer; an opening takes an average of four to seven minutes. It is
also used by 750 Tri-Met buses a day. Hawthorne is the busiest bicycle-
pedestrian bridge in Oregon.

From the Hawthorne Bridge, walk north along the Greenway Trail, part of Eastbank Riverfront Park, toward Morrison Bridge. While 54 percent of Oregon's entire population resides in the upper Willamette Valley, there is still opportunity on the east side for solitary observation, with views to the west across the river of red-tailed hawks flying about the Central Business District. One red-tail regularly lands next to a red light on the northeast corner of the World Trade Center's 20-story roof. Portland's downtown office towers create a canyon effect, supplying updrafts the big birds crave. The largest falcon around is the red-tailed hawk (adults measuring 25 inches from head to talon, while peregrines measure from 15 to 21 inches). Even though a voracious bird of prey, the red-tail is often harassed by the American crow. A witty citizen with more than 23 documented calls, the crow knows how to use pack power. One Portland naturalist reports seeing crows chase an adult red-tail down SW Columbia Street. Crows, starlings, and long-lived pigeons outnumber all other birds, including the proliferating Canada geese which roam Tom McCall Waterfront Park near RiverPlace on the west side, and Eastbank Park, south of Steel Bridge on the east side.

Bridges serve as handy bird hotels. With seven truss bridges in and near downtown, our urban birds have nearly as many overnight accommodation choices as human travelers. Great blue herons are often seen fishing off deadhead logs along the east bank between Hawthorne and Morrison Bridges.

Bridges serve as handy bird hotels. With seven truss bridges in and near downtown, our urban birds have nearly as many overnight accommodation choices as human travelers.

Morrison Bridge

Ascend the circle ramp to gain access to Morrison Bridge, walking across the Willamette from east to west. The Morrison Bridge is a "Chicago-style" bascule drawbridge and opened in 1958. Bascule is a French word that means seesaw. Morrison's huge counterweights are hidden from view. Among the largest mechanical structures in Oregon, the concrete blocks inside each of Morrison Bridge's two river piers weigh 940 tons and are operated by twin gears 36 feet tall. This is the third Morrison Bridge at this location, and the first bridge lighted by the Willamette Light Brigade in 1987. Look cross-river at the Portland harbor wall, just south of Morrison Bridge's west end, and you can see a whitened area about 80 feet long. This mark gives clues as to why the Morrison Bridge does not connect with Morrison Street on its west end. While the extant Morrison Bridge was being built, the second Morrison (in place from 1905 until 1958), which did connect to Morrison Street, was left in place and not removed until today's Morrison opened. The first Morrison Bridge, the first span across the lower Willamette in Portland, opened in 1887. Also a moveable bridge, a sign on its moveable span said, "Walk Your Horses on the Draw."

Morrison Bridge requires an operator on an as-needed basis, since its clearance is greater than Hawthorne's. Many kinds of birds, including Canada geese and great blue herons, use the Morrison Bridge's "starlings" as perches to roost. The word "starlings" dates to the 1600s and refers to the pointed cluster of pilings found upriver on Morrison and Burnside bridges. Starlings protect bridges from floating debris.

The word "starlings" dates to the 1600s and refers to the pointed cluster of pilings found upriver on Morrison and Burnside bridges. Starlings protect bridges from floating debris.

Once across Morrison Bridge, there are several options:

Option #1: Continue walking north through Tom McCall Park to Burnside and Steel bridges.

Option #2: Cross Naito Parkway, east to west, boarding MAX at SW 2nd and Yamhill or in front of Robert Duncan Plaza, SW 2nd and Stark. Ride MAX to Burnside Bridge, then walk across Naito Parkway, west to east, into Tom McCall Waterfront Park, near the site of the Children's Story Garden public area.

The floating Ankeny Street Dock, on the southwest end of Burnside Bridge, is a good place to see activities along Eastbank Riverfront Park across the river, and to see the bottom deck of Steel Bridge, downriver one third of a mile.

Burnside Bridge

Burnside Bridge offers an excellent view of most of Portland's bridges and a good place to see the 30-degree curve of the Willamette River near Steel Bridge. One description for the Central City part of the Willamette is serpentine.

Burnside Bridge is another movable bridge owned by Multnomah County. When it opened in 1926, it was one of the heaviest bascule drawspans in the world, and is still one of the heaviest bridges in the United States. Burnside's counterweights weigh almost twice as much as Morrison's. Morrison's deck is made of open-grate steel, while Burnside's lift span is solid concrete. Burnside is a Strauss-style bascule, designed by Joseph Strauss of Golden Gate Bridge fame, and was designed during the "City Beautiful" movement. The west end tower is where the bridge operator sits. This tower is finished inside with fine hardwood and a circular staircase. Like Morrison Bridge, Burnside has an on-call operator. Under its east end approaches is an internationally-famous public skateboard park. Burnside Bridge is the city's designated emergency route. With the Willamette River, Burnside Street and Burnside Bridge divide Portland north from south and east from west.

Option #3: Ride MAX to Chinatown/Old Town, or ride across Steel Bridge on MAX across the Willamette River to the Rose Quarter. Tri-Met's Fareless Square will be expanded in September 2001, making it free to travel across Steel Bridge.

Steel Bridge

Steel Bridge, opened in 1912, is owned by Union Pacific Railroad. A double-deck vertical lift with decks capable of independent movement, Steel Bridge is unique in the world. The bottom deck, only 26 feet above the Willamette, is the double main-line track for Union Pacific Railroad and carries up to five Amtrak and several freight trains a day. The bridge operator works suspended beneath the wheelhouse, both buildings located on the highway or top deck. The operator opens the bottom deck or train deck by sliding it up inside the highway deck, much like a slide trombone. Lifting the bottom deck does not interfere with MAX, vehicles, or pedestrians using the top deck. If the highway/MAX deck needs to be opened to accommodate taller river traffic, the operator can then lift both decks together, the bottom deck inside the top deck. This second lift, about 90 feet in 90 seconds, displaces almost nine million pounds. Steel Bridge was designed by the firm Waddell and Harrington of Kansas City, who also designed the Hawthorne Bridge and the northbound Interstate Bridge. Steel Bridge is integral to Eastbank Riverfront Park. The city began building a pedestrian/bicycle walkway across the bottom deck of the bridge in 2000.

Burnside is a Strauss-style bascule, designed by Joseph Strauss of Golden Gate Bridge fame, and was designed during the "City Beautiful" movement.

Once at Steel Bridge, choices to return to Hawthorne Bridge along the west side are to take MAX, riding to SW 1st and Morrison, or to walk back south through Tom McCall Waterfront Park. Continuing across Steel Bridge west to east, you can also catch a Tri-Met bus in front of the Oregon Convention Center on Martin Luther King, Jr. Boulevard to travel south to the east end of Hawthorne Bridge, or walk south through Eastbank Waterfront Park.

To continue north along the Greenway Trail from the west end of Steel Bridge, cross the railroad tracks and walk by the 301-unit McCormick Pier Apartments, which extend all the way to Broadway Bridge. At the end of this dock is the Oregon Wheat Commission Center, 1200 NW Naito Parkway. From here is an unabridged view of the Fremont Bridge where, in the springtime, peregrines soar and chicks fledge. Between Steel and Broadway bridges, on the east bank, you can see Cargill and Louis Dreyfus grain elevators, the reasons why Portland fowl, well fed, proliferate. McCormick Pier residents report mallards, wood ducks, coots, great blue heron, cormorants, Canada geese, and river otter. After the 1996 flood, beavers took white birch and small pine down by the waterfront. One McCormick Pier resident enjoys catching and releasing bass—some as large as two pounds—off McCormick Pier dock. He also reports seeing sea lions "swimming down the river."

Broadway Bridge

The Broadway Bridge, opened in 1913, is one of only three Rall-type bascule drawbridges in the United States (the others are in Baltimore and New Jersey). Notice Broadway's counterweights are above deck, rather than below as with Morrison and Burnside. A large bull wheel rolls along as the draw span opens. Its piers are covered in granite, a trademark of its designer, Ralph Modjeski, who also designed the North Portland railroad bridges and the great Oregon Trunk Railroad Bridge across Crooked River Canyon near Bend. Many famous early 20th century bridge engineers designed Portland-area bridges. Built by the City of Portland, Broadway Bridge has been owned and maintained by Multnomah County for nearly 90 years. Its operator is on duty 24 hours a day, due to large grain ships that must pass through to unload and load at the nearby silos. The Willamette Light Brigade and the Mayor of Portland have called for decorative lighting designs for at least three other mid-town bridges to celebrate the millennium and Portland's 150th birthday in 2001.

Birds like Broadway's trusses, and many roost under its supports along McCormick Pier. This is Portland's only red bridge and is scheduled for a $35 million overhaul.

Downriver from the Fremont Bridge is St. Johns Bridge, at rivermile 58. Fremont Bridge is the largest tied-arch bridge in the world and St. Johns is the only major highway suspension bridge in the Willamette Valley. Peregrine falcons began roosting on Fremont in 1993, and on St. Johns in 1999. It is legal to walk and bicycle all Portland's bridges—even the Interstate, Marquam, and Fremont— once a year during "Bridge Pedal."

By Sharon Wood Wortman

For more information, check out Sharon Wood Wortman's *The Portland Bridge Book* (Portland: Oregon Historical Society Press, 2nd ed., 2001). The author also offers guided bridge tours through Portland Parks and Outdoor Recreation, 503-823-5132.

Fremont Bridge Peregrines

At first glance, Portland's Fremont Bridge might seem an unlikely home for one of nature's most spectacular predators. Yet since 1993, a pair of endangered peregrine falcons has chosen to nest and raise young among this tangled mass of green steel girders. Many a visitor to the short stretch of the Willamette Greenway that runs south of the Fremont Bridge has had the thrilling opportunity to see these magnificent birds making their breathtaking dives (known as "stoops") on unsuspecting prey. Clocked at better than 200 miles per hour, the peregrine is the fastest species on earth!

As recently as 1970, one would have been unable to find a peregrine falcon in Oregon. The use of the pesticide DDT during the 1940s, '50s, and '60s caused peregrine falcons to lay eggs with shells so thin that they would crack during incubation. By 1970, there were only a handful of peregrines known to exist in the western United States, and they had been extirpated altogether east of the Mississippi River. The banning of DDT and the provision of increased protection for the peregrine falcon under the Endangered Species Act have brought the peregrine back from the brink of extinction in the United States. Today the Fremont Bridge represents one of only 80 known peregrine nest sites in the state of Oregon.

In modern times, peregrines have occasionally been known to substitute skyscrapers and tall bridges for the large cliffs on which they have historically nested. Bridges such as the Fremont possess two factors critical to peregrine nest site selection, a high inaccessible nesting location, and abundant prey in the form of rock doves (city pigeons) and starlings, which frequent the area.

Peregrine do not build stick nests, but rather scrape out a small hollow in the dirt or sand found on a selected ledge. Since 1993, the Fremont Bridge peregrines have nested in three different locations on the bridge, but seem to favor a site on a steel platform located under the lower deck on the west end of the bridge. In 1995, biologists entered this nest site and added gravel to make the nest a little more accommodating. Biologists also enter the nest site each year before the youngsters fledge to place identifying leg bands on the birds and to collect eggshell fragments for analysis of the continuing effects of pesticides on this species.

Urban nest sites, and especially bridges, pose special hazards for young peregrines. Bridges do not have the updrafts normally found on cliffs that help keep young birds airborne as they learn to fly. Because of this, the young peregrine raised on the Fremont Bridge have usually wound up spending several days on the ground prior to building up their flying skills. Audubon Society of Portland and the Oregon Department of Fish and Wildlife developed a "Peregrine Watch" program in 1996 to monitor the Fremont Bridge peregrines and to try and help ensure that the youngsters did not run into trouble during the hazardous fledging process. There have been several close calls. One youngster was pulled from in front of an oncoming train, another was rescued from the middle of a busy street, and a third was treated for injuries after flying into a window. One youngster even had to be rescued after falling down into a pit that the local homeless community used as a latrine. Of the 15 youngsters raised on the Fremont Bridge, nine are believed to still be flying free!

Although the Fremont Bridge peregrines chose this site of their own accord, their continuing presence is in large part due to a community-wide effort. The businesses located beneath the bridge have altered their habits to accommodate roving, ground-bound peregrine fledglings. Bridge maintenance has been scheduled around the peregrine breeding season. Even disruptive helicopter traffic has been routed away from the bridge during critical nesting periods. The result is that on any given day you might be lucky enough to see one of these magnificent birds of prey perching on an upper-deck lightpost or riding a thermal high above the Willamette River. If you are really lucky, you might see one slicing through the clouds at over 200 miles per hour, taking aim at an unsuspecting pigeon!

Where to Look
Please use caution as these sites are extremely sensitive.

The peregrines are present on the bridge year-round. The best time to observe them is during their courtship displays in late February and March and when the young begin to fledge in early June. Nesting locations on the bridge vary from year to year. The best place from which to observe is along the stretch of Willamette Greenway that runs south from the Fremont Bridge along the west bank of the Willamette River. Take Front Avenue north past Union Station. Just before you reach the Fremont Bridge, find a public parking space, and then walk through the Fremont Place Office Park to the Greenway and seawall. Please be respectful of the fact that you have to cross private property to access this stretch of Greenway and that much of the parking in this area is private property as well. Often you will find them perched up on the arch, on lightposts that line the bridge, or on the blue water tower that stands just to the northwest of the bridge.

By Bob Sallinger

Starlings

To most birdwatchers, starlings are the objects of violent antipathy. Arthur Cleveland Bent described the starling's place in birdwatchers' imaginations as delicately as possible when he said that they were "long suspected to be of doubtful value." Others have shown less restraint. It's hard to understand why a bird barely eight inches long can call forth such passion from such gentle souls. There are reasons, however, and they have their beginnings in New York City, less than 100 years ago.

Before the last years of the nineteenth century there were no starlings, *Sturnus vulgaris*, in the New World. But among the flood of immigrants pouring into the United States were many who missed the songbirds of their native Europe and set about importing them to America. Portland had its own "Songbird Club" which had some success introducing European goldfinches, skylarks, and starlings in the late 1880s and early 1890s.

An excerpt from William Rogers Lord's 1902 book, *A First Book Upon the Birds of Oregon and Washington*, illustrates the rarity of starlings in Portland at the turn of the century:

> The Starling, unlike any of the birds related to it in this country, lives and nests in buildings and not in trees—and in buildings in cities, moreover, which seems quite strange to us. It is, however only a proof of what change in the habits of birds is wrought by civilization. It is difficult to say what our own birds may do in the future, when Americans have won back the confidence of our now truly "wild" birds. In this spring of 1901, the Starlings may be seen around the top of the tower on the Perkins Hotel in Portland, nesting in the gilded ornaments on either end, and also about the Blagen Block, First and Couch streets, nesting in perpendicular holes just over each of the two ornamental heads on the west face of the structure.

Gradually, though, the Portland populations of these exotics were extinguished, as was the fate of most of the introductions during this period.

Westward Ho!

One fabulous exception resulted from the efforts of Eugene Schieffelin and the American Acclimatization Society of New York. In 1890 Mr. Schieffelin took it into his head to bring to America all the birds mentioned in Shakespeare. Taking as his text a line from the first act of *Henry IV, Part I*, he imported 80 starlings and on March 16, 1890, opened their cages, releasing them in Central Park. The following year he released 40 more. For once, the birds really took to their new home, spreading rapidly, and it appears certain that this modern-day Pandora is responsible for the presence of New World starlings.

Within six years the starlings had spread throughout the New York metropolitan area. They had reached north to Nova Scotia by 1915, south to Savannah, Georgia, by 1917, and by 1928 ornithologists considered their range to be all the land east of the Mississippi. The river and Rocky Mountains slowed their westward progress but by the 1940s, they had realized their manifest destiny . . . they started to populate the West Coast. The starlings reached Portland from the east in 1947.

Now, starlings are among the most common birds in the city. They can be seen summer and winter, bobbing and jerking across lawns searching for insects, or perched in large noisy flocks. So common are they that I hesitate to provide a description. For the record, they are slightly smaller than a robin, averaging seven to nine inches long, with a wingspan of 16 inches. They are among the few songbirds whose plumage changes with the seasons. Following the fall molt they are black, spangled with buffy "stars." During the course of the winter these spots wear away, leaving the starlings to face spring with glossy iridescent black plumage. As the breeding season approaches, their bills change too, from the dusky color of winter to a bright yellow.

Starlings—relatives of the mynahs—are among the most amazing vocalists in the animal kingdom.

An Impressive Repertoire

Starlings—relatives of the mynahs—are among the most amazing vocalists in the animal kingdom. Their normal voice consists of a series of creaking, crunching, squeaking, squealing, seething, and whistling sounds. Anyone who has heard a cacophony of starlings roosting at dusk knows what a volume of noise they can produce.

In addition to their normal vocalizations, however, they are amazing mimics. If you hear a redwing blackbird or meadowlark far from its normal habitat, it is likely to be a starling. They have been known to imitate the sounds of killdeer, flickers, robins, crows, and numerous other birds. Dogs, cats, and squeaking doors are also in their repertoire, as is human speech. The fateful Shakespearean passage which led to Schieffelin's misguided efforts reads: "I'll have a starling shall be taught to speak/Nothing but 'Mortimer', and give it him/To keep his anger still in motion."

Feats of Flight

Starlings are also amazing aerialists. They have been clocked during migration at speeds in excess of 50 miles an hour, but their agility in the air is even more noteworthy. John Terres in *The Audubon Society Encyclopedia Of North American Birds* describes a flock of starlings "wheeling, twisting, turning in perfect precision, with no apparent leader, now in loose formation, then in tight ball to frustrate [an] attacking hawk." They also put on impressive flight displays when arriving at communal roosts. Watch for this at dusk on the Broadway Bridge and similar sites in Portland. Individual starlings in flight are easy to identify, even at great distances. Portland State University biology professor Richard Forbes likens their triangular-winged and virtually tail-less silhouette to that of a bomb. It is an apt metaphor, considering how these introduced birds have decimated the populations of certain native species. And that brings us to one of the main reasons for the unpopularity of this otherwise interesting species.

Fierce Competitor

Starlings are cavity nesters. They are also among the most aggressive birds in North America. So during breeding season they are in direct competition with other cavity nesters, including bluebirds, woodpeckers, and swallows. It is a competition they almost invariably win, even with some of the cavity-nesting birds of prey. Consequently, the last 30 years have seen a drastic decline in the populations of these rival species, especially in the starling's urban stronghold. Starlings are also despised because of their tremendous numbers, which, coupled with their filthy habits, can render a starling roost virtually unapproachable, not to mention extremely unsanitary.

In economic terms their record is mixed. These omnivorous feeders can create problems wherever fruit is grown, and, joining with blackbirds in vast flocks, they can be a problem in grain fields. On the other hand, starlings are, according to Bent, "the most effective bird enemy of the clover leaf weevil in America." They are also extremely useful in the control of cutworms, Japanese beetles, and many other insects.

The last word on the starling will not, of course, be written for many years. But it seems certain that over the course of time they will somehow—no doubt very much on their own terms—achieve a balance in the ecosystems of the New World as native species become more adept at dealing with the starling invasion. As they are clearly a species as successful as our own, it is obvious that they are here to stay. Perhaps it's time we worked on creating for them a more hospitable place in our own imaginations.

Starlings

18 or 20 starlings
salt
chervil
basil
thyme
1 cup of dry sherry
1/2 pound butter
18 or 20 sage leaves
   (or pieces of aluminum foil)

Dress the birds and sprinkle them with salt. Let them stand for about five minutes and then sprinkle them with a pinch each of chervil, basil, and thyme—or whatever other herbs you have fresh, except for tarragon and saffron, which are not advised. Melt the butter and combine with the sherry. Brush each bird with the mixture and wrap individually in the sage leaves (or aluminum foil). Seal the edges tightly to keep the juices in. Grill for 15 to 20 minutes in a hot (400°) oven or over coals. Serve them in the wrapping, or arrange over polenta and pour the juice over each bird before serving.

The Starling Gourmet

"It is not generally known," wrote a gourmand from early in the last century, "what a delicious bird the Starling is to eat." A Mr. Carnegie wrote that in 1880, but the secret is still very well preserved, at least in America. Europeans have been eating starlings for years. They were extremely common in London markets during World War II, and as many as 24,000 have been taken in a single night near Verona, Italy for consumption. The *Larousse Gastronomique* lists them as edible, but cautions that their flesh is inferior to that of the thrush.

Former Oregon State Non-Game Wildlife Biologist Joe Pesek recounts the story of a Swiss of his acquaintance who was delighted to learn that starlings were one of the three unprotected birds in America (the others being the house sparrow and the rock dove). As a result he was able to indulge his taste for starlings without paying the stiff price he was accustomed to in Switzerland. Pesek is quite enthusiastic about starlings as a source of protein, although he admits that he has "never had the chance" to try one. His only caution is that starlings, although unprotected, are subject to other game and firearm laws.

After hearing all this I decided that I had to try one. So, procuring and dressing a bird, I prepared it simply, first marinating it, then roasting it in a hot oven. I found the meat very flavorful, but even after more than 24 hours of marinating, it was still unbelievably tough. Subsequently, I came across a recipe for starlings in *The Nero Wolfe Cookbook*, by Rex Stout et al. (Viking Press, 1973), which I am appending. Although the recipe calls for 20 birds, I found one adequate for me and my friends.

By Bob Wilson

Wildlife of the Northwest Industrial Area

One crow leg, the remains of a rock dove, an evening grosbeak wing, a couple of feathers most likely from a cedar waxwing, a fragment of eggshell, more rock dove parts—now a mystery: it is a long leg, looks like some sort of shorebird, maybe a snipe.

We are sitting on a steel platform beneath the lower deck of the Fremont Bridge sifting through several inches of dusty gravel, feathers, and peregrine poop. The platform vibrates as cars and trucks roar by overhead. The peregrines are not here. Their young fledged several weeks earlier. The adults are probably now in "hiding mode" trying to avoid their young, which are capable of fending for themselves but will continue to follow their parents about begging for food nonetheless.

The view from here is one that brings both hope and despair. One hundred and eighty feet below, the murky, gray Willamette River lazily flows the final few miles to the Columbia. Here the river does not have banks; it has walls. In some places, decrepit, old warehouses supported by creosote posts jut out over the water. A tangle of tentacle-like ramps protrudes from either end of the bridge and then fans out into a sea of roadways and railroad yards. There is little here that is green.

Yet since 1993, this is a place that a pair of endangered peregrine falcons has chosen to call home. We are collecting prey remains to see what they are living on. We also are collecting eggshell fragments for analysis to determine whether the pesticide which caused eggshell thinning that nearly drove the peregrine to extinction in the United States is continuing to occur. It is all part of an ongoing study conducted by Forest Service peregrine specialist Joel Pagel. The eggshells from this nest, as it turns out, show low levels of thinning, suggesting that these birds are relatively uncontaminated. However, just downriver at the St. Johns Bridge, where a second pair of peregrines attempted and failed to nest in 1997, a recovered unhatched egg revealed that those birds were very heavily contaminated with three toxins: Dieldrin, DDT, and PCBs. Further investigation revealed that a toxic waste clean-up site located just upriver from the St. Johns Bridge was contaminated with all three of these substances.

The peregrines are not the only wildlife that live here. The prey remains that we excavate from their nest are testament to this fact. Come here early on a spring morning and look out upon the Willamette River from the short stretch of Willamette Greenway trail that runs between the Fremont and Broadway Bridges. On any given day, you are likely to see the peregrines defending their territory from the red-tailed hawks that nest just upriver on one of the grain towers or against the osprey that nest downstream on an old piling. Each year, just across the river, in among the creosote stilts that support an old corrugated metal warehouse, a Canada goose raises her goslings. Several years back, this stretch of river played host to one of the stranger urban wildlife sightings. During the winter flooding of 1994, a young beaver, perhaps dislodged from its home upriver at Oaks Bottom, drifted past this spot hugging a half-inflated basketball. Great blue herons frequent this area, but never seem to land before floating off northward toward Sauvie Island.

Hazards abound here as well. In 1995, a migrating peregrine died just across the river after ingesting a poisoned rock dove. Juvenile peregrines raised on the Fremont Bridge have been killed in collisions with cars and windows. A golden eagle arrived at the 100th Anniversary Celebration of Union Station plastered on the front of a high-speed train. The predominant predator here is not the peregrine falcon flying above, but the feral house cat.

In the rush to preserve and protect the last best habitats, it is sometimes easy to overlook the importance of the spaces that lie in-between and forget the fact that wild animals do not respect the arbitrary boundaries that we create for them. Our city is criss-crossed by invisible wildlife flyways and byways. It is inhabited by a multitude of wild animals eking out an existence in the dark corners and forgotten spaces. The industrial area of Northwest Portland is one such place.

By Bob Sallinger

Rooftop Garden Tour

About 230 buildings are located in Portland's Central Business District (CBD), an area that covers as many blocks. About ten percent, or 20 CBD roofs, carry living lawn or greenery that provides natural and recreational space. Because plants soak up rain and heat, such spaces are becoming more and more desirable as cities seek solutions to managing storm water runoff (helping reduce combined sewer overflows), reducing energy costs, and fighting air pollution.

Seen from the Hawthorne Bridge's west end, the concrete roof of the public bathroom in Tom McCall Waterfront Park is perhaps the smallest rooftop garden in the world.

The National Clean Water Act (1969) and subsequent requirements to address stormwater, triggered Tom Liptan of Portland's Bureau of Environmental Services to look at rooftop gardens and eco-roofs as stormwater management techniques. After a request from a Blue Heron Week committee, Liptan developed a rooftop garden tour (see below). Convinced of the enormous benefits of planted roofs as a way of battling the "impervious surface" problem, Liptan has even planted a rooftop garden at his family home. Impervious areas, like streets, parking lots, and house roofs, do not allow water to filter into the ground. The result is twofold. First, all of the water that runs off into our streams carries pollutants as well. Second, and perhaps even more importantly, the increased volume destroys the normal stream channel by eroding banks and cutting streams into unnatural, deeply incised channels.

Rooftop Garden Tour

For one of the best overall views of a number of west side downtown roof gardens, take the elevator or stairs to the top of the Crown Plaza seven-story parking garage. This garage is located catercorner to the Marriott Hotel, just east of the Civic Auditorium and west of Crown Plaza Office Building (1500 SW 1st Ave.). Walking to each corner of the garage's roof provides several roof garden views.

Getting there: From the west end of Hawthorne Bridge, turn left (south) on Naito Parkway, to SW Clay Street. Turn right (west) on the south side of the Marriott. Enter Crown Plaza parking garage, which takes up a city block, at the corner of SW 1st and SW Clay.

From the Top of Crown Plaza Parking Structure:

■ Northeast corner, looking down, see the Marriott Hotel which has a roof terrace/patio area with large pine trees and many plantings of shrubs and ground cover.

■ Same location, looking due north, see Columbia Square and Sedgewick James roof gardens. From here you can only see the east end of the plantings of pine trees and shrubs. The garden actually continues all along the north side of the building.

■ Southeast corner, looking east, see the roof of Crown Plaza Office Building, with hedges and lawn area in the distance. At this point it is often difficult to distinguish where the roof lawn ends and Tom McCall Waterfront Park lawn begins.

■ Southwest corner, looking north, see the 200 Market Building (Black Box) and its multiple levels of lawn used for recreation, with large birch trees and plenty of ground cover. Compare this to the roof of the adjacent Civic Auditorium, located due west.

Other roof gardens in the vicinity, walking west from the river to mid-town:

■ Mark O. Hatfield Federal Courthouse, 1000 SW 3rd Ave., roof gardens on the 8th and 16th floors.

■ Terry Schrunk Plaza takes up one city block between SW 3rd and 4th Avenues and Madison and Jefferson Streets. This grassy park is at street level and covers the underground parking lot for the Green-Wyatt Federal Building, located one block east at 1220 SW 3rd.

■ Standard Insurance, 1100 SW 6th, between Madison and Main. The planted deck around the building is actually the top of a garage.

■ United Airlines building, 502 SW Madison.

Tom Liptan notes that eco-roofs, also called green roofs, are different from a rooftop garden. Eco-roofs are whole systems involving a thin layer of soil, waterproof membranes, and landscaping to nearly eliminate water runoff during the warm season. Like rooftop gardens, they also reduce energy costs and fight air pollution. A conventional roof in the summer can get as hot as 130° to 150° F, but an eco-roof can reduce that to between 70° and 80° F. To combat ozone and air quality problems, Chicago, Illinois is creating eco-roofs on top of its City Hall and other buildings. Eco-roofs have been long popular in Europe. Two eco-roof demonstration projects exist in Portland: the Housing Authority of Portland's ten-story Hamilton West Apartments, 1212 SW Clay St., dedicated in December 1999, and Prendergast and Associates' 130,000-square-foot residential, parking and retail building, 303 NE 16th. Ave., which opened in early 2000.

By Sharon Wood Wortman

For more information: Portland Bureau of Environmental Services, see Resources.

Squirrels of Park and Forest

Most of the world's 4,800 or so species of mammals, including most of the 60-odd species with which we share the Portland metropolitan area, are small, nocturnal, and rarely seen. Members of the squirrel family, Sciuridae, in general constitute a welcome exception to this rule. Most sciurids, like most humans, are diurnal (day active). Most are large enough to be seen easily; and most—some almost to a fault—are comparatively uninhibited in the presence of a quiet, watchful human. Not surprisingly, sciurids are the wild mammals with which most of us are best acquainted.

Worldwide, more than 270 species of squirrels are recognized. The family has native representatives on every major land mass except Australia, Antarctica, and Greenland. Squirrels are absent from the Arabian Peninsula, the hottest and driest parts of North Africa, and southern South America. They have their greatest diversity in tropical and subtropical Asia, southern Africa, and western North America.

Squirrels are thought to be relatively primitive rodents. They share with other rodents several features: one large, ever-growing incisor at the front of each side of each upper and lower jaw, followed by a prominent gap in each tooth row, then a series of four or five molar-like teeth on each side of the upper jaw and four such teeth on each side of the lower jaw. As a family, squirrels usually have medium to long tails that are well-haired and often bushy. Squirrels' fingers and toes, of which there are four per hand and five per foot, are long and provided with prominent, sharp claws. The young of squirrels are born naked and helpless, with the eyes and ears sealed.

Although many of the squirrels most familiar to us are tree-dwellers, there are also many burrowing forms such as the ground squirrels and marmots, and a number of gliding forms including the two North American species of flying squirrels.

Townsend's Chipmunk

Twenty-one species of squirrels have representatives in Oregon. Two—the fox squirrel and eastern gray squirrel—were introduced from the eastern United States. Of the 19 native species, nine are ground squirrels, five are chipmunks, and four are tree squirrels, including the northern flying squirrel, our only nocturnal sciurid. The yellow-bellied marmot, Oregon's largest squirrel, completes the list.

Of these 21 species, only five native species, plus the fox and eastern gray squirrels, occur in the Portland area. Of the ground squirrel-marmot group, only the California ground squirrel occurs here. The other members of this group occupy various habitats in the mountains, grasslands, and deserts east of us. Of the chipmunk group, only Townsend's chipmunk includes the metro area in its range. The other four species occur east and/or south of the Willamette Valley. Of the tree squirrel group, the western gray squirrel, Douglas' squirrel, and the northern flying squirrel all occur in the metro area. Only the red squirrel, associated with boreal forests east, north, and south of the Cascades and Sierras, does not occur here.

Townsend's Chipmunk: A Familiar Forest Face

Chipmunks' diurnal habits and ability to tolerate human presence make these small mammals popular with many people. Townsend's chipmunk (*Tamias townsendii*)—the smallest squirrel in western Oregon, though large as chipmunks go—is well-known to anyone who watches the feeders at Audubon House, or who lives in or visits forests or cut-over areas in western Oregon. Like other chipmunks, Townsend's chipmunk shows a dark stripe down the middle of the back, two dark longitudinal stripes along each side of the body, and dark stripes on each side of the face. The facial and mid-back stripes distinguish chipmunks from various striped ground squirrels, but none of the latter occur in the Willamette Valley.

Chipmunks are not social, but they may be numerous in suitable habitat, appearing in small groups at times—for example, when the annual litter of two to six young leaves the mother's nest in July. Around Portland, Townsend's chipmunks are active throughout the year, although they may stay in their burrows during periods of particularly cold weather.

Many foods are eaten, but fruit, seeds, nuts, insects, and the fruiting bodies of hypogeous (underground) fungi are most important.

The appetites of chipmunks, mice, and shrews for Douglas fir seeds have occasionally posed problems in reforestation projects. All chipmunks have

Western Gray Squirrel

large internal cheek pouches, which they use to carry food to their underground caches. Predators of chipmunks include weasels, bobcats, house cats, and raptorial birds. Hard winters also seem to take a heavy toll on western chipmunks, whose burrows are not particularly deep or extensive, but a life span of seven years has been recorded for one wild Townsend's chipmunk.

California Ground Squirrel: Underground Architect

The California ground squirrel (*Spermophilus beecheyi*), or gray digger, resembles a tree squirrel in size and in having a long bushy tail. The digger's coat is brownish gray with speckles of white and black, and a dark "V" that extends from its apex between the ears to the middle of the back. California ground squirrels are active throughout the day. They are often seen atop a post, stump, rock, or tree limb taking in the sun. These squirrels are burrowers, and are active within the area of their extensive burrow and trail systems. Large colonies of these squirrels occur where cover, soil, and food are abundant. Sauvie Island's oak savannas seem especially favorable for California ground squirrels. The single annual litter may number as many as 15 for a female in some parts of the range, but half that number is more common here. Predominant foods are green vegetation, fruit, nuts and grain, and occasionally meat such as the road-killed carcass of a fellow colony member.

Farmers have little enthusiasm for gray diggers, since a colony may eat enormous amounts of grain, fruit, and nuts, as well as damaging farmland by their digging and trail making. Predators of gray diggers include coyotes, cats, domestic dogs, and raptorial birds.

Douglas' Squirrel: Seed Cone Gourmet

Douglas' squirrel (*Tamiasciurus douglasii*), or chickaree, is a small, swift, agile tree squirrel familiar to watchers at Audubon House bird feeders. Douglas' squirrels are largely coniferous forest dwellers that feed and nest in the forest canopy. Coat colors vary considerably throughout the species' range. Our local race has a dark reddish-brown back and sides, an orange belly, and a dark stripe between the front and hind leg on each side. A prominent, though small, white ring encircles each eye. The long, dark, bushy tail is often held in a graceful arch over the back and shoulders as the squirrel feeds or watches events in progress. Douglas' squirrels are active throughout the day and, except in the coldest weather, throughout the year. Although these squirrels typically build nests in tree cavities, or may build leaf and twig nests on tree branches, during the coldest weather they may use a subterranean nest, often built right under a cache of cones. The ringing calls of Douglas' squirrels are similar to those of the downy woodpecker, and draw attention to anything unusual in the forest. Other vocalizations include sharp barks and buzzing or growling sounds.

Adults establish and vigorously defend individual territories which normally include enough food for the year's needs. Fruits, nuts, pollen cones, green vegetation, mushrooms, and some flesh are eaten, but the dietary staple of Douglas' squirrels is the seeds of coniferous trees, particularly Douglas fir. Ripe cones are cut in large quantities, allowed to fall to the ground, then gathered into caches. Each squirrel usually has several specific areas within its territory where it opens cones. To get at the seeds, the squirrel nips off the cone scales, which fall to the ground and accumulate in a large pile that marks the feeding station.

In our area, there is usually one litter of two to six young per female per year. The young leave the nest in midsummer, remain in the mother's territory for a while, and disperse by late summer. Bobcats, martens, coyotes, weasels, and raptors probably enjoy their greatest hunting success as the young squirrels seek territories of their own.

Western Gray Squirrel: Treetop Acrobat

Our large native tree squirrel is the western gray, or silver gray squirrel (*Sciurus griseus*). These beautiful pale squirrels have a frosted appearance above, a completely white belly, and a marvelously long, bushy, gray tail. The squirrels seem to flow, rather than run, when they move over the ground. Western gray squirrels are most at home, however, in the trees, where their climbing and acrobatic skills are truly astonishing. Substantial quantities of large seeds and nuts are required to support western gray squirrels, and the animals seem to need access to water all year. Accordingly, riparian hardwood forests or mixed forests with access to oaks, walnuts, or filberts are favored habitats. The squirrels build several large nests of twigs and leaves in tree crowns. Some of the nests are loosely made and used only occasionally. Other nests, and cavity nests, are permanent shelters, carefully lined with fine material such as moss, lichens, and shredded bark. Each adult maintains a territory, but defense is less obvious than is the case for the more vocal Douglas' squirrel. Western gray squirrels are comparatively quiet, even secretive, especially while the young are in the maternal nest in early summer. The annual litter of two to five young leaves the nest in mid-summer.

Regrettably, western gray squirrels seem not to adapt well to human presence. Very few places around Portland are known where they still may be found. The introduced and city-wise fox squirrel is far more successful in town and may be seen in parks and residential areas where there are old deciduous as well as large coniferous trees.

Eastern Gray and Fox Squirrels: Eastern Imports

Eastern gray squirrels, particularly abundant at the capitol grounds in Salem, are also found in a few places in the metro area. As its name suggests, it is grayish, but in contrast to the western gray squirrel's clear gray back, sides, and tail, the eastern gray's coat shows a reddish suffusion on the head, neck and legs and a lot of brown on the tail. Fox squirrels occur in several color phases, but the one introduced here is brownish above with a rusty belly.

Northern Flying Squirrel: Night Glider

As its huge, lustrous black eyes suggest, the northern flying squirrel (*Glaucomys sabrinus*) is the only Oregon sciurid habitually active at night. It is the least known of our squirrels, and even where abundant, its presence is often unsuspected. Smaller than a Douglas' squirrel, the northern flying squirrel looks larger because of its long,

Northern Flying Squirrel

soft brown coat. The belly is yellowish, and the tail hairs stick out straight to the sides like barbs on a feather. The skin between the front and hind legs on each side is loose and may be stretched by extending the limbs to form a gliding membrane. The membrane may be extended further by means of a long cartilage attached to each wrist.

Flying squirrels do not fly, but simply glide from a higher point to a lower one. Before taking off, the squirrels appear to judge the distance of their landing point carefully. They can change direction and the pitch of the body during the glide by moving the feather-like tail. In landing, the tail is raised sharply, the body straightens up, and the hind feet strike first, followed by the front feet. Immediately, the squirrel darts around to the opposite side of the tree trunk, a behavior that may cause a pursuing owl to miss its quarry.

Northern flying squirrels are usually found in coniferous or mixed forests. They are gregarious and as many as a dozen have been reported in one winter cavity nest, presumably as a heat-saving measure. In addition to cavity nests, the squirrels construct nests of leaves, twigs, mosses, and lichens on tree limbs. There is one litter, usually of three to five young, each year. Flying squirrels are omnivorous, but may eat almost exclusively one food if it is abundant. For example, underground fungi may comprise nearly their entire diet in summer and fall. Insects, seeds, fruit, nuts, and meat are also taken.

Predators of flying squirrels include martens, cats, and particularly owls. Once, the severed tails of eight northern flying squirrels were picked up under the feeders at Audubon House over the course of a few days. Owls will usually bite off the tail of a freshly caught squirrel and drop it before carrying the body away to be eaten. It appears that the overnight depletion of seeds in the feeders may have been reduced by a skilled owl!

By Richard Forbes

Willamette Cove

These wetlands were a duck-hunting site that Henry Corbett used 100 years ago. After it was filled for industrial use, it fell into disuse in the 1950s. Various redevelopment schemes did not come to fruition, and the Trust for Public Land picked it up as part of its cooperative efforts with Metro's Greenspaces acquisition program.

The City of Portland has developed a management plan for the 27-acre site. The plan outlines efforts to restore it. It will be used for wildlife habitat and passive recreation. But first the site will have to undergo significant restoration, especially to remove the non-native invasive weeds like Scot's broom and Himalayan blackberry.

Although the current alignment for the Willamette River Greenway is on the bluff above, along Willamette Boulevard, the acquisition of Willamette Cove means a route along the river may be possible in the future. It's also the most logical river-side terminus of the Peninsula Crossing Trail that links Marine Drive to the east with the Willamette. The Peninsula Crossing trailhead is nearby on N Carey and Princeton, a block east of Willamette Boulevard.

Access

The only access, as informal as it may be, is along the railroad tracks from the north at the west end of N Richmond Ave.

How to Get There

Willamette Cove can be reached from North Richmond Avenue. Follow Richmond downhill toward the river until the street ends just beyond the railroad tracks. The park property abuts Richmond. The main trail follows the west edge of the railroad right-of-way for 200 feet before turning right and dropping toward the river, where it branches into a series of braided trails that run parallel to the river. Any of these paths will lead you to Willamette Cove.

By Mike Houck

For more information: Metro Regional Parks and Greenspaces or Portland Bureau of Parks and Recreation, see Resources.

Location
South side of the St. Johns Bridge, on the east side of Willamette River Greenway, upstream of the Burlington Northern Railroad Bridge, at the base of Edgewater St.

Activities
This is an undeveloped Metro-owned Greenspace at this time, but the City of Portland has developed a master plan which will determine how Willamette Cove is used in the future. In the meantime it can be used informally for wildlife viewing.

Highlights
The only semi-natural Willamette Greenway site in this area of Portland.

Public Transit
Tri-Met #40 (along Willamette Blvd.), #75, or #17.

Thomas Guide 565

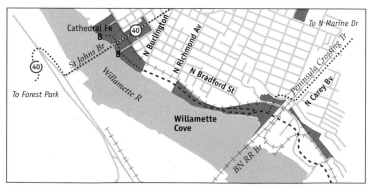

Mt. Tabor Park

When the Olmsted Brothers, America's foremost landscape architectural firm, reviewed Portland's parks and greenspaces in 1903, Mt. Tabor—a Tertiary-era volcanic butte about four miles east of Portland—was one of the areas they chose to single out. By then, the first of several reservoirs for Portland's Bull Run water supply had been constructed on the south side, but Mt. Tabor was still well removed from the city, semi-rural, and covered with orchards. Nonetheless the Olmsteds, visualizing Portland's eastward sprawl, urged the city to protect the hill, and following their recommendation, the Park Bureau began its acquisition in 1909. We can all be grateful for the Olmsteds as, nearly a century after it was envisioned, Mt. Tabor Park not only provides an oasis of urban green, it also knits country and city together better than almost any place in Portland.

At the time of its acquisition there was no suspicion that Mt. Tabor was an extinct volcano. But in 1913 its origins were revealed when a road-building crew discovered traces of volcanic cinders in the northwest corner of the park. Subsequent excavations exposed the throat of the three-million-year-old volcano, which can now be viewed from the edge of the North ("Volcano") Parking Lot.

But Mt. Tabor can be appreciated for more than its geologic history. From the west side of the grassy knoll at its 643-foot summit, visitors can get the best view of Portland on the city's east side, while Mt. Hood and the Cascades can be glimpsed through the trees on the summit's western edge.

Mt. Tabor is also a "hotspot" for resident and migrant birds. Home to such surprising city species as ring-necked pheasants and western screech-owls, Mt. Tabor also contains a remnant forest on the summit's south side which shelters such deep-woods species as winter wrens and chestnut-backed chickadees. The unofficial park list includes nearly 120 birds, two-thirds of the species that regularly occur in the Portland area.

Between March and mid-June, birding opportunities are especially abundant. At that time Mt. Tabor is one of the best places in the city to view spring migrants. On a short stroll from the playground near the volcano parking lot to the summit you will pass through "parkland," tall firs, hedgerows, mature big-leaf maples, and mixed coniferous forest, and you can easily finish your hike with a bird list of 30 species or more. It is such an outstanding time that the Audubon Society of Portland regularly schedules "bird song walks" at the park in March, April, and May.

Mt. Tabor is so close to downtown that gorgeous summer afternoons invariably find the park extremely crowded; but come in the early morning and you will find yourself in nearly sole possession of a rolling, wooded 200-acre estate in the heart of the city.

Location
Southeast Portland, between Belmont and Division on the north and south, and 60th and 71st on the east and west.

Activities
Hiking: Mt. Tabor is more of a "strolling" than a "hiking" park; still, several miles of well-maintained trails and pathways are available.
Biking: One of east Portland's great hill climbs. Park summit is closed to vehicular traffic.

Facilities
Toilets
Wheelchair access
Parking: In addition to marked parking, shoulder parking is available along many of the roadways
Picnic area

Fees and Regulations
Restricted hours:
Mt. Tabor summit is closed to vehicular traffic
Pets on leash; after a couple of years of experimentation, Mt. Tabor is not offering an off-leash area at this time.

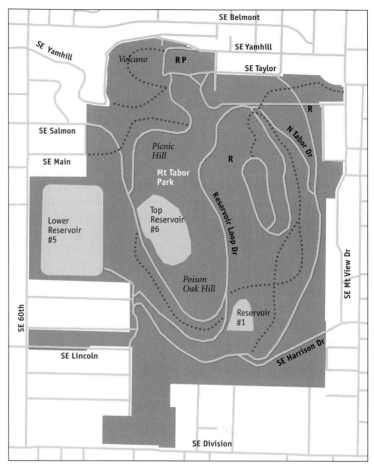

Highlights

Volcano; songbird migration; views. A Tertiary-era volcano at the end of Portland's bustling Hawthorne district, Mt. Tabor provides one of the finest vistas on the east side; it is also the best place in east Portland to view migrant songbirds in April, May, and early June.

Public Transit

Tri-Met #4, Division (exit at 66th and Division and proceed north on 66th into the park); Tri-Met #15, Mt. Tabor (exit at 69th and Yamhill and follow Yamhill into the park); and Tri-Met #71 (exit at 60th and Hawthorne and follow sidewalk past the reservoirs and into the park).

Thomas Guide 596/627

Access

The entire park is criss-crossed with paths. All are well-maintained and some are paved, but the climb to the summit involves a 370-foot elevation gain.

How to Get There

From the west, the easiest approach is along SE 60th, from which several streets enter the park. From the north, follow SE Belmont to SE 69th; turn south on 69th, then right on Yamhill, which enters the park. On the south side of the park, Lincoln (western approach) and Harrison (eastern approach) connect to form a through route.

For more information: Portland Bureau of Parks and Recreation, see Resources.

By Bob Wilson

Tualatin River Watershed

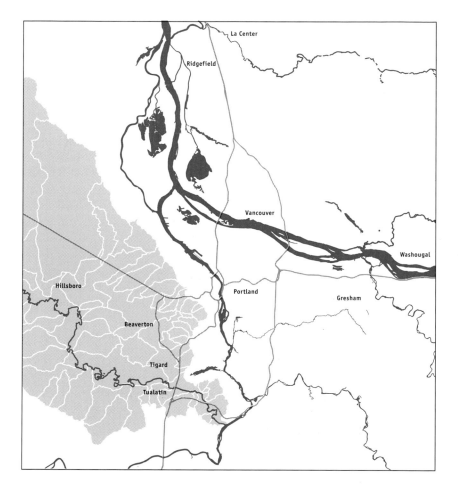

The Tualatin Basin

From its headwaters in the Coast Range, less than 30 miles from Tillamook, to its confluence with the Willamette River in West Linn, the Tualatin River meanders through forest, farm, and city, fed along the way by a network of creeks draining over 700 square miles. The Tualatin, once overlooked and poorly understood, has become a lightning rod for environmental issues in both the urban and rural portions of Washington County. Over one-third of the Tualatin watershed is in forest, both private and state-owned. Fifteen percent, or about 70,000 acres, is urbanized.

Land of the Tuality

Tualatin, or Tuality, meant "slow and lazy" in the language of the Kalapuya Indians. An apt name for a river where languid green pools cover roughly half of its nearly 80 miles. Others trace the name to a word meaning fork or forks, referring perhaps to Fanno Creek, Dairy Creek, Gales, Rock, Roaring, or Black Jack Creek—only a few of the many creeks that join the Tualatin along its meandering route to the Willamette River.

Few Oregonians can claim a relationship to the Tualatin as intimate as those of its native peoples. But in the 1800s, the Tualatin was regarded as a vital waterway for transportation of logs, grains, and other produce of the growing Tualatin Basin. Crude ferries, often little more than rafts of logs, docked at Scholls and Harris Landings. Steamboats like the *Onward*, the *Hoosier*, and the *Yamhill* plied its waters, passing privately owned land adjoining the river. Developed boat ramps at Cook Park in Tigard and Tualatin Community Park now provide the only easily accessible public launches for canoes or kayaks on the entire Tualatin, although Metro has plans for additional access on several sites it has acquired. A partnership of private landowners, community groups, local agencies, and businesses has helped increase public awareness and appreciation of the Tualatin by sponsoring community events highlighting the river and its importance as a regional Greenspace. The Tualatin Riverkeepers-sponsored Tualatin River Discovery Days, the migratory bird festival at the Tualatin River National Wildlife Refuge, and tree planting by grassroots organizations like the Friends of Fanno Creek have changed the Tualatin's image from an alleged eyesore to a resource worth restoring.

The Upper Tualatin

For many, the upper Tualatin remains a mystery. Few have seen the shady gorge at Haines Falls, or watched mergansers fish the clear riffles above Cherry Grove. Here, the Tualatin is a river far different from the slow-moving lower reach. Winter rains falling on the forested hills of the Coast Range send clear, cold water over Haines,

Lee, and Lower Lee Falls. Alder, oak, Douglas fir, and cottonwood line the riverbanks. Osprey hunt its shady course. Salamanders share a quiet eddy with tadpoles and periwinkles.

Below Cherry Grove, the Tualatin flows through rich farmlands. The Tualatin Basin's fertile soils support a checkerboard of over 100 different crops, as well as diverse agricultural enterprises—nurseries and greenhouses, Christmas tree farms, a vast array of small fruit and vegetable farms for both processing and fresh market, filbert orchards, and a variety of livestock operations. Washington County farms raised over $163 million in 1993, ranking fifth in the state in agricultural gross product.

In places, a narrow strip of alder, willow, ash, and other vegetation is often all that remains of a once-extensive riparian forest. Removal of streamside vegetation contributes to soil erosion, especially in winter when the river can swell to 20 times its summer flow. Without the riparian borders, the river cuts deep into valuable croplands, eroding the soil and turning the water muddy brown.

Still Waters Run Deep

Over most of its length, the Tualatin is the slow, pond-like river we glimpse from the many bridges that crisscross its narrow course. Rood Bridge, Shipley, La Follett, and Shamberg are names that reflect the rich history of Washington County, and now offer some of the best viewing spots of the river.

Beneath Stafford Bridge, the Tualatin runs still and green in a pool 20 feet deep. Such pools, a result of the underlying geological formations, are common over a 45-mile stretch where the river drops in elevation only 20 feet. Deep water alternates with shallow reaches where the river's muddy banks are laced with tracks of muskrat and raccoon. An almost imperceptible current swirls around the black branches of fallen trees and irrigation pipes. Crayfish traps attest to an industry that exported 10,000 pounds from the Tualatin to European markets in 1991.

For its last three miles, the Tualatin ripples over rocks and boulders to join the Willamette at West Linn. From the banks of West Linn's Willamette Park, you can watch great blue heron patiently hunt in waters that once flashed with coho and steelhead, and may one day again.

Adapted from "Discovering the Tualatin River," The Wetlands Conservancy, Urban Streams Council

Jackson Bottom Wetland Preserve

Jackson Bottom Wetland Preserve is a 650-acre wildlife preserve located within the city limits of Hillsboro, Oregon. The Preserve was once the typical farmed, degraded wetland often seen throughout the region, but in the 1970s, local residents began to restore the wetlands for habitat and water quality. Today, a non-profit organization operates programs at Jackson Bottom, with a focus to improve wildlife habitat and water quality and provide education, research, and passive recreation opportunities. Jackson Bottom is a huge wetland area located in the Tualatin River floodplain. Songbirds and small mammals, as well as salamanders and rare wetland plants, are dependent on the marshes of the Preserve, which is a sanctuary for both people and animals. The open waters, wet meadows, forested wetlands, and upland ash and fir woods are habitat to thousands of ducks and geese, deer, otters, beavers, herons, and eagles. The forest at the Preserve's eastern boundary supports a thriving great blue heron colony. This is one of the few sites within the urban portion of the region where you can see short-eared owls. During some years both sides of Hwy. 219 are inundated with floodwaters from the nearby Tualatin River and are white with hundreds of wintering tundra swans.

Jackson Bottom is owned jointly by the City of Hillsboro and Unified Sewerage Agency and managed by a non-profit board with broad representation from the community. It is also an important natural resource and information center related to wetlands and aquatic education in the metropolitan region. Thousands of preschool and school-aged children, bird watchers, university staff and students, researchers, and others benefit from the programs and services provided by the Preserve. Water quality, surface water, and habitat enhancement projects in the Preserve have brought visitors from countries such as Poland, Australia, and Italy to Jackson Bottom to learn from research. The innovative water quality program, which uses wetlands to "polish" sewage effluent before it is discharged into the Tualatin River, attracts researchers and wetland ecologists from across the United States.

Currently, no indoor facility is available; however, parking, a portable restroom facility, an area for bus parking, and an extensive trail network are open to the public.

Access

Via Hwy. 219, south of Hillsboro. There are two access points for the general public. The northern site, about 1/2 mile south of downtown Hillsboro, has a covered shelter and offers spectacular views of the wetlands. This shelter meets ADA standards. The southern site is accessed just south of the Unified Sewerage Agency's water quality

Location
South of Hillsboro, Hwy. 219

Activities
Hiking
Wildlife viewing area

Facilities
Toilets (at USA Water Quality Lab, south end of Preserve)
Wheelchair accessible (north viewing platform)
Trail unpaved
Parking
Education programs (Jackson Bottom Staff)
Interpretive information (brochures/maps)

Fees and Regulations
Open dawn to dusk

Highlights
Expansive wetlands in Tualatin River floodplain within walking distance of downtown Hillsboro. Winter migrations bring up to 15,000 aquatic birds to the Preserve, and in the spring it is a prime nesting site for ducks, geese, songbirds, and birds of prey. Frequently filled with tundra swans and nesting bald eagles; great blue heron nesting colony. This is one of the few sites within the urban portion of the region where you can see short-eared owls.

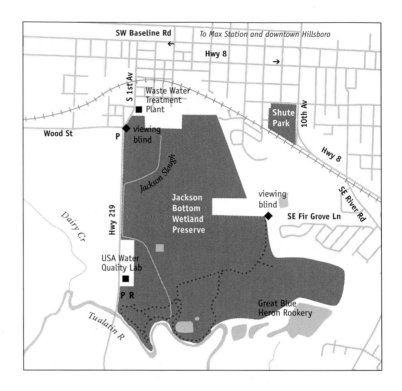

Public Transit
Tri-Met #57 and #91X or MAX light rail; Hillsboro Central, SE 3rd stop is a short walk from the Preserve.

Thomas Guide 593/623

laboratory. There is a small parking area that provides access to another viewing shelter and 2.5 miles of trail.

The majority of the trails at the Preserve are not wheelchair accessible, but great wildlife viewing can be had from both the northern and southern viewing shelters, which are open all year. The lower lying areas, including trails, are often flooded from November through March.

How to Get There

From Hwy. 26, take the North Plains exit (57) and drive south on Glencoe Rd. appx. 6 miles, through Hillsboro. The road will turn into Hwy. 219, which you take south to the Preserve. From the west take Hwy. 8, Tualatin Valley Highway, into downtown Hillsboro; turn south on Hwy. 219 and proceed about 1/2 mile across the railroad tracks and sewage treatment plant; turn left into the paved parking area.

By Pat Willis

For more information: Jackson Bottom Wetland Preserve and Friends of Jackson Bottom, see Resources.

Fernhill Wetlands

Fernhill Wetlands is located near the confluence of Gales Creek with the Tualatin River, just one mile southeast of Forest Grove in Washington County. Managed by the Unified Sewerage Agency and co-owned by USA and the city of Forest Grove, Fernhill was initially the site of three effluent holding ponds which only incidentally attracted a variety of wildlife, especially waterfowl. In several phases between 1991 and 1996, 60 acres of land adjacent to the original ponds were enhanced in order to provide ideal wetland habitat. The land was sculpted for water storage, with dams, islands, snags, bird-boxes, and native vegetation strategically placed. First came "Dabbler's Marsh," a quiet, tree-lined sanctuary with numerous small ponds where beaver make their home. Now, Dabbler's Marsh flows into a series of four large water-retaining "cells," each with its own unique characteristics. This mitigated site is fed by natural groundwater and surface runoff, which is separated from the original ponds (they are no longer used for sewage treatment) by raised dikes. Birders and other outdoor enthusiasts can follow the dikes around the largest lake and along the ponds, cells, and marshy meadows that ultimately feed the nearby Tualatin River.

The Upper Tualatin River meanders along Fernhill's southern border, providing wildlife from the greater ecosystem of the Tualatin River Corridor easy access to and from the wetlands. This proximity to the Tualatin, along with its location at the apex of the Willamette and Yamhill Flyways, contributes to the wildlife diversity for which Fernhill Wetlands is nationally recognized. With its recent additions and enhancements, Fernhill now includes a variety of wetland types in addition to the original lacustrine (lake) habitat, and birders enjoy uniquely unobstructed views both from the raised dikes and from the two viewing shelters built by the Friends of Fernhill Wetlands in 1998–99.

Although Fernhill is well known for the heron, hawks and eagles, beaver, otter and mink, and the many other species that are common year-round, seasonal migrations bring waterfowl, shorebirds, and songbirds by the thousands to the wetlands' lakes, ponds, marshes, and forested areas. Peregrine falcons were sighted frequently during the 1998-99 winter and a pair of bald eagles nested in 1999 and again in 2000. Virginia rails and other rarely-sighted shorebirds are elusive but present. Yet Fernhill provides more than exceptional opportunities for wildlife viewing. Tucked against the northwestern edge of the Willamette Valley in the midst of wine country, it gives visitors a "reach-out-and-touch-it" view of the Coast Range; a dramatic yet pastoral view of the Upper Tualatin River Valley as it ascends to its headwaters; and dazzling, sunset-hued views of Cascade Range volcanoes, including Mounts Jefferson, Hood, Adams, and St. Helens.

Location
Entryway and parking lot located on the east side of Fernhill Road, 200 feet south of the Unified Sewerage Agency Water Treatment Facility at 1345 Fernhill Road, Forest Grove, OR 97116.

Activities
Seasonal tours

Facilities
Wheelchair accessible
Trail unpaved
Parking

Fees and Regulations
Open dawn to dusk
No pets

Highlights
Dikes, ponds, dramatic views of the coast range, marshy meadows teeming with wildlife.

Public Transit
Tri-Met #57 and #91X

Thomas Guide 592

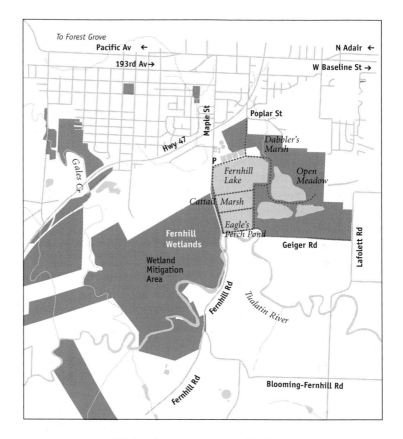

In 1999, an additional 362 acres were officially added to Fernhill Wetlands as a wetland mitigation bank, bringing the total area of Fernhill Wetlands to over 600 acres. A mitigation project of 30 acres in the spring of 2000 initiated the process of transforming this agricultural land into a wildlife-rich, water-cleansing wetland. In addition, planning is in its final stages for the Fernhill Wetlands Research and Education Field Station. With fundraising underway, it is hoped that ground will be broken by the summer of 2002. This facility, a joint venture of the city of Forest Grove, Pacific University, the Forest Grove School District, and the Unified Sewerage Agency, will provide a variety of much-needed public facilities, including restrooms, educational materials, and expansive viewing decks. Yet it is perhaps for the students of the region especially—from the elementary grades through higher education—that the classrooms and laboratory facilities will prove most valuable. For as future mitigation projects move through various stages of succession on their way to becoming exemplary wetlands, students and researchers will enjoy unparalleled experiences "in the field," as, parcel by parcel, this vast floodplain reclaims its original characteristics.

Access

Fernhill Wetlands can be accessed from the public parking area on the east side of Fernhill Road, which is approximately 200 feet past the entrance to Unified Sewerage Agency's water treatment facility.

From the gravel parking lot, visitors can walk nearly 2.5 miles of hard-packed gravel "trails." These trails double as roadways for maintenance vehicles, so they are wide, level, and generally smooth. Motorized wheelchairs, therefore, can easily negotiate the trails, though manual wheelchair users may require assistance. Some portions of the trails flood during periods of heavy rainfall, but access is generally good throughout the year. The loop around Fernhill Lake is just over one mile in length and provides access to both viewing shelters. The East Viewing Shelter, which is .6 mile from the parking area, is in the "middle" of the wetlands, on the dike between Fernhill Lake and the "mitigated" or emergent ponds and marshes, providing a 360 degree view of the wetlands. This access to the "heart" of the wetlands, where visitors are surrounded on all sides by water and wildlife, is a unique feature of Fernhill Wetlands and is its most outstanding characteristic. For visitors who do not wish to take the entire "loop," the West Viewing Shelter is only .2 mile from the parking area, providing extremely easy access to a distinctive vantage point. Perched over Cattail Marsh, the West Viewing Shelter offers a panorama of the Tualatin River's headwaters in the hills to the southwest, as well as a close-up view of "Cattail's" unique wetland habitat. Both viewing shelters are wheelchair accessible and benches provide many resting points along the way.

The East Viewing Shelter provides access to the "heart" of the wetlands, where visitors are surrounded on all sides by water and wildlife. It is a unique feature of Fernhill Wetlands and is its most outstanding characteristic.

How to Get There

Forest Grove is 23 miles west of Portland, by way of either U.S. 26 or Oregon 8 (the Tualatin Valley Hwy.). From US 26 take the North Plains exit (57) and follow the signs toward Forest Grove. However, after turning right at the stop sign onto Verboort Rd., travel just .3 mile and turn left at the first flashing yellow light. Travel 2 miles to the stop sign and turn left. Proceed to the intersection with "TV Hwy." (Pacific Ave. in Forest Grove) and continue south (straight) on the Hwy. 47 Bypass toward McMinnville. Proceed only one-half mile and turn left on Fernhill Rd., then .2 mile to the parking lot on the east side of Fernhill Rd. From Oregon 8, turn left at the Hwy. 47 Bypass just after entering Forest Grove and proceed, as above, to Fernhill Rd.

By Eric Brattain

For more information: Friends of Fernhill Wetlands at 503-357-5890 or Unified Sewerage Agency, see Resources.

Clacking Sticks

Summer is the premier season to observe the multitude of flying insects which inhabit marshes and other wet places in Portland and the surrounding countryside. For size, flying ability, and beauty few insects hold a candle to the dragonfly or its cousin, the dainty damselfly. For thousands of years humans have marveled at dragonflies. They have been depicted in ancient and modern oriental art in paintings, tapestries, and wood-cuttings. The Nootka Indians of the Pacific Northwest conferred the name "clacking stick" on dragonflies and included them in their totems and on personal decorative objects.

Even the uninitiated, would-be entomologist cannot overlook the hovering and darting of these agile predatory insects. The Portland area offers many locations to photograph, observe, and otherwise enjoy the clacking stick.

Insect Kinship

Dragonflies were contemporaries of the first reptiles more than 300 million years ago and were around long before the mammals and flowering plants. Dragonflies and damselflies (collectively referred to as odonates of the insect Order Odonata) share easily observed characteristics which, in combination, distinguish them from the rest of the insects: two equal or nearly equal pairs of wings; large compound eyes; short, threadlike antennae; a long, slender body; and young that are aquatic and develop from eggs to adults through a nymphal stage.

There are also obvious differences between the two odonates: Damselflies (suborder Zygoptera) are delicate and weak fliers. Their wings are held folded over their abdomen, butterfly-fashion, when at rest. Damselfly young obtain their oxygen from the water via three leaf-like "swim fins" (caudal lamella) at the end of the abdomen. Dragonflies, on the other hand, are extremely strong fliers with robust bodies, and their young have internal gills located in their rectum. One of the most obvious field characteristics is the dragonfly's inability to fold its wings over the body when perched. Instead they hold their slightly unequal pairs of wings straight out to the sides like oars. I have sighted dozens of species in the Portland area. There are 84 species of odonates in Oregon, 76 species in Washington, and 93 species for both states combined.

Courting: A Tandem Affair

One of the most often observed dragonfly behaviors relates to courtship and mating, a behavior which is unique among insects and culminates in male and female tandem flights so commonly seen in late summer. This flight is initiated by the male, which first transfers sperm to a special bladder-like pouch on his abdomen. He then pursues a female and attaches the tip of his abdomen to the back of her head; they fly in a tandem coupling, male in front, while the female curls her abdomen to retrieve sperm from the male's storage chamber. Whether eggs are laid while flying in tandem or by the female alone depends on the species. Damselflies mate in the same general manner, except that the male clamps on to the female's thorax rather than the head.

Egg to Adult: the Best of Both Worlds

Dragonfly young, which rival any sci-fi aquatic creature in appearance and method of procuring food, spend their youth underwater catching other insects, tadpoles, and even small fish with their hinged, extendible mouthparts. The amount of time spent preparing for an aerial adulthood may be as long as five years in some cold-water species or as short as a few weeks in warm-water species that live in small, vernal pools that dry up by summer's end. Dragonfly young can be grouped according to their lifestyles as climbers, sprawlers, and burrowers. Climbers are active foragers with streamlined bodies and keen eyesight for stalking prey. They derive their name from their active crawling over submerged vegetation. The sprawlers and burrowers are more sedate, preferring to lie either on top of the bottom ooze and debris or, in the case of burrowers, actually within the silt and muck awaiting unsuspecting prey which they snare with their hooked, prehensile mouthparts.

Ecdysiast

After the voracious young dragonfly has stored enough energy to make the transformation to adult (incomplete metamorphosis without a pupal stage, in contrast with butterflies' complete metamorphosis), it crawls from the water on a stem of emergent vegetation where its skin (exuvia) is shed. This generally occurs under the cover of darkness or in early morning, since this is a particularly vulnerable time in its life. The result is a winged hunter, as ravenous a predator as its younger self, but this time exploiting a new habitat. It is interesting to note that a mosquito missed in its aquatic larval form may now be snatched by the same dragonfly in a different arena. The adult will also feed on a great variety of other insects, but predominantly on species of the fly family (Order Diptera), which they capture while in flight by forming a "basket" with their six barbed legs. They may eat their prey while in flight or after returning to a perch. Sometimes the larger species will also feed on smaller odonates and are themselves food for many species of birds. In their juvenile stage, or if they accidentally fall in the water as adults, they are eaten by fish, aquatic birds, amphibians, and a myriad of other invertebrates.

Dragonfly Watching

Dragonflies become sexually mature within two weeks after emergence and begin the life cycle all over, with males establishing territories near water which they aggressively patrol to seek mates and to ward off intruding males of the same species. Conflicts between different species at the same habitat are often reduced by variations in patrolling and perching habits. Although fights and some mortalities do occur, the aerial battles within and among species help reduce the competition and number of encounters. Females are seldom seen near the water at this time unless they are ready to mate or lay eggs.

Dragonfly watching is best done from the water. In my more youthful days I emulated a pond-dwelling amphibian by submerging myself chin-deep in the nearest marsh, where I literally became a part of the action as aerial battles, "mosquito hawking," mating, and egg laying occurred all around me. Dragonflies do not bite or sting, and their occasional use of my head as a perch was a delight I will never forget. Nowadays I have resorted to the use of chest-waders, which allow the same intimate experience without the discomforts that I enjoyed in my own nymphal age.

Where To See Them

Larger lakes usually have poor odonate populations, except in sheltered areas where wave action is reduced and marshy habitats have become established. The best places to watch dragonflies and catch their young are in marshes, small ponds, warm water streams, and similar places. Beggars-Tick Marsh Wildlife Refuge, Oaks Bottom Wildlife Refuge, Jackson Bottom Wetland Preserve, Fernhill Wetlands, Hedges Creek Marsh, Oregon Episcopal School Marsh, Koll Creekside Marsh, Salmon Creek Wetlands, and the smaller ponds of Sauvie Island and Ridgefield National Wildlife Refuge are good bets for a summer's worth of dragonfly viewing.

Flight

Dragonfly flight is evolutionarily "primitive" compared to the more "advanced," more recently evolved insect groups such as dipterans (i.e. the two-winged flies and mosquitoes). It is ironic that these more "modern" insects make up a significant part of the dragonfly diet. Their amazing aerobatics are made possible because each wing is attached directly to muscles (rather than attached to the thorax as with most winged insects), making it possible to move all four wings independently of one another!

By Ralph Thomas Rogers

It's The Berries...and Seeds and Nuts

A fter alpine meadows have bloomed out late in summer, wildflower enthusiasts usually put away their books and field paraphernalia and retire until the skunk cabbage and Indian plum call them out in spring. In the process, they ignore the world of botanical interest and beauty still to be explored. For fall is the time of fruits and pods—the nuts, berries, achenes, pomes, samaras, and siliques—without which there would have been no point to spring in the first place.

Those who are drawn to wildflowers by their vivid colors will be disappointed with what remains, or they can learn to appreciate the muted hues of autumn. And those who are at ease identifying wildflowers in flower will find themselves on unfamiliar ground without petals, stamens, pistils, and, in many cases, leaves to guide them. To aid in identification, we have prepared a brief compilation of some of the autumn "wildflowers." Most of our descriptions emphasize the ways that plants use wind, water, animals, and humans for dispersal and implantation.

On the Wind

After gravity, wind is the most ancient agent of seed dispersal, and the seeds which have adapted themselves to take advantage of it are countless. Among the most famous are surely the winged seeds common to the maple family. In western Oregon these "helicopters" are found not only on the characteristically maple-ish big-leaf maple (*Acer macrophyllum*), but also on the decidedly eccentric vine maple (*Acer circinatum*). Unlike most of its relatives, the vine maple sprawls and trails along the ground. Even its round, star-shaped leaves are only vaguely maple-like, but its pairs of winged samaras identify it as a maple without question. Pioneer travelers cursed the virtually impassable tangles of vine maple, but today it is a beautiful member of the forest community. You can see examples of the vine maple in Forest Park and along Oaks Bottom's eastern edge.

Another vine which employs the wind in seed dispersal is clematis or virgin's-bower (*Clematis ligusticifolia*). It too is found along Oaks Bottom's eastern bluff, where it climbs for a distance of several meters into many of the trees. In summer it sports lovely white flowers, but in fall it is perhaps even more attractive, as the pistils on the female flowers grow long and develop the feathery hairs which will later be used to catch the wind.

Probably the most numerous wind-borne seeds in the world are the plumed achenes of the thistles (*Cirsium* sp.) and their relatives in the Composite Family. To understand these seeds it is important to realize that Composite "flowers" (e.g. daisies, sunflowers, asters, and dandelions) are actually composed of dozens (or hundreds) of small flowerets clustered together so they resemble a single blossom.

At the base of each floweret is a seed which in thistles is surrounded by a cluster of fine, feathery hairs. As fall approaches, these hairs lengthen and the seeds loosen until finally a gust of wind comes to blow the downy seeds away.

An interesting relative of the true thistles is the dandelion-like sow thistle (*Sonchus* asper). Each seed of the sow thistle bears a small thistle-like plume. In addition, the entire plant, including the seedpods, is covered with stiff bristles. Evolutionary ecologists believe the sow thistle was once dispersed entirely by the wind, but with the advent of gardening it "discovered" that it could achieve more precise dispersal by attaching its seedpods to the clothes of gardeners. So since that time it has been developing its bristly pods while allowing the plumes on the seeds to wither slowly away.

Catching a Ride

Among the plants dispersed on clothing and animal fur, one of the neatest is common burdock (*Arctium minus*). In lieu of the sharp painful bristles so common to similar seedpods, burdock pods are covered with soft hooks identical in form and function to those on a tab of Velcro. In fact, burdock pods inspired the invention of Velcro. Burdock is a common weed throughout the Portland area.

Probably the most useful animal-dispersed device plants have evolved is the edible seed. While walking through the woods in autumn, one will frequently come upon a pile of brown scales on a stump or alongside the trail. This is a sure sign that a squirrel has been feeding on Douglas fir cones (*Pseudotsuga menziesii*). As the squirrel removes the seeds from the cone, some will be eaten, others will be cached. If the tree is lucky, some of these caches will be forgotten and the seeds will survive to germinate in spring.

Other plants carry this strategy much farther. By enclosing their seeds in an attractive, frequently sweet, fleshy berry or pome, they can appeal to many more animals. Animals who eat these fruits either spit out the seeds or swallow them, passing them through their digestive system intact and depositing them some distance away. Some of the producers of fleshy fruits include blackberry (*Rubus* sp.), blue elderberry (*Sambucus cerulea*), and false Solomon's-seal (*Smilacina racemosa*). Most of the soft fruits are quite perishable, but keep an eye out for the more long-lasting rose hips (*Rosa* sp.).

By no means are all fruits edible by humans, but this doesn't stop them from being attractive to animals and hence useful as agents of dispersal. Among the most interesting of these is poison oak (*Rhus diversiloba*). Given my reaction to this innocuous-seeming plant with the three malignant leaflets, it is impossible for me to imagine eating one of the drupe-like fruits; but many birds, including flickers, kinglets, hermit thrushes, and downy woodpeckers, find them delightful. Anyone wanting to get a close look at poison oak will find it growing in profusion along the railroad tracks near Oaks Bottom.

Empty seedpods clinging to Scot's broom (*Cytisus scoparius*) illustrate how plants can disperse their own seeds. Notice that each half of the empty pod is coiled in a different direction. During early summer the pressure in the oppositely-coiled pod halves increases. Finally, by midsummer it becomes unbearable and the pods snap open, scattering seeds in every direction.

If you take the time to visit various parks and greenspaces in fall, you can look for seed dispersal in action and perhaps you will discover (or rediscover) that the Plant Kingdom is a vast, fascinating world about which there is still a lot left to learn. Even in fall. Even in the city.

By Bob Wilson

Hyland Forest Park

Hyland Forest Park is a 30-acre natural area in the heart of southern Beaverton. This rectangular site, three-eighths of a mile long and one-eighth of a mile wide, was acquired by the Tualatin Hills Park and Recreation District (THPRD) when most of the surrounding area was undeveloped. Today, Hyland Forest Park is a forested island providing habitat for urban wildlife and a sanctuary from the residential sprawl of Beaverton. The 60-year old second-growth Douglas fir trees that dominate the site provide a canopy that shades an understory of smaller trees and shrubs such as big-leaf maple, red elderberry, red alder, ocean-spray, thimbleberry, snowberry, hazelnut, salal, and Oregon grape. Unfortunately, some of the fir trees have been removed because of an infestation of laminated root rot, a native fungus that weakens the root structure of the tree, making it vulnerable to blow-down. Native groundcover species such as trillium, yellow wood violet, duck's foot, and several types of fern (sword, wood, lady, and bracken) blanket the forest floor—at least where English ivy, invading from adjacent residential landscaping, hasn't smothered it. Most of the park is upland, but the northeastern corner contains a wetland of Oregon ash and slough sedge. Patches of camas lilies, Willamette Valley bittercress (endemic to the Willamette Valley), and Indian hellebore make this an interesting area to visit. Water from the wetland flows into a man-made pond before continuing to Beaverton's Johnson Creek. In January and February the pond is used by the northern red-legged frog as a breeding site. Their gelatinous grapefruit-sized egg masses can be seen attached to branches and vegetation under the water surface.

Location
Just northeast of the intersection of SW Murray Blvd. and SW Sexton Mountain Dr. in Beaverton.

Activities
Hiking

Facilities
Interpretive information (brochures available from Tualatin Hills Park and Recreation District)

Fees and Regulations
Open dawn to dusk
Pets on leash

Highlights
Hyland Forest Park is an isolated woodland in the midst of heavy residential development that contains both wetland and upland habitat. This 60-year-old, second-growth Douglas fir grove provides an island sanctuary for woodland birds and even affords foraging habitat for the pileated woodpecker. The northern red-legged frog uses the pond in the northeast corner of the park as a breeding site.

Public Transit
Tri-Met #62 runs along SW Murray Blvd.

Thomas Guide 624/625

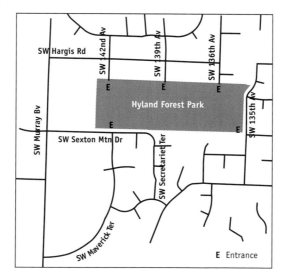

The trails are lined with banks of enchanter's nightshade, fringecup, and non-native, but nevertheless charming, pink flowered geraniums. Stumps, logs, and the contorted trunks and roots of trees growing along the trails provide interesting places to stop and listen for birds. Some of the woodland birds that are frequently observed include red-breasted nuthatch, chestnut-backed and black-capped chickadee, varied thrush, northern flicker, downy woodpecker, spotted towhee, Bewick's wren, winter wren, and common bushtit. Raccoons and Douglas' squirrels are common mammal residents.

Access

There are multiple entrances to approximately 1.5 miles of chipped trails that wander throughout the park. The eastern boundary of the park has two entrances off SW 135th Ave. near Davies Rd. The south end of the park has three entrances off SW Sexton Mountain Dr. The northern boundary has three entrances, all from dead-end streets: SW 136th Ave., SW 139th Ave., and SW 142nd Ave. The main trail through the park skirts the perimeter where the backyards of adjacent homes can be glimpsed through the vegetation.

The main trail is wide and covered with a layer of wood chips, making it easy to scan the foliage for woodland birds without tripping over uneven terrain or slipping in mud. A network of secondary trails penetrates the interior of the park.

How to Get There

From Tualatin Valley Highway, go south on SW Murray Blvd. to SW Sexton Mountain Dr. and turn left. Look for the THPRD sign for Hyland Forest Park on the left.

By Elayne Barclay

For more information: Tualatin Hills Park and Recreation District (THPRD), see Resources. Contact the Natural Resources Office to get a brochure with a map of the trails.

Brookhaven Park and Lowami Hart Woods Park

Location
The parks are located
between SW Davis Rd. and
SW Hart Rd. near SW
152nd Ave. in Beaverton.

Activities
Hiking

Facilities
Wheelchair accessibility:
approximately .2 mile
paved trail

Fees and Regulations
Open dawn to dusk
Pets on leash

Highlights
These parks are part of
a string of protected
natural areas along
Beaverton's Johnson
Creek. The parks include
relatively undisturbed
upland and wetland
habitat harboring many
species of plants unusual
in the thick of the
suburban development of
Beaverton. The natural
areas provide breeding
and nonbreeding habitat
for the northern red-
legged frog, nesting
habitat for cavity nesting
birds, and foraging habitat
for pileated woodpeckers.

Brookhaven and Lowami Hart Woods Parks are undiscovered natural area treasures that are part of a string of protected greenspaces along Beaverton's Johnson Creek. Together the two parks make up around 50 acres of wetlands and uplands containing open water, meadow, riparian, and forested habitat. The creek enters Lowami Hart Woods near its southwestern corner and flows northward through Brookhaven Park on its way to join Beaverton Creek. Unfortunately, even though the two parks are contiguous, there is no trail connecting the two sites. A short walk along a residential street will give you access to a trail entrance to explore each site.

The main trail from Barcelona for Lowami Hart Woods forks, one trail leading up, along, and then back down the slope north of the creek. The other fork leads down to the creek, over a bridge, and up the slope south of the creek. Most of the park is covered with a forest of 90-year-old Douglas fir trees on steep slopes bordering the fast flowing creek. Under the canopy of fir trees are vine maple, cascara, serviceberry, Oregon grape, California hazelnut, salal, Indian plum, ocean-spray, wild roses, thimbleberry, red elderberry, snowberry, and red huckleberry. The forest floor is carpeted with sword-fern, duck's foot, wood violet, enchanter's nightshade, false Solomon's-seal, and wildflowers such as trilliums, fawn lilies, and camas lilies. Pacific madrone and Oregon oak can be found where there is more sun, and the riparian corridor is vegetated with Oregon ash and slough sedge. Beaver activity is usually evident along the creek, sometimes causing problems for homeowners adjacent to the creek. Chipmunks and Douglas' squirrels scamper through the conifers, and raccoons hang out in the large firs during the day. Lots of warblers and woodpeckers take advantage of the park. Banana slugs and roughskin newts are abundant throughout the site and red-legged frogs can be found in the wetland areas.

Those who grew up in Beaverton may have fond memories acquired during summertime rompings in the woods of Camp Lowami, a Camp Fire day camp used until 1992. Camp Lowami must have been a magical place for kids. Former day campers may remember the "Sing Ring", Kalesse Lodge, and the "Bird's Nest". Remnants of its use as a day camp can still be found, such as several fire rings lined with rocks that are now covered with moss and lichens, a flagpole and bridge in the central meeting place, and a pile of bricks—all that's left of the lodge built in the 1950s. The property was acquired in 1996 using joint funds from Metro's Greenspaces bond measure for the City of Beaverton and the Tualatin Hills Park and Recreation District. The perseverance of the Friends of Beaverton's Johnson Creek was instrumental in almost doubling the size of the park with the recent addition of a parcel of land that had been slated for development.

In contrast to the primitive trails of Lowami Hart Woods, a 10-foot-wide paved "path" leads through the woods of Brookhaven Park. The pathway leads through some forested upland of Douglas fir, salal, thimbleberry, California hazel, Oregon grape, and ocean-spray. The trail leads to a bridge that gives wonderful views up and down the riparian corridor of Johnson Creek. The corridor is riddled with an impressive number of snags and is a good place to see wood ducks, kingfishers, green heron, and flycatchers. The creek is lined with Oregon ash, willow, twin-berry, and red-stemmed dogwood. Where the non-native reed canarygrass hasn't invaded, a nice blanket of slough sedge covers the wetland on either side of the creek. After crossing the creek, the paved route leads up through the woods east of the creek. Chipped and natural substrate trails lead off of the paved path to explore a forested arm of the park that goes all the way to Murray Boulevard. Before entering a residential neighborhood, the paved trail crosses a small tributary of the creek. From the tributary, there is a good view downstream. An old beaver dam previously held back Johnson Creek before it left Brookhaven Park, forming a large pond and wetland area just south of the Davis Road bridge. An enhancement/maintenance project of the Unified Sewerage Agency to increase the storage capacity for run-off from the area, along with

Public Transit

Tri-Met #88 runs along SW Hart Rd., giving access to Lowami Hart Woods Park from the south. Tri-Met #62 runs along Murray Blvd. and with a short walk gives access to Brookhaven Park or Lowami Hart Woods Park.

Thomas Guide 624

road and bridge improvements by the City of Beaverton, has changed the site considerably. The beaver dam had to be removed, and consequently the large area of open water is gone, but the area has been replanted with native vegetation and should still be a good place to observe waterfowl such as green-winged teal, mallard, American wigeon, and wood duck and, in the winter, hooded merganser and common egrets. Red-winged blackbirds and nutria are always abundant. Common yellowthroat, great blue heron, green heron, belted kingfisher, and otter are frequently seen. This area is best seen from the Davis Road bridge or from access off SW Ivy Glen Court.

Access

A 10-foot-wide paved walkway through Brookhaven Park can be accessed from the west side of Beaverton's Johnson Creek by a formally marked entrance at the north end of SW Barcelona Way and from the east side of the creek off SW Nehalem Ln. Access to a rough informal trail and views of the site from the west can be found off SW Daphne Ct. An access to informal trails from the east is found off SW 146th Ct.

Lowami is an invented Camp Fire word derived by compiling the first two letters of three chosen words: "lo" for love, "wa" for warmth, and "mi" for mine.

There is a formally marked but steep and muddy entrance off SW Barcelona Way that leads to approximately two miles of unmaintained natural substrate trails through Lowami Hart Woods. There are several unmarked entrances to these trails from SW Hart Rd. between SW Dunsmuir Ln. and SW 152nd Ave.

The primitive trails through Lowami Hart Woods are often very muddy and some are fairly steep.

How to Get There

From Tualatin Valley Highway, go south on SW Murray Blvd. to SW Davis Rd. and turn right. After Davis Rd. crosses Beaverton's Johnson Creek, turn left on SW 152nd Ave. Follow 152nd to SW Barcelona Way and turn left. Access the paved path through Brookhaven Park where Barcelona makes a 90-degree turn to the right. To get to Lowami Hart Woods Park, continue on Barcelona until it makes another 90-degree turn to the right; look for a THPRD (Tualatin Hills Park and Recreation District) sign on the left.

By Elayne Barclay

For more information: Tualatin Hills Park and Recreation District (THPRD), see Resources. Contact the Natural Resources Office for maps of both sites.

Bethany Lake Park (Rock Creek Open Space)

Bethany Lake Park is contiguous with over 100 acres of interconnected open areas in the Rock Creek Watershed that provide a corridor for wildlife movement. Bethany Lake itself is an eight-acre artificial pond with a maximum depth of about six feet. A dam at the western end of the lake was built in 1953 to provide a source of irrigation water for farming. Water rights are still retained by the adjacent Rock Creek Country Club to irrigate the turf of their golf course. A paved pathway adheres closely to the entire southern shoreline. During a walk along the almost 2,800 feet of lakeshore, expect to see several species of swallows (tree, barn, and violet-green), red-winged blackbirds, house finches, cedar waxwing, great blue heron, and a wide variety of waterfowl (northern shoveler, hooded and common merganser, American wigeon, wood duck, and Canada goose), depending on the season. Also easily observed are nutria, bullfrogs, carp, and if you are lucky, the family of otters that frequents the lake. Other wildlife that can be seen include green heron, belted kingfisher, mink, common garter snake, and tree frogs. Evidence of the presence of raccoons and beaver is easy to find around the edge of the lake. The paved path crosses a bridge over Rock Creek, continues west through a wetland meadow, and then enters the golf course of the Rock Creek Country Club. There is a public easement through the golf course, but watch out for errant golf balls. Red-tailed hawks, ring-necked pheasant, and coyote are species that can be seen during a walk. Northwest of Bethany Lake, the park contains a wonderful chunk of riparian habitat along the main stem of Rock Creek. There is no formal access to this area, but it is well worth a trip off the paved path for a visit. This grove

Location
Bethany Lake Park is just southwest of the intersection of NW West Union Rd. and NW 185th Ave. in Beaverton.

Activities
Hiking
Fishing
Canoeing
Biking

Facilities
Portable toilet in summer months
Parking areas
Picnic area
Wheelchair accessible, Paved trails

Fees and Regulations
Open dawn to dusk
Pets on leash

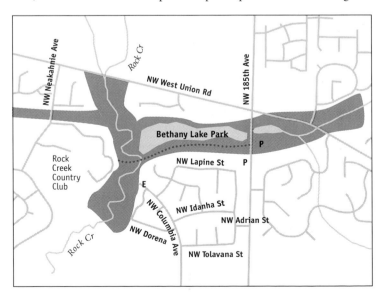

harbors one of the few places maidenhair fern and false lily-of-the-valley have been seen within the natural areas of the Tualatin Hills Park and Recreation District. Large-diameter western red cedar trees are another reason to investigate the area. Many fallen trees provide a means of crossing Rock Creek for further exploration: look for pockets of camas lilies and clusters of Pacific yew. Red-legged frogs and Douglas' squirrels are plentiful, and a bobcat has been seen and photographed by residents of the adjacent neighborhood! Rock Creek continues to flow through the park downstream from the lake, but the paved path follows only for a short distance before it dumps you onto a dead-end street. There is no formal access to the rest of the park and large thickets of Himalayan blackberry discourage further exploration.

Tualatin Hills Park and Recreation District acquired Bethany Lake Park in 1977. Work to improve the site by rebuilding the dam and dredging accumulated sediments from the bottom of the lakebed was completed in 1997. Lakeshore viewing platforms are planned for the future and there is an ongoing grant project to revegetate the southern shoreline with native species.

Highlights

Bethany Lake Park provides easy access to open water that allows visitors good wildlife viewing opportunities as well as providing an urban fishing site. For the more adventurous, there are opportunities to explore less accessible areas of the park with the possibility of discovering less frequently observed plants, such as camas lilies, maidenhair fern, false lily-of-the-valley, and large-diameter western red cedars. Also, you can observe otters and perhaps be lucky enough to spot a bobcat, which has been seen several times.

Public Transit

Tri-Met #52 runs along NW 185th Ave.

Thomas Guide 564/594

Access

Bethany Lake Park can be accessed from the east directly from NW 185th Ave. There are two small parking areas, one on each side of NW 185th Ave. (be careful crossing this busy street). The park can also be accessed from the end of NW Columbia Ave.

How to Get There

From Hwy. 26, go north on NW 185th Ave. Bethany Lake Park is on the left before NW West Union Rd. under the power lines and just before 185th crosses the tributary that feeds the lake.

By Elayne Barclay

For more information: Tualatin Hills Park and Recreation District Natural Resources Office, see Resources.

Willow Creek

Willow Creek's headwaters are formed from a series of marshes and boggy meadows on Bonny Slope, just south of Thompson Road near the boundary between Multnomah and Washington County. Although encroached upon by high-density development, many of the marshes remain in a natural state thanks in part to long-time residents whose lots form a barrier to the surrounding urbanization. Shaded by tall fir, oak, and aspen, the bogs are covered in delicate native plants including camas, trout-lily, and marsh buttercup and are home to upland mammals, such as raccoon, squirrel, and possum.

The creek's upper reaches flow rapidly down the slopes of the Tualatin Mountains, passing through more high-density development in Northwest Portland before entering Beaverton. The creek passes under Highway 26 between Murray and Cornell Road, then flows under NW 158th, where it enters Willow Creek Nature Park.

At this point in its journey the character of Willow Creek has changed. The stream is slower and wider, and it meanders. Its banks are surrounded by wide swaths of reed canarygrass, and the delicate plants from its upper reaches give way to larger, heartier shrubs including blackberry, red-osier dogwood, Douglas spirea, and common snowberry. Here the stream has enough water to support aquatic mammals—nutria and muskrat.

This section of the creek is the most accessible to viewing. A boardwalk runs from the entrance of the nature park through a series of developments—Waterhouse, Stonegate, and Winthrop. There's a short gap in the boardwalk at Moshofsky Woods, but a trail leads between the two sections of the walk. The boardwalks were built by developers, but the walks and their associated parks are maintained by the Tualatin Hills Park and Recreation District.

The Moshofsky Woods are themselves worthy of note because of the rare western wahoo that is found there. A member of the maple family, the western wahoo is similar to the vine maple but has an oval, serrated leaf instead of the more common maple-shaped leaf. The Moshofsky Woods and the woods adjacent to the Stonegate subdivision are high-quality remnant forest habitat dominated by Oregon ash, black cottonwood, red alder, and Douglas fir. This is the largest block of forest left on the creek.

At NW 173rd, the stream flows under the street to Apollo Ridge Park. Apollo Ridge Park is the first in a series of parks that include Salix Park, Willow Creek Park, and Chantal Village Park. These parks are undeveloped and serve as natural area buffers for the stream and the wildlife it supports. Chantal Village Park is the site of Willow Creek's confluence with Beaverton Creek. This marks the end of Willow

Creek, as the stream retains the name Beaverton Creek until it flows into Rock Creek, which drains to the Tualatin River.

Just before it enters Beaverton Creek, there is a small dam on Willow Creek. Behind the dam is a pond that supports cutthroat trout, bass, crappie, bluegill, and catfish. A canopy of Douglas and grand fir, Pacific yew, willow, and alders shades the pond and provides habitat to a variety of birds including great horned owl, winter wren, and song sparrows. Seasonally the park is an excellent site for spotting warblers and waterfowl migrating through the area.

From start to end, Willow Creek runs about six miles and draws from a watershed of five square miles. New development is rapidly urbanizing the stream. Local requirements, including erosion control and a 25-foot buffer along the stream and its associated wetlands, help preserve Willow Creek for the moment. However, future implementation of wider buffers in Metro's Title 3 and Goal 5 regulations may be needed to maintain the creek's integrity and allow it to continue supporting the great variety of wildlife that depends on it.

By Thomas E. Hanrahan

Willow Creek Nature Park

Willow Creek Nature Park lies at the base of the Waterhouse development at NW 158th and Cornell Road in Beaverton. Offering one of the best sites for viewing Willow Creek, the major man-made feature of the park is a boardwalk that follows the course of the stream.

The creek and boardwalk, which run east to west, are bounded to the north by a ridge and to the south by fences of the Waterhouse development. The east end of the park is marked by its main entrance at NW Waterhouse Avenue, and its western boundary abuts Moshofsky Woods.

Shaded by a canopy of ash and Douglas fir, the park is well segregated from the traffic and activity that surround it. The canopy above the creek and the adjacent woods provide excellent habitat for migrating song birds during the spring and early summer. It's a good place to spot orange-crowned and Wilson's warblers. Year-round, you can find flickers and downy woodpeckers high up in the trees.

The understory consists of reed canarygrass nearest the creek, followed by blackberry, especially along the north ridge. These are heavily populated by sparrows and finches. Along the fence bordering Waterhouse are red-osier dogwood and Douglas spirea, which provide shelter for Bewick's wrens and spotted towhees. On the creek side of the boardwalk, there are several areas where bittersweet nightshade is threatening to overtake native vegetation.

Water in the creek is also a draw to birds. Violet-green and barn swallows arc over the stream during spring and summer. It's fairly common to find a great blue heron at the western end of the park where the creek spreads and forms shallow pools. Early in the migration season, the creek is a stopover point for waterfowl including mallards and an occasional hooded merganser.

In the park, the meandering water of Willow Creek is interspersed with small islands. Gnawed trees are visible on the islands and along the creek—just one indication the park supports a variety of aquatic mammals including beaver, nutria, muskrat, and river otter.

The southwest corner of the park is dominated by a stand of Pacific crabapple that provides food for cedar waxwings, flickers, and raccoons.

Access

Access to the park, including wheelchair access, is excellent. The park can be entered from four locations—NW Waterhouse Ave., NW 161st Pl., NW Jeffery Pl., and from the Waterhouse soccer fields at NW Mission Oaks Dr.

The MAX stop at Merlo/SW 158th is nearby and an asphalt trail leads directly from the station to the park.

Location
Waterhouse Ave. near 158th and NW Cornell Rd., Beaverton.

Activities
Walking

Facilities
Wheelchair accessible

Fees and Regulations
Pets on leash
Tualatin Hills Parks and Recreation District rules apply

Highlights
A boardwalk follows the flow of the stream. Shaded canopy provides habitat to song birds and woodpeckers. Good variety of trees and other plants. Nearby Moshofsky Woods and the woods adjacent to the Stonegate subdivision are high-quality remnant forest habitat dominated by Oregon ash, black cottonwood, red alder, and Douglas fir. This is the largest block of forest left on the creek. The rare western wahoo, similar to vine maple, is found in the Moshofsky Woods.

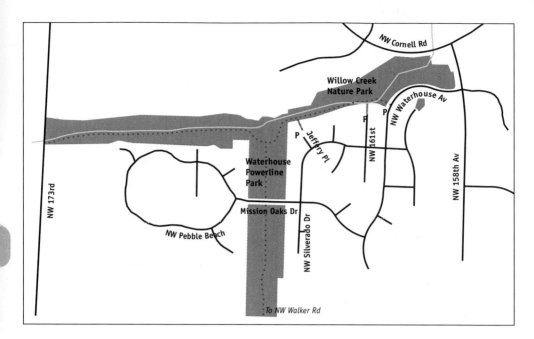

Public Transit

The Merlo MAX light rail stop is about one mile to the south, and there is a very nice asphalt path that goes directly to Willow Creek park along the west side of NW 158th. Merlo is also next to Tualatin Hills Nature Park, so you could combine two nice nature tours from this light rail station.

Thomas Guide 594

How to Get There

Take Hwy. 26 to Cornell Rd. exit. Take NW Cornell Rd. west to NW 158th Ave. Go south on 158th to NW Waterhouse Ave. and turn west on Waterhouse. You can park on Waterhouse at the curve as it turns south for the main trailhead. Other parking is on street at the cul-de-sac ends of NW 161st and Jeffery Pl., both off Silverado Dr. There is also access off NW 173rd to the west and from the south on the Powerline Trail from NW Walker Rd.

By Thomas E. Hanrahan

For more information: Tualatin Hills Park and Recreation District (THPRD), see Resources. Contact the Natural Resources Office to get a brochure with a map of the trails.

Blackberries: A Thorny Issue

It's hard to malign the blackberry while savoring a mouthful of fresh blackberry pie. Even so, those juicy fruits don't come without a price—both physical and ecological.

It takes careful maneuvering and a thick hide to battle the barbed brambles of the Himalayan blackberry (*Rubus procerus*) and harvest a bucketful of juicy, ink-black berries. The Himalayan blackberry, our main source of berries, is widespread in Oregon, where it clambers along stream banks and fence rows, skirting woodlands and pasture like a thorny petticoat, but this species is not native. Nor is the evergreen blackberry (*Rubus laciniatus*), which, like the Himalayan, escaped from cultivation to become an invasive, tenacious shrub.

The Himalayan and evergreen blackberry have a similar growth habit. Both form dense thickets of thumb-thick canes covered with large flattened thorns. The character of the leaves is the best method for distinguishing these two species. Both vines have leaves composed of five leaflets; those of the Himalayan have toothed leaf margins with fuzzy white undersides, while the evergreen blackberry has delicate, deeply cut leaflets.

Will the "Real" Blackberry Please Stand Up?

Of the three species of blackberries common to western Oregon, only one is native to the Northwest, the Pacific blackberry (*Rubus ursinus*). The Pacific blackberry has toothed leaf margins resembling the Himalayan variety, but each leaf is characteristically composed of three leaflets rather than five. Unlike its introduced cousins, the Pacific blackberry is a rather inconspicuous plant, though not without its noisome habits. It grows as a thin, thorny vine along the forest floor where it grabs tenaciously at the exposed ankles and calves of hikers.

For the diligent berry hunter, the native blackberry is well worth scratched legs. Its small berries are reportedly much more savory than the large introduced fruits. In fact, horticulturists used the Pacific blackberry as the parent material for loganberries, boysenberries, and other tasty derivations. Not every vine you trip over will reward you with fruit—our native blackberry bears separate male and female flowers.

The Pacific blackberry is frequently found in open, wooded areas in the Cascades or Coast Range, usually from 2,000 to 6,000 feet. Here it shares the understory with salal, Oregon grape, huckleberries, rhododendrons, and other native shrubs. It can also be found in less pristine urban environments such as vacant lots or the roadside tangle favored by the Himalayan and evergreen varieties.

A Thorny Issue

Himalayan and evergreen blackberries are exotic, invasive species. The prolific vines replace an ecologically healthy, diverse shrub community with thickets of thorny canes. Their presence often indicates a disturbed habitat. Volunteer groups, such as The Fans of Fanno Creek, have begun the seemingly Sisyphean task of replanting our urban stream corridors with native shrubs. Blackberry briers have been hacked back, replaced with seedlings of salmonberry, willow, and other natives, all staked and girded with the best of intentions. But given the blackberry's tenacious habits, these exotic vines may remain a thorn in the side of Portlanders for years to come.

By Connie Levesque

Salix Park

Salix Park is one of a series of undeveloped parks along the lower reaches of Willow Creek. It is a small but important link in the Willow Creek wildlife corridor. Reed canarygrass dominates the banks, the result of work associated with placing two sewer lines through the park. The reed canarygrass, an invasive exotic weed, crowds out less hearty native plants. However, both the Unified Sewerage Agency and Tri-Met are making ongoing efforts to restore the park. One of the more successful areas of recovery lies off the stream's bank in the southeast corner of the park. Here, Douglas fir, Douglas spirea, ash, willow, and cottonwood are all beginning to make comebacks. Up the slope from the reed canarygrass, Himalayan blackberry, another non-native vegetation, takes over.

Red elderberry, osoberry (also known as serviceberry), and Indian plum are found throughout the park in scattered locations, along with Pacific ninebark, beaked hazelnut, Douglas hawthorn, and ocean-spray. The predominant trees in the park are Oregon ash, several species of willow, red alder, Douglas fir, and red cedar. Several large Pacific yews grow on the east side of the creek.

The park draws a wide variety of birds throughout the year, including sparrows, chickadees, nuthatches, and jays. Red-tailed hawks frequently pass overhead during the day and great horned owls hunt along the banks at night in search of the voles and deer mice that occupy the park. The stream supports several species of fish, among them cutthroat trout, sculpins, and shiners. These in turn draw belted kingfishers and great blue herons. The *Gambusia affinis* (gambusia) was introduced into the creek for mosquito abatement. Usually one-half to three-quarters of an inch in length, this tiny fish has a voracious appetite that leads to a feeding frenzy reminiscent of piranhas when they discover beds of mosquito larvae.

Willow Creek also supports a freshwater clam that in turn draws a healthy population of mammals, including raccoons. It's fairly common to see raccoon footprints and broken clam shells along the stream's banks. Occasionally deer and coyote pass through the park in route to larger forested blocks.

Access

You can access the west side of the park from SW Salix Ridge. The park has plenty of downed trees, and it's often possible to cross over the creek from the Salix side and reach the trail system, but wear boots when you want to spend time hiking in the park.

Access is relatively poor, mostly unmaintained trails on the east side of the park. There are difficult, unmaintained trails.

Location
Salix Ridge near NW Baseline Rd. and 185th, Beaverton

Activities
Wildlife viewing area

Facilities
None

Fees and regulations
None

Highlights
Very natural setting. This is an unmaintained park meant to serve as habitat link along Willow Creek, so human access is de-emphasized here.

Public Transit
The Willow Creek/185th Avenue MAX light rail station is about 1/2 mile southwest.

Thomas Guide 594

How to Get There

Take Hwy. 26 to NW 185th and turn south; just north of SW Baseline Rd., enter Salix Park residential area on Salix Terrace. Turn right on Salix Ridge and go to the end of the cul-de-sac.

By Thomas E. Hanrahan

For more information: Tualatin Hills Park and Recreation District (THPRD), see Resources. Contact the Natural Resources Office to get a brochure with a map of the trails.

Autumn Arachnids

For the more than 20 percent of us whose fear and loathing of insects and spiders borders on phobia, fall is the time to heed the words of Theodore Roosevelt: "Speak softly and carry a big stick." Fall is spider season, and those blissful hikes through the autumn leaves can suddenly bring you face to face with eight legs, eight eyes, and a sticky web that has the effect of a brick wall on a die-hard arachnophobe. However, if you quell your panic long enough to take a good look at the much-maligned spider, you'll see a fascinating animal emerge from its shroud of bad press.

Spiders 101

Every school kid knows that spiders have eight legs, spin webs, and have something to do with water spouts and tuffets. Thanks to black widows, tarantulas, and Hollywood special effects, they also believe spiders to be evil, venomous creatures, even though the 30,000 spider species identified to date are mostly harmless, inconspicuous animals that can't even pierce human skin. Of course it hasn't helped their image that spiders are related to scorpions and ticks as members of the class Arachnida.

Arachnid is derived from Arachne, the name of a young Greek woman who incurred the wrath of the goddess Athena when she beat her at a weaving contest. All arachnids have four pairs of legs and two body segments—a cephalothorax (head plus thorax) and an abdomen. The abdomen of spiders contains the silk glands and the spinnerets (not a bad name for a rock band), and is usually their most prominent feature, sometimes dwarfing a tiny cephalothorax.

We all tend to fear what we don't understand, and our understanding of spiders has been hampered by a paucity of research. Research on Northwest and urban species in particular has been sadly lacking, although one finds representatives of most major spider groups lurking around the metro area. Several species are particularly prominent in fall as the males mature and wander in search of mates. These include the familiar web-spinning spiders and the often over-looked hunting spiders.

Web Spinners

To most of us, the spider's one concession to beauty is its web. Perhaps the most beautiful web is the classic, symmetrical jewel of the orb weavers. Orb weavers figured conspicuously in Native American legend and myth. As Dr. Willis J. Gertsch recounts in his excellent book, *American Spiders*, "To the Dakotah the orb web is the symbol of the heavens; the corners of the foundation lines point in the four directions from which come the thunders, while from the spirals of the orb emanate the mystery and power of the Great Spirit."

Fall is the perfect time for observing orb weaving spiders and their mystical creations. More than half a dozen species mature in autumn here. With a leg span of up to four inches and a bright gold-and-black body, the golden garden spider is one of the largest orb weavers you'll encounter. While introduced to Oregon, this species is common in the Willamette Valley, particularly in blackberry patches, where they invariably spin their beautiful webs in front of the choicest berries.

Oregon's native orb weavers, primarily forest dwellers, also mature in the fall. Their huge orb webs can reach two feet in diameter and may be suspended between trees 15 to 20 feet apart. These are the real heart-stoppers when you encounter them while jogging down Forest Park's Wildwood Trail.

Hunting Spiders

Hunting spiders, such as the wolf spider, are common in the Portland area and occupy a variety of habitats, including the surface of ponds. Most species are typically seen lurking under rocks, vegetation, or old boards. They often move in short, quick bursts, sometimes seeming to hop rather than run. Wolf spiders feed by pouncing on insects and crushing them in powerful pincer-like jaws called chilicerae.

Unlike web spiders, whose feeding techniques limit them to a sedentary life, hunting spiders wander considerably and are highly efficient daytime hunters with extremely acute vision. Their use of silk is restricted to reproduction and to construction of a drag line. This silken strand, used by all spiders, is anchored to twigs or walls and acts much like a safety line does for a mountain climber.

Cobwebbers and Their Kin

The familiar "cobweb" spiders, so abundant on our lawns and in those hard-to-reach corners of our homes, are actually a member of the hunting spider group. Unlike most hunting spiders, this species spins a funnel-shaped web. A series of trip lines alerts the spider in the apex of the funnel to a meal's presence. The spider then races out and subdues its prey in the same manner as the wolf spider. During the fall, male funnel-web spiders are maturing and these tan-and-black checkered spiders with legs up to two inches long may be running around your home or yard in search of the smaller female.

A careful search through the sword-fern may produce one of the Cribellate spiders. You'll find the tiny triangle spider, barely one-sixth of an inch long, patiently manning a strand of silk attached to the apex of its web, waiting to ensnare a hapless insect in the Velcro-like tangles called hackle bands that are characteristic of all Cribellate webs. Hackle bands are produced by combing silk through a special sieve-like plate, the cribellum, located on the abdomen.

Suburban Portland residents might happen upon still another type of spider usually found in forested areas or along river banks, *Antrodiaetus*, the folding trap-door spider. Males of this species abandon their subterranean burrows in search of mates during the fall.

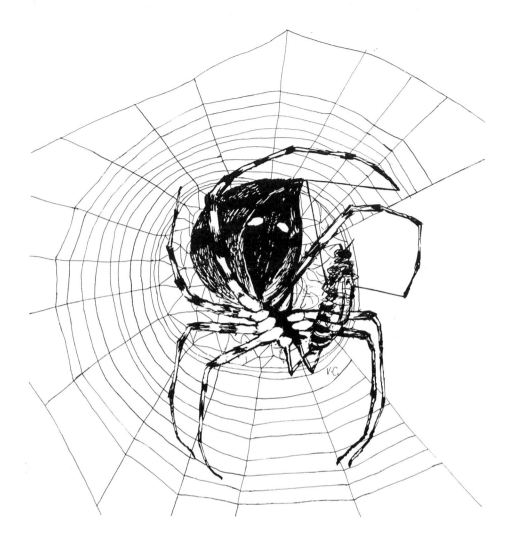

Charlotte's Sad Saga

Fall is an active time in the spider realm as courtship, mating, and egg laying must take place before winter sets in. Like E.B. White's beloved Charlotte, many female spiders die after reproducing, but some species live on to guard their egg sacs or attend to the young. Female wolf spiders are amazingly dedicated mothers. The egg sac is carried about attached to her spinnerets and she will actively defend it or seek to regain it if it is lost. Despite their sharp vision, female wolf spiders have been known to accept egg sac substitutes such as pieces of cork or cotton offered by curious, if not sadistic, scientists. When the spiderlings are ready to hatch, the female wolf spider opens the egg sac and the young clamber onto her back, where she will carry them until they have molted and become independent.

Baby Ballooners

Baby spiders demonstrate a phenomenon also seen in small adult species—ballooning. After climbing to a high perch on a twig or fence post, spiderlings spin strands of silk that are played out by the wind until they are buoyant enough to lift the spider. Ballooning is a major means of dispersal, and some species can surpass the flight of insects by lofting over 200 miles at elevations of over 10,000 feet. In the words of Walt Whitman:

> A noiseless, patient spider,
> I mark'd where on a little promontory it stood isolated,
> Mark'd how to explore the vacant vast surrounding,
> It launch'd forth filament, filament, filament, out of itself,
> Ever unreeling them, ever tirelessly speeding them.

Take Two Spiders and Call me in the Morning

While cobwebs are now considered a sign of poor housekeeping, they were once welcome in the home. Spiders and spiderwebs were valued for their medicinal qualities, and cobwebs were considered to impart a certain immunity from disease. Funnel webs were used as a substitute for gauze and were purported to have wound-binding properties. Spiders and spider derivatives were applied to the skin or taken orally to cure all sorts of ills.

If the thought of spider therapy sends a shiver down your spine, consider the fate of little Miss Muffet of nursery rhyme fame. Patience Muffet was actually the daughter of the naturalist Dr. Thomas Muffet, whose love of spiders was obviously not inherited by his daughter. Forced to swallow her father's medicinal spider remedies, it's small wonder she bid a hasty retreat from her tuffet at the sight of a spider.

The only spiders in our medicine cupboards these days got there on their own eight legs, not in a bottle. They are, thankfully, no longer important medicinal products. Spiders are, however, extremely abundant and efficient predators that may offer us an alternative to toxic pesticides.

By Connie Levesque

Masked Marauders

Most mammals conduct important activities such as foraging and mating at night. Thus, we light-loving humans rarely see them and are unacquainted with even common and abundant nocturnal species. There are, of course, exceptions. The striking white-on-black coats of skunks, for example, are easily recognizable even in poor light. So too are the definitive markings of raccoons, sightings of which have become commonplace in and around Portland.

The seven living species of raccoons are native only in the western hemisphere. The common raccoon, *Procyon lotor*, occurs in wooded areas, usually near water, from southern Canada to Panama. It has been introduced into at least five areas in Europe and Russia where surprise!—it has become somewhat of a pest. A close Latin American relative, the crab-eating raccoon, occurs from Costa Rica southward into Peru and Uruguay. Each of four Caribbean islands has its own unique raccoon species, as do the Tres Marias Islands off the western coast of Mexico.

All seven, however, are unmistakably raccoons. Their grizzled brownish to blackish coats are distinctively marked by a black facial "mask" and by alternating light and dark rings around the moderately long, furry tail. These markings, along with the raccoon's rotund body, are sufficiently endearing to make the manufacture and sale of plush raccoon stuffed toys, fake fur "coonskin" caps, and other items in a raccoon motif a small but long-standing industry.

For some who must deal with these furry felons, however, the frontier notion of a real raccoon hide nailed to the wall finds occasional support. Last year my wife and I moved into a home on a wooded acre that included an attractive pond occupied—temporarily, as it turned out —by half a dozen medium-sized koi (i.e., expensive carp). We beautified the pond with potted emergent aquatic plants, and we pampered the fish with tender floating plants and special food. One August morning we were awakened by sounds of serious squabbling outside our bedroom window. Investigation revealed two young raccoons, apparently sent into the cruel world by their mother.

"Cute," I thought.

"I don't like raccoons," said my wife who, as an impressionable child, had once been served baked raccoon, courtesy of a well-meaning neighbor.

A few mornings later, we awoke to find that our potted emergent plants were now unpotted submergents, that many of the floating plants were part of the forest litter, and that even special treats could not coax any fish into view. Raccoon tracks and small piles of fish scales around the pond indicated the fate of the fish. Over the next several weeks the raccoons returned regularly despite a bright yard light, a "hot wire," and my worst threats, until destruction of the pond's macrobiota was complete.

The episode illustrated several well-known aspects of raccoon biology. Raccoons are curious, resourceful, and able to take advantage of nearly any opportunity to obtain food and shelter. They are adept climbers, frequently denning in hollow trees. Other den sites have included hollow logs, other animals' burrows, brush and rock piles, muskrat lodges, spaces beneath buildings, and the chimney of an unused fireplace. Interestingly, only during extended winter naps or in the case of a female with young is a den used for more than a few days before it is deserted for different quarters. Although it is common for raccoons to den alone, there is one record of 23 individuals using the same winter den.

Raccoons do not have to wash their food before eating it—they eagerly eat sunflower seeds at my bird feeder. Much of their natural food, however, is aquatic animals which are captured in the water and, like most prospective food items, thoroughly manipulated and investigated chiefly by the raccoon's exceptional sense of touch. Raccoons reportedly have more tactile receptors on their fingertips than does any other mammal. Other raccoon foods include table scraps, pet foods, garden crops, fruit, seeds, and nuts. The main requirement, apparently, is that the food be of suitable quality (no hay, thanks) and quantity (the more the better).

Raccoons accumulate considerable fat, perhaps even doubling their lean body weight, before the onset of winter, but they do not truly hibernate. Although they may spend much of the winter asleep, raccoons' body temperatures, heart rates, and metabolic rates remain high. Emergence in late winter or early spring is followed by mating as solitary adult males roam over an area that may include the home ranges of several adult females, each of which tends to avoid the others. About two months after mating, the females give birth to several (rarely as many as six or seven) blind, helpless youngsters which, though only scantily haired, already show their distinctive markings. The young remain in the mother's den for about two months, soon after which they begin to accompany her on foraging excursions. Youngsters may separate from their mother in late summer or fall, or remain with her during their first winter. Although yearling raccoons are sexually mature, they are not likely to mate until their second year.

Still sought by hunters and trappers, raccoons are also taken by large predators and are susceptible to a variety of parasites and diseases, some of which can be passed on to humans or our pets. In urban areas, however, the main killers of raccoons are motor vehicles. Raccoon road kills now far outnumber those of the former road kill leader, the Virginia opossum.

Nevertheless, it is clear that raccoons are here to stay, even in the city. Most residential dwellers, and even the proprietors of some downtown eating establishments, have raccoon tales to tell. Far from having its numbers diminished by contact with urban society, the masked marauder, icon of the American frontier, continues to adapt, survive, and thrive as a fascinating and occasionally exasperating member of our urban wildlife.

By Richard B. Forbes

Snug Bugs

When it's time for us to batten down the storm windows, add an extra layer of insulation, and put in the antifreeze, many insects do the same thing. Unlike humans, though, insects are ectotherms, or "cold-blooded," and unable to elevate their body temperature much above that of their environment. To keep from freezing, insects employ an amazing array of behavioral and physiological strategies.

Whether they winter as eggs, larvae, nymphs, pupae, or adults, they enter an almost comatose condition called diapause. Their metabolism slows, and they cease to feed and grow. It is now known that decreasing hours of daylight can cause the depressing wintertime blues in people. The same changing ratio of daylight to darkness also stimulates diapause in insects.

Monarch butterfly

Getting Away From It All— Migration

Like human "snowbirds" that flock to tropical resorts, western monarch butterflies head south to retreats near Pacific Grove, California. There, they pack together in trees, conserving fat reserves for the partial return trip the next spring. Other insects make vertical migrations, from lowlands to mountains. Ladybird beetles are known to do this in the Sierras of California, and in Colorado. They, too, huddle in dense masses. Locally, smaller clusters of ladybirds can sometimes be found in clumps of grass or wedged in the furrows of tree bark.

Other beetles, true bugs, many flies and mosquitoes, and queen yellowjackets find shelter in any cozy nook or cranny, especially under bark. The Audubon Society of Portland Nature Store even sells butterfly houses to urban naturalists wishing to shelter mourning cloaks and other tortoiseshell butterflies that hibernate as adults.

Blackberry Knot gall

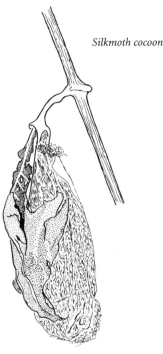
Silkmoth cocoon

Insect Insulation

Woolly bears, the caterpillars of the Isabella tiger moth, are well-insulated by their dense coat of hairs. The width of the central orange band does not, contrary to the old wives' tale, indicate the severity of the approaching winter. Curled up in leaf litter or under bark, woolly bears wait until spring to spin cocoons.

Giant silkmoths, like the polyphemus, do snuggle as pupae in cocoons that trap air between layers of dense, protective silk. Many caterpillars forego cocoons, instead burrowing underground to change into the pupal state.

Insect Antifreeze

Besides acting differently, insects can use their body chemistry to endure harsh cold. They can even manufacture their own antifreeze. Secretions of alcoholic compounds, glycerol, and some complex proteins lower the freezing point of water in an insect's cells. By actively excreting water, other insects reduce the risk of the formation of ice crystals that could puncture cells. Still another option is to permit the water between cells to go ahead and freeze.

Insect Wake-Up Call

While we may wait for the groundhog to wake, and predict the time left until spring, how insects determine when to emerge is somewhat more mysterious. The prevailing theory is that a chemical accumulates in the insect's body, signaling the onset of diapause. During the winter chill, the chemical breaks down, and its elimination from the system causes the resumption of normal activity.

It may take more than hormones to stir a fair-weather urban naturalist, but observing the still-life of insects in winter can be rewarding!

By Eric R. Eaton

Apache Bluff Wetland

This is a Tualatin River floodplain wetland that holds water all winter, but goes partially or totally dry in the summer months. Waterfowl include Canada geese, mallards, wood duck, hooded merganser, bufflehead, and wigeon. Other birds recorded at this site are great blue heron, green heron, American bittern, snipe, killdeer, Bewick's wren, red-winged blackbird, and several species of swallows. The wetland contains dense brush and remnant apple trees from an old farmstead which support deer, raccoon, and beaver.

Two trails provide access along the west and south sides of the marsh. The Apache Bluff neighborhood flanks the wetland on the south bluff above the marsh.

Access

Trails lead to the left (west) along the open water portion of the marsh and right (south) from the lower end of the panhandle access trail. The south pathway which skirts the scrub-shrub wetland is very muddy after wet winters.

How to Get There

Take I-5 south to Tualatin exit #289. Turn right on Nyberg Rd. (becomes Tualatin-Sherwood Rd.). Follow Tualatin-Sherwood Rd. to 90th Ave. Turn right on 90th to Tualatin Rd. (T-intersection at Tualatin Country Club). Proceed left to SW Cheyenne Way; turn right onto Cheyenne Way. Park at the end of Cheyenne and walk to the right down slope to the wetland.

By Mary Anne Sohlstrom

For more information: The Wetlands Conservancy, see Resources.

location
At end of SW Cheyenne Way, off SW Tualatin Rd., Tualatin, OR

Activities
Wildlife viewing
Hiking

Facilities
None

Highlights
This is a seasonal wetland, flooded by the Tualatin River in winter, which dries completely in summer. It is part of a larger greenway made up of Cook Park (Tigard), Tualatin Community Park, Durham City Park, and the Tualatin Country Club.

Public Transit
Closest Tri-Met routes are #37 and #38 to Tualatin-Sherwood Rd. and Martinazzi St. in downtown Tualatin. Walk west on Tualatin-Sherwood to 90th Ave.

Thomas Guide 685

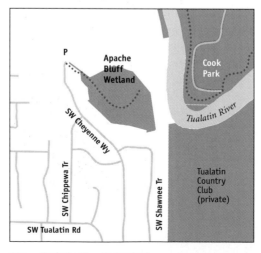

Bunnies and Briers

S tories of Bre'r Rabbit and the brier patch contain at least one germ of truth. When danger threatens, true rabbits, compactly built and relatively short-legged, bolt for cover or a burrow. To rabbits, a thicket of blackberry canes penetrated by a maze of rabbit-sized runways is the essence of safety. In contrast, the rangier and longer-legged hares (including "jack rabbits") depend on speed and endurance for their getaway. Hares neither build nor use burrows; running room is their refuge.

We have no hares in the Portland metropolitan area, but three species of rabbits, two of them introduced, occur here. The domestic rabbit (*Oryctolagus cuniculus*), of European origin, is the largest of the three and has become established through releases of pets. The disastrous introduction of this rabbit in Australia, New Zealand,

and elsewhere provides a plain lesson on the dangers of transplants. Artificial selection has produced domestic rabbits with coat colors ranging from black to white to multicolored, but their wild color is grayish-brown.

The eastern cottontail (*Sylvilagus floridanus*), also introduced, is widely established in the Willamette Valley. Good sprinters, eastern cottontails forage in fields and pastures but still depend on cover for refuge. They are grayish-brown and do not show the color polymorphism seen in local colonies of domestic rabbits.

The only native rabbit in western Oregon is the brush rabbit (*Sylvilagus bachmani*). The western Oregon race was described from a specimen collected in Beaverton in 1890. The smallest, darkest, and most secretive of our rabbits, brush rabbits rarely stray more than a meter or two from dense thickets. Often they escape notice by remaining motionless. So dependent are brush rabbits on dense cover that their home ranges conform closely to the shape and size of these retreats. Female home ranges average only about 20 meters in radius; those of males are larger but overlap more.

In summer, brush rabbits eat green herbaceous vegetation supplemented by fruit such as blackberries and thimbleberries. Winter diets include green vegetation supplemented by the leaves, buds, twigs, and bark of woody plants. Rabbits also eat moist, green pellets taken directly from the anus. This practice, analogous to cud chewing, helps rabbits meet their nutritional needs, especially in winter. The familiar hard, brown pellets are of material that has been through the rabbit twice.

The reproductive potential of rabbits is legendary, and brush rabbits are no exception. They breed from mid-February through mid-August. A female may produce five litters averaging three bunnies each in a year. The young are born in a nest the mother builds of dry grasses and her belly fur. Blind and helpless at birth, the babies grow quickly and become mature by the following year.

Young or old, rabbits are food for many kinds of dogs, cats, weasels, hawks, and owls. Along with disease, predators are an important check on the rabbit's prodigious reproductive potential. But as long as there are briers, bunnies will be bolting for them and—if they make it—making more bunnies.

By Richard B. Forbes

Brown's Ferry Park

Brown's Ferry Park is located at the confluence of Nyberg Creek and the Tualatin River. It is named for Zenas J. Brown, who laid a claim to the land in 1850 and started the first ferry in the Tualatin vicinity. Interpretive signs are mounted on posts along paved trails in the park and offer information about cultural and natural history. The park is a great place to walk, picnic, launch or dock a canoe, and view wildlife. It includes a variety of wildlife habitats and their associated species. Nyberg Creek and the Tualatin River support lush riparian communities dominated by Douglas fir, big-leaf maple, Oregon ash, willow, red elderberry, and snowberry. You can often see belted kingfisher and great blue heron hunting fish along the river and red-tailed hawks soaring above the trees. The trails loop around a meadow that the city is trying to restore to a native prairie. On the east end of the meadow is a pond that attracts winter waterfowl. A wildlife viewing blind is located on the south end of the pond adjacent to Nyberg Lane. Vegetation surrounding the pond is diverse and includes soft rush, meadow foxtail, American speedwell, slough sedge, creeping buttercup, mannagrass, and sawbeak sedge. Shrubs were planted around the pond in 1998 to provide additional food and cover for wildlife. East of the pond the trail narrows and continues as an unpaved path through a dense mixed deciduous/coniferous forest with wetland pockets of skunk cabbage, water-parsley, and lady-fern.

Access

Gentle trail; mostly paved; no seasonal restrictions. From the parking lot trails lead to Nyberg Creek and the Tualatin River.

How to Get There

Take I-5 south to Tualatin exit (#289); left at signal onto Nyberg Rd.; continue on Nyberg about .5 mile.

By Christie Galen

For more information: City of Tualatin Parks Department, see Resources.

Location
5855 SW Nyberg Ln.; north of Nyberg Ln. between SW 65th Ave. and 50th Ave.

Activities
Hiking
Biking
Canoeing, boating

Facilities
Toilets
Wheelchair accessibility
Paved and unpaved trail
Parking
Interpretive information
Picnic area
Dock, canoe launch (no boat trailer access)

Fees and Regulations
Open dawn to dusk

Highlights
Canoe launch and dock. Trail along Tualatin River. Pond attracts winter waterfowl including dabbling and diving ducks. Interpretive signs on cultural and natural history. The trails loop around a meadow which the city is trying to restore to a native prairie.

Public Transit:
Tri-Met #96, #76; depart bus at Seneca, walk south to Nyberg Rd. and east to the Park about 1 mile.

Thomas Guide 685

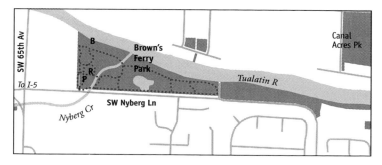

Atfalati Park

Atfalati Park, named for a tribe of the Kalapuya Indians, is located near the headwaters of Saum Creek, which flows into the Tualatin River east of I-5. The park is a great family place that combines active and passive recreation. It includes a large play structure, basketball courts, tennis courts, and sports fields. There's a paved trail that loops around the park. On the south end of the park the trail overlooks Saum Creek Greenway. Along the trail are interpretive signs describing the wetlands along the creek. Vegetation along the creek consists of an alder/willow canopy with reed canarygrass dominating the understory. Mallard, song sparrow, red-winged blackbird, and bullfrog are often observed.

Access

Trails are paved and gently to moderately sloped with interpretive signs. No seasonal restrictions.

How to Get There

Take I-5 south to Tualatin exit (#289); turn left at signal onto Nyberg Rd., right on 65th Ave., then right on Sagert to parking lot.

By Christie Galen

For more information: City of Tualatin Parks Department, see Resources.

Location
6600 SW Sagert;
southwest of SW
Sagert/SW 65th

Activities
Hiking
Biking
Large play structure
Basketball courts
Tennis courts
Sports fields

Facilities
Toilets
Wheelchair accessibility
Trail paved
Parking
Interpretive information
Picnic area

Fees and Regulations
Open dawn to dusk
Pets on leash

Highlights
A great family place that combines active and passive recreation. Small wetland.

Public Transit
Tri-Met #96; depart bus at Sagert, walk east on Sagert about 1/2 mile.

Thomas Guide 685

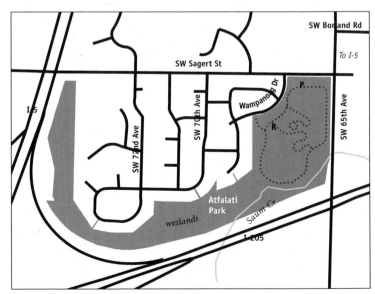

Moles and Gophers

Many small mammals build or at least use burrows, but moles and pocket gophers are our most highly specialized burrowers and common residents in urban orchards. Moles and gophers share features such as small eyes and ear openings, soft fur, cylindrical bodies, short but powerful forelimbs, small hindquarters, sensory hairs on snout and appendages, and solitary habits. They differ, however, in details of their form, digging styles, and diets.

Moles

Our large Townsend's mole has a long, tapering, flexible snout and extremely broad hands with out-turned palms and stout foreclaws. This species, which is well adapted to digging in heavy Willamette Valley soils, is the mole most likely to occur in local

orchards. Moles' dark, thick fur lies equally well in any direction, allowing easy forward and backward movement in their tunnels. They feed on many soil animals but prefer earthworms, and build two kinds of tunnels. Shallow tunnels are represented by winding ridges of soil pushed up by the mole as it forages. These tunnels are not reused by moles but may be used by other small animals. A mole's permanent home is an extensive system of tunnels and chambers one to two feet underground. Soil from this system is pushed up vertical shafts and accumulates on the surface as hemispherical mounds. Spring and summer are times of most digging activities as the tunnels are cleaned and extended and the spring's young are driven from their mother's burrows to establish their own homes.

Gophers

Pocket gophers have blunt snouts, down-turned hands with long claws, and strong, protruding, ever-growing incisors, which are used to loosen hard soil. Dirt is kept out of the mouth by furry lips, which close behind the incisors. A gopher's yellowish-to-black fur slopes toward the tail. To reverse direction in a tunnel, a gopher executes a vertical hairpin turn in which head and shoulders pass beneath and slightly beside the small pelvis. Gophers have external fur-lined cheek pouches, which are used to

carry the strictly vegetarian fare to underground storage chambers. Gophers dig extensive shallow tunnel systems while foraging, but their permanent homes are one to two feet underground. Soil from these tunnels is pushed to the surface through a slanting shaft and thrust out, forming a crescentic mound around the tunnel entrance, which is usually plugged with loosened soil. Of the two species of pocket gophers in the Portland area, the Camas pocket gopher is by far the larger and most likely to occur in urban orchards. The small western pocket gopher is more typical of mountains and foothills surrounding the Willamette Valley.

Looking at Their Good Side

Orchardists, gardeners, and groundskeepers dislike moles and gophers, but their digging tills the soil and their tunnels help air and water enter the soil. Moles consume many pestiferous soil invertebrates. Gophers reduce the numbers of dandelions and stimulate plant growth in established fields. Next time you see the tell-tale mounds and tunnels of these subterranean mammals, keep their positive contributions in mind.

By Richard B. Forbes

Tualatin River National Wildlife Refuge

The Tualatin River National Wildlife Refuge owes its existence to a visionary group of local citizens who recognized the value of natural areas to the community and future generations. Through a grassroots movement, the citizens conceived a plan to create an urban refuge. The Tualatin River National Wildlife Refuge—a jewel for wildlife in an urban setting—is an example of what individuals can accomplish when they take responsibility for their own place.

Traditionally, fish and wildlife agencies have focused most of their pro-active conservation efforts on lands and waters outside of urban areas. However, protection of these valuable habitats not only sustains the species that depend on them, but can also provide important public benefits such as open space, recreation, environmental education, aesthetics, flood storage, and water quality enhancement. Recognition of these issues culminated in 1991, when the work of Metro, local governments, conservation organizations, and citizens resulted in the initiation of a feasibility study to determine if a National Wildlife Refuge could be established in the Portland region. The Tualatin River National Wildlife Refuge is one of the major accomplishments that stemmed from that local support.

The Refuge was officially established in 1992, when a private landowner made a generous donation of 12 acres of property. Since that time, over a third of the 3,058 acres approved for purchase for the Refuge have been acquired (as of February 2000). The approved Refuge boundary straddles the urban growth boundary. Almost all of the targeted land had been modified for agriculture, and development in the vicinity has encroached upon adjacent floodplains and wetlands, resulting in habitat loss, increased pollution, and flood problems. The Refuge will allow for the protection, restoration, and enhancement of riverine floodplains and associated wetlands, riparian areas, and uplands adjacent to the Tualatin River from approximately river miles 22 to 23 and 13 to 20, and along Rock Creek. In addition, water rights included with land purchases will be used for restoration and the maintenance of streams and wetlands. A variety of migratory birds, resident fish and wildlife, threatened and endangered species, and the public will benefit from the management of these lands with a focus on natural resource values. One of the goals of a National Wildlife Refuge is the protection of endangered species. Bald eagles breed and winter on the Refuge.

Two high-priority areas of management emphasis are to restore native habitats associated with the Tualatin River floodplain and to provide wildlife-dependent public use which emphasizes environmental education and interpretation. Land acquisition and habitat restoration continue to dominate Refuge activities during these still-early stages of Refuge development. In 1998, the Refuge completed the first phase of

Location

Refuge Headquarters, 16340 SW Beef Bend Rd., Sherwood, Oregon, approximately 15 miles southwest of downtown Portland near the city of Sherwood. Most of the Refuge sits on the edge of the urban growth boundary, and along the Tualatin River.

Activities

The Refuge is not yet open to the public. Pre-arranged activities and special events are offered at this time. Areas will open once adequate parking, trails, and interpretive signage become available. Currently, the U.S. Fish and Wildlife Service works with groups like the Friends of the Refuge and Tualatin Riverkeepers to pre-arrange recreational activities such as canoe trips, bird watching, and revegetation projects. Look for special tours, events, and volunteer opportunities throughout the year. (For information, contact the Friends of the Tualatin River National Wildlife Refuge at 503-972-7714.)

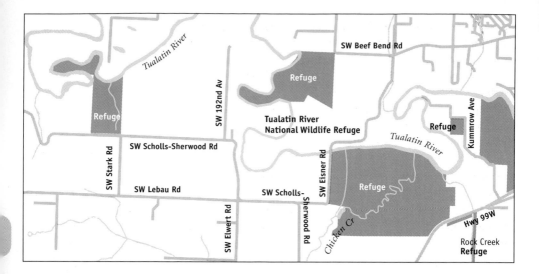

floodplain restoration on 400 acres of wetlands to enhance wildlife habitat, improve water quality, provide flood storage, and allow for the slow release of water back into the river. The U.S. Fish and Wildlife Service worked in partnership with the Bureau of Reclamation, Ducks Unlimited, and numerous volunteers to accomplish this project.

Natural Resources

Typical tree species of the forested riparian stands include red alder, Oregon ash, big-leaf maple, western red cedar, cottonwood, and Douglas fir. The shrub layer typically includes snowberry, ocean-spray, elderberry, vine maple, Oregon grape, willow species, spirea, rose species, red-osier dogwood, honeysuckle, Indian plum, Pacific dogwood, and cascara. Several invasive, non-native species, such as Himalayan blackberry, reed canarygrass, and Scot's broom, pose problems at the Refuge by competing with the native plants that provide higher quality and more diverse wildlife habitat. It is hoped that restoration projects will reduce the extent of encroachment by these invasive species.

During the wet season from fall through spring, the open water, wetlands, and floodplains provide habitat for thousands of migrating ducks, geese, tundra swans, and shorebirds that crowd onto the Refuge wetlands. Noisy flurries of flapping, feeding, and socializing bring the tranquil countryside alive, filling the air with raucous crescendos of quacking. Dominant ducks consist of northern pintail, mallard, and wigeon. Canada geese include dusky and cackling sub-species. The Refuge supports significant breeding populations of wood duck and hooded mergansers, and to a lesser extent, cinnamon teal and mallard. Common wading and shorebirds include killdeer, snipe, lesser yellowlegs, and spotted sandpiper. It is also a significant breeding area for neotropical migratory birds, such as the black-throated gray warbler, Wilson's warbler, western tanager, Swainson's thrush, and several species of swallows.

Mid-spring brings song and color to the Tualatin Valley. Feisty little warblers and other migratory songbirds literally burst onto the scene, arriving from their winter homes in Latin America. Yellowthroats, tanagers, juncos, song sparrows, grosbeaks, and red-winged blackbirds sing up a storm as the magic of spring graces the valley.

Threatened, endangered, and other at-risk species that frequent the area include peregrine falcon, bald eagle, Aleutian Canada goose, western pond turtle, and the northern red-legged frog. Listed and at-risk fish species that use the Tualatin River and tributary streams include winter steelhead, fall coho and spring chinook salmon, and resident cutthroat trout.

The woody riparian habitat and emergent marshes support mammals such as beaver, mink, river otters, and muskrats, as well as numerous small animals like deer mice. Many amphibians and reptiles such as Pacific treefrogs and garter snakes are also dependent upon these habitats. The forests are home to upland passerine birds in addition to those dependent upon water edges such as green-backed and great blue herons, belted kingfishers, wood ducks, winter wrens, and varied thrush. Hawks and owls roost and nest in these forests. Deer graze the marsh and pasture grasses.

Interesting geological and biological features occur on the Refuge due to the effects of the Missoula Floods. This series of catastrophic flood events took place between 11,000 and 18,000 years ago, and created the Tonquin Scablands located between Sherwood and Tualatin. Soils in portions of this area are extremely thin, with barren exposures of basalt rock due to the scouring caused by the flood waters. These conditions support relatively drought-resistant plants that are unusual for this area of Washington County. Evidence of Tonquin Scablands within the Refuge can be seen in scoured bedrock knolls and channel walls along Rock Creek, and by plant communities dominated by the less common Oregon white oak and Pacific madrone.

Water

The Tualatin River is designated by the Oregon Department of Environmental Quality as "water quality limited." Pollution problems are compounded by relatively impervious soils and a high, unconfined groundwater table throughout the Tualatin Valley. In the spring and winter, the groundwater occurs at a depth less than ten feet under much of the valley, and ranges from 15 to 30 feet in the summer and fall. However, significant groundwater level declines have been documented.

Fees and Regulations
Not yet open to the public

Highlights
In May, a portion of the Refuge is opened to the public for the annual Migratory Songbird Festival. (For information, contact the Refuge headquarters at 503-590-5811.) A stunning view of Mt. Hood looms from various vantage points on the Refuge.

The Tonquin Scablands (located between Tualatin and Sherwood) are a unique geologic relic from the Missoula Floods (a series of catastrophic flood events 11,000-18,000 years ago). Scouring caused by the floodwaters left soils extremely thin with barren exposures of basalt rock. Evidence of the Scablands within the Refuge can be seen in scoured bedrock knolls and channel walls along Rock Creek, and in plant communities dominated by the less common Oregon white oak and Pacific madrone.

The Refuge's first restoration project has been to turn a large-operation dairy farm back into permanent and seasonal wetlands. Chicken Creek, which had been straightened out and used as a runoff ditch, is once again a meandering, naturally flowing creek.

Public Transit
When the Refuge opens to the public, the main entrance at Hwy. 99 will be accessible by city buses that currently run along that route.

Thomas Guide 684

Cultural Resources & History

The first people of the Tualatin were the *Atfalati*, a tribe of the Kalapuyan Indians. *Atfalati* was also their name for the river which eventually became *Tualatin*. The Kalapuyan hunted with bows of yew wood, fished with woven traps, and gathered plants and berries, a lifestyle they continued as the first white settlers began arriving in the early 1800s.

Historic accounts indicate that the Tualatin Valley, especially the area around the Refuge's Wapato Lake Unit, supported at least 20 native Kalapuyan winter villages, which eventually disappeared as settlers homesteaded the lowlands for farms, mainly growing hay, grain, and onions, and using fields to graze livestock. Wapato, a tuberous plant traditionally harvested by the Indians as an important food source, is being considered for replanting as part of the effort to restore native vegetation on the Refuge.

Access

To be determined, but the main access will likely be located off of Hwy. 99 just north of the Tualatin-Sherwood Rd.

How to Get There

The Refuge headquarters can be reached from either I-5 or State Hwy. 217 by taking the exit for Hwy. 99 westbound. Drive through Tigard until and turn right onto Beef Bend Rd. Continue for approximately 3 miles until the road makes a sharp 90-degree curve to the right. Go straight at this curve into the driveway of the headquarters office.

By Jennifer Thompson and Nancy Pollot

For more information: Tualatin River National Wildlife Refuge, Tualatin Riverkeepers, or Friends of the Tualatin River NWR, see Resources.

Tualatin Hills Nature Park

Tualatin Hills Nature Park is an extraordinarily diverse urban greenspace. Its nearly 220 acres of marshes, meadows, ponds, creeks, and forested wetlands and uplands have been influenced for thousands of years by disturbances caused by humans, first through fire, and later through logging, farming, grazing, the installation of sewer lines, and most recently the development of a permanent trail system and Interpretive Center. Despite these disturbances, the Nature Park retains much of the biodiversity indigenous to the Tualatin Valley. For thousands of years, the area where the Nature Park is now located was used by native Indian tribes of hunters and gatherers. They intentionally set fires to maintain meadows for better foraging opportunities. These people lived off what the land provided until the first settlers arrived in the mid-1800s. A family from Maine, John and Lydia Elliot, with their ten children, arrived in 1850 to stake claim to a 640-acre parcel which included the current Nature Park site. John died shortly after arriving in Oregon, and a few ancient apple trees are the only visible evidence of their homestead. In 1859 the property was purchased by the Catholic Church and in 1891 it was used by the Church to provide a home for boys in need—St. Mary's Home for Boys. The site is still known as "St. Mary's Woods" to some people. For the next 50 years the property underwent many changes: it was actively farmed by the boys' home until the 1940s for carrots, strawberries, cabbages, and onions; Beaverton Creek was ditched; a large herd of cattle grazed the site; and sections of the park were logged.

Despite all this past disturbance, in 1975 the land was identified by the City of Beaverton as a regional park site. A few years later, a citizens' committee was formed to promote acquisition of the site for preservation, and in 1980 a bond measure passed that allowed for the purchase of most of the property that makes up the Nature Park today. In 1994 another bond measure provided funds to develop the trail system. In addition, the construction of an interpretive center was also funded. The Nature Park Interpretive Center opened in 1998 and offers environmental education classes, a Nature Store, a reference library, and an interpretive display that explains the region's ecology, habitats, and watershed. New classrooms opened in spring of 2001.

The Nature Park can be artificially divided into several sections based upon habitat type or physical separation from each other via Beaverton or Cedar Mill Creek. The five main sections of the park are the Big Fir Woods, the Wildlife Preserve Area, the North Woods, the West Woods and the South Woods. The main trail from the Interpretive Center first leads you through the most recently logged area of the park, filled with a dense brushy re-growth of ocean-spray, California hazel, and wild rose.

Location
15655 SW Millikan Blvd.

Activities
Hiking
Biking
Wildlife viewing

Facilities
Toilets
Wheelchair accessibility:
    paved and unpaved trails
Parking
Interpretive center
Interpretive information
    (brochures, signs, maps,
    newsletter, environmental
    education program)
Picnic area

Fees and Regulations
Open dawn to dusk
No pets
Bikes restricted to paved
    trails only, must obey
    speed and helmet
    regulations

Highlights
The Nature Park
Interpretive Center opened
in 1998 and offers
environmental education
classes, a Nature Store, a
reference library, and an
interpretive display that
explains the region's
ecology, habitats, and
watershed.

Big Fir Woods

The change in light, temperature, and vegetation is dramatic when the trail enters the Big Fir Woods, the most mature forest found in the park. A walk through these shady glens often gives the stroller an opportunity to eavesdrop on pileated woodpeckers and winter wrens. These birds take advantage of the habitat provided by Douglas fir, western red cedar, and grand fir close to 100 years of age. Indianpipe, a fascinating and easy-to-recognize plant because of its lack of chlorophyll, can be found near some of the trails through the Big Fir Woods. Adjacent to the Big Fir Woods is the Big Pond, where you may find waterfowl, great blue and green herons, turtles, nutria, beaver, river otter, mink, and muskrat. Search the shrubs and grasses nearby for songbirds. In late summer, blooms of one of the largest stands of wapato left in the Tualatin Valley can be seen at the water's edge.

West Woods

Beaverton Creek separates the West Woods from the rest of the Nature Park, but a bridge allows access to this isolated chunk of the park. A grove of western red cedar makes a visit to this area worthwhile.

Tracks left along the muddy banks of Beaverton Creek near the Cougar Trail have been verified by experts as the footprints of cougar, confirming at least their occasional use of urban creeks as travel corridors. Belted kingfishers and red-breasted nuthatches are easily observed permanent residents of this section of the park.

In late summer, at the edge of Big Pond, blooms of one of the largest stands of wapato left in the Tualatin Valley can be seen. Along the muddy banks of Beaverton Creek near Cougar Trail, cougar footprints have been sighted. Lily Pond is one of the most pristine areas of the park and an important breeding habitat for sensitive native amphibians such as the northern red-legged frog and northwestern salamander.

Public Transit

There is a MAX light rail stop that provides immediate access to the northwest entrance of the park. Tri-Met #67 runs to the Merlo Garage, which is adjacent to the northwest entrance as well. The Interpretive Center is a short walk down Millikan Blvd. from the West Beaverton Park and Ride at 160th Ave. and Tualatin Valley Highway.

Thomas Guide 594/624

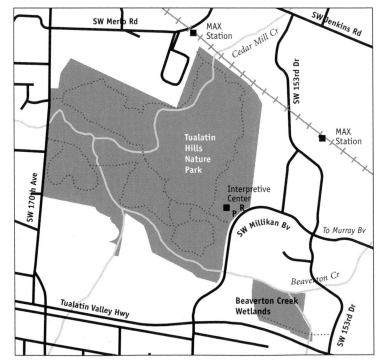

North Woods

The North Woods refers to the area of the park north of Beaverton and Cedar Mill Creeks. A walk through these woods is especially rewarding in the spring. You will be serenaded by a chorus of Swainson's thrush as you walk. Look for clumps of the rare sessile trillium along the trail. Unlike the more conspicuous western trillium, commonly seen in our forests, the sessile trillium has a much smaller flower attached immediately above the three dark, leathery, maroon mottled leaves. Cottonwoods add a sweet scent to the air and downy woodpeckers are busy in the Oregon oak and ponderosa pine that are abundant. A section of the trail follows the bed of an old wagon road and passes through a forested wetland of Oregon ash and slough sedge. The North Woods also contain the Lily Pond. This seasonal pond is one of the most pristine areas of the park and an important breeding habitat for sensitive native amphibians such as the northern red-legged frog and northwestern salamander. The surrounding ash forest attracts cedar waxwings and black-headed grosbeaks in addition to lots of warblers.

South Woods

(Editor's addition) At the time the District purchased the park land from the Archdiocese of Portland one of the few access points was an eroded, muddy path in the future nature park's southwest corner. Twenty-one years later a citizen-led campaign resulted in the purchase of the 22-acre inholding by Metro and THPRD. What was once the last remaining "hole" in the park now boasts a soft-surface, bark-chip loop trail that was constructed by the same citizen volunteers who helped make the park whole.

"Perched" wetlands throughout the south woods result in an unusual juxtaposition of dry-site trees, like ponderosa pine and white oak, immediately adjacent to wetland species, like ash and black cottonwood. Indian plum, hazlenut and sword fern dominate the scrub-shrub understory. During migration hordes of warblers, siskins, finches, and tanagers can be heard singing from the tree canopy. And, for reasons that are not entirely clear, this is one of the surest places in the region to hear the mellifluous, rolling song of the Purple Finch. Red-tailed hawks nest in the forest adjacent to Beaverton Creek. Their unique, high-pitched cry can be heard almost anytime of the year, although during early summer the insistent screeching of their hungry young drown out the adults.

Wildlife Preserve Area

If you enter the park via the Merlo Road entrance, look along the side of the trail for large boulders with images etched in them; these boulders, along with the bronze plaques embedded in the handrail of the boardwalk over the Cedar Mill Creek floodplain, and the hand-crafted "bird poles" installed in groups in several locations through the park, were installed with funds from the construction of the Westside Light Rail Project.

The trail leads along the edges of the Wildlife Preserve Area, a portion of the park that will remain without trails to provide a large area for wildlife to have sanctuary from human disturbance. Most of the area is made up of the cattail marsh, a large wetland where Cedar Mill Creek slows after its rush down from the West Hills and spreads out over a wide floodplain. Open water and clear vistas are not found here. Visitors must be content to listen for the abundant birdlife or look along the muddy wetland edges for signs of other wildlife, such as the abundant footprints of deer and raccoons or the gnawing marks of beaver. Great horned owls are often seen in the ponderosa pine and Oregon oak trees along the trail that skirts this area. Striped coral-root, an orchid, can be seen close to the trail. A short loop trail ventures under a set of power lines. This corridor was the most recent addition to the park, and the loop trail gives views of a mitigation project that is intended to provide breeding habitat for native amphibians, the northern red-legged frog in particular.

Access
The trails of the Tualatin Hills Nature Park can be accessed from several locations. The main entrance and the only parking area is off SW Millikan Blvd. Another formally signed entrance is near the Merlo/SW 158th Ave. light rail stop. There are two entrances off SW 170th Ave.

There are five miles of paved, graveled, and natural substrate trails for passive recreation and to allow individuals of all ages and physical abilities to enjoy the park. The trails are lined with many beautiful interpretive signs.

How to Get There
From the north take Murray Blvd. to SW Millikan Way. Turn right (west) on Millikan and proceed past SW 154th Terr., cross the railroad tracks and turn right into the Nature Park parking lot. From Tualatin Valley Highway turn north onto SW Millikan Way and proceed north until Millikan curves to the right. Foot access is via trails off SW 170th Ave. that borders the park's western boundary and from the Merlo light rail stop.

By Elayne Barclay

For more information: Tualatin Hills Nature Park Interpretive Center, see Resources.

Jordan Park

Cedar Mill Creek runs through more than 15 undeveloped acres of trees, shrubs, and other native plant life. The property was logged approximately 80 years ago and not replanted. Big-leaf maples and red alder now dominate, but there are several cedar, fir, and a few Oregon ash scattered throughout. More than three dozen bird species have been spotted here ranging from bushtits, hummingbirds, and winter wrens on the small end, to red-breasted sapsuckers, downy and hairy woodpeckers in the middle, and pileated woodpeckers and Cooper's hawks on the large end. Most of the trees are large and 70 to 80 years old. The shrub and ground cover layers have good native representation including nettles, trillium, Oregon grape, vine maple, salmonberry, and elderberry.

Access

All of the trails are unimproved dirt, mud, or grass, and conditions vary by season. The trails start at the end of NW 107th. The initial section, which has branches leading to the east and west, slopes gradually, but all of these paths become steep and difficult. There are also trees across the trail. Several of the trails scale down into raccoon trails and are nearly impassable by humans. The trails near the creek require boots most of the year. There are no bridges across the creek, but it can be crossed on rocks much of the summer or when there has been no rain for a week or two.

The park boundaries are not marked. Most private property surrounding the park is unfenced and semi-wild to wild and blends in with the park, so consideration with unleashed pets (and humans) is in order.

Location
3 blocks north of NW Cornell Rd. at the end of NW 107th.

Activities
Hiking

Facilities
Trail unpaved

Fees and Regulations
None

Highlights
Very rustic and unmanaged. Owls can be heard at night and some local residents have been lucky enough to spot the occasional flying squirrel gliding between the trees.

Public Transit
From the Sunset light rail transit center, take Tri-Met #60 to the intersection of NW 107th and Cornell Rd. Walk north on 107th for about 3 blocks to the park. Or Tri-Met #89 will get you as close as 113th and Cornell. Walk from there to NW 107th and then north on NW 107th for about 3 blocks to the park.

Thomas Guide 595

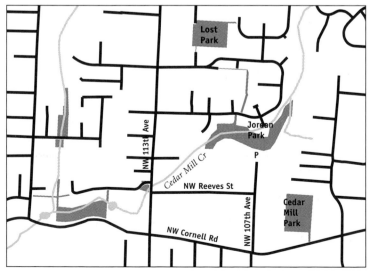

How to Get There

Take the Sunset Highway (Hwy. 26) to exit 68 (Cedar Hills Blvd.).
Take Cedar Hills Blvd. north to NW Cornell Rd. Turn right (east) on
NW Cornell Rd. Turn left (north) on NW 107th and proceed north
to the end of 107th.

By Bruce Godfrey

For more information: Tualatin Hills Park and Recreation District
(THPRD), see Resources. Contact the Natural Resources Office to get
a brochure with a map of the trails.

Cedar Mill Creek Watershed Watch has worked with park district and
local residents to clear non-native plants (primarly blackberries),
plant native trees and shrubs, and plant native willows for stream
bank stabilization, see Resources.

Fanno Creek Watershed

After receiving water from its Tualatin Mountain tributaries, Fanno Creek meanders 15 miles through residential, commercial, and industrial lands of west Portland, Beaverton, Tigard, and portions of Washington and Clackamas Counties. Its 32-square-mile watershed collects water from 117 miles of streams. Ash, Summer, Vermont, Ball, Woods, Sylvan, and Red Rock Creeks all contribute their flows to Fanno's main stem before it empties into the Tualatin River at Durham City Park. As with all our urban waterways, Fanno provides important scenic, wildlife, and recreational resources. Even cutthroat trout, though relatively few in number these days, remain in breeding populations, and steelhead were recently observed spawning in the lower reaches of Fanno. With more protection, restoration of channelized sections, and improved water quality, Fanno Creek could become one of the region's premier greenways.

Down Fanno Creek

Fanno's headwaters in Portland's West Hills flow through thickly wooded, mostly privately-owned residential properties. Here, where shade cools shallow, gravel-bottomed tributary streams, cutthroat trout still spawn. Postage-stamp wetlands, lush with skunk cabbage and lady-fern, remain here as well. A mile or so downstream, after paralleling Beaverton-Hillsdale Highway, Fanno takes its first plunge through massive underground culverts, resurfacing in Bauman Park, west of Oleson Road. While abuse is heaped on Fanno throughout its short run under the highway, it emerges into a huge wetland and riparian complex at Montclair Elementary School and flows, unfettered by culverts and development, through the Oregon Episcopal School marsh at Nicol Road. Extensive wetland and riparian habitats border Fanno Creek throughout this reach.

It's no accident that more than 140 species of birds, beaver, muskrat, nutria, and other wildlife can be found along Fanno between Oleson and Nicol Roads. The broad, wetland-rich floodplain is carpeted in spring and summer with yellow, pink, and purple wildflowers. Oregon ash and black cottonwood dominate the thick riparian zone and higher, drier islands of hawthorn provide a dense thicket for foraging and nesting wildlife.

Just downstream, after flowing through a narrow culvert, Fanno is again subjected to the ignominy shown all too may urban waterways. As it courses through the Portland Golf Club, Fanno is relegated to a sterile cement channel devoid of riparian vegetation and so strait-jacketed that all vestiges of the broad, fertile floodplain just a few feet upstream are eliminated. It isn't until Fanno reaches Vista Brook Park that it again resembles a natural stream.

Downstream of Vista Brook access to the creek is limited, although there are plans to put a trail here in the next few years. All along Allen Boulevard there are excellent views of western red cedar and Douglas fir which represent the most extensive riparian forest downstream of the Oregon Episcopal School marsh. Dense stands of skunk cabbage, horsetail, and lady-fern dominate the understory between Scholls Ferry Road and Highway 217.

From Denny Road to SW Hall Boulevard, Fanno Creek Park links the dense riparian corridor north of Hall Boulevard with marsh and open water habitats of Creekside Marsh and Greenway Park to the south of Hall. Both Koll Creekside Marsh, a small wildlife refuge to the east of Fanno, and the more manicured Greenway Park to the west parallel Fanno Creek between Hall and Scholls Ferry. Wildlife abounds in the upland, Douglas fir and big-leaf maple forest, emergent marsh, meadows, and riparian habitat at Creekside. Common mergansers, green-winged and cinnamon teal, common snipe, Virginia rail, sora, and mourning doves are common. Red-tailed hawks and great blue herons frequently roost in the Douglas fir forest on the marsh's eastern boundary.

Augustus Fanno, who drained much of the original wetlands to plant onions, built his New England-style house here in 1859. Occupied by the Fanno family until 1974, the homestead and surrounding 83 acres were purchased for an office park in 1979. The house and 14 acres, including a scenic stand of Garry oak and ponderosa pine, were then donated to the Tualatin Hills Park and Recreation District in the late 1980s. The old Fanno Farmhouse is now the meeting hall of the Fans of Fanno Creek, a grassroots citizen nonprofit organization dedicated to improving Fanno's water quality and habitat.

South of Greenway Park, Fanno Creek is carried through culverts under Scholls Ferry. To the west along Hiteon Creek are Englewood Park (City of Tigard) and Hart Lake (private), two important remnant wildlife habitats. Englewood Park has a small skunk cabbage marsh and numerous snags which harbor cavity-nesting birds. The Fans of Fanno Creek and Unified Sewerage Agency have undertaken extensive habitat improvement at Englewood Park just south of Scholls Ferry. Hart Lake provides open water, marsh, woodland, and riparian habitats. Further south, Summer Creek enters Fanno after flowing through the Reflections at Summer Creek Development and Summerlake Park. Fanno then flows into the Tualatin River just downstream from Cook Park at Durham City Park.

Adapted from "Fanno Creek, Urban Streams: Wetlands, Wildlife, Water Quality;" Aubudon Society of Portland

Oregon Episcopal School Marsh

The 16-acre Oregon Episcopal School (OES) marsh is nestled between two small knolls that flank Fanno Creek where the West Hills give way to the flat, broad Tualatin River floodplain. Fed mostly by springs and stormwater runoff from the adjacent Willowmere neighborhood, its open water and emergent marsh areas are home to over 100 species of birds and other wildlife. This wetland area was purchased by OES in 1985 to protect it from development and to provide an outdoor educational environment for the community.

The OES Marsh is in the historical floodplain of Fanno Creek and is part of a continuous riparian zone that extends east to Oleson Road. Due to increased urbanization and stormwater runoff, this stretch of Fanno Creek is deeply incised and is no longer directly connected to its historic floodplain. Several different plans over the last few years have been put forward to reconnect this stretch of the creek.

One of the most striking examples of the state of urban waterways can be seen at the bridge crossing of Nicol Road over Fanno Creek. To the east, a dense canopy of trees and shrubs, including Oregon ash, creek dogwood, and willows, provides an intact riparian zone. To the west, the creek becomes a concrete ditch as it flows for the next mile through the Portland Golf Club. Here, with no shade and with fairways that carry pesticides and herbicides to the creek, water quality takes a big hit.

Location
Just west of Oregon Episcopal School, 6300 SW Nicol Rd., on SW Nicol Rd. (north).

Activities
Wildlife viewing area

Facilities
Wheelchair accessible (along SW Nicol Rd.)
Trail unpaved

Fees and Regulations
None

Highlights
Beautiful floodplain marsh with open water and emergent vegetation. Intact riparian zone along much of Fanno Creek.

Public Transit
Tri-Met #56 on SW Scholls Ferry Rd.

Thomas Guide 625

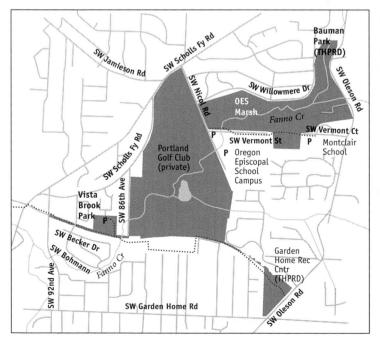

Although the views from Nicol Road are fantastic, a short walk to a small blind provides a quiet experience for watching and listening. No permission is needed to use the blind. Access beyond this point requires permission from OES. The school also owns a small wetland just off SW Oleson Road across from Hideaway Park (THPRD) that has produced Virginia rail and other marsh birds. The access road to OES's tennis center provides access to what is one of the most pristine wetlands, from a native vegetation perspective, in the watershed.

Listen for the distinctive call of sora, a small chicken-like marsh bird that sounds like a horse whinnying.

No outing to the marsh would be complete, however, without a stroll down SW Vermont to Montclair School, to the east of OES. Fortunately, Vermont is still discontinuous between the OES campus and SW Oleson Road. Partway down this still-graveled, dead-end section of Vermont, you can access the OES sports field through a break in the trees and shrubs. Continue east, staying to the edge of the fields, until you pass through a band of Douglas fir and hawthorn trees onto the Montclair Elementary School fields. You can continue on this route to SW Oleson Road; the marsh is the extensive floodplain to your left (north). The tree-lined route is great for purple and house finches, Bewick's wrens, and wintering fox, golden-crowned, and song sparrows. Cedar waxwings and robins are abundant during fall and winter on the red-fruited hawthorn trees that dot Fanno's floodplain.

This route is also an alternative way to get to the OES marsh if you happen to be on bicycle or foot from SW Oleson Road. You cannot drive this route since Vermont does not connect with SW Nicol Road. You can park at Montclair Elementary, however.

Access
SW Nicol Rd., just off SW Scholls Ferry Rd. It's best to just park along Nicol Rd. or at the small turnout just north of SW Vermont (a dead-end unpaved road that provides access along the west side of the OES athletic fields).

How to Get There
From Beaverton-Hillsdale Hwy. head south on SW Scholls Ferry Rd. and turn left (south) onto SW Nicol Rd., which dead-ends at Oregon Episcopal School campus.

By John LeCavalier

For more information: Oregon Episcopal School, see Resources.

Vista Brook Park

When I taught at Oregon Episcopal School during the late 1970s, one of our favorite cross-country and track workouts was to run down SW Scholls Ferry Road (probably only a lunatic would do such a thing these days) and through a little-known bower-covered trail to the western edge of the Portland Golf Club. From there we'd scale a barbed wire-topped, chain-link fence and lope back to the OES campus along the old abandoned interurban rail line, always on the lookout for errant golf balls and groundskeepers.

Vista Brook is classified as a wildlife park, although the athletically-minded naturalist can combine some hoops and a set or two of tennis or flip a frisbee on the large grassy area that's also a nice picnic spot. Meanwhile, kids can play on the children's play set. Thick willows that now nearly block the view of the pond are the best place to look for black-headed grosbeaks, cedar waxwings, western wood-pewees, Bewick's wrens, and warbling vireos during the late spring and early summer. The brushy trail margins are excellent for overwintering sparrows the rest of the year.

The trail immediately to the south of the park is an ADA-compliant, fully accessible trail that serves as a critical link in the Willamette-to-Tualatin Fanno Creek Greenway trail. It provides access to the west, across Fanno Creek and south of the Portland Golf Club all the way to THPRD's Garden Home Recreation Center on SW Garden Home Road. To the east the trail is complete as far as SW Allen Boulevard. From there, until new trail segments are constructed, most likely along Fanno Creek, the next publicly accessible trail is south of SW Denny Road to the west of Highway 217.

Access
The park may be accessed via a wood chip trail off SW 92nd at SW Allen Blvd. or from the west off SW 86th.

How to Get There
The best access if you are driving is from SW 88th, which is south off SW Scholls Ferry Rd. The park may be accessed from either the east or west via a newly constructed, ADA-compliant asphalt path. *See map on page 213*

By Mike Houck

For more information: Tualatin Hills Park and Recreation District (THPRD) or City of Tigard Parks, see Resources.

Location
SW 88th Ave. off SW Scholls Ferry Rd.

Activities
Hiking
Wildlife viewing area
Basketball courts
Tennis courts
Children's playground
Large grassy area, perfect for frisbees and picnics

Facilities
Wheelchair accessible (only to pond)
Paved and unpaved trail
Parking
Picnic area

Fees and Regulations
None

Highlights
Small pond harboring wood ducks and green heron, and future important Fanno Creek Greenway Trail access.

Public Transit
Tri-Met #56 stops on the west side of SW Scholls Ferry Rd. across from SW 88th Ave. If you want to walk from the Garden Home Recreation Center on Oleson you can catch Tri-Met #45 which stops at the corner of Garden Home and Oleson Rds.

Thomas Guide 625

A Bee? Or Not a Bee?

A great many flies and other insects as unlikely as moths, beetles, and true bugs masquerade as winged stingers. The real bees and wasps are known as *models*, while their look-alikes are *mimics*. Predators that munch a model will quickly learn to associate the color patterns and behaviors of such insects with an unpleasant experience of the palate! Thus, "wannabees" of various other insect orders gain protection by looking and acting similarly. This sheep-in-wolf's-clothing ploy is called Batesian mimicry, after the late Henry Walter Bates, an observant English naturalist. One could hardly blame the uninitiated urban naturalist, however, for being duped!

Flies . . . Master Mimics

Flower and hover flies (Syrphidae family) are masters of disguise. One species even sounds like a wasp, with a wingbeat nearly identical in frequency to its model. These flies share yet another quality with their weapon-wielding counterparts, being important pollinators of flowering plants.

The dronefly, *Eristalis tanax*, is a dead ringer for a honeybee, except for having only two wings (as all flies have) to the bee's four. There are also subtle differences in antennae, eyes, and other anatomy. Dronefly larvae are aquatic, scavenging bottom sediments in shallow pools. Known as rat-tailed maggots, they breathe through a telescoping appendage that connects them to the surface.

A convincing bumblebee impostor is the bulb fly, *Merodon equestris*, the immatures of which feed in the hearts of bulbs and are occasional pests of narcissus. Other species' larvae, on the other hand, are beneficial. Green with yellow stripes, the large syrphid larva is well camouflaged as it inches along stems searching out aphids to eat.

The bumblebee costume of some robber flies (family Asilidae) serves a dual purpose, protecting them from assault while making them appear harmless to their prey. This aggressive mimicry is practiced by *Laphria astur*, which may be found in sun-splotched woodlands, where it perches on logs to wait for a passing meal. A sharp, stout beak delivers the lethal bite. Female flies lay their eggs in the bark of rotting logs and stumps, and the larvae bore within, feeding on decaying vegetable matter and other insects.

Besides impersonating bees, the fuzzy bee flies of the family Bombyliidae parasitize them. A female bee fly will seek the burrow of a solitary bee species, hover over the entrance and, with the flick of her abdomen, lob eggs down the hole. If the bomber misses her target, a persistent newly hatched larva will crawl down the tunnel and into a cell. There it may feed on the nectar and pollen stored for the bee's offspring. It then transforms into a sedentary maggot that feasts on the larval or pupal bee. Eventually, an adult fly emerges, taking to the air and sipping nectar through a long, straw-like beak. The large bee fly, *Bombylius major*, is common around barren patches of soil, where its hosts excavate their nests.

"I've Got You Under My Skin" could be the theme song of animals plagued by the parasitic Cuterebridae, or robust bot flies. The adults are large insects that closely resemble bumblebees. The maggots, or bots, live in rabbits and other rodents, feeding just under the skin. They ultimately exit the host to pupate in the soil. The adult flies have no mouthparts, their activity being fueled solely by the nourishment imbibed by the larvae. These are supposedly rare insects, but look for them in the south fill at Oaks Bottom, where a large rodent population sustains a fair number of bots.

Moth Mimics

Flies do not have a monopoly on the mimicry game. Take the Sesiidae, or clearwing moths, for example. The narrow, transparent wings and waspish body clad in black and yellow scales are a totally convincing imitation of a yellowjacket. The similarity is reinforced by their day-flying, flower-feeding habits. The caterpillars are borers, feeding in roots, stems, or the wood of various plants. Two years are often required to complete development, culminating with the eruption of a new moth from the pupal case, poking like a periscope from the branch, trunk, or cane.

One member of the family Sphingidae is a bumblebee fraud. It carries off the hoax with clear, narrow wings, fuzzy black and olive-yellow body, and rather clumsy flight. The bumblebee sphinx moth, *Hemaris diffinis*, frequents the flowers of vetch and other legumes, while its caterpillar feeds on the snowberry.

When a Beetle Is a Bee

An insect of a totally different order, the beetle, also travels incognito. Believe it or not, the scarab beetle, *Lichnanthe rathvoni*, is a stunning bumblebee mimic in three color combinations: yellow and black, orange and black, or all black. Their dense coat of long hairs and powerful flight belie their true identities. Look for them cruising along sandbars and along the shores of major rivers. The grubs live underground, feeding on decaying leaves and other debris, taking a leisurely three years to reach maturity.

Some kinds of longhorn beetles, family Cerambycidae, pass themselves off as wasps. The flower-loving *Anoplodera crassipes* is a good counterfeit of a yellowjacket, and the slender species of *Necydalis* have short wing covers, the better to expose their membranous hindwings. Longhorn grubs bore in dead or dying timber.

Bugs and Bees

Even true bugs of the order Hemiptera can pull off a hoax. The broad-headed bugs of the family Alydidae actually mimic two different insects. As wingless nymphs crawling on the ground they easily pass for carpenter ants. In the adult state, they look like spider wasps, flying actively and, when at rest, flicking their wings and bobbing their antennae, just like the real McCoy! Throughout life they use their beaks to feed on the juice of weeds and flowers.

Scientists are quick to point out that any similarities between models and mimics are probably coincidences of evolution, but it is tempting to think that mimics know exactly what they are doing. After all, in nature, imitation is more than the sincerest form of flattery... it's a strategy for survival!

By Eric R. Eaton

Koll Center Wetlands

Although it is better known these days as Creekside Marsh, THPRD calls the 13-acre wetland Koll Center Marsh, after the Koll Construction Company which proposed to fill it in the early 1980s for development. Fortunately, this land use battle had a relatively happy ending. Once it was established that the marsh could not be filled, Creekside Corporate Park took form on the upland areas and the marsh was preserved, more or less intact. Unfortunately, saving the marsh's extensive wetland area did not keep it pristine. All the lush, forest-green bulrush, sedges, and cattails have been lost to an invasive reed canarygrass mat, the all too common result of urban stormwater that has disrupted the normal hydrology. That said, Creekside Marsh is still aesthetically pleasing and wildlife-rich.

It's good birding any time of year. During winter the marsh is full of wintering waterfowl, including hooded and common merganser, gadwall, American and the occasional Eurasian wigeon, wood duck, divers like ring-necked duck and bufflehead, and the omnipresent mallard. Belted kingfisher frequently patrol the marsh margins looking for tiny sculpin, or sit patiently on the many snags that ring the wetland. In recent years great blue herons have taken up residence in the forest stand of Oregon white oak and Douglas fir that ring the parking lot at Creekside VI. There's no better place to view herons nesting from the time they begin courtship and nest rebuilding in mid-February until the young fledge or leave the nests in late June. There is a nicely designed kiosk with interpretive signs at Creekside VI that affords excellent, elevated views of both the wetlands and herons. The office managers at Creekside V, just north of Creekside VI, more often than not allow eager birders access to the balcony overlooking the marsh.

The best views are from the grassy knoll at the marsh's south end. From this vantage you have an overview of the entire marsh system. It is a very short walk here from Creekside VI. Although their usual perching snag has long since rotted away, red-tailed hawks can routinely be seen wheeling over the short-grass meadows between the marsh and Fanno Greenway Park or hanging idly in the breeze over the great blue heron nesting colony. The red-tails have nested near the herons some years, and sometimes strafe the heron nests. In recent years great egrets spend winter and early spring in the marsh, where herons are frequently seen chasing these newcomers off their mud flats.

Near the tennis courts on the north side of the marsh, there are great views of tree and violet-green swallows that have taken to the artificial nesting boxes that have been placed on poles throughout the shallower-water wetland margins. Common snipe, a secretive shorebird that also feeds on the mud flats with their stout-billed

Location
South of SW Hall Blvd. and west of Hwy. 217 at Creekside Corporate Park

Activities
Hiking
Biking
Wildlife viewing area
Tennis courts
Volleyball sand court

Facilities
Wheelchair accessible (on Greenway Trail only and parking lots next to Creekside V, Creekside VI, and Creekside Corporate Park, main campus)
Trail paved
Parking
Interpretive information (kiosk with signs)
Picnic area

Fees and Regulations
Pets on leash

Highlights
Simply put, it's one of the most beautiful urban wetlands in the region and the largest marsh in Beaverton. The forest at Creekside VI office building on the east side of the marsh has a new great blue heron nesting colony in the Douglas firs. The adjacent Fanno Greenway trail provides access up and down Fanno Creek.

Public Transit
Tri-Met #78 on Hall Blvd.

Thomas Guide 625

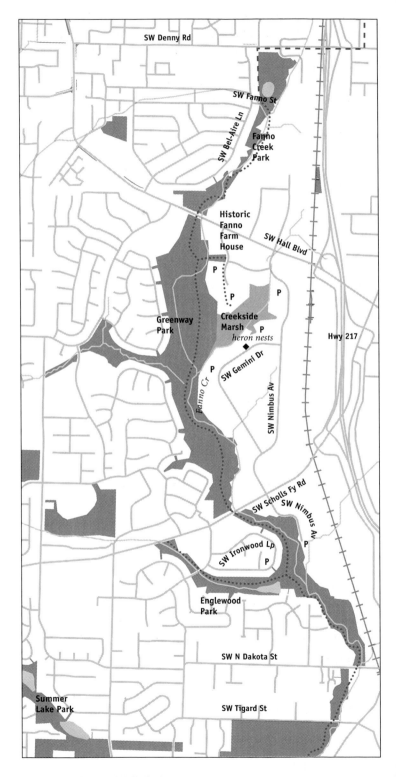

SW Denny Rd

SW Fanno St

SW Bel-Aire Ln

Fanno Creek Park

Historic Fanno Farm House

SW Hall Blvd

P

P

P

Greenway Park

Creekside Marsh

heron nests

P

Hwy 217

P

SW Gemini Dr

Fanno Cr

SW Nimbus Av

SW Scholls Fy Rd

SW Nimbus Av

SW Ironwood Lp

P

P

Englewood Park

SW N Dakota St

Summer Lake Park

SW Tigard St

brethren, the dowitcher and sandpipers, are seen here, although more often they are flushed in the short meadow wetland between the open water and Fanno Creek. The tennis court fence is usually adorned with flocks of mourning doves.

To fulfill the conditions imposed on the Koll Construction Company as mitigation for development around and, in the case of the parking lots, in the marsh, the wetland was donated to THPRD along with funds to construct a small dam to control the marsh's water level so that mud flats are exposed during the migratory season to provide shallow, muddy feeding areas for migratory shorebirds and waterfowl. Indeed, it is possible to see voracious, flight-starved dowitchers, least sandpipers, western sandpipers, spotted sandpipers, and other shorebirds gorging on microscopic prey during the early spring and fall.

Access

The 13-acre marsh can be accessed from several directions. From the Fanno Greenway Park trail the marsh is accessed via a footbridge just south of SW Hall Blvd. Cross the footbridge and walk uphill through the Oregon white oak grove past the historic Fanno Farmhouse (home to Fans of Fanno Creek and owned by THPRD). Turn right and walk south through the office park to the tennis courts and volleyball sand court just south of the extensive parking lot.

The most spectacular views are from the grassy knoll at the marsh's south end. To get there, if you are driving, continue up the short hill on SW Nimbus and turn right onto SW Gemini. Proceed to the first parking area past Creekside VI and turn right into the parking lot. From this vantage you have an overview of the entire marsh system. It is a very short walk here from Creekside VI.

How to Get There

If you are coming from the north, take the Progress exit off Hwy. 217 and head west on SW Hall Blvd. Turn left (south) at the first traffic light after crossing the railroad tracks, onto SW Nimbus. You can either turn into the main Creekside Corporate Park campus and make your way to the north side of the marsh and park behind the buildings or continue south on SW Nimbus to either Creekside V or VI, both of which provide excellent views from the east side of the marsh.

By Mike Houck

For more information: Tualatin Hills Park and Recreation District (THPRD), see Resoures.

A Hoover Hog by any other name: The Opossum

Opossum vital statistics: Length—25" to 40"; Tail—10" to 21"; Weight—4lbs. to 14lbs.

The opossum has 50 teeth, more than any other North American mammal.

Opossum young are born after a gestation period of only 13 days. Following birth they must make their way to their mother's pouch where they remain, attached to a nipple, for two months until they are fully developed.

The opossum has a prehensile tail which it uses for climbing and carrying nesting material. It is strong enough to support the opossum's full weight for a short time.

In spring, the thoughts of Portland's residents for many years have turned to opossums, for it is then that they have been most frequently observed. Unfortunately, most of the opossums we see at this time are dead, having perished in an unsuccessful effort to cross the street. But despite their notorious unwillingness to stop, look, and listen, we don't seem ready to run out of opossums quite yet. It must be admitted, however, that their numbers appear to have dwindled in recent years, and although no conclusive explanation has emerged, automobiles for once appear to be off the hook. There is, however, a rather suspicious correlation between the decline of opossums and the rise in the population of urban raccoons. But despite their decline, it is amazing that animals with brain cases one-seventh the size of a raccoon's can survive at all in the fast lane of city life.

In delving into opossum survival skills, one thing that immediately emerges is that they will eat almost anything—even bits of inedible rubbish have been found in their stomachs. This is not to say that they don't have favorite foods. Fruits, seeds, and bulbs make up a large part of their diet. They also seem fond of invertebrates such as earthworms, snails, and slugs. In the city, pet food attracts them. So does garbage, although this bears qualifying. Many believe that urban opossums gorge themselves at dump sites and unattended garbage cans, but one study of Portland's opossums discovered that garbage made up less than 10% of their diet. By far the most commonly eaten food of our urban population turned out to be mammal flesh. As the opossum has little skill at hunting, it is presumed that the bulk of this was scavenged from road kills. It turns out that they will even eat other, less fortunate, roadside opossums.

Our mild climate also favors this remarkable animal's ability to exist in Portland. Although opossums have expanded their range quite far north, they don't always do well in regions of extreme cold, frequently succumbing to frostbite where the mercury spends a lot of time below freezing.

The city opossum worries little about predators. Most of its natural enemies—foxes, bobcats, great horned owls, and 'possum hunters—are rare or absent in its habitat, although urban coyotes no doubt eat opossum, and dogs will also take one occasionally. But perhaps the most important reason for the opossum's survival is its spectacular reproductive rate. A single female may rear up to 13 young at one time, and evidence suggests that breeding may take place three times annually in our temperate climate. This would make each female capable of adding nearly 40 opossums to the population each year. Litter sizes are usually closer to eight, which still leaves an impressive reproductive capacity. Why their fecundity hasn't maintained their historically high numbers is something of a mystery right now.

The opossum has done so well in Portland that it would be natural to assume it has been here since the beginning, but it is actually a very recent addition to the fauna of the Pacific Northwest. All of the New World marsupials originated in South America, and it is there—and in Central America—that most of them remain. Of its order, only the Virginia opossum (*Didelphis virginiana*) ventured north of the border, and at the time of the European settlement it was restricted to the southeastern quarter of the country where it resided in streamside woodlands, and figured in the diet of Indians and settlers alike. Since then it has dramatically extended its range north- and westward, following the spread of civilization.

The Pacific Northwest population, however, is not part of this natural westward expansion. Our opossums were brought here by humans. The earliest recorded instance of an opossum's release in Oregon dates from around 1910. In the following decade a half dozen or so more were released—enough, some early investigators thought, to establish a population. But it was not until the 1930s that the population explosion began. At that time, numerous Civilian Conservation Corps workers from the southeast brought these animals with them (perhaps as a food source). By the time the CCC was terminated, many of these had escaped or been released, providing the base of the Oregon population. Even so, it was not until the early 1950s that opossums took up residence in Portland where by now, of course, they have become a fixture.

So what does the future hold for opossums in the city? There is no reason to believe that they will entirely disappear in Portland, even if they don't return to their former prominence in our neighborhoods—and our roads. They've already learned all they need to know about obtaining food and shelter, and who knows, in time, they may learn how to avoid automobiles as well. In the meantime, we can only wait to see if their brisk reproductive rate will keep the city well supplied.

Some naturalists regret that opossums were ever introduced to the Northwest and welcome the news of their lower numbers. But it's a little early to applaud their demise. It's likely that, for better or worse and despite their dwindling numbers, opossums are here to stay. Meanwhile, our time might be better spent in observation, trying to answer some of the numerous questions about the opossum's life in the city, and above all simply enjoying this visitor from the wild.

By Bob Wilson

The opossum is the only marsupial in North America.

Besides monkeys and humans, the opossum is the only animal with an opposable digit. The rear foot has an opposable toe, allowing the opossum to grasp branches and climb trees with ease.

The opossum will frequently respond to aggression by "playing 'possum." In this behavior it will collapse into an involuntary catatonic state, which usually induces the attacker to abandon the "corpse."

"Opossum" is the Algonquian name for the animal as rendered into English by Captain John Smith. It is also known in some parts of the country as the Hoover Hog.

Summerlake Park

Summerlake Park is a 24-acre community park dedicated to the city as a condition of development of the Summer Lake and Ari Green subdivisions. The park includes a small, two-acre grove of Douglas fir, red cedar, and deciduous trees.

An old, still-standing, rotted-out Douglas fir, riddled with what appear to be decade-old pileated woodpecker cavities, stands sentinel to what must have once been spectacular forested habitat, but is now a series of impoundments surrounded by residential neighborhoods. Nonetheless, Summerlake is a highly used park and natural area for residents who literally surround the park. Getting there for a non-resident, however, requires circumnavigation of a confusing network of roads that encircle the park.

From what used to be a free-flowing stream and a major tributary to Fanno Creek, Summer Creek has been transformed into two large ponds, the upper one of which is surrounded by paved paths and crossed by bridges. Efforts are now underway by Unified Sewerage Agency to diversify the reed canarygrass-dominated habitat and to plant more trees and shrubs at the margins of the lakes. There are also emerging plans to replace the culvert under SW 121st, at the park's extreme downstream border, and replace an old dam to allow for fish passage. The recent sighting of a 22-inch cutthroat trout makes an even stronger case for returning Summer Creek to a free-flowing urban stream.

Local residents have fought these efforts in order to preserve their views and what they perceive to be a "beautiful" park. However, if park and local stormwater agencies are successful in putting together a decent restoration plan, which would include returning the stream to seasonal inundation so that waterfowl would flourish in the winter and stream temperatures would be reduced in the summer, Summerlake Park and the wildlife that use it would benefit greatly.

In the meantime, the Summerlake ponds and adjacent western red cedar and ash forest provide some of the best remnant wildlife habitat in this residential neighborhood.

The lakes are rimmed with a paved, wheelchair-accessible path. During the winter, the lakes are filled with waterfowl. The forest adds significantly to the habitat diversity of the park and hosts species you'd expect to find in a mixed coniferous and deciduous forest. The bridge to the south affords a beautiful view across the larger of the two lakes.

While you might assume an artificial and highly regulated pond system would have very little wildlife, a group of senior birders from Audubon's monthly "magpie" group were astonished to see a sora being escorted by wigeons that paddled convoy-like on either side of it until they all reached the safety of one of the upper pond's islands.

Location
Tucked in among cul-de-sacs off SW Glacier Lily and SW Winter Lake Dr., south of SW Scholls Ferry Rd.

Activities
Hiking
Biking
Wildlife viewing area

Facilities
Wheelchair accessible
Paved and unpaved trail
Parking (on street)

Fees and Regulations
Open dawn to dusk
Pets on leash

Highlights
Huge, open-water ponds or lakes with an adjacent red cedar forest. The only remaining Greenspace in this densely developed residential area.

Public Transit
Tri-Met #62 on SW Scholls Ferry Rd.

Thomas Guide 655

Next up was an American bittern and great egret. Local residents report Cooper's hawks, sharp-shinned hawks, pine siskins, willow flycatchers, and yellow warblers using the thick willows around the pond margins. Of course red-winged blackbirds, barn swallows, violet-green swallows, and tree swallows are abundant.

Access

There are several trailheads, all of which are between houses on cul-de-sacs. From the north enter off SW Glacier Lily Dr. From the south enter off Winter Lake Dr. The lakes are rimmed with a paved, wheelchair accessible path which is used heavily by power walkers of all ages as well as binocular-laden parents and kids. There is also a forest trail that is not wheelchair accessible.

How to Get There

From SW Scholls Ferry Rd. turn south on N Dakota, right onto SW Springwood Dr., and then immediately left onto Glacier Lily Circle. However, if you miss that left you can pick up Glacier Lily a short distance west and turn left.

By Mike Houck

For more information: City of Tigard Parks, see Resources.

...senior birders from Audubon's monthly "magpie" group were astonished to see a sora being escorted by wigeons that paddled convoy-like on either side of it until they all reached the safety of one of the upper pond's islands.

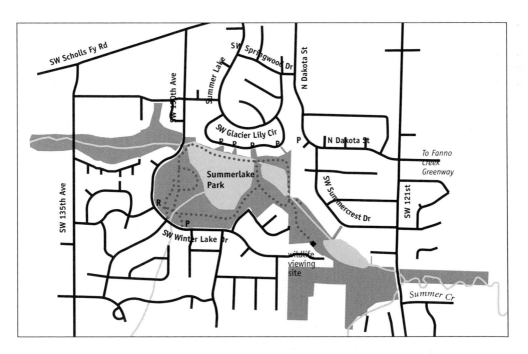

Cook Park

This 79-acre multipurpose park has about 14 acres of undeveloped natural area. The natural area is heavily wooded with thick riparian and wetland vegetation.

There is a huge multi-field soccer field on the right as you enter and a large open field to the east that abuts wetlands and streams. Extensive wetlands are at the base of 92nd Avenue which is an obvious sign to even the casual observer that you have entered the Tualatin River floodplain. Signs read, "Please be sensitive to wildlife in wetlands, no dogs allowed," although there is a specified area for "dog exercise" at the west end of the main parking lot by volleyball courts.

Cook Park is situated on the north side of the Tualatin River in a large meander that on a map looks like a small version of Big Bend National Park on the Rio Grande. As you descend into the park along SW 92nd both sides are dominated by forested and emergent wetlands. The wetlands have a lot of open water as a result of wetland mitigation work that was required of Tigard Parks for locating soccer fields in wetlands and floodplain. The wetlands to the east of SW 92nd is a large cattail marsh, bordered by willow wetlands. To the west are open ponds which have obviously been excavated.

The rest of the park is taken up with picnic shelters, lots of picnic tables, two Tigard Little League baseball fields, a playground for kids, and volleyball and basketball courts. There is a lot of parking. The active recreation area is situated between the soccer fields and the river. There are myriad soft wood-chip trails that wind through the small forest between the picnic area and the Tualatin River. The forested area immediately adjacent to the river is a combination of forested wetland and riparian habitat. Ninebark, red-osier dogwood, Oregon white ash, and reed canarygrass grow here, whereas the upland forest in the picnic area consists of ponderosa pine, big-leaf maple, and western red cedar.

A paved path runs parallel to the road that leads down another bench, a lower floodplain area, to the developed boat ramp. There are porta-potties at the boat ramp and numerous plumbed bathrooms in the picnic area. Another paved trail runs downstream along the river midway between the ball fields and boat ramp. This new trail was created with part of Metro's regional Greenspaces bond measure funds.

A metal marker denoting the height of the flood of 1996 is affixed to pilings next to the boat ramp. When you stand at the river's edge the flood marker is an impressive 15 feet over your head. A fresh landslide across the river, at the base of the Tualatin Country Club golf course, has a belted kingfisher nest. Their nests are easily recognized from the four to five-inch hole with two parallel grooves

Location
17005 SW 92nd, south of SW Durham Rd. on SW 92nd Ave., past Tigard High School

Activities
Hiking
Canoeing, boating
Fishing
Wildlife viewing
Soccer
Baseball
Children's playground
Basketball
Volleyball

Facilities
Toilets
Wheelchair accessible
Paved and unpaved trail
Picnic area
Dock, canoe launch
Volleyball courts
Soccer fields
Baseball fields
Children's playground

Fees and Regulations
Hours: 8 A.M. to dusk summer,
8 A.M. to 4 P.M. winter
Note: Gates are locked other hours so be sure to check if you are going canoeing because sometimes the gate is locked after the official opening time
Pets on leash: There is a specified area for "dog exercise" at the west end of the main parking lot by volleyball courts.

worn at the bottom of the opening where the bird's feet "stick" as the kingfisher enters the nest each time.

Access
Only two access points: one by road at SW 92nd and one by the Tualatin River at the dock. A paved path runs parallel to the road that leads down to another bench, a lower floodplain area, to the developed boat ramp. There are many soft wood-chip trails that wind through the small forest between the picnic area and the Tualatin River. Another paved trail runs downstream along the river midway between the ball fields and boat ramp.

How to Get There
By Car: From I-5 take Boones Ferry Road west to SW Durham Road. Take SW Durham to SW 92nd, just past the Tigard High School, and turn left (south) onto 92nd and follow down a steep hill to the park. If you get there before the gates open there is a large parking area just outside the gate.

By Mike Houck

For more information: City of Tigard Parks, see Resources.

Highlights
Tualatin River Access, nice wetlands in upper park area, and riparian zone along the Tualatin. Lots of sports facilities as well as river access for fishing, boating, and canoeing.

Public Transit
Tri-Met #76 stop on the corner of SW Hall Blvd. and SW Durham, about .5 mile east of SW 92nd.

Thomas Guide 685

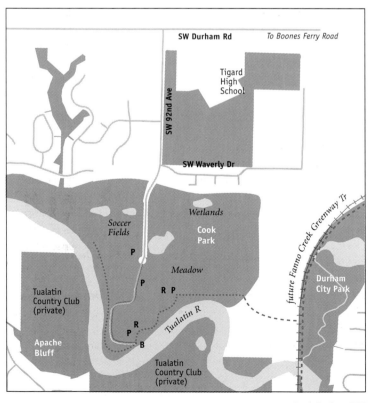

The Freeway Falcon

Most birds are best seen on a solitary walk in the field, but your first view of an American kestrel is as likely to be from a car. Fond of perching on roadside power lines, kestrels—with their small size and striking steel-and-cinnamon plumage—may at first be mistaken for a songbird. But a closer look will reveal the erect posture and hooked bill of a falcon. American kestrels (*Falco sparverius*) were originally called sparrow hawks because early settlers mistook them for a close relative of the European sparrowhawk, an accipiter similar to our own sharp-shinned hawk.

American kestrels will in fact take sparrows and other small birds. But they feed more commonly on insects, mice, and small reptiles and amphibians. Their most distinctive hunting maneuver is to hover on rapidly beating wings and hang like a kite over the ground, alert for the movement of mice or insects. In fact, any smallish bird seen hovering in open country is almost certain to be a kestrel.

Kestrels can frequently be seen right in town in such city parks as Oaks Bottom, Mt. Tabor, Powell Butte Nature Park, Laurelhurst, West Delta Park, and Tualatin Hills Nature Park. But your best bet for seeing a kestrel is to hop in the car and head for the open country right at the edge of the city. Keep an eye on the power lines and fields lining Portland's suburban highways and before long you are likely to spot the small attractive form of the "Freeway Falcon."

By Bob Wilson

Clackamas River Watershed

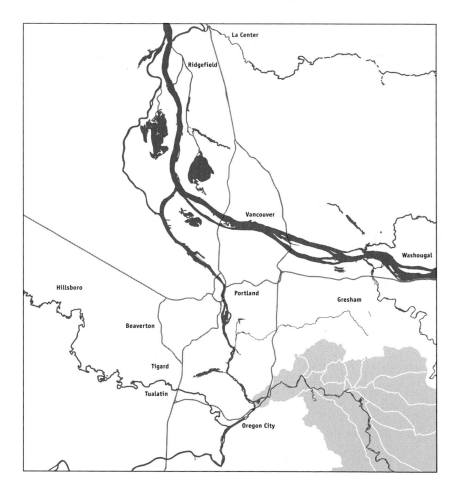

Clackamas River Watershed

As with the Sandy River to the north, the Clackamas River has its origins 6,000 feet in the high Cascades. The Clackamas flows over 80 miles from its source at Olallie Butte to near sea level in Gladstone at Clackamette Park, where it joins the Willamette. Its watershed, draining almost 1,000 miles, collects runoff from the Collawash River, Fish Creek and Roaring River, Eagle Creek, Deep Creek, and Goose Creek.

The Clackamas supports spring and fall chinook salmon, coho salmon, cutthroat trout, and both summer and winter steelhead. It provides drinking water to almost 200,000 people in the metropolitan area and is viewed as a long-term source of drinking water for the entire region.

The Clackamas River's scenic qualities and natural resource values led to 50 miles being federally designated as "wild and scenic" between Big Spring near Olallie Butte and the North Fork reservoir just above Estacada. Fourteen miles of the Roaring River are also a federal wild and scenic waterway. Four reaches are designated as scenic waterway: 12 miles of the North Fork-Clackamas, four miles of the South Fork-Clackamas, 54 miles of the main stem from Olallie Lake to North Fork Reservoir, and the more urbanized 12-mile stretch between River Mill Dam, just below Estacada, downstream to Carver.

From "Clackamas River Watershed Atlas," Metro, December 1997

Eagle Fern Park

Eagle Fern Park lies at the confluence of the North Fork and main stems of Eagle Creek in rural, north Clackamas County. Undoubtedly among the most beautiful and pristine of this region's rural forested parks, Eagle Fern is primarily characterized by its magnificent old-growth forest and the streams that run through it. Western red cedars, Douglas firs, and western hemlocks tower over its 171 acres. Flowing through the park, Eagle Creek and the North Fork are both salmon- and steelhead-spawning habitat.

The conjunction of old-growth forest and free-running streams is impressive in overview, but the magic of Eagle Fern is found in the more subtle details of nature's invention. Although the variety of tree and fish species in our region's forests and streams is not notable, diversity, though often hidden, abounds for those who seek it. Kinglets, creepers, voles, and flying squirrels inhabit the firs, cedars, and hemlocks, while centipedes, salamanders, and truffles lie hidden in rotting logs and forest soil. Orchids and violets compete for countless pollinating insects, and mosses and lichens seem to quietly cover almost every thing. In the streams, myriad mayfly, stonefly, and caddisfly larvae lie hidden under rocks, logs, or within their stone and stick cases. The lucky or careful observer may even see tailed-frog tadpoles adhered to stones in fast-moving water.

About one-fourth of the park is roaded and developed as a dispersed picnic area, leaving more than 100 acres accessed only by trails or cross-country hiking. A footbridge over Eagle Creek near the park's main entrance leads to the trail system. The long, cable-slung footbridge is suspended over the stream and offers unique and beautiful views of old-growth riparian forest. From the bridge you may see dippers which nest nearby, a common merganser hen and her tight-trailing brood, or even one of the ospreys that nest at the park. Once across the bridge, a variety of loop trails guides you along the stream and through the forest. Big-leaf maples cloaked with epiphytic mosses and licorice-fern shade natural gardens of trillium and wood violet. The beautiful stair-stepping feather moss, *Hylocomium splendens*, grows diminutively under massive Douglas firs more than six feet in diameter. Here almost anything is possible. There has even been a sighting of a spotted owl!

Visit the park on a cool and damp fall, winter, or spring day. The old-growth forest needs to be wet to properly show off its lichens and mosses. Avoid the park on summer weekends, when large family or company picnics often mean a crowd. Take a companion to the park if you must, but go alone if you can, at least for your first visit. You won't need help to enjoy the quiet beauty and solitude of the forest, or the stoic dignity of the great old trees.

Location
Eagle Fern Rd. and Kitzmiller Rd., near Estacada at Eagle Creek.

Activities
Hiking
Fishing
Nature study

Facilities
Toilets
Wheelchair accessible
Trail unpaved
Parking
Picnic area

Fees and Regulations
Parking fees: $2 per car on weekends and Memorial and Labor Days

Highlights
Outstanding old-growth forest, beautiful streams, exceptional picnic area. American dippers can be seen in the park's pristine streams.

Public Transit
Tri-Met #31 stops at Eagle Creek Grange on Wildcat Mt. Rd. and from there it is a 3.5-mile hike or bicycle trip to the park.

Thomas Guide 720

Access

Hiking trails begin near the park entrance at a footbridge over Eagle Creek. Wheelchair access trail is across the footbridge and is about 1/4 mile in length. The hiking trail is about 1 mile long.

How to Get There

Take I-205 to Estacada exit (Hwy. 224) in Clackamas. Head toward Estacada and take a left at Wildcat Mt. Rd. south of Hwy. 224 and Hwy. 211 junction. Follow Wildcat Mt. Rd. east about 2 miles and take a right (south) on Eagle Fern Rd. It's about 2 miles to the park entrance.

By Bruce McCullough

For more information: Clackamas County Parks, see Resources.

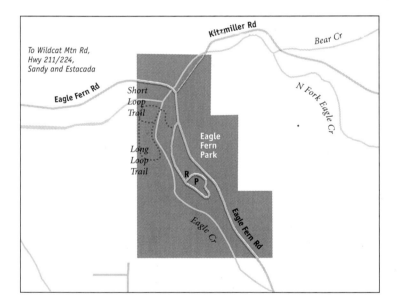

Evergreen Ferns

Drizzle, damp, and cold can't keep inveterate naturalists and botanists from pursuing our avocations. By late November, the showy majority of plants that usually catch our attention have been reduced to so much wilted detritus slowly slipping into a less aesthetic part of the carbon cycle. It is now that certain hardier types become more noticeable and perhaps more interesting in the absence of the abundant fair-weather competition. The modest blossoms of salal and the downright homely catkins of western hazel are more easily appreciated against the somber background of winter.

A few members of another group of often-overlooked plants stand out, modestly, during this time: the evergreen ferns. Although most ferns die back in fall just like their more advanced flowering relatives, a few species retain green, living foliage through the winter.

The ferns' reliance upon a less flamboyant form of sexual reproduction than that of the flowering plants has somehow made them difficult for some to identify. Many amateur botanists who have no trouble with the hundred-plus members of the rose family are totally intimidated by the 40-odd fern species they're likely to encounter in Oregon and Washington. The winter study of evergreen ferns is an easy introduction to this group of plants.

Sword-Fern

If you haven't seen this one, you've been walking through the woods with your eyes closed. The sword-fern (*Polystichum munitum*) may be the most common fern west of the Cascades. Anywhere in the Portland area where there are a few Douglas firs with a natural ground cover, you will almost certainly find this fern. All through Forest Park their dark green whorls of fronds dominate the forest floor. Examine a single frond and you will find the basic pattern for almost all ferns: a central mid-rib (rachis) with a rank of leaflets on either side, much like a feather. In this particular species, each leaflet stands free on its own stalk and has a small, pointed ear-like projection at its base pointing toward the tip of the frond. The prickly-toothed margins of the leaflets give members of this group the name "holly-ferns."

Licorice-Fern

This fern looks its best during fall and winter because the new fronds are produced from midsummer to fall. If you haven't tasted it, be sure to try it. Take a small piece of the "root" (which is actually a creeping underground stem), peel it, then taste. Some insist it tastes like licorice, others say it just tastes bad. The fronds of licorice-fern (*Polypodium glycyrrhiza*), although smaller and softer, look very similar to those of the sword-fern. However, a closer look reveals that the leaflets, rather than standing free on their own stalks, are broadly attached at their bases to the rachis of the frond. Instead of growing in circular clumps, this plant creeps with branching stems through the mossy cover of rocks and tree trunks, especially on big-leaf maples. Magnificent growths of licorice-fern can be seen on the rocky banks along Terwilliger above Duniway Park, on the north-facing banks along West Burnside and Northwest Cornell Roads, and on the cliffs just south of the bridge on Highway 43 leading out of Lake Oswego toward West Linn.

Deer Fern

Like the sword-fern, the fronds of deer fern (*Blechnum spicant*) grow in a circular rosette, but in this case, the evergreen fronds grow flatter to the ground. The same feather-like arrangement of leaflets is present, and they are broadly attached at their bases like those of the licorice-fern. However, they have very blunt, rounded tips as opposed to the more pointed tips on the leaflets of sword- and licorice-ferns. At this time of year you are likely to find only the withered remains of a second kind of frond on the deer fern. These are the remnants of the spore-producing fronds, which grow as a feathery, erect tuft from the flat rosette of evergreen fronds. Finding deer fern in the city is a matter of luck. They can be found in scattered groups in Forest Park in places that remain relatively damp year-round but not so damp as to encourage the larger and more robust lady-fern (*Athyrium filix-femina*). Segments of Forest Park's Wildwood Trail that pass near streamlets or into shady, moist gullies are a good place to find it.

Gold-back Fern

Although this is generally considered a species for drier east Cascades and southern Oregon situations, it does show up in drier microhabitats in the West Hills. Careful examination of the licorice-fern colonies just west of the first tunnel on Cornell Road will turn up some examples of this little gem. The small triangular fronds are a pleasant soft green above, but if you take the trouble to turn one over, you'll find the shocking sulfur yellow that gives the fern its name. Winter and spring are the best time to see the gold-back fern (*Pityrogramma triangularis*) since its habitat preference usually results in its being dried and shriveled by midsummer. Even then the exposed undersides of the leaves on their wiry black stems make it easy to identify.

Come spring there will be many other ferns crowding the forest floor, but during these few slow, cold months you can gain a basic familiarity with the group by taking a look at this hardy foursome.

By Roger Yerke

Salamanders

Frogs, at least as adults, are easily recognizable even by small children. The large heads, big eyes, and short, sturdy forms of most frogs are child-friendly enough to serve as models for plush and bathtub toys, hand puppets, and cartoon characters. Frogs' cool, moist skins are simply ignored.

In contrast, I've never seen a plush salamander, nor a salamander bathtub toy, hand puppet, or cartoon character. Perhaps salamanders' long bodies, long tails, and flattened heads remind many people of lizards and snakes, neither of which is a big hit in the child's toy or cartoon business. And, although most kinds of salamanders live their entire lives on land, those we usually see live in ponds where some species breed and where their larvae will develop to adulthood. Others can be found under boards, leaves, or rocks.

As an aside, Linnaeus (circa 1700s), often called "the father of taxonomy," made no distinction between amphibians and reptiles and seemingly had little use for either group. He used words (in Latin, of course) such as "foul and loathsome" and "filthy skin" to describe the animals, and "squalid habitation" to refer to their habitats. In any case, the morphological features of salamanders apparently have not been sufficiently endearing to overcome Linnaean-era biases against animals with cool, moist skins.

Nevertheless, salamanders are often important members of the biological communities in which they occur. The biomass of salamanders in one recent study area in the Great Smoky Mountains was twice that of all the breeding birds and equal to that of small mammals present. Another study in a redwood forest in California yielded similar results, yet most of us encounter salamanders only rarely. Why?

One reason is that salamanders, like frogs, quickly lose water by evaporation from their skins. Therefore, they must live in moist habitats to avoid drying out. Moreover, most of the world's—and the Pacific Northwest's—species of salamanders belong to the family Plethodontidae, a group distinguished by having no lungs. They respire only through their moist skins and so are especially tied to dark, cool, moist microhabitats. Finally, unlike most frogs, nearly all salamanders lack a voice, so even those that form breeding aggregations in ponds are silent and may escape notice.

Worldwide, there are just over 400 species of salamanders, compared to more than 4,100 species of frogs. Despite its large geographic expanse, Western North America has fewer than 40 species of salamanders, some of which are known only from very restricted areas. Oregon has 19 species of salamanders, more than any western state except California, and 11 of these have been recorded in or just outside the Portland metropolitan area. In fact, there are more species of salamanders in and near the city of Portland than can be found in all the western plains and Rocky

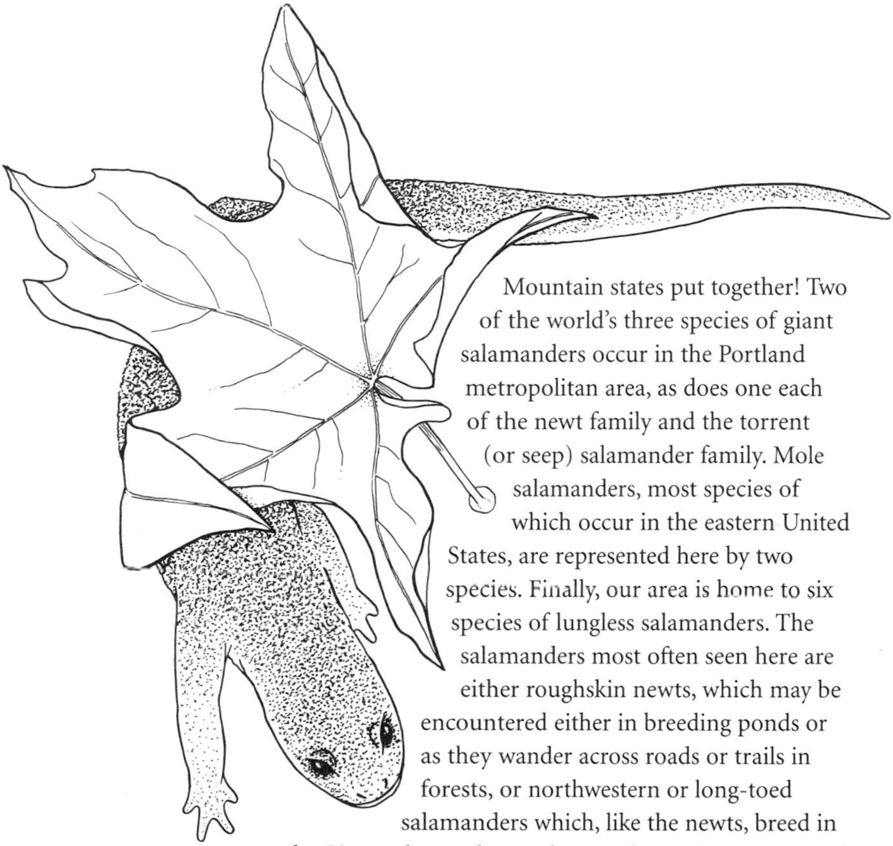

Mountain states put together! Two of the world's three species of giant salamanders occur in the Portland metropolitan area, as does one each of the newt family and the torrent (or seep) salamander family. Mole salamanders, most species of which occur in the eastern United States, are represented here by two species. Finally, our area is home to six species of lungless salamanders. The salamanders most often seen here are either roughskin newts, which may be encountered either in breeding ponds or as they wander across roads or trails in forests, or northwestern or long-toed salamanders which, like the newts, breed in ponds. Giant salamanders and seep salamanders are strongly associated with cold mountain streams, where they live as larvae, and at stream edges, where they live as adults. The lungless salamanders, even where they are abundant, are rarely encountered unless one looks beneath stones, boards, or fallen leaves, or in decaying logs or stumps.

Salamanders, like all other amphibians, have poison glands in their skins. In particular, the poison glands of northwestern salamanders and roughskin newts are abundant, and their secretions can cause death should one be so foolish as to put one of these animals in one's mouth. As is true for all wild animals, it's best to let these creatures go about their business unmolested. If you must handle one, be sure to wash your hands thoroughly afterward.

Small, silent, and secretive as they are, salamanders nevertheless are very important both as predators upon some smaller animals and, for some larger predators, as prey. They may never pass the plush-pet or cartoon character test, but their quiet, efficient, yet important lives are worthy of our respect—perhaps even our admiration.

By Richard B. Forbes

Johnson Creek Watershed

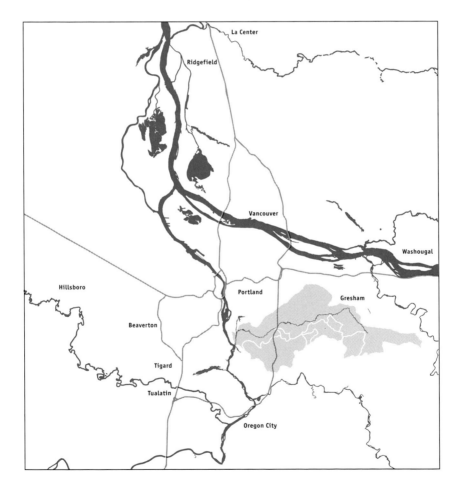

Johnson Creek Watershed

Johnson Creek flows 24 miles and is fed by runoff from a 54-square-mile watershed from its origin near Orient, east of Gresham, to its confluence with the Willamette River. The last completely free-flowing urban stream within the city of Portland, Johnson Creek cuts across political boundaries of Portland, Clackamas County, Multnomah County, Gresham, and Milwaukie. What begins as a gentle swale in a farm field east of Cottrell Road rapidly becomes a full-fledged rural stream. Although the rural fields provide a scenic backdrop to Johnson Creek, they also contribute pollutants from agricultural, nursery, and grazing activities along the stream. Creek residents, regional park advocates, planners, and water quality agencies have recently formed a coalition to address flooding, degraded water quality, and loss of fish habitat. This effort also has the potential to capitalize on opportunities to protect and enhance open space, fish and wildlife habitat, recreation, scenic vistas, and property values throughout the Johnson Creek Corridor.

Down Johnson Creek, Along the Springwater Corridor Trail

The newly established 16.8-mile Springwater Corridor Trail, a segment of the 40-Mile Loop regional trail system, provides access to parks, wildlife habitat, and cultural landmarks. In 1903, when the Olmsteds were riding trains back and forth between Portland and Seattle to write park master plans, the Springwater Line was used by passenger trolleys and locomotives that hauled freight and produce between Portland and Estacada, a popular tourist destination at the time. After the Estacada line ceased in the 1930s it received limited use to haul lumber to Boring mills until 1990. When Oregon Department of Transportation (ODOT) studied improvements at SE McLoughlin Boulevard and SE Spokane in the Sellwood area, they determined it would cost $3 million to replace the old interurban railroad bridge over McLoughlin. Astute trail advocates and park planners pointed out to ODOT that it would cost roughly half that much to buy the entire rail line from McLoughlin to Boring, 18 miles of public right-of-way as compared to 100 feet or so of bridge repairs.

ODOT agreed that not only was a savings of nearly half a million dollars in the public interest a wise investment, but it would complete one of the most long-sought legs of the 40-Mile Loop. This represented the first urban rails-to-trails effort in Oregon. The state also owns the rail line from Boring to Estacada, so one day it will be possible to bicycle or hike from the downtown Portland center to Estacada and from there to the Pacific Crest Trail.

Adapted from "Johnson Creek, Urban Streams: Wetlands, Wildlife, Water Quality;"
Audubon Society of Portland

Gresham Main City Park

Located in the core of downtown Gresham, this park is the oldest and most established park in the city. It was once called Camp Ground because the Portland Methodists held annual meetings there in the 1880s. Early maps of 1911 and 1922 show that the site was the location of the original township.

Gresham Main City Park is easy to find, has ample parking and bus service, and has good access to the Springwater Trail. It would also be a good base to begin explorations of other parks, trails, and open space in Gresham. For hikers and bikers doing a long jaunt on the Springwater Trail, this attractive park would be a nice place to take a rest or pick up refreshments in downtown Gresham.

The 17.5-acre site is a community park designed for multiple uses. The level, paved trails meander through a grassy and landscaped space with scattered benches and picnic areas, including a covered group picnic area, as well as ball fields, horseshoe courts, and a playground. There is a Japanese garden on a small island connected to the main park with a graceful arching bridge. The park was created around a meander of Johnson Creek, and visitors can enjoy watching ducks and the natural riparian aspects of the site. The edges of the park have been kept in a natural state, which provides for wildlife habitat.

Access
From Main St., downtown Gresham at Powell Blvd., or from the Springwater Corridor Trail.

How to Get There
From Portland take I-5 to SE Powell Blvd. and head east to downtown Gresham; turn south at Main St. into the Park.

By Diana Bradshaw

For more information: Gresham Parks, see Resources.

Location
Powell Blvd. at the end of N Main St.

Activities
Hiking
Biking
Baseball field
Horseshoes
Exercise course

Facilities
Toilets
Wheelchair accessible
Paved and unpaved trail
Parking
Picnic area (includes covered group site; call 503-618-2485 for reservations)
Playground
Japanese garden
Food concessions

Fees and Regulations
Open dawn to dusk
Pets on leash

Highlights
The park's core is highly decorative and landscaped. The edges are more natural. A small island with Japanese garden connected to the park. A major jumping-off point for the Springwater Corridor Trail, with parking.

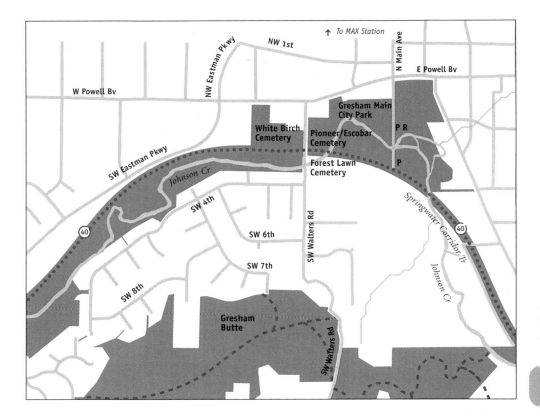

↑ *To MAX Station*

NW 1st

NW Eastman Pkwy

N Main Ave

E Powell Bv

W Powell Bv

Gresham Main
City Park

White Birch
Cemetery

Pioneer/Escobar
Cemetery

P R

SW Eastman Pkwy

Johnson Cr

Forest Lawn
Cemetery

P

40

SW 4th

Springwater Corridor Tr

40

SW 6th

SW Walters Rd

Johnson Cr

SW 7th

SW 8th

Gresham
Butte

SW Walters Rd

Public Transit
Take MAX light rail to
Gresham Transit Center,
end of the line, about
1/4 mile north of the
park, or Tri-Met #9 on
SE Powell Blvd.

Thomas Guide 629

Gresham Main City Park   243

Gresham Butte

This site is probably the crown jewel of the Gresham area open spaces because of its size, degree of naturalness, and beauty. At about 180 acres, it is the largest of the open spaces in the Gresham area and is directly south of downtown Gresham. It is a wonderful mature second-growth forest, a haven for wildlife and native vegetation; a haven, too, for visitors seeking quiet and nature. The real surprise is the Gresham Butte trail. It is big and seems a small version of Forest Park. The first two birds I saw when I first visited the site were hermit thrush and Cassin's vireo, and that was about 25 feet down the trail! Those were followed by Hutton's vireo, orange-crowned warbler, spotted towhee, downy woodpecker, ruby-crowned kinglet, and black-capped chickadee. The recently completed wide gravel trail provides access across the center of the butte through a saddle. It offers a quiet place where all one hears is birds singing.

This trail is the first phase of an extensive network of walking and hiking trails planned to loop and meander around the butte and provide access at several places. These trails will provide visitors an excellent opportunity to experience nature and see birds, wildlife, and native vegetation. The plans also call for future trails to ascend to the top for views to the south, east, and west. There are plans as well to connect the Gresham Butte Trail system to the Springwater Trail near Gresham Main City Park and the trailhead at Hogan Road.

Metro Regional Parks and Greenspaces has targeted the Boring Lava Domes in the Gresham area for a significant amount of Greenspace acquisition, so there will be more areas like this in the near future.

Location
SE 19th Dr. and SE 19th St. (on the east off SE Regner Rd.) or end of SW 19th Dr. and SW Towle on the west, Gresham.

Fees and Regulations
Open dawn to dusk
Pets on leash

Highlights
Lots of birds, great place for newly arrived spring migrants. Excellent example of Boring Lava Butte with a mature upland forest.

Public Transit
If you are willing to walk about a mile from SE Powell Blvd., take Tri-Met #9.

Thomas Guide 629

Access
Trail is wide, loose gravel, newly built, and in excellent condition. The trail passes through a saddle on the butte and is gently hilly with a couple of short, steeper areas.

How to Get There
From Portland take I-205 and head east on SE Powell Blvd. Go south on Eastman Pkwy., which becomes SW Towle Ave. Turn left (east) on SW 19th Dr. From the east take SE Powell Blvd. to SE Roberts and turn right on SE Regner; take a right onto SE 19th St. and another right onto SE 19th Dr.

By Diana Bradshaw

For more information: Gresham Parks, see Resources.

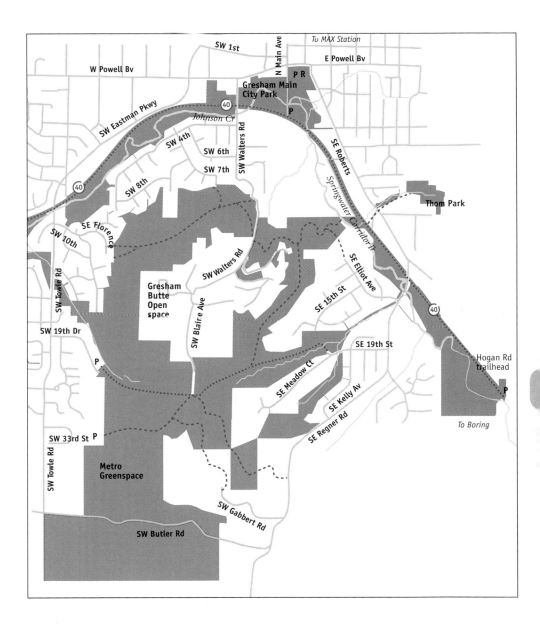

W Powell Bv

SW 1st

N Main Ave

To MAX Station

E Powell Bv

P R

Gresham Main
City Park

SW Eastman Pkwy

Johnson Cr

40

P

SW 4th

SW 6th

SW Walters Rd

SW 7th

SE Roberts

40

Springwater Corridor

Thom Park

SE Florence

SW 8th

SW 10th

SW Walters Rd

Gresham
Butte
Open
space

SW Blaire Ave

SE Elliot Ave

SE 15th St

SW Towle Rd

SW 19th Dr

SE 19th St

Hogan Rd
trailhead

P

SE Meadow Ct

SW 33rd St P

SE Kelly Av

SE Regner Rd

P

To Boring

SW Towle Rd

Metro
Greenspace

SW Gabbert Rd

SW Butler Rd

Gresham Pioneer Cemeteries

Gresham Pioneer and Escobar cemeteries are on the east side of SW Walters and adjacent to each other, but the sign lumps them together. They were founded separately, but the founders wanted them to remain distinct, so at this time, nearly 150 years after their founding, they have separate names; however, unless one is able to find the ground marker which separates the two, they seem as one. White Birch Cemetery, only one-half acre in size, is on the west side of Walters. It was founded in 1888.

These peaceful old cemeteries on Johnson Creek provide riparian habitat along with the big old trees, mostly Douglas fir. They offer the visitor a chance to stroll among the ornate grave markers and contemplate the history of the area and the lives of the people buried here. There is Frank Escobar, a colorful character of early Gresham, who, ironically, was not buried in his own namesake cemetery. He is remembered as being well-off and big-hearted, but frugal. It is said that he lived in a ramshackle cabin with no indoor or outdoor facilities, but that he had a very nice garden! On the markers of these old cemeteries are the names of familiar place-names like Powell. There is the grave of the founder of a college and that of a college professor so well liked that his monument was placed by his students. There is the grave of Miyo Iwakoshi, the first Japanese woman to settle permanently in Oregon. She married Andrew McKinnon and they lived east of Gresham, in Orient, so named for her place of origin.

Access

There are three pioneer cemeteries located one block west of the Gresham Main City Park: Gresham Pioneer Cemetery, Escobar Cemetery, and White Birch Cemetery. They can be reached from the park by way of the Springwater Trail which passes by the park and the cemeteries, or by way of SW Walters Rd. and Powell Blvd.

How to Get There

Take I-205 to SE Powell and take Powell east to Gresham. South on SW Walters Ave., one block west of Main. *See map on page 243*.

See map on page 243.

By Diana Bradshaw

For more information: See Metro's *GreenScene* for programs. To get the *GreenScene* or to get information about field trip programs for schools and youth groups, contact: Metro Regional Parks and Greenspaces, see Resources.

Time Stains of the Plant World

Needing little more than a forbidding rock on which to anchor and minute amounts of water on which to grow, lichens are one of our hardiest plant forms. Robust and adaptable, lichens are pioneer plants that spread into areas where conditions are unfavorable for more complex plants. Pioneer plants like lichen start the process of growth and decay that prepares the soils required for higher order plants to later follow. Typically slow growing and long living, some lichen colonies are estimated to be over 2,000 years old. Their longevity, in fact, and the peculiar shapes that varieties adopt are why lichens are aptly referred to as "time stains."

The Nature of Lichens

Lichens are not distinct individual plants. They are actually two plants, an alga and a fungus, living together in a symbiotic union. Lichens are commonly cited as the epitome of mutualism, each component assisting the other for the common good. Recent research, however, indicates the fungus might actually be parasitic on its algal partner. The organism's fungal component is its most conspicuous part. Forming the outer layers of the lichen's thallus, or main body, the fungus helps prevent dehydration during times of drought and supplies both itself and its partner algal cells with water and minerals, which it collects from rain or absorbs from the air. The algal component of the lichen usually resides in the inner core amidst the fungal fibers, and, through photosynthesis, serves to produce sufficient amounts of carbohydrates to support both itself and its fungal counterpart.

Lichens are generally divided into three basic types: crustose (powdery or crusty), foliose (leafy), and fruticose (stalked or branching). Crustose lichens are the flaky encrustations that you frequently see on tree trunks, decaying wood, rocks, or soil. They vary greatly in color—pale to dark green, rust brown, white, gray—and are the most primitive of the lichens. According to local lichenologist Glen Walthall, the easiest way to identify a crustose-type lichen is to try to scrape off a tiny bit of it from its host. Crustose lichens generally adhere so strongly to their hosts that it is impossible to remove the lichen separately.

Foliose lichens are the most common in the Portland area. These have a spreading, leaf-like appearance and are the type most readily identifiable as lichens. Foliose lichens are bound much less tightly to their hosts than are the crustose type. They are attached either by many tiny root-like strands or at a single central point. Foliose lichens can be peeled off from their hosts fairly readily and their undersides are generally much darker than their exposed upper surface.

The most specialized types of lichens are the fruticose species. These are characterized by branching forms, having very small thalli and long stem-like growths, and by stalked forms, which have crusty or leafy thalli out of which grow upright stalks.

Formal classification and naming of lichens is greatly complicated by the fact that they are not really individual plants. Naming a plant consisting of two or more plants is forbidden by the International Code of Botanical Nomenclature, but many "species" of lichen had been named before the discovery of their dual plant nature was made. Abandoning literally thousands of old names and having to coin an equally great number of new ones would have been a massive and confusing undertaking, so it has become the custom among botanical taxonomists to apply the old lichen names to the lichen's fungal component only.

The Practical Side—So What's It Good For?

Over the ages, lichens have been used for many medicinal purposes simply because of their superficial resemblance to other objects. The term lichen, which comes from the Greek word for leprous, was given to the plant by the Greek physician Pedanios Dioscorides (c. 68 A.D.) in his book *Materia Medica*. Dioscorides thought that lichens looked like a leper's skin and might be a potential treatment for the disease. Later, in the middle ages, the lichen *Lobaria pulmonaria* was sought as a cure for lung diseases because of its physical resemblance to lung tissue. As with many other folk remedies, there appears to be an element of reason behind such medicinal uses of lichens. We have found more recently that the fungal components of some lichens can be used effectively to produce antibiotics.

Historically at least, a more fruitful use of lichen has been in producing vegetable dyes. As early as biblical times, lichens were used to dye the royal purple garments worn by kings and monarchs. Because of their low production costs, synthetic dyes have now generally replaced lichen dyes, but not entirely. Harris tweeds manufactured in Scotland are still produced using traditional lichen dyes, and a variety of small local cottage industries continue relying on lichen-based colors. Lichen dyes can be easily produced at home; the process mainly involves fermenting the lichen thalli in a warm solution of water and ammonia.

Lichens and Air Quality

It has long been known that lichens are particularly sensitive to air pollution. Over a hundred years ago, scientists noticed a significant lack of lichens in London, Paris, Bonn, and other major manufacturing centers in Europe. Further research led to the discovery that lichens are especially sensitive to sulfur dioxide. William C. Denison, a professor at Oregon State University, studied the effects of air pollution on lichens in the Willamette Valley several years ago. He established four classes of lichen, ranging from most resistant (class I) to least resistant (class IV), and charted the entire Willamette Valley according to the presence or absence of lichen species as a means of correlating degrees of air pollution and lichen sensitivity. Denison found that although it is not a quantitative test, monitoring air quality with lichens gives us an early indication of the encroachment or retreat of air pollution in any given area. The contrast between the lichen-rich trees in the Sandy River Gorge and depauperate lichen community in Oregon City is an excellent local example of this phenomenon.

Where to See Them In Portland

By far, the three most common lichens that you will see in the Portland area are the cracked-shield lichen (*Parmelia sulcata*), the short-beard lichen (*Usnea subfloradana*), and the mealy ramalina (*Ramalina farinacea*). Cracked-shield lichen is a leafy type that is usually seen on branches of trees or along old wooden fences. It often looks as though a hurried house painter had scraped his brush across the host and left globs of thick gray-green paint to dry and crack in the weather. The short-beard is a fruticose lichen of the branching variety. It too is most often found on the branches of trees. In winter, the short-beard lichen can envelop entire orchards and seems to be particularly fond of filbert trees. As with all lichens, the short-beard is not a parasite and is in no way harmful to its host. The mealy ramalina isn't quite as common as the other two, but is found in most areas in which the short-beard lichen appears. Like the short-beard, the mealy ramalina is a branching variety of fruticose lichen, but the two are easily told apart by their branches. Branches of the short-beard lichen are all rounded and those of the mealy ramalina are flat.

Specific examples of other types of lichen are scattered throughout town. The trees along 19th Avenue in Northwest Portland between Flanders and Glisan support all three basic types of lichens. In addition to the cracked-shield lichen (foliose) and mealy ramalina (fruticose) they are coated with varying shades of powdery-paint lichen (*Lepraria membranacea*), a crustose-type lichen that is fond of moist, shady environments. The Sellwood Bridge is covered with splashes of rock-flame lichen (*Caloploca saxicola*), whose common name aptly describes its bright yellow-orange color.

To find rarer species and those that are especially sensitive to air pollution, you must go to the usual places for viewing wildlife within Portland. The delicate goblet lichen (*Cladonia pyxidate*), a fruticose lichen of the stalked variety, prefers rotting wood and can be found among the damp trails of Oaks Bottom. Dog lichen (*Peltigera canina*) and the British soldier lichen (*Cladonia cristatella*) can be found in some areas of Forest Park, Tualatin Hills Nature Park, and around Audubon House. Dog lichen is primarily a ground-growing foliose lichen with a large thin greenish-gray or brown thallus. British-soldier lichen is a stalked lichen with red cushion-like caps at the ends of its stalks. The premier lichen (and moss) localities in the Portland area are Sandy River Nature Conservancy, Oxbow County Park, Tryon Creek State Park, and Forest Park.

Lichens grow year-round, but are usually more active during the winter months when a lot of other plant life is dormant. And lichens prefer wet temperate climates, which explains why Portland currently has such an abundance of "time stains" on display.

By Thomas E. Hanrahan

References

Bland, John H. *Forests of Lilliput.* Englewood Cliffs, NJ: Prentice-Hall, Inc., 1971.

Bolton, Eileen M. *Lichens for Vegetable Dyeing.* London: Studio Books, 1960.

Denison, William C. *A Guide to Air Quality Monitoring with Lichens.* Corvallis, OR: Lichen Technology, Inc., 1973.

Hale, Mason E. *How to Know Lichens.* The Pictured Key Nature Series. Dubuque, IA: Wm. C. Brown Co. Pub., 1979.

Jenne Butte

Jenne Butte Open Space is a large parcel atop one of the lava buttes. It is a recent acquisition of the Gresham Parks District, and the trail system has not yet been developed. At the present time there is an unimproved trail looping through an open, mostly red alder forest with groves of western red cedar and an understory of ferns. There are plans for a paved wheelchair-accessible loop trail and scenic viewpoint which will provide views to the north and east toward the Columbia River Gorge. A longer walking/hiking trail loop is planned which will allow hikers to explore the gentle slopes of this butte and will connect to the Jenne Butte Community Park, which is also yet undeveloped. The plans call for access by way of the Springwater Trail just east of Powell Butte and another access by way of a trailhead to be located at SE Jenne Road and SE 174th Street. This site has a different feel from the other nearby buttes, Powell, Gresham, and Grant. It is airier, with large expanses of second-growth deciduous trees, and has an open understory. It is large enough for visitors to spend some time, experience the forest, and get away from the city. It is a valuable preservation of open space in this area of rapid growth. Its proximity to the Springwater Trail will make it a great place for a side trip into nature.

Location
SW Equestrian Dr. and SW Nancy Dr.

Fees and Regulations
Open dawn to dusk
Pets on leash

Highlights
A large parcel atop one of the lava buttes with a unique landscape from the other nearby buttes.

Thomas Guide 628

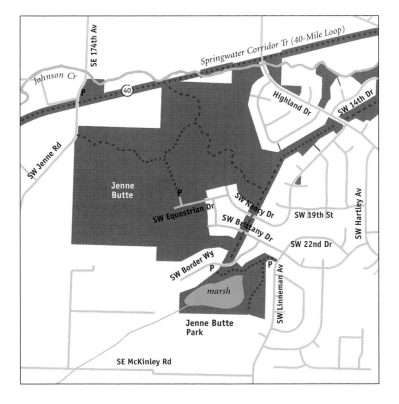

Access
Currently unimproved dirt trails as this is a new park.

How to Get There
From Portland take I-205 to SE Powell and head east on Powell to Highland Dr. Take a right (south) on Highland Dr. Turn right on SW Nancy Dr. and follow it to its end at SW Equestrian Dr. The trailhead is at each end of Equestrian.

By Diana Bradshaw

For more information: Gresham Parks, see Resources.

Butler Creek Greenway and Johnson Creek

This greenway is a linear strip of open space which connects the Springwater Corridor Trail with Butler Creek Park and follows Butler Creek northward from its confluence with Johnson Creek. It can be accessed from several places, but the preferred route would be to park along Powell Loop which connects Pleasant View Drive to Powell Boulevard, then walk the Springwater Trail to the east, about 1/4 mile, to one of the two trailheads on the right. Here the trail, about 3/4 mile in length, winds across an expanse of the Johnson Creek floodplain of willow and cottonwood to a viewpoint of Johnson Creek, near where Butler Creek flows into Johnson Creek. The trail then passes through upland forest of Douglas fir and western red cedar, salmonberry, elderberry, and wildflowers such as bleeding heart. It climbs and crosses Johnson Creek on a new high bridge which provides nice views of the creek, and continues, crossing SW 14th Drive and SW Binford Lake Parkway. The trail and Butler Creek go through a small canyon in the middle of a neighborhood, but the big old trees and snags give the feeling of a bit of wilderness. The trail comes out in Butler Creek Park, a multi-use community park with playgrounds, paved trails, and picnic areas in the center of a subdivision. In the upper park the creek has been impounded to form small lakes or ponds where one can see mallards, wigeon, and bufflehead. This site is a strip of riparian woodland, a wildlife corridor, and a pleasant natural area for an upland side trip from the Springwater Trail.

Access

Park along Powell Loop which connects Pleasant View Dr. to Powell Blvd., then walk the Springwater Trail to the east about 1/4 mile to one of the two trailheads on the right. Powell Loop is also just across SE Powell Blvd. from the headwaters of Fairview Creek and the Columbia Slough watershed to the north. Gravel trail along Butler Creek involves a moderate climb. When the trail emerges in Butler Creek Community Park there is a level paved trail suitable for wheelchairs.

How to Get There

From Portland go east on SE Powell Blvd. and south on Powell Loop. *See map on page 254.*

By Diana Bradshaw

For more information: Gresham Parks, see Resources.

Location
About 1/4 mile walk from SW Powell Loop

Activities
Hiking
Biking

Facilities
Toilets (portables)
Wheelchair accessible (only in Butler Creek Community Park)
Paved and unpaved trail (paved in Butler Creek Park only)
Picnic area (Butler Creek Community Park)

Fees and Regulations
Open dawn to dusk
Pets on leash

Highlights
The riparian woodland and greenway corridor offers a very peaceful trip through the adjacent neighborhoods. The confluence of Johnson and Butler Creeks is a broad open space. The upper reach of Butler Creek is more developed with two small ponds.

Public Transit
Tri-Met #9 on Powell or #82 on Eastman and 182nd Ave. (weekdays only from Rockwood Transit Center to Gresham Transit Center). Tri-Met #82 stops at SW 14th Dr. and SW Binford Ave.

Thomas Guide 628

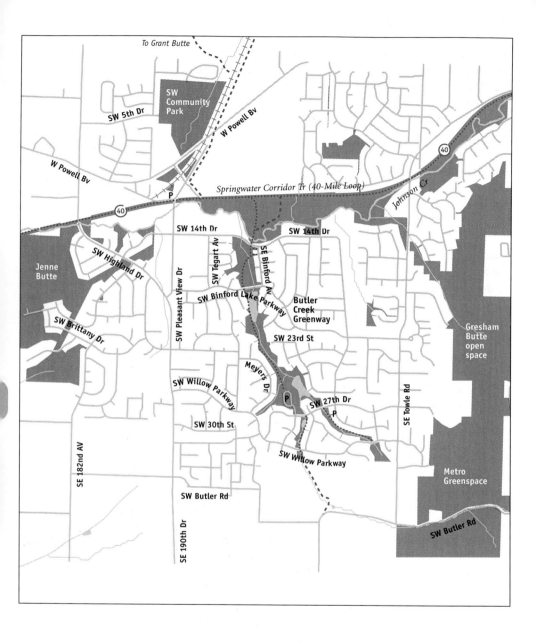

To Grant Butte

SW Community Park

SW 5th Dr

W Powell Bv

W Powell Bv

40

Springwater Corridor Tr (40-Mile Loop)

Johnson Cr

40

P

SW 14th Dr

SW 14th Dr

SW Highland Dr

Jenne Butte

SW Pleasant View Dr

SW Tegart Av

SE Binford Av

SW Binford Lake Parkway

Butler Creek Greenway

Gresham Butte open space

SW Brittany Dr

SW 23rd St

Meyers Dr

SW Willow Parkway

P

SW 27th Dr

P

SE Towle Rd

SW 30th St

SE 182nd AV

SW Willow Parkway

Metro Greenspace

SW Butler Rd

SE 190th Dr

SW Butler Rd

Powell Butte Nature Park

Powell Butte, owned by Portland Water Bureau and cooperatively managed with Portland Parks and Recreation, has over nine miles of trails that accommodate hiking, equestrian, and bicycle recreation. The Springwater Corridor Trail passes by the butte's south boundary and connects to the lower end of the Pioneer Orchard Trail. Picnic tables are located in the pioneer orchard at the top of the butte, as well as at the parking lot and restroom area on the north slope. A visitors' information kiosk is also located near the parking lot and features information on Portland's water supply, park trails information, and park history. The Mountain View Trail, which begins at the parking lot, is paved and wheelchair-accessible.

Butte Habitats

The 600+ acre extinct volcano has a diversity of habitats that support an abundance of wildlife. Over 100 species of birds as well as a variety of mammals, reptiles, amphibians, invertebrates such as the ochre ringlet and red admiral butterflies, and many other insects occur on the butte.

The summit, at 630 feet, is dominated by an open, gently rolling grassy meadow with scattered copses of black hawthorn and Himalayan blackberry. The meadow supports a wide variety of native and non-native grasses and wildflowers. An old orchard of walnut, apple, and pear trees occupies the highest point of the meadow, which was used for years as forage for cattle grazing from a nearby dairy. In addition to affording spectacular views of Cascade peaks— Mt. St. Helens and Mt. Adams to the north, Mt. Jefferson to the southeast, and Mt. Hood to the east—the butte is a premier area to observe American kestrel and, frequently, red-tailed hawks "kiting" or hovering into the strong winds from the nearby Columbia River Gorge. At the northeast corner of the orchard is a "mountain finder" which highlights the regional buttes and mountains. Coyote, deer, northern shrike (winter), and northern harrier also forage in the open, grassy habitat and along the meadow's margins. The insect-like song of the savannah sparrow is one of the most common spring and summer sounds of the meadow. The brilliantly marked lazuli bunting can also be seen on occasion near the orchard. Other rarer meadow/ orchard species include western meadowlark, short-eared owl, and northern bobwhite.

The flanks of Powell Butte support mixed forest, with some large western red cedar and Douglas fir in isolated pockets. There are basically two types of forest on the butte. The first occurs on steeper slopes on the north, west, and south slopes, and is predominantly Douglas fir with some big-leaf maple and Oregon white ash, with red alder occurring in wet seeps. The second forest type is dominated by

Location

The main entrance to the park is off SE Powell Butte at SE 162nd Ave. (The entire area lies immediately north of the Springwater Corridor Trail, within the Johnson Creek Watershed). See map on page 257.

Access road hours:
June 1–August 31:
  6 A.M.–10 P.M.
September 1–late October:
  7 A.M.–8 P.M.
Late October–early April:
  7 A.M.–6 P.M.
early April–May 30:
  7 A.M.–8 P.M.

Activities
Horseback riding
Hiking
Biking
Wildlife viewing area

Facilities
Toilets
Wheelchair accessible
Trail paved (Mountain View trail only)
Parking
Interpretive information (brochures/maps)
Picnic area

Fees and Regulations
Restricted hours
Pets on leash
Trail use designations

big-leaf maple and is restricted to the flatter area near the summit on the drier south slope. This habitat hosts an assemblage of birds, mammals, herps, and invertebrates typical to many forested areas in western Oregon. Most notable include nesting great horned owls, pileated woodpeckers, Swainson's, varied, and hermit thrushes, and several species of warblers (i.e. yellow-rumped, Wilson's, orange-crowned, black-throated gray, and Townsend's). Common winter residents include winter wren, song and fox sparrows, spotted towhee, American robin, black-capped and chestnut-backed chickadees, dark-eyed junco, and Steller's jay.

Butte History

The butte was first logged in the late 1800s. With subsequent sustained grazing by Meadowland Dairy herds, the upper portions of the butte have remained in open pastureland. The flanks of the butte support regenerated forest. Former City Commissioner John Mann is credited with first having seen the butte's water storage, open space, and recreational opportunities. Mann instigated the city's purchase of the butte from George Winston in April of 1925 for $135,000. Since then there have been numerous plans for the site. In 1935 an airport and federal radio receiver towers were proposed. In 1938 part of the land was leased to Powell Valley Road Water District for their water reservoirs, three of which are presently on the Butte's lower northeast corner. A prison farm for alcoholics and drug addicts was proposed in 1946.

The butte saw Mann's original intent begin to materialize in 1977 when design of reservoirs for Portland's water supply was started. Today there is one buried 50 million-gallon reservoir measuring 385 by 641 feet in area and 32 feet at its deepest point on the north side of the butte. It supplies up to 40% of Portland's daily water use. There are projections for at least three similar reservoirs, all arrayed along the north face. Total cost for the first reservoir, including associated piping, was $9.5 million.

By the early 1980s, primarily due to interest in the butte by citizens and Portland Parks and Recreation, management considerations, and other factors, the Water Bureau suggested a cooperative management scheme by both bureaus. Funds were obtained from the Land and Water Conservation Fund and planning was started with a citizens' advisory committee and public hearings. Ultimately, a management plan was devised, and Powell Butte Nature Park became a reality in July 1990.

Butte Geology

Portland is the only city in the continental United States that has a volcano within its city limits. Powell Butte is a cinder cone that is part

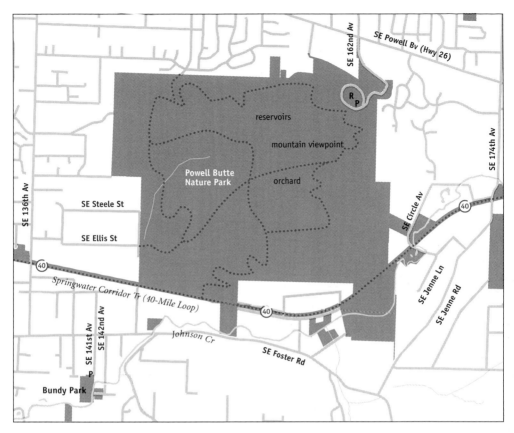

of the Boring Lavas, a system of over a hundred small vents, cinder cones, and shield volcanoes (i.e. Mt. Sylvania and Larch Mt.) in this region created during the Pliocene, one to five million years ago. Cinder cones are not actually uplifted volcanic cones, but are the result of vents, which allowed lava to ooze over the landscape. This hot material interacted with water and surrounding soils to create erosion-resistant landforms which remain after adjacent land has given way to eons of wind and water erosive forces. The result is the peaks which dominate east Portland: Rocky Butte, Mt. Tabor, Kelly Butte, the Sandy River bluffs, and Powell Butte. Most of the material that can readily be seen on the butte today is the cobbley, sandy Troutdale material. Construction of the water storage reservoir required the excavation of more than 350,000 cubic yards of this formation, which was then placed in a valley on the south side of the butte. A stroll over this portion of the butte will reveal the rounded rocks characteristic of the Troutdale formation.

Portland is the only city in the continental United States that has a volcano within its city limits.

Access

Main trailhead begins at the public parking area, and includes a .6 mile paved, 5% grade path that ascends to the orchard at the top of the butte. There are over nine miles of trails throughout the upland meadow and forest habitats, as well as linking with the Springwater Trail that runs along the south boundary of the butte.

How to Get There

Heading east on SE Powell Blvd., turn right at SE 162nd Ave. and travel south on the main park entrance road to the parking lot, about midway up the north side of the butte. You can also hike or bicycle to the south entrance to the park along the Springwater Trail, approximately .75 mile east of SE 136th Ave. There are other less formal access points along the west (i.e. at SE Ellis St. and SE Holgate Blvd.) and east (i.e. SE Circle Ave.) park boundaries.

By Ralph Thomas Rogers

For more information: Powell Butte Nature Park is owned by the Portland Water Bureau, but under cooperative agreement, the natural resources and recreational activities are managed by Portland Bureau of Parks and Recreation. Or contact: Friends of Powell Butte, see Resources.

Bundy Park

A bit difficult to locate, and parking is greatly limited, but worth the effort for those seeking solitude in a shady riparian environment. This 3.47-acre undeveloped Portland park which borders Johnson Creek is dominated by mixed evergreen and deciduous trees that provide forage and nesting sites for a variety of passerine (perching) birds. The sound of running water combined with the songs of Swainson's thrush and varied thrush adds to the meditative atmosphere of this little-known haven.

There is a single, informal out-and-back trail paralleling the creek channel. Much of Johnson Creek within the park is well shaded by the mostly native riparian vegetation. In addition, the riffle-pool complex along this stretch of the creek is reminiscent of what much of Johnson Creek must have been like prior to human settlement. Under the Douglas fir and western red cedar-dominated canopy is a fairly natural understory and groundcover, except along unshaded sections of the trail (especially near the trailhead) and at a couple of openings in the forest canopy, where several exotic species have become established. The most notable exotics include Himalayan blackberry, English ivy, common hawthorn, and American holly. The native understory species include red alder, Indian plum or osoberry, snowberry, salmonberry, and chokecherry.

Access

Entrance to the park is at the south end of the single-lane, unpaved 141st Ave. that dead-ends at the trailhead. Since public parking is greatly limited at the park entrance (room for one vehicle along the side of SE 141st without blocking residential driveways and traffic), it may be best to park along SE Foster and walk down SE 141st to the park entrance. There are no restroom facilities at this park.

How to Get There

Heading east on SE Foster Rd., turn right (south) onto SE 141st Ave. (be aware that the sign for SE 141st is on the north side of the road). This road is an unpaved single-lane road that is easily missed, since it looks like a long driveway mostly lined with rows of mixed evergreen and deciduous trees. Proceed for approximately 1/4 mile to the gated entrance to the park. *See map on page 257.*

By Ralph Thomas Rogers

For more information: Portland Parks and Recreation, see Resources.

Location
Approximately 1/4 mile south of SE Foster Rd. on SE 141st Ave. in Portland.

Activities
Hiking (short trail)
Wildlife viewing (limited)

Facilities
Parking (very limited on site)

Fees and Regulations
Open dawn to dusk
Pets on leash

Highlights
Solitude with great streamside sitting areas within a relatively intact riparian corridor along both sides of Johnson Creek.

Public Transit
Tri-Met #10 (Harold) stop at SE Foster Rd. and SE 122nd Ave. is the closest stop to Bundy Park. From that stop walk east along SE Foster to SE 141st, turn right (south), and walk the 1/4 mile to the gated entrance to the park.

Thomas Guide 628

Leach Botanical Garden

As the name implies, this Portland park is for plant lovers. Because of the diversity of habitats, however, wildlife viewers also flock here. Established paths and the tranquil Johnson Creek setting provide easy access for a wide range of users.

This nine-acre botanical garden specializes in preserving the original Leach collection as well as Northwest native plants. The collection of over 2,000 species, hybrids, and cultivars can be enjoyed on a self-guided tour that winds about the Manor House and down along Johnson Creek.

This site is located in a woodland hollow bisected by Johnson Creek. The colorful Wilson's warbler and many other riparian species can be seen along the creek's edge.

Access

Entrance to Leach Botanical Garden is at 6704 SE 122nd Ave. However, parking is off-site in a nearby lot just to the southwest of the bridge crossing Johnson Creek. Note the vegetated swale at the edge of the parking lot nearest the creek. The swale was constructed with Metro Restoration Grant money and matching funds from Portland Bureau of Environmental Services as a water quality treatment area for the parking lot runoff. Within the gardens there is a short network of established paths from which to enjoy both the maintained gardens and the natural habitat areas.

How to Get There

Heading east on SE Foster Rd., turn right (south) on SE 122nd Ave. and drive up the hill approximately 1/2 mile to the main gate, then veer right and cross the bridge over Johnson Creek. The parking lot is immediately to the right. *See map on page 263.*

By Ralph Thomas Rogers

For more information: Leach Botanical Garden, Portland Parks and Recreation or Leach Garden Friends, see Resources.

Location
Gated entrance to the Garden is at 6704 SE 122nd Ave., 3 blocks south of SE Foster Rd.

Activities
Hiking
Wildlife viewing areas

Facilities
Toilet
Wheelchair accessible (limited)
Trail paved
Parking (short walk from main gate)
Interpretive center
Interpretive information

Fees and Regulations
Restricted hours
No pets

Highlights
Botanical garden with large variety of exotic and native Pacific Northwest flora (over 2,000 species, hybrids, and cultivars); trails through relatively natural forested riparian habitat adjacent to relatively undisturbed and unaltered stretch of Johnson Creek.

Public Transit
Exit Tri-Met #10 (Harold) or #71 at SE Foster Rd. and SE 122nd Ave. Travel south along SE 122nd Ave. for approximately 1/2 mile to the Garden main gate.

Thomas Guide 628

Beggars-Tick Marsh Wildlife Refuge

Once zoned for industrial development, this 21-acre open space was officially dedicated in April of 1990 by Multnomah County as its first official urban wildlife refuge. The refuge is currently owned and managed by Metro Regional Parks and Greenspaces. As unlikely as it seems, in the midst of an industrial neighborhood, this is one of the most pristine wetlands in the Portland metropolitan area. Because of its limited access during most of the year, and the dense woody vegetation which buffers it in many places from excessive human interference, Beggars-Tick harbors a diversity of native, relatively undisturbed plant communities, which in turn support varied wildlife.

The name Beggars-Tick is derived from the common name of two plant species of the Genus *Bidens* that occur in the marsh. Those species (*Bidens frondosa* and *B. cernua*), which are members of the sunflower family (Asteraceae), bloom as the marsh is drying out in late August and into September. The double-barbed seeds of beggar-ticks are a classic example of "stick-tight dispersal" whereby the seeds hitch a ride on the clothing of passing hikers or the fur of passing four-legged mammals; hence the name beggar-ticks.

Beggars-Tick is predominantly a wetland with three easily identifiable plant communities: shrub-scrub which is dominated by spirea or hardhack (*Spirea douglasii*), willow (*Salix* spp.), swamp rose (*Rosa pisocarpa*), and beggar-ticks; emergent marsh in the heart of the wetland with a thick mat of smartweed or knotweed (*Polygonum* spp.) and small patches of the once abundant cattail (*Typha latifolia*); and a willow/red alder (*Alnus rubra*) swamp that surrounds the other wetland communities. In the late fall, winter, and early spring, much of the wetland is essentially a large, shallow pond offering ideal habitat for a variety of migratory and wintering waterfowl. Most of the ponded area usually drains by late spring, exposing the vegetated marsh until re-flooding begins again during late fall.

The site was once farmed, with blueberries being one of the major cash crops. It has also been used for horse grazing, and in 1968 was purchased by Multnomah County as a storage basin for local stormwater runoff. Today, in addition to being important habitat for a diversity of fauna and flora, the refuge is an important component of water quality and floodwater management within the Johnson Creek watershed by storing stormwater and removing the associated sediment and pollutants.

The marsh and its associated wildlife are not easily viewed from any of the surrounding roads. The newly contoured and revegetated south fill was once used as a handy place to dump construction debris. The significant annual flooding (up to five feet in some areas) makes this area relatively inaccessible during the winter and early spring.

Location
SE 111th Ave. just north of SE Foster Rd. and south of SE Harold Rd. (The entire area lies immediately north of the Springwater Corridor Trail and west of SE 111th Ave.)

Activities
Hiking
Wildlife viewing area

Facilities
Wheelchair accessible (only one portion adjacent to Springwater Trail trailhead)
Trail unpaved
Parking
Interpretive information (brochures/maps)

Fees and Regulations
Pets on leash

However, during the dry season the habitat mosaic and vegetative screening offer excellent opportunities to closely observe the plant and wildlife communities and their interrelationships.

Emergent Marsh
This habitat is best accessed from the north parking area just off of SE 111th Avenue. When this area is flooded, a variety of waterfowl are easily observed including gadwall, northern shoveler, wood duck, mallard, American wigeon, bufflehead, green-winged teal, American coot, Canada goose, pied-billed grebe, hooded merganser, ring-necked duck, and scaup. As the ponded water decreases, waterfowl use decreases but other species become more obvious including nesting red-winged blackbirds, sora, and Virginia rail. At its driest in late summer, the vast bed of smartweed blossoms is visited by tens of thousands of honeybees and other pollinating insects. Above the wetlands large numbers of swallows and dragonflies can be seen hawking their insect meals. There are also some isolated areas vegetated with a variety of sedges (*Carex* spp.) and bulrushes (*Scirpus* spp.).

Shrub Scrub
Mostly located along the south and west side of the refuge, this habitat is best viewed and accessed from the restoration area in the southeast corner of the refuge. In addition to the spirea, willow, and beggar-ticks, other plants include small amounts of reed canarygrass (*Phalaris arundinacea*), spotted jewelweed (*Impatiens noli-tangere*), and soft rush (*Juncus effusus*). This is the habitat to observe the cedar waxwing, red-winged blackbird, scrub jay, brown-headed cowbird, rufous hummingbird, spotted towhee, ring-necked pheasant, and a variety of sparrows, warblers (yellow, common yellowthroat), and flycatchers. Green heron can be observed stalking prey along the edge where the shrub habitat borders the marsh.

Forested Swamp
The forested wetlands that serve as a buffer along the east and west boundaries of the refuge are predominantly willow, but also contain black cottonwood (*Populus balsamifera* ssp.*trichocarpa*)and red alder. Here is where you may see or hear the Bewick's wren, black-capped and chestnut-backed chickadees, bushtit, warblers (yellow-rumped, Wilson's, and orange-crowned), sparrows, purple and house finches, and band-tailed pigeon. This habitat also provides good perches from which the red-tailed and sharp-shinned hawks can survey the open wetlands below.

Upland

Much of the restoration area in the southeast corner is a grass-dominated upland area surrounding excavated ponds becoming overgrown with willow and cottonwood. The filled site bordering the fence along the Foster Auto Parts wrecking yard in the southwest corner of the refuge is also an upland, supporting a variety of mostly exotic herbaceous species including wild carrot (*Daucus carota*), bull thistle (*Cirsium vulgare*), Canadian thistle (*C. arvense*), common tansy (*Tanacetum vulgare*), chicory (*Chicorium intybus*), common St. John's-wort (*Hypericum perforatum*), white clover (*Trifolium repens*), red clover (*Trifolium pratense*), curled dock (*Rumex crispus*), Japanese knotweed (*Polygonum cuspidatum*), and vetch (*Vicia* sp.). Himalayan blackberry (*Rubus discolor*) and Scot's broom (*Cytisus scoparius*) are the dominant upland shrubs. Goldfinch, sparrow, and junco frequent this old field habitat.

Access

Access is year-round to the two main wildlife viewing areas and the limited formal trail system. One viewing area with off-street parking for about 4-5 vehicles is accessed from the west side of SE 111th, approximately 1/2 mile north of SE Foster Rd. in Portland.

The other viewing area is located in the southeast corner of Beggars-Tick with access via the short formal loop trail that begins at another off street parking area at the junction of SE 111th and the Springwater Trail.

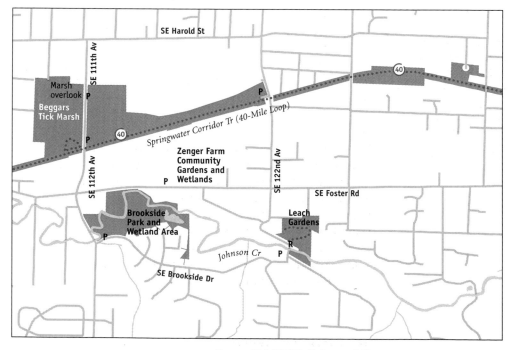

There is also an extremely informal path that runs north off the Springwater Trail, approximately 100 yards west of SE 111th. That path goes behind the Foster Auto Parts wrecking yard and provides additional wildlife viewing locations along the eastern boundary of the wildlife refuge, although it has more recently become overgrown with Himalayan blackberries.

How to Get There
Heading east on SE Foster Rd., turn left onto SE 111th Ave. at the traffic light (be aware that the road to the south at this intersection is SE 112th, so look to the left for the sign for 111th Ave.) and drive north a short distance to either of the two designated parking areas west of SE 111th. You can also hike or bicycle to Beggars-Tick along the Springwater Trail.

By Ralph Thomas Rogers

For more information: Formerly owned by Multnomah County Parks, Beggars-Tick was transferred to Metro Regional Parks and Greenspaces. Metro has a brochure on Beggars-Tick, runs some interpretive programs, and is involved in restoration projects at the site.

Zenger Farm

Recognized as an important component of floodwater and water quality management within the Johnson Creek Watershed, Zenger Farm was purchased by Portland Bureau of Environmental Services in July 1994. In addition to preserving the stormwater storage capabilities, protecting the site from future development also preserved important natural resources, including a spring that flows year-round from the base of the upland slope. That spring supplies clean, clear, cool water to the wetlands that comprise the northern half of the site as well as down-gradient wetlands including Beggars-Tick Marsh. This spring flow is particularly important during the summer and early fall when the wetland would otherwise be dry.

This 15.85-acre site was once a small-scale dairy farm where cows grazed on the upland meadow and seasonally on the emergent marsh. A row of orchard trees with a few evergreens runs east-west through the property, and marks the boundary between the wetlands on the northern half and the sloping upland meadow and farm buildings that occupy the southern half.

The wetland consists of a mosaic of emergent marsh and shallow ponds which provide resting, feeding, and/or nesting habitat for several species of waterfowl, most notably mallard, gadwall, northern shoveler, green-winged and cinnamon teal, American wigeon, and American coot. Although reed canarygrass (*Phalaris arundinacea*) is the most obvious of the marsh vegetation, there is a surprising diversity of other grasses, plus sedge (*Carex*), rush (*Juncus*), spike-rush (*Eleocharis*), and bulrush (*Scirpus*). Shrubs are scarce and mostly limited to a discontinuous row of Douglas spirea (*Spiraea douglasii*) and willow (*Salix* sp.) along the northern boundary where the wetland abuts the Springwater Trail.

Most years Virginia rail and common snipe can be heard and less commonly seen in these wetlands. Occasionally sora are also found here. Other common species utilizing the wetland include red-winged blackbird, marsh wren, common yellowthroat, and ring-necked pheasant. This is a great location for watching a variety of swallows rapidly darting low over the marsh in pursuit of the abundant insect inhabitants. Any large mammals seen swimming in the marsh are likely to be nutria, which are fairly common in this wetland and the adjacent marshes in this watershed.

The adjoining upland meadow is mostly grasses, but many invasive exotics, herbaceous and shrub species, are becoming more abundant. In addition, a sizable area of upland has been leased and subsequently converted to an organic gardening enterprise. Still, the surface of the remaining upland meadow is riddled with rodent holes and connecting runways where voles, mice, and shrews are occasionally picked off by patrolling red-tailed hawks, American

Location
Site entrance is at 11741 SE Foster Rd., although there is no public access. The entire site lies north of Foster Rd. and south of the Springwater Corridor Trail, which forms the northern boundary.

Activities
Hiking (Springwater)
Wildlife viewing area

Facilities
Wheelchair accessible (Springwater)
Trail paved (Springwater)

Fees and Regulations
No pets
No on-site public access

Highlights
Easy viewing of an extensive emergent marsh/open water habitat complex. On-site spring provides year-round water. Virginia rail frequently nests here.

Public Transit
Tri-Met #10 runs eastbound on SE Harold, southbound on SE 122nd Ave., then westbound on SE Foster. Exit at SE 111th and travel north approximately 1/4 mile to the Springwater Trail, then travel east on the trail approximately 1/4 mile.

Thomas Guide 628

kestrels, and even northern harriers which are infrequent visitors to this site. In late summer, American goldfinch and pine siskins feed on the abundant thistle (*Cirsium*) seed.

The aforementioned perennial spring at the base of the upland slope fills an excavated depression, forming a deep pool that overflows through a channel that disperses the water to other parts of the marsh, and ultimately flows under the Springwater Trail to the wetlands to the north. Any excess water then flows westward toward Beggars-Tick marsh. The spring pool and overflow channel are densely vegetated with watercress (*Nasturtium officinale*) where aquatic insects abound.

Zenger Farm wetland is contiguous with a wooded wetland/ pond complex to the east where wood ducks find shelter and nest sites. Another emergent marsh/pond complex and a shrub-scrub wetland can be easily observed immediately to the north of the Springwater Trail.

Access
There is no official public access to the site itself. Wildlife viewing can be done from the Springwater Corridor Trail that forms the north boundary of the site, approximately 1/4 mile east of SE 111th Ave.

How to Get There
Heading east on SE Foster Rd., turn left onto SE 111th Ave. at the traffic light (be aware that the road to the south at this intersection is SE 112th, so look to the left for the sign for 111th Ave.) and drive north a short distance to the Beggars-Tick Marsh Wildlife Refuge designated parking area where the Springwater Corridor Trail crosses SE 111th Ave. Hike or bicycle east approximately 1/4 mile to the north boundary of the site. *See map on page 263.*

By Ralph Thomas Rogers

For more information: Portland Bureau of Environmental Services. Urban Bounty Farm leases and operates the organic garden at the upper reach of the upland meadow. See Resources.

Reflections and Techniques of an Odonate Watcher

Early one late-spring morning at the edge of a Southeast Portland pond, a small creature crawls from beneath the water to be reborn. No, it is not a religious ceremony of baptismal rebirthing. It is a dragonfly performing one of nature's most splendid spectacles, known as emergence. It is the final stage of incomplete metamorphosis, whereby one lifestyle of the dragonfly is literally shed like an old coat and a new lifestyle unfolds. Dragonflies of the order Odonata have been doing this magical transformation for more than 300 million years, beginning sometime during the Carboniferous period of the Paleozoic era. To put this into perspective, dragonflies are as old as the first reptiles, and much older than flowering plants, which evolved a mere 100 million years ago.

The dragonfly emerging from the pond in Southeast Portland is the green darner (*Anax junius*), one of the largest and most widespread of the 400 species found in North America (there are about 5,000 species known worldwide, mostly from the tropics). I watch by flashlight as the totally aquatic nymph, about two inches in length, climbs a cattail (*Typha latifolia*) until it is nearly 12 inches above the water's surface. After anchoring itself to the cattail by means of its clawed feet, the darner appears to test its grip by swinging vigorously from side to side. For nearly an hour nothing outwardly happens until, finally, the swelling body splits the larval shell (exuvia) and the head and thorax of the adult dragonfly emerge. The abdomen, which remains in the nymphal skin, supports the upper body as it hangs downward for almost 30 minutes while the legs harden. The dragonfly then rights itself, re-grasps the cattail, this time with the adult legs, and pulls its abdomen free. By now a flashlight is no longer needed to witness the finale, as blood, surging from the body, expands the crumpled wings. Forty minutes later the wings have dried, and the adult green darner, about three inches in length and with a wingspan slightly over four inches, makes its maiden flight. Think of the possibilities had this specimen been a giant paleo-dragonfly of the Carboniferous period emerging from that same pond in Southeast Portland. The nymph would have been approximately 15 inches long and the adult would "hawk" over the terrain with a wingspan of over 30 inches! That's slightly larger than a present day sharp-shinned hawk (*Accipiter striatus*).

Powers of Observation

One of the best ways to learn about the behavior of an organism is to observe, quietly and motionlessly from a concealed vantage point within or near the critter's habitat, and at a time of day and season when it is likely to be visibly present. Dragonflies are ideal organisms for urban naturalists to study. Compared to many other insects, they are large and easily observed. The adults have complex and interesting territorial, mating, and egg-laying behavior. In addition, the larvae can be easily reared and observed in a home or school aquarium.

When observing dragonflies, keep in mind that they are daytime hunters, and although some species fly late into evening, most are active only in sunshine. In fact, during cloudy periods or inclement weather, dragonflies will generally settle in trees and shrubs and await better flight conditions.

Concealment is not a necessity for observing dragonflies, but remaining motionless once positioned at an observation post is important, particularly when observing reproductive behavior. For the true hard-core odonate watcher, the best vantage for observation is to remain motionless, chin-deep in pond water or veiled within the emergent marsh vegetation. This technique is particularly rewarding as other organisms such as snakes, turtles, newts, frogs, other aquatic insects, and even waterbirds come within close range of the observer.

Two easily observed activities of adult dragonflies are feeding and reproduction. Reproductive behavior can be divided into three categories: territorial defense, mating, and egg-laying. During feeding, these airborne dragons fly with their six spiny legs bent forward to form a "basket" which captures small flying insects, such as flies, midges, and mosquitos. Although most often found "hawking" around ponds, streams, lakes, and wetlands, dragonflies range far afield in search of prey, and have even been observed low to the ground beating their wings to flush insects from the vegetation. Observe when and how each species forages for prey, and whether one species of dragonfly preys on another. Remember, it is important while observing wildlife behavior that you ask yourself why the organism is behaving as it does.

Unlike feeding, dragonfly spawning, or egg-laying, occurs exclusively around water, be it permanent or ephemeral. Males can be observed competing for territories at the potential spawning sites and actively driving off intruding males of the same or sometimes different species. By contrast, the female dragonfly often feeds and roosts varying distances away from the spawning locations and occasionally flies within the male-guarded territories, where she is aggressively pursued by several males and mated. Observe how the males of different species defend their territories, and whether they mate with several females or a single female, which is guarded until the eggs are deposited. Observe how egg-laying strategy varies among the species.

By Ralph Thomas Rogers

Tideman Johnson Park

Stretching along a long segment of Johnson Creek, Tideman Johnson is a fantastic find in inner Southeast Portland. Steve Johnson, who lives just across Johnson Creek in what could only be called "Hobbitville-on-Johnson," is of the Johnson family that donated the park to Portland in the early 1940s. Since then Steve and his family and friends have kept an eye on this six-acre park, which fortunately no longer suffers from rowdy gang use.

Thankfully, with increased attention to fish restoration and improving water quality in what has been a severely polluted stream, Tideman Johnson took a decided turn for the better beginning in the mid-1990s when Steve, other citizens and some local businesses, and the Portland Bureau of Environmental Services created the Johnson Creek Watershed Council.

The most striking thing one notices now is that formerly eroded banks have been replanted in creek dogwood, spirea, red alder, and other native plants. When I think of my birding experiences at Tideman Johnson, the nearby fish ladder, and downstream at the Eastmoreland Racquet Club, the species that immediately spring to mind are great horned and screech owls, band-tailed pigeons, mourning doves, and belted kingfishers. It's great in winter for song, golden-crowned, and white-crowned sparrows. A solitary great blue heron can usually be seen skulking about near the fish ladder or just downstream. Northern flickers are thick at times, gleaning insects from the ground in the open grassy areas in the heart of the park.

Johnson's home-made fish hatchery attracts green heron, which are persistent and ingenious. Once after he stretched netting over his holding pond, which was crammed with fingerling trout, Steve watched a green heron stand on the net until it sagged just enough for the heron to snap up several fish. After he adjusted the net until it was racquet-taut, the heron returned and literally bounced off the netting. To hear Steve tell it, he wasn't sure who was more shocked, he or the bird.

If you enter the park from SE 37th the nicest walk is straight into the park, across the grassy interior to the stream. Then stroll along a very rustic, unimproved path that parallels the creek downstream where you pass under the Springwater Corridor Trail that runs across the bridge overhead. This puts you onto the bridge, once a nice wooden structure that was unfortunately torched a few years ago and replaced by a fire-resistant metal bridge. From the bridge is some of the best birding, especially in late spring and early summer when the big-leaf maple, cottonwoods, and alders can be alive with Wilson's warblers, black-headed and evening grosbeaks, softly-cooing mourning doves, and the almost grunt-like, deep call of band-tailed pigeons.

A short walk down the paved path toward the Eastmoreland Racquet Club is great for sapsuckers, downy woodpeckers, black-

Location
Mile marker 6 on the Springwater Corridor Trail, south of SE 37th Ave.

Activities
Hiking

Facilities
Trail unpaved
Parking (in surrounding neighborhood off SE 37th and Crystal Springs Blvd.)

Fees and Regulations
None

Highlights
One of the best access points to a natural area on Johnson Creek. Shady, open with newly restored creekside vegetation. One of my favorite birding sites over the years.

Public Transit
Tri-Met #19 or #75

Thomas Guide 627

capped chickadees, bushtits, and other commonly seen forest species. Then head back across the bridge, and either continue east on the Springwater Trail or back to SE 37th. Within a few years it will be possible to continue west on the Springwater to the Willamette River, but not before three bridges are replaced and the right-of-way between SE Umatilla and SE McLoughlin is purchased.

Access

Via the Springwater Trail from the east, at SE 45th and Johnson Creek Blvd. (the segment west of here will not be completed for a few years); from SE Berkeley Way and a path behind the Eastmoreland Racquet Club; or the easiest access is from the south end of SE 37th off SE Crystal Springs Blvd.

How to Get There

From the Sellwood area take SE Bybee over the McLoughlin overpass; turn right at Eastmoreland golf course onto SE 28th and head south on 28th to Crystal Springs Blvd. Continue east to SE 37th and turn right. Park along 37th or Tenino. Walk south to the end of 37th and take the path across the Springwater Trail and into the park.

By Mike Houck

For more information: Portland Parks and Recreation or Portland Bureau of Environmental Services, Johnson Creek Watershed Manager, see Resources

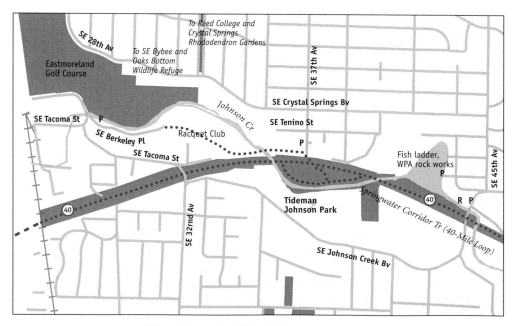

Reed College Canyon

Do not be deceived by the Reed College Canyon's small size (15 acres) or by the manicured landscape of the Reed College campus that surrounds it. The Reed College Canyon is a wild, unruly place that virtually bursts out of its shallow confines (the "Canyon" is only forty feet deep at its deepest). It is the place to go for those wishing to catch a faint glimpse of what inner-city, east-side Portland might have looked like before it was paved over and built upon.

Formed by a series of underground springs scattered throughout and above its eastern half, the canyon transitions from swampy marsh to shallow lake to fast-running creek before exiting the campus. From there the creek enters a culvert, crosses through a small farm and under 28th Avenue, and then feeds into the Rhododendron Test Gardens, which in turn feeds into Johnson Creek and ultimately the Willamette River.

The canyon, then pastureland for cows, was donated to Reed College in 1910. A conservation ethic and prohibitive costs saved the canyon from a plan to convert it into the "centerpiece of an artful landscape of Tudor Gothic quadrangles and formal gardens," and in 1913 it was declared a wildlife refuge by the State Game Commission, a designation it still holds today.

In spring, summer, and fall, the swampy marsh that forms the canyon's eastern end is so lush that you often do not notice the water until an accidental misstep sinks you up to your knees in muck. An easy-to-follow loop trail skirts the edge of the marsh. Numerous labyrinth-like side trails lead into (but not necessarily out of) its dense interior. The canopy here is populated with trees evident throughout the canyon: Douglas fir, big-leaf maple, red alder, and western red cedar. Shrubs such as red elderberry, Oregon grape, and black hawthorn, and herbs such as trillium, Pacific water-parsley, hardhack, skunk cabbage, and stinging nettle are common in the understory. Wildflowers abound in spring (over 50 different species have been identified in the canyon). Among the more common ferns are sword and bracken. Also, look in the drier areas for the somewhat uncommon gold-back fern.

Many of the 80+ bird species that have been sighted in the canyon, including great blue herons, green herons, kingfishers, and seven different species of warbler (orange crowned, yellow-rumped, black-throated gray, Townsend's, MacGillivray's, Wilson's, and common yellowthroat), can be found in this area. This is also a good place to call for western screech owls.

As the marsh transitions into the deeper, but quite silted, Reed Lake, signs of beaver become evident. Beaver-chewed stumps abound and from the lake's northeast edge a beaver dam is visible. River otter and muskrat have also been sighted in the canyon. The

Location
This site is located on the campus of Reed College in Southeast Portland. Reed is bordered by SE 39th Ave. (east), SE Woodstock Blvd. (south), SE 28th Ave. (west), and SE Steele St. (north).

Activities
Hiking

Facilities
Trail unpaved

Regulations
Pets on leash
Reed College campus is a private institution and the canyon is private property. The college has always welcomed birders and nature enthusiasts. Please return the courtesy by respecting private property.

Highlights

Over 80 different avian species have been sighted at the Reed College Canyon. It is a great place to see green herons and belted kingfishers. The Reed Canyon offers a nice juxtaposition to the nearby Rhododendron Gardens. Visit the manicured Rhododendron Gardens to learn to identify local waterfowl and then visit the Reed Canyon to see if you can sight them in a more natural setting.

Public Transit

Tri-Met #75 runs along SE 39th Ave. Tri-Met #10 stops near Reed's north parking lot on SE Steele St.

Thomas Guide 627

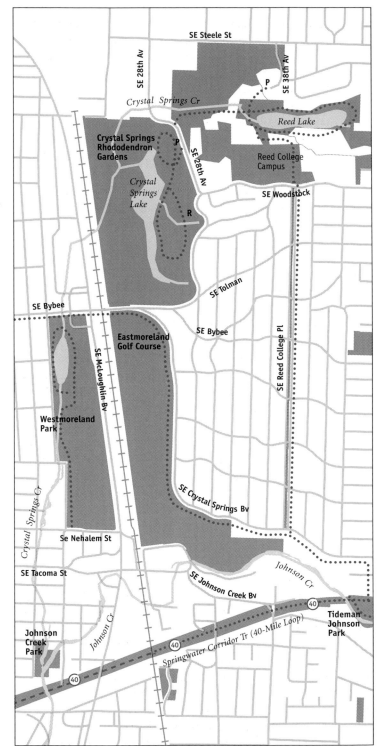

damp underbrush of the southeast side of the canyon is home to the canyon's only known amphibian, the terrestrial *Ensatina* salamander. Look throughout the lake for ducks. Mallards are obvious, but look also for wood ducks, American wigeon, bufflehead, and lesser scaup. Common merganser, green-winged teal, and ruddy ducks are here as well. In winter look for hooded mergansers.

The western end of Reed Lake was deepened to create a swimming area in 1915. Although swimming no longer occurs here, do not be surprised if you happen to see the occasional papier-mache dragon or even a naked Reed student emerging from the primordial ooze. In spring and summer, barn, violet-green, and tree swallows abound here. A dam built in 1929 forms the western boundary of Reed College Lake and routes the flow of water around the Reed Swimming Pool.

Just beyond the pool, note the coho salmon incubator box. Since 1996, a joint project between Reed College and the Oregon Department of Fish and Wildlife has been attempting to reintroduce coho salmon into this stretch of creek. Historically, this creek has been home to coho and chinook salmon, steelhead, and cutthroat trout and there is a possibility that a remnant population of landlocked steelhead still persists. In the spring, look for the coho salmon fry in the shallow backwater areas of the creek.

Reed's efforts to restore native fish species to the canyon have been coupled with removal of invasive, non-native plant species such as reed canarygrass, Himalayan blackberry, clematis, and English ivy. It is Reed policy to forgo the use of chemical controls, so all clearing is done by hand.

Beyond the salmon incubator, the creek is narrow, shallow, and fast. Beyond a stairway leading up to the Reed College Theater, the understory becomes dense with common horsetails, and in late spring the creek sometimes disappears beneath a carpet of skunk cabbage. Two hundred feet further on, the western edge of the campus is reached and the trail dead-ends.

Access

The canyon bisects the Reed College campus in an east-west direction. There are several points of access to the canyon depending on where one parks. Consult the large colorful campus maps located at each parking area to orient yourself to the closest access point.

The easiest access point can be reached by parking in Reed's west parking lot along SE 28th Ave. From here a short walk northward beside the tennis courts and across narrow Botsford Dr. will bring you to the Reed Theater. A large staircase next to its entrance descends into the canyon. From here, a trail heads westward along a fast-running creek. This single track runs for approximately 800 feet before it reaches a dam that bisects the canyon and forms the west boundary of Reed Lake. A loop trail (approx. one mile long) departs from either end of this dam.

Editor's Note:
As of fall 2000 Reed College had realigned the Reed Canyon trails to take them out of the wetlands onto adjacent uplands. Significant restoration work has also begun to replace invasive non-native plants with native species.

How to Get There
Travel south on McLoughlin Blvd. (99E) and take the Reed College exit. Turn right onto Bybee Blvd. Bybee Blvd. will quickly curve around to the left and become 28th Ave. Pass Woodstock Blvd. on the right. The next right-hand turn is the Reed College parking lot recommended above for access to the canyon. Additional parking areas are located along Woodstock Blvd. and along Steele St.

By Bob Sallinger

For more information: Reed College, see Resources. The Reed College Canyon is private property owned by Reed College.

Crystal Springs Rhododendron Gardens

As with Tideman Johnson Park, size sometimes is very deceiving. Crystal Springs is only seven acres in size, but seems to cram a lot into the space. It is first and foremost a manicured, highly managed garden, not a natural area. It is billed as having "an outstanding collection of rare species and hybrid rhododendrons, azaleas, and other lesser known ericaceous plants, as well as many companion plants and unusual trees."

Before it got all gussied up with rockeries, waterfalls, and extensive ramps to accommodate wheelchairs, the "rhody garden" was just a great place to go look at winter ducks. It still is. There has been a long-standing battle to save at least a vestige of natural habitat since the Portland chapter of the American Rhododendron Society co-founded the park with Portland Parks in 1950. Now that the gardens have been completely renovated, what to the gardeners undoubtedly seem an offensive eyesore, the brambles and unkempt willows, still remain. It seems that urban naturalists have won that small but important concession.

While the rest of the gardens is just that, a lovingly tended and truly beautiful garden, the wildlife-attracting and messy-looking rough patch of shrubs, submerged logs, and emergent marsh vegetation remains on the left as you walk across the low bridge which crosses the pond. It is here that you look for a gang of wood duck, and where green herons have nested, providing the only readily-accessible view of young green herons being fed by parents that I know of in Portland.

The past feeding of ducks with tons of hand-me-down bread from eager visitors has, thankfully, been replaced with small packets of cracked corn available at the park. It would be better if the ducks were not fed at all, but some people are simply driven to feed them, so the Park Bureau compromised by supplying cracked corn.

If you're interested in a variety of ducks, don't bother with the rhody gardens during the summer. About the only residents are a few squirrels or mongrelized mallards hanging around for a handout. However, it's still a nice cool walk among the stream and rhodies which are evergreen. In spring, of course, there are lots of migrant warblers which are attracted to the lush vegetation, and there is an astonshing display of blossoms, some of the rhododendrons as huge as trees. You may want to avoid weekends, as there are crowds. Otherwise, you can virtually get lost, awash in a forest of color.

Absolutely the best time to bird here is during the winter, when huge flocks of waterfowl and gulls congregate on and around the artificial pond that is fed by the amazingly clear springs that bubble up in the creek's headwaters on the Reed College campus. The Rhodendron Society's brochure describes it as a "multiplicity of birds." Hard to argue with that, given that their official checklist counts 94

Location
SE 28th, north of SE Woodstock across from Reed College campus and adjacent to Eastmoreland Golf Course.

Activities
Hiking

Facilities
Toilets
Wheelchair accessible
Trail paved
Parking
Interpretive information
  (brochures/maps)
Picnic area

Fees and Regulations
Entrance fees: Membership is $10 for individuals and allows you and a friend in free; From March 1 through Labor Day there is a modest fee per visit for those without membership, Thursday through Monday, 10 A.M. to 6 P.M.; free Tuesdays and Wednesdays; children under 12 are always free. Restricted hours: 7 days a week, dawn to dusk

species. They've got all but two of the state's grebes: pied-billed, horned, red-necked, and western. Great blue heron, green heron, and black-crowned night-heron are all on the list, as are a plethora of ducks which include, in addition to the common species, lesser scaup, greater scaup, redhead, ring-necked, northern pintail, Eurasian wigeon, and blue-winged teal. And this is the only place now that you can routinely see ruddy ducks and canvasback. Look on the Eastmoreland Golf Course, which meanders around the gardens, for Eurasian wigeon where they can be seen, two to four at a time, grazing among flocks of one to two hundred American wigeon, and an equal number of Canada geese who love to loll on the fairways.

Virtually all of Portland's gulls have been seen here: mew, ring-billed, California, herring, Thayer's, western, and glaucous-winged.

The fairly extensive upland forest attracts red-breasted nuthatch, rufous hummingbird, Anna's hummingbird, black-capped and chestnut-backed chickadees, brown creeper, and several warblers. A veritable chorus of thrushes includes Swainson's, hermit, American robin, and varied. Not a bad assemblage for a garden!

Access
From SE 28th Ave. Entrance is located off the large parking area.

How to Get There
Take SE Bybee east across McLoughlin and bear north on SE 28th past Woodstock. The parking lot is on the west side of SE 28th Ave.
See map on page 272.

By Mike Houck

For more information: Crystal Springs Rhododendron Garden or Portland Parks and Recreation, see Resources.

Highlights
Amazing rhododendron and azalea displays and perhaps the most easily accessed, inner-city winter waterfowl viewing area in Portland.

Public Transit
Tri-Met #19 on Woodstock stops one block from the gardens.

Thomas Guide 627

Cold Feet, Warm Heart

Most birds and mammals that live in cold environments have thick coats of feathers or fur that reduce heat loss from their bodies. In contrast, the feet and lower legs of these animals are thinly insulated or bare. There are good reasons for this. Heavily insulated limbs would hinder running and swimming, and birds and mammals need these "thermal windows" to eliminate excess heat.

At rest, animals can keep their feet warm by drawing them close to their well-insulated bodies. But how do birds swimming in icy water or standing on snow keep their feet and lower legs warm? They don't! Instead, they allow these extremities to cool to temperatures as low as freezing. This conserves heat that would be lost if the feet were kept at normal body temperature, and avoids problems created by warm feet melting holes into the ice.

The cold-feet trick is accomplished partly by varying the amount of blood flowing to its appendages. Excess heat can be "dumped" by increasing the flow of blood through the lower legs and feet. Under cold conditions, the flow can be restricted, reducing heat loss.

Nature's Heat Exchanger

Birds must, however, circulate enough blood through their feet to keep them from freezing. The keys to doing this without losing too much heat are networks of tiny arteries and veins, called *retia mirabilia* ("wonderful nets"), in the well-insulated upper leg. There, arteries carrying warm blood toward the foot divide into many small branches, each of which is surrounded by several tiny, highly branched veins bringing cold blood from the foot back toward the heart. Because heat flows from where there is more of it to where there is less, arterial blood arriving in the bird's foot has already given up most of its heat to the venous blood returning from the foot. These arrangements of blood vessels are called vascular countercurrent heat exchangers, other examples of which are found in the flippers of marine mammals, the noses of caribou, and the shoulders and thighs of arctic foxes. Heating engineers design similar systems to capture furnace heat that would otherwise be lost through chimneys.

These circulatory adaptations reduce heat losses, but a bird or mammal must still retain full use of its feet even when they are very cold. Adaptations in nerve and muscle functions and the fact that fats in the lower legs and feet remain soft at low temperatures make normal use of cold appendages possible.

Birds and mammals maintain a balanced heat budget in the cold by insulating the body but letting appendages remain unencumbered and cool. Think about that the next time you put on your down vest in the cold weather!

By Richard B. Forbes

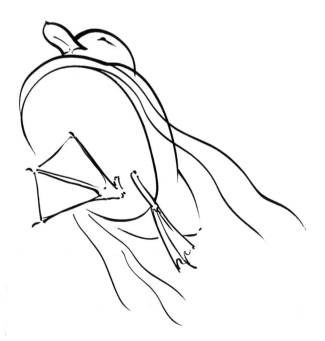

Columbia Slough Watershed

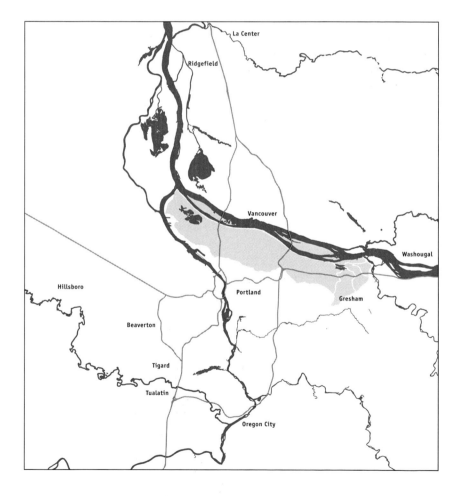

La Center

Ridgefield

Vancouver

Washougal

Hillsboro

Portland

Gresham

Beaverton

Tigard

Tualatin

Oregon City

The Columbia Slough—A Landscape in Transition

A "low piney country with an emence quantity of Geese, Brants, Ducks and sea otters, Swan and cranes," is how Lewis and Clark described the Columbia River floodplain in the autumn of 1805. By 1820, there was a lively enterprise in otter and beaver fur for the Hudson Bay Company; in the 1850s pioneers arrived to farm it; and between 1917 and 1921, dikes and levees "reclaimed" its floodplain for urban development. One hundred and ninety years after the Corps of Discovery, the Slough bears little resemblance to the lush Columbia River floodplain that dominated Lewis and Clark's vista.

Once a braided network of sloughs to the Columbia River, the Upper Slough is now moved and discharged via huge pumps. The Lower Slough, while also diked and drained, still is free-flowing and under tidal influence from the Columbia and Willamette. The entire watershed is touted by the Columbia Corridor Association and Port of Portland as the hub of a $3 trillion Pacific Rim economic engine, but it's also a priceless greenspace, providing canoeing, hiking, and bicycling opportunities near home and work.

The extant greenspaces form a narrow band of riparian forest, scattered wetlands, a few large natural enclaves, and newly planted forests and wetlands that dot the landscape along this 18-mile waterway, which drains over 23 square miles from Fairview Lake in the east to its confluence with the Willamette River at Kelley Point Park.

While it is Oregon's largest industrial area, with 17,800 acres, 2,850 businesses, and 45,000 jobs, it is just as much home to river otter, osprey, peregrine falcon, painted turtles, bald eagles, and hundreds of other birds, mammals, and other wildlife. Although the network of railroads, freeways, and airports may be more obvious to the casual observer, the watershed is also criss-crossed with a natural network of cottonwood, ash, and creek dogwood woodlands, and willow-lined sloughs.

Adapted from "Exploring the Columbia Slough," Audubon Society of Portland

Gresham-Fairview Trail

Location
West side of SE Powell
Blvd. east of SW Duniway
Ave. and east of W
Powell Loop.

Activities
Hiking

Facilities
The 37-acre park is
  undeveloped at this time
Trail unpaved (informal
  trails only)
Parking: SW 5th St. at
  dead-end on west side
  of Southwest Park

Fees and Regulations
Open dawn to dusk
Pets on leash

Highlights
Wetland mitigation area
and trail connector
between Springwater Trail
and Gresham-Fairview
trail system. Near
headwaters to Fairview
Creek which flows into
Fairview Lake to the
Columbia Slough.

Public Transit
Tri-Met #9 on Powell or
#23 on SW 182nd.

Thomas Guide 627

The meandering stream and wetlands were restored within the last five years and are rapidly maturing into a marsh, attracting wildlife, ducks, and other wetland birds while also improving the water quality of Fairview Creek. While Fairview Creek headwaters has been posted with a sign to keep people out, the City of Gresham Parks has plans for an interpretive trail as part of its plans to develop Southwest Community Park and the proposed Gresham-Fairview Trail.

The adjacent Southwest Community Park was only recently acquired and has yet to be developed or opened. The plans call for a nature park and community park at this site. To the north is Grant Butte, where the Gresham Parks Department plans to create a trail to its summit through Douglas fir and western red cedar forest. Grant Butte was not as heavily logged as many of the nearby buttes and has retained, relatively undisturbed, many large old native trees, understory plants, and wildflowers. The top of Grant Butte is nearly inaccessible because of stinging nettles. Although all of these sites are undeveloped as *Wild in the City* goes to press, they already offer views of wildlife, marshes, wetlands, and forests.

The Gresham-Fairview Trail is planned to go from the Springwater Trail at SE Powell Boulevard and Powell Loop, by way of the Southwest Community Park, along the wetland of the Fairview Creek headwaters, past access points for Grant Butte trails. It remains to be seen whether the trail will follow an old abandoned railroad bed at the wetlands. Once past the wetlands, the trail will proceed north to connect with the 40-Mile Loop Trail at Fairview and Blue Lakes. This trail between Powell and SE Division will provide an excellent opportunity for people to enjoy the Fairview Creek headwater's marsh and wildlife.

Access

Southwest Park, City of Gresham, W Powell Blvd. You could also depart from Gresham's Main City Park, where there is plenty of parking and access to Springwater Trail and other sites. *Also see map on page 254.*

How to Get There

From Portland, take SE Powell Blvd. east past SE 182nd Ave. As Powell curves to the northeast, the wetland and Southwest Park are on the left (west). Access to the wetlands will not be completed for a while, and there is no parking on Powell. The best way to access the wetlands prior to trail construction is via SW 182nd Ave., north from Powell and either the dead-end at SW 5th or 2nd St. off SW Hartley. Turn right onto SW 5th just south of Centennial High School. From Gresham Main Park, ride west to View Drive and take W Powell Loop to SE Powell Blvd. This is closed to the public.

By Diana Bradshaw

For more information: Gresham Parks, see Resources.

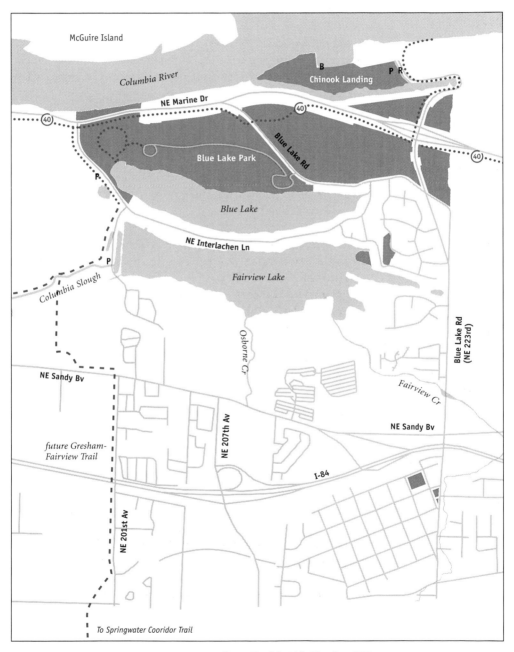

Blue Lake Regional Park

Those familiar with Blue Lake Regional Park would probably not think of it as a good spot for wildlife, since it is by far the most developed site in Metro's Parks and Greenspaces system. Most of the park is mowed lawns and playing fields with large picnic shelters and playgrounds. The lake itself has swimming facilities and boat rentals. While it is true that the part of the park intensely managed for human recreation provides little habitat diversity, as usual, there is more wildlife in the park than most visitors imagine.

Location
Blue Lake Regional Park is about 12 miles east of Portland between Sandy Blvd. and Marine Dr., west of 223rd Ave.

Activities
Hiking
Biking
Canoeing, boating
Fishing
Wildlife viewing
Volleyball
Basketball
Archery
Softball

Facilities
Toilets
Wheelchair accessible
  (most areas)
Trail unpaved
Parking
Interpretive information
  (brochures/maps)
Picnic area (sheltered
  areas and tables)
Dock, canoe launch
Concessions

Use of Blue Lake Park is very seasonal and during most of the rainy season there are few visitors. During these quiet months, Canada geese and gulls hang out on the lawns by the hundreds, the geese peacefully grazing while the gulls work the turf for any animal tidbits they can find, from worms to dead mice. Almost any of the ducks that winter in the Portland area can be seen from time to time on Blue Lake itself. Great blue herons and red-tailed hawks fly over regularly, and in winter are joined by an occasional bald eagle, with summer bringing osprey and turkey vultures. A careful observer may find evidence of coyote, raccoon, red fox, or river otter visiting the park during the quiet times.

But the area that provides the best wildlife habitat and some surprising wildlife activity at Blue Lake Park is the wetlands at the west end of the park.

The far west end of Blue Lake Park is the site of a wetland creation project, and there are two ponds encircled by a paved path about half a mile long. There is a wide, flat, mowed path between the ponds that also allows easy access and viewing. Wetland plants like cattails, willows, and rushes provide habitat for common freshwater marsh birds such as red-winged blackbird, common yellowthroat, and the ever-adaptable song sparrow. In the warm months, swallows frequently fly over the ponds and nearby Blue Lake, snatching flying insects from the air. On summer evenings their look-alike, the Vaux's swifts, can often be heard and seen high overhead.

The pond area is extensively "naturescaped" with native plants, many producing edible berries. Trees include cottonwood, alder, dogwood, willows, and young conifers. Shrubs are abundant with elderberries, flowering currant, thimbleberry, snowberry, spirea, and Oregon grape. During spring migration almost any of the common migrants passing through Portland can be seen in the trees, bushes, and wetland vegetation in this end of the park. As the dandelions in the lawn go to seed, you may see large flocks of American goldfinches and house finches feasting on the fluffy bounty.

Evidence of mammal activity around the ponds is usually easy to find. Muskrat trails through the water lilies and other pond plants are usually obvious, as are their trails leading out of the water at the

Fees and Regulations
Entrance fees
No pets
Restricted hours: open
from 8:00 A.M. until
legal sunset. Entrance
fee for each vehicle. No
alcohol without special
permit (fee). For more
information or to reserve
shelters call Metro Parks,
503-797-1850. Park
office phone is
503-665-4995.

Highlights
The unexpected wetland
area for wildlife watching.
Swimming in Blue Lake
with sandy beach area,
boat rentals. Seasonal
education programs are
provided by Metro's
naturalist staff.

Public Transit
Closest is Tri-Met #24 on
NE Halsey to the south.

Thomas Guide 598/599

pond's edge. Quiet and patient observers have seen muskrats active just before sunset. The little tunnel-like trails of voles, also known as meadow mice, are usually easy to find along the edge of the mowed paths. Raccoon footprints can be found in the mud at pond's edge. And now and then your searching might be rewarded with a big, fresh coyote scat!

Access
Getting to the wetlands area is easy. From anywhere in the park just walk toward the west end of the lake until you see cattails or the ponds themselves. The closest parking is currently the small parking area for the archery range.

Most areas are wheelchair accessible including the fishing dock.

How to Get There
Blue Lake Regional Park is about 12 miles east of Portland between Sandy Blvd. and Marine Dr., west of 223rd Ave. The entrance is on Blue Lake Rd. which is off NE 223rd. From I-84 take exit #14 and follow the signs to the park. ***See map on page 283.***

By James L. Davis

For more information: Blue Lake Regional Park. See the current *GreenScene*, Metro Regional Parks and Greenspaces, for programs. To get the *GreenScene* or to get information about field trip programs for schools and youth groups, contact Metro, see Resources.

Chinook Landing Marine Park

Location
On the Columbia River just north of Blue Lake Regional Park, off Marine Dr. The entrance to Chinook Landing is essentially the end of NE 223rd Ave., just north of the intersection with Blue Lake Rd.

Activities
Canoeing, boating
Wildlife viewing

Facilities
Toilets
Wheelchair accessible
Picnic area
Dock, canoe launch

Fees and Regulations
Entrance fees
Restricted hours: varies
  seasonally
No pets

Highlights
Major boat-launching facilities. A variety of wildlife viewing opportunities, especially large birds—osprey, bald eagle, great blue heron, Canada geese, and double-crested cormorant. The real fun at Chinook is mammal tracking.

Public Transit
Closest is Tri-Met #24 on NE Halsey to the south.

Thomas Guide 599

Chinook Landing is Oregon's largest public boat launching facility, with six launching lanes and parking for 300 vehicles with boat trailers. All kinds of boats can launch here, from kayaks to cabin cruisers. Few people come here other than to launch their boats, but fishing is allowed from the shore and there are a few picnic tables. There are, however, some interesting wildlife watching opportunities.

This highly developed facility in Metro's Regional Parks and Greenspaces system is another unlikely place to imagine seeing much wildlife but, as usual, there is more than meets the eye at first glance. There is a whole other side to Chinook Landing, literally—the east side. East of the entrance road is a small restored wetland that once again demonstrates the amazing tenacity and adaptability of some wildlife if they are given enough suitable habitat.

Chances are good that you'll see some large birds—in the Columbia, on shore, or flying overhead. Canada geese have started to hang out at Chinook year-round and are even nesting here. All the birds common along the river can be seen from time to time including double-crested cormorants, great blue heron, gulls, killdeer, belted kingfisher, osprey, Caspian tern (summer), and bald eagle (mainly winter). Red-tailed hawks and kestrels are often seen over the open, grassy areas, and higher overhead turkey vultures are a regular summer sight. Occasionally northern harriers can be seen flying low over the marshy spots in typical teetering flight. Snipe have been seen in the tall grasses near the pond and are suspected to nest here. The trees, shrubs, and wetland vegetation are well-populated with the songbirds typical of Portland.

The real fun at Chinook is mammal tracking, and this is where the careful, patient observer will be rewarded. Look along all the edges, where the blackberry and unmowed grasses meet the mowed path. It is usually easy to find rabbit and mouse trails. If you see trails significantly larger than rabbit trails coming up from the river, through the blackberries, and off into the wetland, they are probably river otter, which have been quite active here lately. Beaver are also common. Coyote regularly hunt for mice in the grass, and they often leave their scat deposited right in the middle of the path in their typical "calling card" fashion. This area has been studied very little and exciting discoveries await those who spend some "dirt time" here.

As you might expect, use of Chinook Landing is very seasonal. Don't even think about coming on a sunny summer day unless you love crowds, boats, and trailers. But much of the year if you come on a cloudy weekday, and even some weekends, you will have the wetland area all to yourself.

Access

From NE Marine Dr. there are well-marked exits. To get to the wildlife areas, turn right and park in the small parking lot just inside the entrance gate. Areas of mowed grass along the blackberry brambles on top of the steep riverbank are the best for searching for animal signs.

How to Get There

There are well-marked exits for the landing coming from both directions on Marine Dr. From I-84 take exit #14 and follow signs to Blue Lake and to Chinook landing. *See map on page 283.*

By James L. Davis

For more information: Metro Regional Parks or Blue Lake Regional Park, see Resources.

Big Four Corners Wetlands and 40-Mile Loop Access

The large cottonwood woodland is the last remaining forest of any size on the eastern ends of the Columbia Slough. This area is rich in both cultural and natural resources. Numerous Native American habitation sites have been recorded in this area of the Columbia Slough. The black cottonwood-dominated forest is home to western screech and great horned owls, and northern saw-whet owls have been nesting in the artificial wood duck boxes at the ponds.

Swainson's thrush, brown creeper, winter wren, and other forest birds also use the forested habitat. Deer are frequently seen, and northern harriers have been observed nesting in the open fields. It is unlikely the harriers will remain much longer, unless they take to the wetland mitigation areas to the south of Airport Way. The site, which is now relatively rural due to the still-existing farm operations, will soon change dramatically as the entire area changes to commercial and industrial office parks.

There is a short but very pleasant walk along a spur of the 40-Mile Loop on the south side of Airport Way. The trailhead is at a Portland Bureau of Environmental Services data-collecting facility. Walk south on this trail past stormwater ponds. A wetland mitigation area is on the west side of the Columbia Slough, which takes a sharp bend to the south at this site before swinging east again from where it receives its water from Fairview Lake.

Access

The only access is along Airport Way, where parking is not allowed. But you can bicycle to the site on Airport Way or park at the nearby kiosk and boat landing just to the west and walk back to the wetlands and 40-Mile Loop access. Look for the 40-Mile Loop logo on the north side of Airport Way next to the large wetland mitigation ponds. The 40-Mile Loop access is across the street on the south side of Airport Way. This unpaved path dead-ends at the Columbia Slough.

How to Get There

You can get to this site from the east and south by taking Airport Way north from NE Sandy, across from NE 181st Ave. From the west and north get on Airport Way from Sandy or Marine Dr. at NE 148th Ave. *See map on page 289.*

By Mike Houck

For more information: Portland Bureau of Environmental Services or Columbia Slough Watershed Council, see Resources.

Location
Airport Way, west of NE River Side Pkwy. and east of NE Mason Ct.

Activities
Hiking
Wildlife viewing area

Facilities
Parking (limited to side streets)

Fees and Regulations
None

Highlights
The large, open water ponds to the north of Airport Way are immediately adjacent to the largest remaining forested habitat on the Columbia Slough. The short 40-Mile Loop trail on the south side of Airport Way provides the only access to the Slough at this site.

Public Transit
Tri-Met #23 on NE Sandy to the south.

Thomas Guide 598

40-Mile Loop Trailhead and Canoe Launch

This is the only formal, publicly accessible canoe access on the east end of the Columbia Slough. Not only does this site provide convenient canoe/kayak put-ins, but it is also the only walking path that connects the Slough with the 40-Mile Loop bike and pedestrian path on NE Marine Drive.

There is a kiosk, and interpretive signs line the wood-chip trail to the west that extends from NE 158th Avenue to the Marine Drive. The Portland Bureau of Environmental Services has installed numerous signs that describe how replanting of trees and shrubs along the Slough will help reduce water temperatures by providing

Location
16550 NE Airport Way

Activities
Hiking
Canoeing, boating

Facilities
Wheelchair accessible
Trail unpaved
Parking
Interpretive information
    (brochures/maps)
Picnic area
Dock, canoe launch

Fees and Regulations
None

Highlights
This is one of the most important publicly accessible spots on the Columbia Slough as well as a significant trail connector from the Slough to NE Marine Drive.

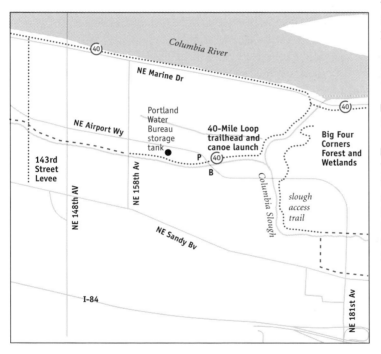

additional shade. The use of native vegetation for water quality improvements also restores wildlife habitat to the Slough.

A floating dock is just a short distance from the parking area at the end of a short but steep graveled path. The dock has been re-designed several times to better accommodate canoes and kayaks, although it is still a bit high off the water for an ideal launch site. The dock and trail facility is a cooperative project of Portland Parks, Portland's Bureau of Environmental Services, and the Portland Development Commission. This project is part of the city's requirement that the 40-Mile Loop be installed as development occurs along the Slough.

From here it's possible to canoe upstream to within a few feet of Fairview Lake (a sewer line crossing prevents access to the dam at Fairview Lake) or downstream to the 143rd Street cross levee.

The Columbia Slough is very narrow and densely vegetated between the floating dock and Fairview Lake. A variety of willows, ash, cottonwood, spirea, red-osier dogwood, and other shrubs and trees forms a dense riparian canopy in some places. I have seen black-crowned night heron, yellow-breasted chat, and ash-throated flycatchers here as well as lazuli buntings. More commonly seen species include wood duck, green heron, great blue heron, belted kingfisher, cedar waxwings, song sparrow, golden-crowned sparrow, spotted towhees, orange-crowned warbler, and yellow-rumped warbler.

Public Transit
Tri-Met #23 on NE Sandy or #201 to the west on Airport Way (transit will improve as businesses expand along Airport Way).

Thomas Guide 598

Access
A soft wood-chip trail to the west extends from NE 158th Ave. to Marine Dr. There is a kiosk, and interpretive signs line the path.

How to Get There
You can get to this site from the east and south by taking Airport Way north from NE Sandy, across from NE 181st Ave. From the west and north get on Airport Way from Sandy or Marine Dr. at NE 148th Ave.

By Mike Houck

For more information: Portland Parks and Recreation or Columbia Slough Watershed Council, see Resources.

Little Four Corners and Prison Pond

They don't come any more "informal" than this one, and how often is a premier wildlife viewing site juxtaposed with a prison? Multnomah County's Inverness Jail is just across the Slough at what has affectionately become known as the "prison pond" wetlands by local neighborhood Slough enthusiasts. This is also one of the few natural areas available to the nearby Wilkes Neighborhood, one of the most active of Columbia Slough advocacy groups.

This is one of several unofficial canoe launch sites for the upper Columbia Slough. Put in on the downstream side of the rapidly deteriorating wooden bridge. It's a difficult put-in and not for the fainthearted or physically challenged. But it's well worth the effort and hassle. From here you can paddle downstream, being sure to take the first sharp right-hand turn to get to the main channel.

During the winter, flotillas of waterfowl congregate in the open water upstream of the bridge. Commonly seen species include gadwall, American and Eurasian wigeon, wood duck, northern shoveler, ring-necked duck, lesser scaup, and hooded merganser. There is almost always a belted kingfisher perched on overhanging willows or electrical wires. Pied-billed grebes also ply the shallow, clear water for minnows. This is perfect habitat for the wily green heron, so be on the lookout for this reclusive, red-necked and green-backed relative of the great blue.

Location
NE 112th

Activities
Canoeing, boating
Wildlife viewing area

Facilities
Parking (NE 112th residential area)
Dock, canoe launch (very informal; a narrow bridge, not a dock, per se)

Fees and Regulations
None

Highlights
A wonderful, shrubby-scrubby section of the Slough that is filled with wintering waterfowl. You can see groundwater welling up from the Slough's depths from the small footbridge.

Public Transit
Tri-Met #12 to the southwest or #201 to the northeast.

Thomas Guide 567

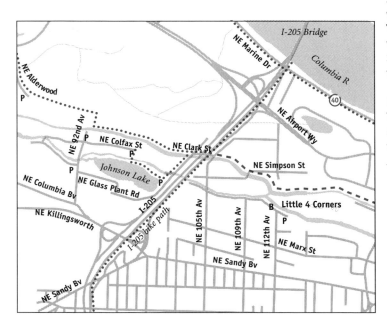

Access

Off NE 112th and NE Marx, north of Sandy Blvd. This is a residential neighborhood and access is about as informal as it gets.

How to Get There

Take NE 112th from NE Sandy and head north, across NE Marx, and down a small hill to the residential area. You need to park back from the Slough along NE 112th.

By Mike Houck

For more information: Multnomah County Prisons or Portland Bureau of Environmental Services, see Resources. Multnomah County Prisons owns the north side's Inverness Jail. Portland Bureau of Environmental Services owns a small part of the north shore.

Johnson Lake and Woodlands

Portland Parks and Recreation owns the forest and a portion of Johnson Lake's north side. The woodlands north of the lake have been planted with western red cedar, black cottonwood, ash, and Douglas fir.

Hooded merganser, northern shoveler, double-crested cormorant, ring-necked duck, pied-billed grebe, and lesser scaup are common in winter. Vaux's swifts dart about the lake's surface in summer, as do all of the swallows. Osprey nest in the cottonwoods and great horned owls are seen all year.

On a secluded walking path between NE Clark and Alderwood Corporate Park, to the west along an asphalt trail (negotiating a chain-link fence), you can walk through open fields at Portland International Airport and along dense riparian forest next to a blind slough. Spotted towhee, Bewick's wren, song sparrow, cedar waxwing, and common yellowthroat all share the local airspace with the "gashawks," albeit at lower altitudes. Even with the noise of ascending and descending aircraft and the occasional roar from Air National Guard jet fighters, it's a surprisingly pleasant trail from which you can see, and believe it or not hear, ring-necked pheasant, increasingly rare western meadowlark, savannah sparrow, and other grassland species that inhabit the open meadows adjacent to the runways.

Access

The forest can be accessed from a cul-de-sac off NE Colfax from NE 92nd from the west and from Glass Plant Rd. from the east. The best place to view Johnson Lake is from the east side on NE Glass Plant Rd.

Location
West of I-205 off NE Glass Plant Rd.

Activities
Hiking
Biking

Facilities
Paved and unpaved trail
Parking (on street)

Fees and Regulations
None

Highlights
The only true lake on this reach of the Slough. Scenic and full of wildlife.

Public Transit
Tri-Met #12 runs on NE Killingsworth to Columbia Blvd.; #201 runs on NE Bennett, south of Marx.

Thomas Guide 567

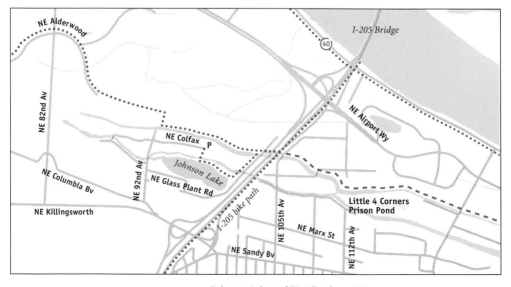

There is a wonderful, hidden walking path between NE Clark and Alderwood Corporate Park, to the west. The trail is accessed under I-205 at NE Clark on the east, at the dead-end at NE 92nd, through a chain-link fence, or from the west at NE Alderwood Corporate Park. The trail is a two-mile asphalt path that runs south of open fields at Portland International Airport and along dense riparian forest next to a blind slough.

There is also a connection with the I-205 bicycle path at NE Clark and 105th.

How to Get There

This one's tricky. During weekday business hours the easiest access is via NE Glass Plant Rd., which provides access to the glass recycling facility off NE Columbia Blvd. A more circuituous route is off NE Clark west of NE 105th and NE Marx, under I-205.

You can access Glass Plant during the week off NE 92nd from the west or from NE Clark west of NE 105th and NE Marx.

By Mike Houck

For more information: Portland Parks and Recreation, see Resources.

Whitaker Ponds

Whitaker Ponds is one of those places you stumble on and find yourself continually going back to. It is a 13-acre publicly-owned greenspace bounded on the north by the Columbia Slough. There are two ponds, neither of which is visible from the street. Part of the site was once a junk yard full of scrap metal, old cars, and 2,000 tires. After public acquisition by Metro Parks and Greenspaces the junk was removed, and the site has since been restored with thousands of native plants.

A black cottonwood forest stretches eastward from NE 47th between the two ponds and the Columbia Slough. While the westernmost pond adjacent to the interpretive center is more accessible and scenic, it is the eastern pond that typically produces more wildlife sightings.

Brown-headed cowbirds, willow flycatchers, and Bewick's wrens are all common around the pond, and the usual suspects among the waterfowl hang out during the winter months: gadwall, wigeon of both persuasions, mallards, and pied-billed grebes.

Whitaker Ponds is a great example of what collaborative partnerships can achieve. Some of the land was purchased by Metro; just over two acres were donated by Ned Hayes in 1997; the land in the middle of the site is owned by Portland Public Schools; and Portland's Bureau of Environmental Services provides youth and adult education programs. More than 2,000 school kids visited the site in 1998. BES is also working to improve water quality in the adjacent Slough and ponds.

Location
7040 NE 47th Ave., 1/4 mile north of NE Columbia Blvd.

Activities
Hiking
Wildlife viewing area

Facilities
Toilets
Parking
Interpretive center
Interpretive information (brochures/maps)

Fees and Regulations
Restricted hours
Note: No fishing is allowed at Whitaker Ponds. The Oregon Health Division has issued a fish advisory urging people to avoid eating fish caught in the Columbia Slough.

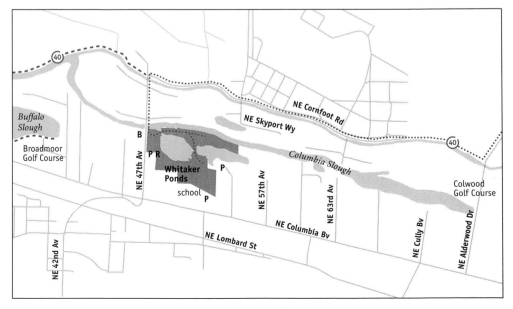

By the fall of 2001 the City of Portland expects to have replaced the culverts under NE 47th with a new bridge. This will greatly improve water quality and open up many miles of the Slough to canoeing and kayaking.

Access

Best access is off NE 47th. A small house on the site serves as an interpretive center, classroom, and work space and headquarters for Columbia Slough Watershed Council. A second access point is from the former Whitaker Middle School, now called Turnaround School, an alternative school operated by the Portland Public Schools. It is at 5135 NE Columbia Blvd. and you enter the parking lot east of the school. If the gate is open, go north on a lane that winds through several baseball fields.

How to Get There

Take NE Columbia Blvd. to NE 47th and turn north. The entrance to the parking area and house is about 1/4 mile north, on the east side of 47th.

By Mike Houck

For more information: Columbia Slough Watershed Council, Portland Bureau of Parks and Recreation, Portland Bureau of Environmental Services. For environmental education programs, contact Portland Bureau of Environmental Services, see Resources.

Children's Arboretum

The arboretum features every state tree, all of which were planted by Portland Public School students; it is bounded on the south by an arm of the Slough and reed canarygrass wetlands and on the north by rapidly developing residential subdivisions. This small gem of a greenspace is thick with Himalayan blackberries in the summer, which nearby families harvest. The arboretum is a local birding favorite, with northern flicker, downy woodpecker, and western wood-pewee being gimme's. In fact, the flickers, which routinely grub about on the ground for ants and other insects, can be positively thick on the arboretum's expansive grassy meadows.

The arboretum was considered by the Portland Public School District as "surplus" property, and at one point might have been sold for development. Fortunately, the City of Portland Parks Bureau negotiated a deal with the District to bring a number of sites, including this one, into public park ownership.

Access
NE Meadow Ln. off NE Meadow Dr. Park here and walk down Meadow Ln. to the entrance gate.

How to Get There
Take NE 13th Ave. south from NE Marine Dr. and turn right (west) onto NE Meadow Dr. NE Meadow Ln. is to the left.

By Mike Houck

For more information: Portland Bureau of Parks and Recreation, see Resources.

Location
NE Spring Ln., off
NE 13th Ave.

Activities
Hiking

Facilities
Trail unpaved
Parking (on street)

Fees and Regulations
Pets on leash

Highlights
This arboretum was owned by Portland Public Schools and was planted with every state tree. It is the only greenspace for the surrounding neighborhood and one of those unexpected green gems that makes urban trekking such a pleasure.

Public Transit
Tri-Met #6 to the west of the site.

Thomas Guide 566

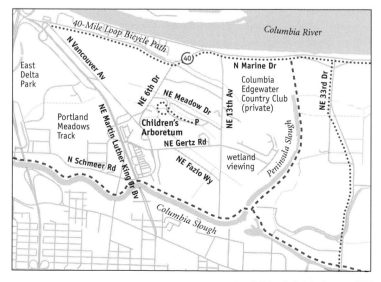

Heron Lakes Golf Course

Location
West of I-5, off of
N Broadacre St. and
N Force Ave.

Activities
Hiking
Wildlife viewing area
Golf

Facilities
Toilets
Paved and unpaved trail
Parking
Interpretive information
  (brochures/maps)
Food at the clubhouse

Fees and Regulations
Restricted hours
No pets

Highlights
Great blue heron rookery,
waterfowl of Force Lake,
36-hole golf course.

Public Transit
Tri-Met #5 and #8

Thomas Guide 566

Between 1942 and 1945, 650 acres of Columbia River floodplain were transformed to a city of 40,000 people, 9,000 dwellings, and 19 miles of streets. Vanport, Oregon's second largest city, was wiped out by floodwaters May 30, 1948, through a break in the levee at N Portland Road. Portland Parks purchased this property in 1960 and built the 18-hole West Delta Golf Course in 1970. Nine holes were added in 1986 and the course was renamed Heron Lakes after Portland's city bird, the great blue heron. Nine more holes were added in 1992. The original 18 holes were named "Green Back" after the green heron and the newest 18 are "Great Blue," after the great blue heron.

Interpretive signs at Force Lake, named after pioneer George Force, provide the history of the Vanport Flood and local wildlife. Great blue herons nest in the northwest corner of the course. Wildlife viewing is excellent, especially at Force Lake and the heron colony. Connections between the 40-Mile Loop at the Slough and Marine Drive are planned, as are interpretive signs and trails on the golf course. Heron Lakes has improved habitat and water quality through use of native vegetation.

I like to think of it as "par three" birding when I take groups to Heron Lakes. Some of my most pleasant birding experiences have come from a small patch of cottonwoods lining the par-three seventh fairway of the green-back nine at Heron Lakes Golf Course.

You should start your walk at the maintenance facility, midway between Force Lake and the clubhouse. A short stroll takes you to the black cottonwoods, which are alive with buzzing house wrens and warbling purple finches, and the wetlands that border the golf course from Force Lake to the heron colony. Always exercise common courtesy to golfers by allowing them to hit their tee shots without interference, and keep to this preferred access route.

From behind the maintenance shed proceed along the asphalt path to the northwest and follow the path to the extreme northwest corner of the course, past the bathrooms (open seasonally) to the seventh fairway. To the right is a cottonwood forest with shrubby, weedy verges of teasel and other weeds.

The nearby half-mile linear wetland is always a good bet for cinnamon and green-winged teal and an occasional green heron. From here you can watch herons glide lazily to their nests as they return from feeding forays at nearby Smith and Bybee Lakes. It's an amazing sight to witness a heron as he deftly insinuates his bulky, six-foot wingspan among a tangle of cottonwood limbs, and settles into a loosely constructed stick nest high up in a constantly swaying cottonwood.

When young are in the nest, a cacophony of bill clacking, guttural squawks, and elaborate neck and plumage displays greets the

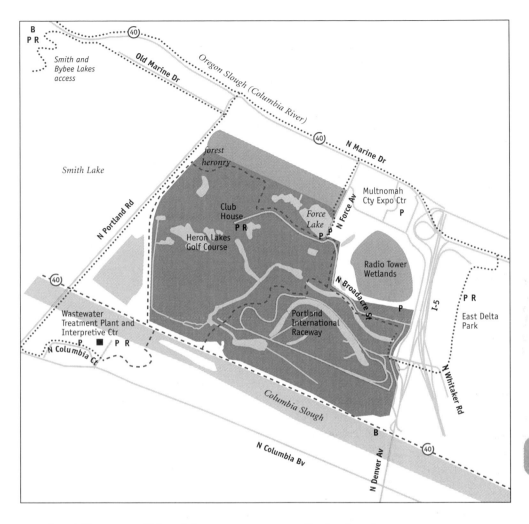

pterodactyl-like parent. Although herons nest communally, they brook no intrusion on their individual nest! During early courtship the male proffers a twig to the waiting female. They both tug for a few seconds, then she ritualistically takes it and weaves it into the nest, and the male is off again, frequently being chased by two crows and a mixed flock of violet-green and tree swallows.

Meanwhile, in the background, the cottonwood forest reverberates with bird songs. Dazzling yellow-and-black American goldfinches snatch seeds out of teasel flower heads. Melodious, flute-like songs of Swainson's thrushes echo from behind a blue elderberry where cedar waxwings, black-headed grosbeaks, and downy woodpeckers gather seeds and insects. The cottonwood canopy is alive with black-throated gray, orange-crowned, and yellow-rumped warblers, and the marsh buzzes with the common yellowthroat's "witchity, witchity" call. An occasional marsh wren may scold an intrusive red-winged blackbird.

If you listen carefully, you'll hear the unique "fitz-beew" of the willow flycatcher, which may be perched on a nearby willow twig.

Access
Off N Force Ave. The parking area for Force Lake interpretive signs is immediately on your right as you enter the golf course. The clubhouse is at the end of the access road.

How to Get There
Take I-5 to Delta Park exit. From the south turn left at the stop sign and pass back under I-5 to N Expo Rd. Take N Expo Rd. north and turn left (west) on N Broadacre St. Drive west (a remnant slough is to your left) to N Force Ave. and bear left into the golf course.
See map on page 299.

By Mike Houck

For more information: Portland Bureau of Parks and Recreation, see Resources.

Herons of Portland – Stalking the Stalkers

Picture the scene: You're frantically chasing a mystery warbler singing tantalizingly out of sight between you and the slough. You're moving fast to keep up with the warbler, as quietly as you can. Although you are making considerably less noise than a cattle stampede, the warbler continues to retreat before you. Finally, just as you catch a glimpse of yellow, the air is split by a mighty "GRAAAWNK;" the warbler is gone, along with your wits; the trees empty; and you're aware only of an airborne great blue heron, its broad wings powering a dignified retreat from a favored fishing hole.

Herons

The great blue heron is a member of an ancient order. Most ornithologists believe that herons are among the most "primitive" of North America's terrestrial birds. Herons and their relatives—including egrets, bitterns, and, at some remove, ibis, spoonbills, and storks—are large, long-legged waders, numbering among them some of the continent's tallest birds. They are not, however, related to cranes, with which they are frequently confused—especially great blue herons. All the herons,
five of which can be found in Portland, are still-hunters
and stalkers of fish, frogs, and small mammals, and they spend much of their time standing and waiting for dinner to drift by.

great blue heron

Great Blues

Great blue herons (*Ardea herodias*) love the flooded fields and watery byways that surround and penetrate the metropolitan area, making them the perfect City Bird for us. For something that stands four feet tall, it's surprising how many people are unaware of their august blue-gray presence. But those in the know frequently observe "GBHs" huddling over the carp that lurk in Oaks Bottom Wildlife Refuge, cruising above the Willamette River bridges, or standing sentinel in wet meadows along the Columbia Slough, alert for straying mice, frogs, and snakes.

They are perhaps most notable when they gather each spring to breed, following the herons' sociable custom of nesting in "rookeries"— large colonies containing anywhere from a dozen or fewer to several hundred nests. Their elaborate courtship rituals can be observed each spring, early to mid-February.

Green Herons

Compared to the relatively conspicuous great blue, green herons (*Butorides virescens*) are the kings of low profile. Rarely found perched in the open, they prefer to seclude themselves at the margins of wooded ponds and streams, where, save for their spectacular orange feet, they are very hard to spot. Consequently, they are seen a

green heron

fraction as often as the larger great blues. In addition, they are far less numerous. So, while their numbers have dramatically increased since Ira N. Gabrielson and Stanley G. Jewett assembled a mere six records for the state in 1940, they are still considered "uncommon" in the Portland area. After a decade of calling them "green-backed herons," ornithologists have decided they are green herons after all. But while the ornithologists can't make up their minds, the herons themselves don't seem to care one way or the other, preferring to skulk along tree-lined waterways, far from the fury of ornithological debate. Not only are these summer residents less common and less conspicuous than GBHs, they are even more solitary. It is unusual to see more than one at a time, and they rarely nest communally. In the Portland area, green herons can be seen, among other places, along the Columbia Slough, at Oaks Bottom, and at Crystal Springs Rhododendron Garden, where they fly back and forth between the wooded verge of Crystal Springs Lake and the densely wooded "back country" of Reed College Canyon. They are also seen on the Tualatin River, where they have become the official mascot of the Tualatin Riverkeepers, and along the shores, canals, and backwaters at Ridgefield National Wildlife Refuge.

Night-Herons

Black-crowned night-herons (*Nycticorax nycticorax*) are perhaps Oregon's most beautiful herons. These elegant birds, sporting black, white, and gray plumage, accented by a scarlet eye and two or three white plumes descending from the back of their head, are a well-loved sight in the marshes of eastern Oregon. But in Portland they are truly rare. Furthermore, in contrast to green herons, night-heron numbers have dramatically decreased in recent decades.

In the early 1900s a rookery near Portland contained 200 nests. Nowadays, night-herons are not known to nest west of the Cascades, although they winter here and occur in Portland in small but fluctuating numbers year-round. They are perhaps most conspicuous in winter, when a modest but stable population can be found in north Portland, in the narrow riparian area along Bridgeton Slough, north of the Columbia Slough proper.

Heron Relatives

Two close relatives of the herons that can occasionally be found in the Portland area are American bitterns (*Botaurus lentiginosus*) and great egrets (*Ardea alba*). Bitterns are secretive marshland birds. Their brown-streaked plumage makes them very difficult to see in the tall marsh grass that they favor. When discovered, they point their beaks to the sky, holding absolutely still, transforming into a clump of marsh grass. More prevalent in migration than at any other time, bitterns can be seen in marshes on Sauvie Island and a few other places around Portland, including Heron Lakes Golf Course's Force Lake.

Great egrets, the statuesque white "herons" of eastern Oregon, are the only other member of the family that can regularly be seen in Portland. Although their numbers in western Oregon have recently been on the increase, it is still exciting to see them in the metro area. During the winter of 1995-96 nearly 100 egrets could be found on Sauvie Island, Oaks Bottom, Smith and Bybee Lakes, Creekside Marsh in Beaverton, Jackson Bottom Wetland Preserve in Hillsboro, and elsewhere in the region, making it a good candidate for "the year of the egret."

Meanwhile, as you continue to sleuth the slough, silence has returned. The heron is back. Pausing in the chase, you try to duplicate its silent vigilance. Lured by the quiet, the trees begin to fill with birds again. And from the heron you learn something about hunting.

By Bob Wilson

black-crowned night-heron

Great Blue Herons: Their Status and Natural History

Joe Pesek, now retired, Holly Michael of the Oregon Department of Fish and Wildlife, and several Audubon volunteer heron watchers provided the following statistics on Portland-area heron colonies. On the Columbia River: Deer Island (90–100 nests); Government Island (50 nests); Sauvie Island (7–8 nests); Burlington Bottoms (3 nests); Clark County's Bachelor Island (300 nests); and Frenchman's Bar (250 nests). Closer to downtown Portland, Heron Lakes Golf Course has had as many as 30 nests in good years, but more recently the colony has dwindled to four well-screened nests. Ross Island consistently has around 55 nests. Goat Island, upstream from Ross Island, has 40–50 nests. A new colony on the Clackamas River has 7–8 nests. Molalla River State Park has over 100 nests. In the Tualatin River basin new colonies have been established at Jackson Bottom Wetland Preserve (7–10 nests); along Rock Creek, just south of Hwy. 26; and at Creekside Marsh in Beaverton, where there are 5 nests on the east side of the marsh. And a breeding bird survey at Ridgefield National Wildlife Refuge netted 528 nests.

Heronries are transitory over many years, as rivers switch channels, nesting trees grow and fall, and food sources either disappear or, much less frequently, become more abundant. New colonies start with fewer than ten nests and, if conditions are favorable, they grow in size. Every year there are reports of new, one- or two-nest "starter colonies," but few of these take off as a viable colony. What would appear to be an ideal nesting site may be selected by pioneer herons and then abandoned for no apparent reason.

In addition to changing sites, heronries are not static within a nesting area. They will move around, amoeba-like, in a grove of trees over time. The prime nest tree in our area, the black cottonwood, is extremely brittle and subject to loss of branches during windy weather. Cottonwoods are also short-lived, and dead trees leave returning herons without the previous year's nest site. This makes "buffers" which are left around colonies problematic unless enough room is left for expansion or even relocation of a colony. In fact, the Ross Island colony seems to be moving north on the island since a 300-foot buffer was established in the mid-1970s as a condition on gravel extraction activities of Ross Island Sand and Gravel. The Heron Lakes colony has also been unstable during recent years, with herons expanding to the northwest from their original nesting sites. The strong winds of December 1998 seem to have disrupted this colony even more than usual, and it remains to be seen how long herons will continue to nest at Heron Lakes.

Heron Neighbors

While herons dominate their colonial-nesting site, they often share space with other birds, especially raptors. At Heron Lakes Golf Course a great horned owl pair has nested almost every year, smack dab in the middle of the colony. Being earlier nesters, the owls already have fuzzy-headed young peering over the edge of their nest when herons have just begun nest-building and courtship. Many heronries have a pair of red-tailed hawks nesting among the herons or nearby. Both Heron Lakes and Ross Island have nearby red-tailed hawk nests, and Ross Island also has bald eagles and osprey nesting within a quarter mile of the colony. Aside from occasional strafing forays, the hawks don't seem to bother the herons much. Similar attacks by an immature golden eagle at Audubon Canyon Ranch heronry at Bolinas Lagoon, California, led to nest abandonment by several hundred herons, and reports out of British Columbia document depredation of heron colonies by bald eagles.

Who Eats Herons?

While adult herons present a formidable opponent, their young can fall prey to predators in and around their nests. The primary predators on nesting herons are crows and gulls. Increased gull predation at Heron Lakes Golf Course came about

the same time the St. Johns Landfill was being closed, but has trailed off since the landfill ceased operation. Coyotes have been observed feeding on young fledgling herons, especially if a windstorm has blown nests from the brittle treetops. Fourth of July fireworks displays in Gladstone might be responsible for startled young herons showing up on residential lawns in the Milwaukie and Gladstone area. The Audubon Canyon heronry was also devastated two years in a row by marauding raccoons, until the sanctuary manager placed six-foot-high strips of stainless steel strapping around the base of the coast redwood trees the herons and great egrets share for their nesting colonies.

Aside from people calling wanting to know why that crazy robin keeps attacking itself in their window, one of the most frequent questions I get is "Did you know we had cranes in our backyards or all up and down the Willamette?" While some people are disappointed when I tell them cranes fly with their necks "craned" out, in front of them and that they instead have a heron stalking koi in their backyard pond, most people are content to know that the great blue heron also likes their backyard naturescape or nearby stream or wetland.

The heron is everyone's favorite city bird. No sight can match the lumbering, powerful strokes of a great blue heron's wings as it cruises in a long graceful arc from the banks of the Willamette high in the cottonwood trees of Ross Island's nesting site, its neck carefully tucked away in the characteristic s-shape that, among other things, distinguishes it from the sandhill crane.

Its scientific name, *Ardea herodias*, is a redundant moniker if ever there was one. *Ardea* means "heron" in Latin and *herodias* denotes "heron" in Greek. As to local colloquialisms, the great blue heron goes by "blue crane," "shyte poke" (presumably after its habitat of unloading a huge fecal mass when taking flight), "Poor Joe," "sentinel bird," or "Indian Hen," depending on what region of the country you are in. I personally prefer "Big Cranky." Have you ever seen any creature, be it bird or human, look as utterly out-of-sorts as a heron hunkered down on a mudflat during a cold winter drizzle? And their loud, guttural squawk when aroused by a passing birder or kayaker does nothing to diminish their image as an out-of-sorts curmudgeon.

Measured from tip of beak to tip of tail, the heron is about four feet long, and from wingtip to wingtip is up to six feet wide. The heron's huge wingspan and tall stature belie the fact that it is a relatively lightweight bird, weighing in at between five and eight pounds.

They eat virtually anything they can get their formidable six-inch, dagger-like bills around or through. They do in fact spear their prey much of the time, and one heron was reported to have pierced a three-inch thick canoe paddle. Fish are by far the biggest part of a heron's diet, but I have seen them spearing Townsend's ground squirrels at Malheur and tossing small voles and other rodents into the air before gulping them down in one bite on the grassy fields at Portland International Airport. While it was probably not feeding on it, former Audubon Society of Portland director Mike Uhtoff once observed a great blue spear a green heron that had the temerity to land on an adjacent rock.

While they feed on upland farm fields, golf course greenways, and the extensive meadow-like habitat at the airport, they are most often seen feeding around water where they gobble up frogs, snakes, and fish. There is no doubt they will snatch a young red-winged blackbird nestling, given half a chance. That's undoubtedly why herons are so often seen being escorted through a marsh by successive waves of nesting blackbirds, yellowthroats, and wrens.

Breeding and Nesting

While they hunt individually, they prefer the company of other herons when nesting, sometimes creating nesting colonies of several hundred nests. In our region, the nest tree of choice is typically black cottonwood. That's because it is the dominant riparian tree. In other areas willow, Douglas fir, and whatever other species is handy is used. The Bolinas Lagoon, Audubon Canyon Ranch colony has flattened the tops of coast redwood trees, which they share with a great egret colony.

Theories differ regarding why they, and many other species of birds, have chosen the colonial nesting lifestyle. Some researchers feel that this makes it more likely that information regarding a good food supply will be shared. The most reasonable explanation is that there is safety in numbers and that a colony will ensure there is always a sharp, stout beak to fend off potential predators.

Their nests are always built of sticks and measure three to four feet across, and are usually either at the top of a tree or within 10 to 12 feet of the top. In other regions they have been observed nesting in short shrubs like sagebrush, or even on the ground if there is no woody vegetation at hand. Their nests are built not closer than a neck-stretch from each other, and transgressions of this space are met with a swift clack and strike with the beak. Nests are reused each year, or rebuilt from scratch if they are severely damaged during winter storms. I watched one nest totally stripped of twigs by one enterprising pair that dismantled the nest above theirs, with the male pulling twigs out and dropping them to his mate below. When the other pair finally arrived at the colony, they had to start from scratch, which explained why they still had nestlings well into July, long after the other nests had fledged their young.

Nest building is one of numerous behaviors that contribute to pair bonding between a male and female great blue heron. I have watched as what I assume was the male brought fresh twigs back to the nest at Heron Lakes. She seized the twig. He tugged back. This went on for several minutes until he relinquished the new material to the female, who then deftly wove it into the nest's growing bulk. In addition to this twig-tugging, neck-stretching, bill snapping, neck-arching, preening, bill dueling, and crest-raising are all part of an incredibly ritualistic set of behaviors designed to ensure the couple stays together through copulation, egg-laying, and raising of young. Great blues, like most birds, are serially monogamous. The elaborate courtship ensures they remain true to one another during each breeding season, but they will pair up with another mate the following year. Researchers have observed, however, considerable philandering by males when their mates are away from the nest.

Their three to seven pale blue-green eggs are laid in early March, and incubation is an equal-opportunity activity between the sexes, as is feeding of the young later. Incubation is 28 days on average; both parents turn the eggs every two hours to ensure the egg's heat from the incubating adults is spread evenly, without which the chick embryo would not develop properly. This behavior can actually be seen at the Audubon Canyon Ranch colony, as the trail and observation deck are situated above the trees. Young begin to emerge in early to mid-April, sequentially as they were laid.

Nothing looks quite as bizarre or ridiculous as a young great blue heron, with a "buzz cut" appearance to its head and a "punked-out" mien. Early on, both adults regurgitate food into the nest and put smaller morsels into the chicks' mouths. Later the young birds insert their own bills into the adult's gullet to get their food, and eventually, after the young have larger, more dangerous bills, the adults simply disgorge whatever they have, including an entire carp, into the nest and the young are on their own. From the din emanating from any heron colony, it is clear that nest mates vie aggressively for food, and there is no doubt that the first-born get the heron's-share of food. Nevertheless, two or three young usually survive from each nest.

It takes around eight weeks of continual care by the adults before the young herons are ready to venture from the nest, the longest nestling period of any heron. It will be three years before this hatch of young will be sexually mature and ready to use their own repertoire of neck stretches and bill-clasping to initiate their own nesting cycle. Young herons are easy to tell from adults, as they lack the distinctive head plumes that hang down the back of their neck. Experts can differentiate among fledgling, juvenile, yearling, and adult herons. During their first year as many as two-thirds are lost to predation, the weather, or starvation. Once they make it to sexual maturity, they stand a good chance of living as long as 20 years.

By Mike Houck

Smith and Bybee Lakes

"I can't believe we're in the middle of Portland!" Although these words can be spoken at several of the places in this book, they fit Smith and Bybee Lakes to a tee. Although it is an almost 2,000-acre regional park, this little-known wetland is surrounded by warehouses, Port of Portland terminals, the old St. Johns Landfill, and other industrial sites, making it one of the biggest secrets in town. There are other reasons for the low profile. The only developed part of the wildlife area is the small parking lot and the Interlakes Trail. The only other public access to the rest of the lakes is by boat. There is currently a primitive launching area from the parking lot that involves a subsequent portage, but Metro is planning a new boat launching site that will make access easier. If you want more information on boating at the lakes, call Metro. The easiest way to get to know the lakes from the water is by going on a guided boating trip with the Friends of Smith and Bybee Lakes.

Most people are amazed at the wildlife that can be seen here, "in the middle of North Portland." The mammals you can actually see at the lakes, especially by boat, are really surprising. The careful, and lucky, wildlife watcher might see nutria, beaver, river otter, cottontail rabbit, raccoon, muskrat, mule deer, and even mink. The coyotes at the lakes seem to be particularly cautious, but their tell-tale scat is a fairly common sight.

Bird life is abundant and almost all water birds from the region can be seen at one time or another. Winter is great for waterfowl and bald eagles. The songbird migration through the riparian woodland in the spring is outstanding. Just about every migrant seen in the metropolitan area shows up at Smith and Bybee, and there are some birds that are much more conspicuous at the lakes than in most of Portland, such as the house wren and yellow warbler. Even red-eyed vireos have been singing along the Interlakes Trail. Singing American goldfinches ring the meadow along the trail in May. Great horned owls and red-tailed hawks nest in the cottonwoods. In fall, dozens of great egrets may show up for a few weeks, and some days you can see 1,000 double-crested cormorants at once.

The most famous resident at Smith and Bybee Lakes is the western painted turtle. The healthy population of these beautiful reptiles is probably the largest in the lower Columbia River drainage. Their numbers have plummeted in the last few decades, and they are classified as sensitive, one step away from protection under the Endangered Species Act. Habitat loss and predation of hatchlings by the introduced bullfrog have played a major role in their decline, and the turtles are being carefully monitored at the lakes. They are easy to see basking on logs near the trail, and even from the parking lot, on warm, sunny days from April through September.

Location
Smith and Bybee Lakes Wildlife Area is 2.5 miles west of I-5 on N Marine Dr.

Activities
Hiking
Canoeing, boating
Fishing
Wildlife viewing

Facilities
Portable toilet
Wheelchair accessible
Trail paved
Parking
Interpretive information (brochures/maps)
Canoe launch

Fees and Regulations
Open dawn to dusk
No pets
No bicycles

All plants and wildlife are protected, but fishing is allowed in compliance with state regulations. All boats must be people-powered, with the exception of electric trolling motors. For more information call Metro Regional Parks and Greenspaces.

Note: The Oregon Health Division has issued a fish advisory urging people to avoid eating fish caught in the Columbia Slough.

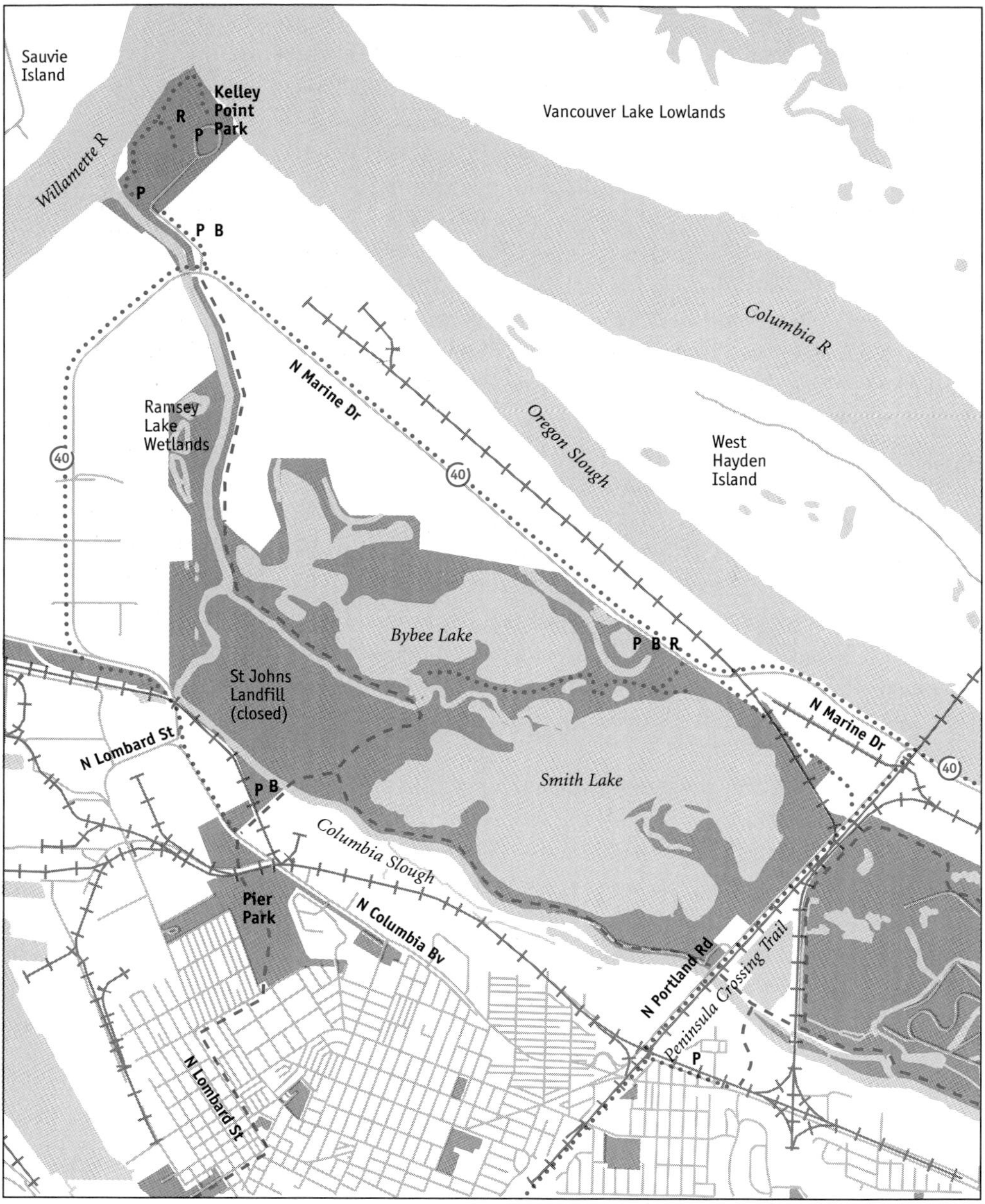
Sauvie Island
Kelley Point Park
R
P
Vancouver Lake Lowlands
Willamette R
P
P B
Columbia R
N Marine Dr
Oregon Slough
Ramsey Lake Wetlands
40
40
West Hayden Island
Bybee Lake
P B R
St Johns Landfill (closed)
N Marine Dr
40
N Lombard St
Smith Lake
P B
Columbia Slough
Pier Park
N Columbia Bv
N Portland Rd
Peninsula Crossing Trail
P
N Lombard St

Access

The Interlakes Trail is about half a mile long, one way. It is paved, level, and universally accessible. There are two wildlife viewing blinds on the trail.

How to Get There

Going north on I-5 from Portland, take exit #307, the Delta Park/Marine Dr. West exit. Take the left fork of the exit road, following the sign for Marine Dr. West. After you loop under I-5 you will come to a large intersection with traffic lights. Turn right and go west on Marine Dr. past the Expo Center and past the light at N Portland Rd. Watch for the small parking area on your left as you come down off the railroad overpass.

By James L. Davis

For more information: Metro Regional Parks and Greenspaces or Friends of Smith and Bybee Lakes, see Resources.

See Metro's publication *GreenScene*, see Resources

Highlights

Hidden lakes offering superb canoeing and wildlife observation. The most famous resident at Smith and Bybee Lakes is probably the western painted turtle.

Education programs are provided by Metro's naturalist staff, and canoe/kayak trips are led by the Friends of Smith and Bybee Lakes.

Thomas Guide 535/536/566.

Tracking Mammals

It's easy to know what birds live in an area because they are so conspicuous. Birds are active, diurnal, colorful, and noisy, and there are lots of different kinds, so it is no surprise that there are literally millions of active bird watchers in America. Mammals, however, are a completely different story. People love to see mammals but it's really tough to get a look at many, let alone actually watch them go about their normal lives. There are less than half as many different kinds of mammals as there are birds. Half of all mammals are rodents, and a quarter are bats. Most of these are small, dark-colored, and nocturnal (bats famously so), making them very hard to observe. Most other mammals are also nocturnal, and all are generally secretive and stay out of sight of people. Given all this, how can you ever get to know them?

The key is to become a super nature detective. Mammals leave many different kinds of evidence that are clues to their identity. The general term for studying animal signs to identify the animal and figure out what it was doing is "tracking." When people hear the term tracking, they tend to think of looking at animal footprints and figuring out who made them, but there is much more to tracking than just identifying prints. Other clues or signs to look for include scat (feces), trails, fur, chewing or digging marks, feeding debris, food caches, rubbings or scratchings on trees, dens and nests, and even smells. In trying to identify animal signs it is important to have some basic knowledge of the natural history of the possible animals—their preferred habitat, diet, activity periods, and behaviors. All these clues help the tracker "build a case" for the identity of the animal. But tracking doesn't end here.

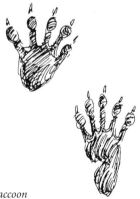

raccoon

More exciting and complex than identifying the prints of an animal is interpreting the tracks and all the signs to learn what the animal was doing, where it was going, and even why it behaved the way it did. People develop a whole new awareness of animals through tracking. In essence, skilled trackers learn to think like the animals they study. Tracking is "whole brain" or holistic learning; it greatly increases your observational skills and your awareness of the world around you. It is not surprising that many naturalists experience profound connections with the natural world through tracking.

"Wow, this sounds great," you're thinking; "How do I get started?" Fortunately, we are in the midst of a tracking renaissance, following the success of Tom Brown's books. The Northwest seems to be one of the hotbeds of tracking activity and expertise. Jon

Young was mentored by Tom Brown and has established the Wilderness Awareness School in Washington, and students of both Tom and Jon are teaching classes in the Portland area. The key to learning tracking is getting as much "dirt time" as possible, doing the real thing outdoors. The Tracking Club (of Portland) has at least one dirt time every month, and tracking classes are offered by Metro Regional Parks and Greenspaces, Audubon Society of Portland, and Tualatin Hills Parks and Recreation District, among others. There is no better way to get started than to go outside with an experienced tracker!

beaver

The increased popularity of tracking has brought a flood of new books, making it hard to choose. Experienced trackers highly recommend starting with *Tom Brown's Field Guide to Nature Observation and Tracking* by Tom Brown, Jr., with Brandt Morgan. After you have read some Tom Brown and had some dirt time, you may want to get *A Field Guide to Mammal Tracking in North America* by James Halfpenny, considered by the pros to be the single most comprehensive, authoritative, yet concise book on the subject.

Tracking usually focuses on mammals, but other animals also leave evidence behind. Some tracking books will discuss some birds, a few general types of tracks made by reptiles and amphibians, and even the more common trails left by insects. The classic "Peterson's guide" from 1954, *A Field Guide to Animal Tracks* by the great naturalist Olaus Murie, has a good selection of these and is still a favorite of many naturalists.

Then it's outside for more dirt time. Remember, just as with bird watching, the most important way to understand and appreciate nature is to get out into it and experience the real thing.

river otter

To find out about The Tracking Club, write PO Box 40722, Portland, OR 97240-0722.

By James L. Davis

Kelley Point Park

Kelley Point Park's, and that's with two e's please, namesake is Hall J. Kelley, a New Englander, who was an ardent Oregon booster in the first half of the nineteenth century. Although Kelley's effort to establish a city where Kelley Point Park now stands failed, his advocacy for Portland over Oregon City and Sellwood was obviously more successful.

This nearly 100-acre park was created by dredge spoils that were deposited by the Port of Portland, which covered the North Portland peninsula with millions of tons of sand that were dredged from the Columbia River and deposited to create a marine industrial port facility. It looks quite different from when Lewis and Clark camped here in their 1805–1806 Corps of Discovery visit to the Portland area. The park that Kelley had envisioned as a city is now merely the peninsula's northwest tip.

The Port of Portland transferred Kelley Point to the City of Portland Parks in 1984. There is handy access to sandy beaches at the mouth of the Columbia Slough. Treacherous currents here have claimed several lives in recent years, so be careful if you decide to take a dip.

Caspian terns are commonly seen diving headlong into the Willamette River here, and the black cottonwood forest is usually alive with house and Bewick's wrens. Fruit trees, remnants from the old Biddle estate, are riddled with parallel lines of sapsucker holes. You may even see a coyote working the Sauvie Island shoreline from this spot as well.

Location
North Portland Peninsula, off N Marine Dr. at the confluence of the Columbia Slough, Willamette River, and Columbia River.

Activities
Hiking
Canoeing, boating
Fishing

Facilities
Toilets
Wheelchair accessible
Paved and unpaved trail
Parking
Picnic area
Dock, canoe launch

Fees and Regulations
Restricted hours
Pets on leash
Note: The Oregon Health Division has issued a fish advisory urging people to avoid eating fish caught in the Columbia Slough.

Highlights
Best views of the Columbia River ship traffic in the metro area. Access to the lower Columbia Slough. Great views of Sauvie Island.

Public Transit
Tri-Met #6.

Thomas Guide 535

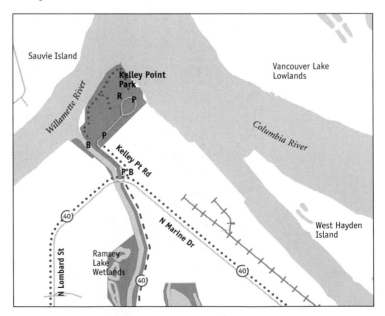

From the last parking lot you can stroll along paved paths through picnic meadows and on to promontories overlooking the Columbia River. Osprey, double-crested cormorants, and gulls are commonly seen from here, if you're not totally distracted by the passage of huge ocean-going freighters.

Kelley Point is either the end of the line or your point of departure for a circumnavigation of the 40-Mile Loop by foot, bicycle, or kayak.

Access

Off N Marine Dr., Kelley Point Park Rd. Just inside the entrance road on the left is an informal but serviceable canoe launch site. The surface is rutted dirt but it's only a short portage to the Slough.

Farther along Kelley Point Park Rd. are two parking areas. The first, on the left, provides excellent access to sandy beaches at the mouth of the Columbia Slough. Beware of treacherous currents, however. You can walk to the tip of the park from here along informal, unpaved paths.

The paved paths, restrooms, and picnic areas—and gorgeous views of the Columbia River—are best had from the second parking area. From the parking lot, it's a short walk past the commodious restrooms and a grassy picnic area to the shoreline of the Columbia.

How to Get There

Take I-5 north to Marine Dr. and take Marine Dr. west to Kelley Point Park Rd.

By Mike Houck

For more information: Portland Bureau of Parks and Recreation, see Resources.

St. Johns Landfill Canoe Launch

Location
9003 N Columbia Blvd.
Just east of Rueben's
Import Auto Wrecking and
west of the Stockyard Café.
Across N Columbia Blvd.
from the city's Stanley Parr
Archives and Records
Center at Chimney Park.

Activities
Canoeing, boating

Facilities
Parking (umimproved)
Dock, canoe launch

Fees and Regulation:
None

Highlights
Only existing formal, semi-
developed canoe launch
east of Kelley Point Park
on the lower Slough
(another is planned at N
Denver Ave. near Portland
International Raceway).

Public Transit
Tri-Met #4 on Fessenden is
the closest.

Thomas Guide 535

This site includes a semi-developed canoe launch just west of the entrance to the now-closed St. Johns Landfill. After all environmental issues associated with closure of the landfill are dealt with, this is likely to be an important 40-Mile Loop connector. For now, the best way to explore the area is by canoe or kayak from this boat ramp. This is a convenient point to explore downstream to Kelley Point Park, about a 2-3/4 mile paddle. Or, you can go as far east as the "plug" that separates the lower and upper Columbia Slough near NE 13th and Gertz Road, about a 12-mile round trip.

The launch is used routinely for the annual Columbia Slough Regatta, traditionally held the last Sunday of July. Other canoe launches in the vicinity are at Kelley Point and Smith and Bybee Lakes. Another launch will soon be added near N Denver Avenue.

About the St. Johns Landfill: The 238-acre St. Johns Landfill represents a classic example of landfill practices of the past. More than 238 acres of wetland and floodplain habitat of Smith Lake was filled 50 years ago by the City of Portland to serve as the metropolitan region's garbage dump. Nowadays we would call it a solid waste facility. Unfortunately, not only were significant wetlands lost in the process but we have, until recently, continued to reap the negative impacts of siting the landfill next to the Columbia Slough and in Smith Lakes Wetlands. Leachates, or filtered pollutant-laden water, have worked their way through the landfill after rain penetrated the soil cover, until Metro instituted a more advanced system after it assumed closure responsibility from the City of Portland in 1990. Metro has closed the landfill with rain-retarding layers of plastic and clay soils that are designed to prevent rainwater from penetrating the underlying waste and carrying pollutants into the Slough and Smith and Bybee Lakes.

All that covers the landfill at this time is a protective layer of grass. As you paddle by the landfill, you may catch a glimpse of sheep, which Metro is using as a non-mechanical means to keep the grass "mowed." You may also see llamas which were brought in to discourage coyotes in a non-lethal way from eating the organic lawn mowers. Metro plans to diversify the habitat throughout the landfill once it has settled and methane generation ceases. One day, the St. Johns Landfill will provide 200 acres of upland meadow and shrub habitat to complement the 2,000-acre Smith and Bybee wetlands and lakes. In the meantime, we can take solace in knowing garbage is no longer being dumped into the lakes.

Access
N Columbia Blvd. From the dead end which takes you to a large grassy field (it is less than 1/4 mile from the railroad crossing), you will find a steep asphalt boat ramp. There is no dock, simply a ramp sloped to the

Columbia Slough just downstream from the bridge that provides access to the now-closed landfill.

The parking area is unimproved and the launch includes a deteriorating ramp. But it is perfectly suitable for launching canoes or kayaks.

How to Get There

Take I-5 north and head west on N Columbia Blvd. to the St. Johns Landfill. Take the right just past the landfill entrance and proceed along a rough-looking access road. Cross the railroad tracks (there is a lighted signal) and bear left onto the gravel road that goes slightly downhill, opposite the Union Pacific Railroad Automobile Distribution Center sign on the right. Note: trains can take 5 to 10 minutes to pass this point, so plan accordingly. This informal-looking road that looks more like a driveway will take you to a large grassy field and, finally (it is less than 1/4 mile from the railroad crossing), to a steep asphalt boat ramp. *See maps on pages 310,319.*

By Mike Houck

For more information: Metro, Regional Environmental Management: St. Johns Landfill Section or Metro Regional Parks and Greenspaces, Smith and Bybee Lakes Program. For the Columbia Slough Regatta contact: Columbia Slough Watershed Council or Friends of Smith and Bybee Lakes, see Resources

Peninsula Crossing Trail

The Peninsula Crossing Trail follows an old road right-of-way that was constructed across North Portland to provide bicycle and pedestrian access between the Willamette and Columbia Rivers. It also connects important Greenspaces along the way, including Willamette Cove, Smith and Bybee Lakes Wildlife Area, Columbia Slough, and, eventually, Heron Lakes Golf Course.

The trail is more about traversing the Peninsula than a nature hike, although there are small nodes of habitat and a fairly extensive linear natural area that lines the upper reaches of the railroad cut. I've seen Cooper's hawks, sharp-shinned hawks, and a host of warblers, vireos, and chickadees in the big-leaf maple and other trees that line the trail north of Carey.

Art On The Trail: There are a number of art pieces along the trail that were installed through the One Percent for the Arts public art program. Portland artist Brian Borrello has designed steel sheets with cut-out silhouettes of hawks to cast shadows on the seating at Columbia Court. He also carved seats out of Columbia River Basalt that are at the trailheads on N Lombard and N Columbia Blvd.

The Peninsula Crossing Trail is a perfect example of how citizen-based organizations, in this case North Portland neighborhoods and the 40-Mile Loop Land Trust, can work with government agencies to develop a vision and put a project on the ground in a relatively short period of time.

The trail was funded by Metro's 1995 bond measure, federal ISTEA transportation funds, and Portland's Bureau of Environmental Services, which is constructing the segment of the trail that runs through the Columbia Boulevard Wastewater Treatment Plant site.

Access

Various points along the 3-mile linear trail, with trailheads at: Corner of N Princeton and N Carey, one block north of N Willamette Blvd.; N Lombard, west of Macrum; N. Fessenden; and Columbia Ct. and N Columbia Blvd. Eventually, along N Portland Rd. to the west and from the 40-Mile Loop at the Columbia Slough and Heron Lakes Golf Course feeder trails.

Absolutely flat for easy accessibility.

How to Get There

From the south take Willamette Blvd. to N Carey and Princeton, just east of the railroad cut. From the north, from the city's Wastewater Treatment Facility off N Columbia Blvd.

By Mike Houck

Location
Extends from Willamette Blvd. at N Carey and Princeton to the Portland Bureau of Environmental Services Wastewater Treatment Facility on N Columbia Blvd. and along N Portland Blvd. to Smith and Bybee Lakes to NE Marine Dr.

Activities
Hiking
Biking

Facilities
Wheelchair accessible
Interpretive information
 (brochures/maps)
Picnic area

Fees and Regulations
Pets on leash

Highlights
There are a number of art pieces along the trail that were installed through the One Percent for the Arts public art program, and include seats carved out of Columbia River Basalt on the trailheads. More of a connector than a nature trail, it is the only north-south connector that extends from the Columbia to the Willamette across the North Portland Peninsula.

For more information: Metro Regional Parks and Greenspaces or Portland Parks and Recreation, see Resources.

For information about access to Columbia Boulevard Wastewater Treatment Plant and future access around the plant to the 40-Mile Loop Columbia Slough footbridge, contact: Portland Bureau of Environmental Services or Friends of the Peninsula Crossing Trail, see Resources.

Public Transit
Tri-Met #40 on Willamette Blvd.; #75 on Lombard; #4 on Fessenden.

Thomas Guide
565/566/536

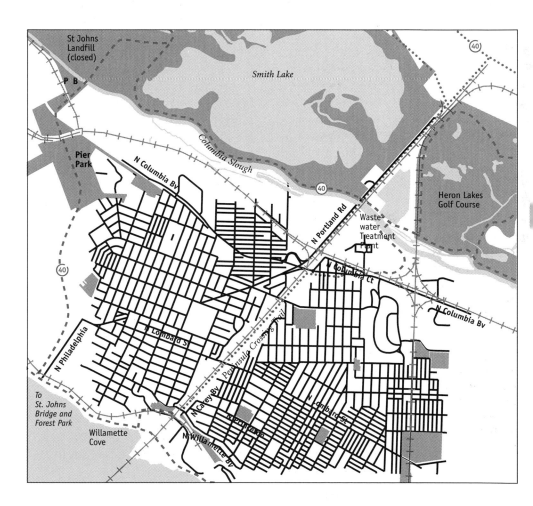

Lower Columbia River Watershed

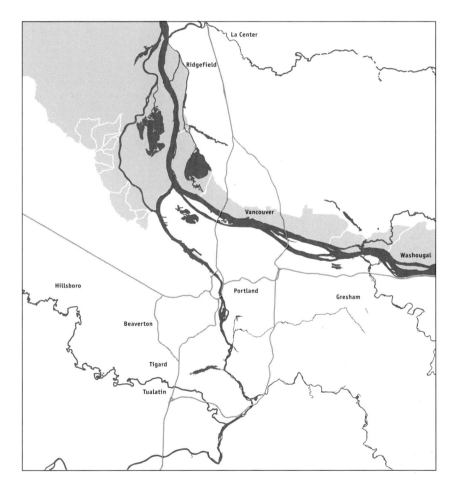

Sauvie Island

From the Pleistocene era a million years ago sediments from the mountains upriver washed down with the rains and snowmelt, to come to a stop at a ledge of large rocks. Through those aeons, soil accumulated in minute increments, and the ledge became an island's northern end. Each year the inundation continued, with annual freshets layering mud and sand, to a depth of 30 feet, in some places 50. Eventually the earth was shaped into soft, rolling contours, peppered with dozens of lakes and ponds. The resulting island is unique in the West.

Sauvie Island lies at the confluence of the Willamette and Columbia Rivers, a mostly narrow body of land approximately 15 miles long and four miles wide, almost identical in size and shape to Manhattan Island. But Sauvie's 24,000 acres are much differently settled—home to about 500 households of humans and 300 species of wildlife. The southern half of the island is graced with fertile farmland, sprouting Farm Markets, and U-Pick berry and flower businesses that produce bountiful, luscious harvests.

The 12,000 acres of the northern half are managed as a Wildlife Area by the Oregon Department of Fish and Wildlife. Aimed at preserving and developing habitat for wintering waterfowl, the Area is a major stop on the Pacific Flyway and its land and waters are host to astounding wildlife spectacles.

A birdwatcher's journal on a single day might show counts of 21 bald eagles, a flock of 1,000 snow geese, 250 sandhill cranes, 800 Canada geese, and 700 pintail ducks. A morning jaunt to a few favorite spots might turn up rough-legged hawks, red-tailed hawks, northern harriers, dozens of songbirds, bufflehead ducks, ring-necked ducks, wood ducks, and a pair of American kestrels.

Native to the island were the Multnomah tribe of the Chinook Indians. At one time they numbered about 2,000, living in villages of cedar long houses. The distinguished people of the tribe were "flatheads," a name derived from the custom of tying newborn babies to a flat board with a piece of wood across the brow, pressuring the skull to flatten in a continuous line from crown to nose.

They lived barefoot and bare-legged, clothed in animal skins and cedar bark. One of the food mainstays was wapato, a wetland tuber with arrow-shaped leaves, also known as arrowhead or wild potato. Roasted fresh on embers, dried and stored, or traded, wapato were harvested by the tribeswomen, who waded out alongside a canoe, and dug with their toes to find and loosen the mud-bound bulbs. Small patches of wapato can still be found today along some of the island lake shores.

Wapato Island was the name given by Lewis and Clark, who literally put the place on the map during their explorations of 1805 and 1806. They camped across the river from the island and in their journals bemoaned being kept awake by the

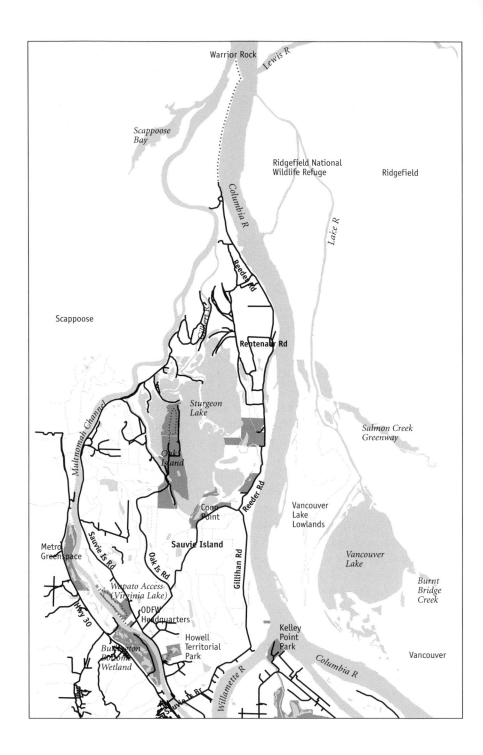

"horid" noise of the geese, ducks, and swans. Over the next decades, the native population weathered outbreaks of diseases, including smallpox and tuberculosis, brought by the white man. Then in 1828 a horrifying epidemic of a fever known as the "ague" swept across the land, and within three years all the Indians had died.

In time, the island came to be named for Laurent Sauvé, a French dairyman who had worked for the Hudson's Bay Company less than a decade later at Fort Vancouver. Four hundred head of cattle were swum across the Columbia River from the fort to produce butter and cheese that the company sold to Russian settlements in Alaska.

The island was resettled in the 1850s, when emigrants arrived and divided parcels based on the new Donation Land Act, which allowed a married couple to claim 640 acres. A number of working farms on the island today can be traced back to pioneers who set out from Missouri across the Oregon Trail.

The farming tradition continues across the southern half of the island, protected from flooding by surrounding dikes. The 12-mile loop of Gillihan-Reeder-Sauvie Island roads is a popular bike route, a flat road past scenic farm fields with a stunning backdrop on a blue-sky "Four Mountain Day" of Mounts Hood, Adams, St. Helens, and Rainier.

The northern Wildlife Area is one of few remaining vestiges of something akin to the region's original wetlands, with 21 lakes, plus streams, sloughs, and channels, and the meandering Gilbert River. It's a paddler's paradise. Boat ramps are located at Oak Island, the Gilbert River, and Steelman Lake, and there's the Old Ferry Boat Ramp with access to the Multnomah Channel, and St. Helens boat ramp with access into Cunningham Slough and Sturgeon Lake. The possibilities for gunkholing are endless, and likely to result in sightings of a multitude of great blue herons, belted kingfisher, and maybe a beaver, osprey, or bald eagle. Beaver-gnawed trees dot the shorelines, the remains finely sculpted with hundreds of tiny chiseled curves.

Along the Columbia River are some of the metropolitan area's finest sand beaches, with one section clothing-optional. Crowded in summer or a gorgeous day in any season, the miles of beaches offer serene strolls in the off-season or under gray skies.

Because the Wildlife Area was purchased and is maintained by hunting license fees and firearm taxes, one of its main purposes is to provide public hunting. Except for the northernmost section, which is open year-round, the Wildlife Area is off-limits during hunting season, typically from October 1 to mid-January. Various closures to keep the enormous flocks of geese from devastating early farm crops can extend the closures at some sites until April 15. A check with ODFW at 503-621-3488 can provide current status.

On Sauvie Island, the seasons unfold with magnificent flourish. In spring, trees and wildflowers burst into bloom, and avian courtship dances are choreographed in the sky. The wild roses of summer sweeten the air and scrumptious trail-side blackberries tempt with thoughts of whipped-cream cobblers. Fall, like spring, brings the great Flyway migration, and a landscape speckled in brilliant golds and scarlets. Winter reveals nests in bare branches, ponds newly-created with each rainy day, and once in a while a carpeting of snow, daintily etched with the tracks of wild creatures.

By Donna Matrazzo

Wapato Access Greenway State Park Trail

Location
NW Sauvie Island Rd.,
approx. 3 miles from the
Sauvie Island bridge.

Activities
Horseback riding
Hiking
Biking
Fishing
Canoeing, boating
Birdwatching

Facilities
Wheelchair accessibility
  (gravel trail; may
  require assistance)
Parking
Picnic area
Wildlife viewing blind
Dock, boat ramp

Fees and Regulations
Parking fees: none
Restricted hours: day
  use only
Pets on leash

One of the park's most interesting features is the seasonal lake, which is rich with abundant and extraordinary birds in winter and typically non-existent in summer, with water fluctuations sometimes noticeable from day to day. Locals recall ice skating on the lake in years past. A viewing blind near the southern end of the lake provides a concealed spot for waterfowl watching.

The park is managed as a natural area, the trail curving past wildflower meadows, an upland forest that contains mostly big-leaf maple, western red cedar, and western hemlock, and a coniferous forest of Douglas firs and an Oregon ash wetland. Sweet-scented wild roses, bursts of lupine, and tall golden stalks of mullein stipple the landscape, while August transforms the path into blackberry-picking heaven.

A spur trail leads to Hadley's Landing, a floating dock and boat tie-up on the Multnomah Channel. Wapato Park is part of the Willamette River Greenway and a portion of the trail follows the Multnomah Channel, with views of the Tualatin Mountains beyond.

Birding is excellent year-round, including bushtits, red-breasted nuthatches, Bewick's and winter wrens, American goldfinches, ruby-crowned kinglets, and western tanagers. The frog chorus is raucous in spring. Brush rabbits are commonly seen; rarer are sightings of coyote, fox, and black-tailed deer.

Access

An unpaved path heads out from the parking area and makes a two-mile loop around a seasonal lake. The trail is uneven but wheelchair-accessible (although it would be rough and narrow in some parts). Woodland sections become very muddy in winter and unusually high water will flood the trail at its most northerly and southerly points. A spur leads down to a floating boat dock at Hadley's Landing on the Multnomah Channel.

How to Get There

Take Hwy. 30 northwest to the Sauvie Island Bridge. Follow NW Sauvie Island Rd. (which parallels the Multomah Channel) north for approximately 2.5 miles, where you come to the junction with NW Reeder Rd. Continue on Sauvie Island Rd. for approximately .5 mile. The park will be on your left.

By Donna Matrazzo

For more information: Oregon Parks and Recreation, see Resources; the area is managed out of Tryon Creek State Park.

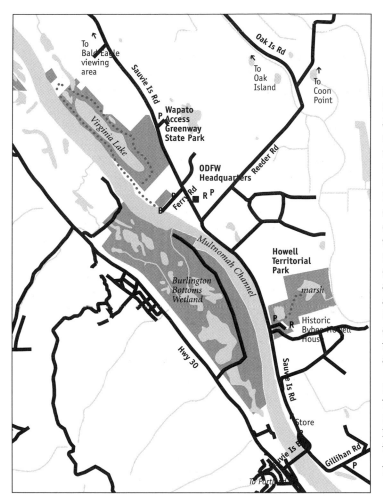

Highlights

From November through January or February, depending on the lake's water level, an abundance of striking birds can be observed—including bufflehead, ring-necked duck, great egret and the occasional cattle egret, wood duck, northern pintail, northern shoveler, green-winged teal, hooded and common mergansers, and cinnamon teals. Pileated woodpeckers and great blue herons are frequently seen, as well as bald eagles.

Public Transit

Tri-Met #17 to the parking lot beneath the Sauvie Island bridge. From there it's approx. 3 miles.

Thomas Guide 504/535

Howell Territorial Park and Howell Lake

Location
NW Sauvie Island Rd.,
approx. 1 mile from the
Sauvie Island Bridge

Activities
Wildlife watching

Facilities
Toilets
Wheelchair accessibility
Parking
Interpretive center
  (interpretive information)
Picnic area
Historic house

Fees and Regulations
Restricted hours: day
  use only
No pets

Highlights
Most of the seasonal
ponds and lakes on Sauvie
Island dry up in summer. A
recent restoration of
Howell wetlands included
the installation of a well
and pump, making this
one of the few places on
the island for consistently
great bird-watching in the
drier seasons.

Public Transit
Tri-Met #17 to the parking
lot beneath the Sauvie
Island bridge. From there
it's a one-mile walk or
bicycle ride.

Thomas Guide 535

The graceful and authentically restored Bybee House, centerpiece of Howell Territorial Park, is Sauvie Island's only remaining house built by Oregon Trail homesteaders. In 1873, the Bybees sold the property to John and Joseph Howell, who founded a successful dairy farm on the site.

Today the 93-acre park showcases Oregon's cultural and natural history in a pastoral setting that features an agricultural museum and an orchard of fruit trees planted with cuttings from historic 19th-century trees. A pasture includes seven oak trees which comprise a remnant of the Savannah oak communities historic to island uplands.

Howell Lake is actually a freshwater wetland. The two dominant plant species are reed canarygrass and soft rush, but wapato—the wild potato that was an important food source for Native Americans—still grows along the eastern edge. One of the few places west of the Cascades to spot yellow-headed blackbirds, the Lake is home to dozens of species of birds including green-winged teal, wood ducks, great blue herons, American coots, and common mergansers.

Large white gourds suspended from high posts near the lake provide nesting sites for purple martins, a sensitive species that once nested mainly in tree cavities in old growth forests.

A section of the Gilbert River defines the park's eastern boundary, and the site also contains other large natural wetlands and small mixed deciduous forest areas. Combined, these create good habitats for a multitude of species such as California quail, barn owls, and ring-necked pheasants, and amphibians like the western fence lizard.

While California ground squirrels are the most visible mammal, readily seen scurrying about the meadows and trees, other mammals frequently spotted are black-tailed deer, red foxes, coyote, and beaver.

Access
A planned 1,200-foot paved trail and a 3,000-foot unpaved trail leading to the wetlands and marshes and other park facilities are in the works.

How to Get There
Take Hwy. 30 northwest to the Sauvie Island Bridge. Follow NW Sauvie Island Rd. for approx. 1 mile and turn right on Howell Park Rd. *See map on page 327.*

By Donna Matrazzo

For more information: Howell Territorial Park or Metro Regional Parks and Greenspaces, see Resources.

Bald is Beautiful

In the damp pre-dawn of winter, three vans halt at the narrow edge of Sauvie Island Road. Van doors slide open and a dozen passengers file out into the cold morning air. The bundled figures lining the roadside look like commuters awaiting a bus. Actually, they have come looking for this morning's real commuters—bald eagles on their dawn flight onto Sauvie Island. The eagles are returning from their forest roost to the west to search the island's lakes, ponds, and wetlands for food.

It's 7:00 A.M., and the Sauvie Island Bald Eagle count is just beginning. In the dim morning light, the volunteer counters peer out over Multnomah Channel. Several gulls and a double-crested cormorant fly low over the water and, to the north, a rough-legged hawk quietly glides toward the island. From the island's interior comes the echoing "pop pop" of shotguns. Several counters exchange glances, but most ignore the duck hunters and continue to scan the western horizon, looking for incoming eagles.

After nearly ten minutes, someone points excitedly to the distant silhouette of a large bird . . . hoping for an eagle. In an instant the entire group turns to the line of sight, collectively straining to see in the dim light. The bird approaches quickly. Large, finger-like feathers and a touch of white on the head and tail cinch it. With a few powerful wing beats, the immature bald eagle moves rapidly toward the reddening eastern sky.

The counters turn and chatter excitedly for several minutes, but soon gaze back to the west to look for the next arrival. By 8:30 they have finished for the day. Thirty eagles, more than have been seen all winter, have passed over the Multnomah-Columbia County line this morning.

The Eagle Mystique

Getting out of bed to count birds during the coldest and darkest months may seem like a strange avocation, but humans have long been fascinated with eagles. For centuries, these huge birds have been held as symbols of strength and courage. The eagle was an emblem of ancient Sumerians and appeared on the King of Ur's seal. In the Old Testament, God said to Moses on Mt. Sinai, "Ye have seen . . . how I bare you on eagle's wings and brought you unto myself."

To the ancient Greeks, the eagle was Zeus' messenger and the bird of heaven. To the Romans, it marked their legion's military might, and to us, of course, the bald eagle is a national symbol.

But being a symbol is not always easy. Living symbols often get bad press, and the bald eagle is no exception. In Alaska, the territorial legislature put a price on its

head, alleging that eagles were responsible for reduced salmon runs. More than 60,000 eagles were slaughtered as a result. Benjamin Franklin, disappointed with its selection as our national symbol, once wrote his daughter:

> . . . the Bald Eagle . . . is a bird of bad moral character; he does not get his living honestly; you may see him perched on some dead tree; where, too lazy to fish for himself, he watches the labor of the fishing-hawk; and, when that diligent bird has at length taken a fish, and is bearing it to his nest for the support of his mate and the young ones, the Bald Eagle pursues him and takes it from him.

Moral character notwithstanding, the bald eagle is a beautiful bird. Although an agile predator, the eagle will take what comes most easily and often eats dead fish or waterfowl, especially during the cold winter months. The Sauvie Island eagles are on the lookout for ducks and geese that have been killed by hunters or succumb to the winter elements. Since ingestion of as few as three to four lead pellets can kill an adult eagle, Sauvie Island is one of several steel-shot zones in the Northwest.

In summer, eagles are territorial and nest over a wide range. During the winter months, however, they gather into communal roosts, which in Oregon and Washington are frequently stands of old growth forest. The thick canopy provides shelter and moderates temperatures. When the feeding territories of several roosts overlap, it makes it more difficult to obtain accurate counts for a single group.

The Sauvie Island population is one of several roosts in the Pacific Northwest, but locally, the greatest variety and abundance of raptors occurs here, where the concentration of winter waterfowl and small mammals attracts a large population of these winged predators. These are mainly birds that nest along the lower Columbia River but also include eagles from Washington and British Columbia. Each morning, just before dawn, the eagles leave their roost and fly roughly 20 miles to the island. They spend the day feeding on waterfowl and resting in the tall black cottonwoods that grow in the island's wet soils. At dusk, the eagles return to their roost singly or in pairs.

Dawn is the best time for viewing eagles since their normal "commute" is from a specific direction . . . from the west. The evening flight is more difficult to pinpoint because it is dispersed throughout the island and as far as Ridgefield National Wildlife Refuge in Washington.

There are smaller roosts near Astoria and at the Yale and Merwin Reservoirs in Washington. The Klamath Falls, Bear Valley roost is the largest winter gathering of bald eagles in the contiguous United States.

The bald eagle is staging a comeback in some parts of the state, but the lower Columbia River population remains in decline due to habitat losses. Fortunately, Sauvie Island still offers a rare opportunity to appreciate the bald eagle. In our unique setting, it's possible to take a few minutes from one's own commute to watch this majestic bird on its daily commute . . . and still make it in time for work!

By Thomas E. Hanrahan

Coon Point Viewpoint

The viewpoint at Coon Point is spectacular for its panorama and multitude of habitats visible in one wide sweep. To the west are farm fields, prime haunts for sandhill cranes feeding in harvested fields. Foreground trees are favorite perches for American kestrels. A low seasonal pond due north might be the day's choice spot for shorebirds like greater or lesser yellowlegs. Then comes the expansive Sturgeon Lake, with a multitude of great blue herons standing sentinel as hundreds, or maybe thousands, of ducks float and dabble. Tundra swans are abundant in winter. Good binoculars or a spotting scope might focus on eagles, red-tailed hawks, or other raptors in distant trees.

And then, the sky. Vast numbers of Canada geese, myriad species of ducks, and sandhill cranes wing their way overhead in flocks small and immense. During spring and summer migrations, the sheer numbers of birds in the sky are astounding, and the cacophony delightfully outrageous.

As if all that isn't enough, on clearer days there's the backdrop of Mt. St. Helens over the vista of Sturgeon Lake in one direction, and miles and miles of the lovely forested Tualatin Mountains dominating the other.

On occasion, especially in summer, when the pond is dried up and the lake shallower and more distant, it's possible to arrive on the platform and not immediately spot any wildlife. But patience pays off and one rarely leaves without a few enticing sightings.

Access

A paved ramp with a handrail slopes gently up to a paved viewing area at the top of an island dike. Between October 1 and April 15, there's no access beyond the paved area. The remainder of the year, flat grassy trails to either side of the paved area are accessible for a short distance (approx. a quarter of a mile).

How to Get There

Take Hwy. 30 northwest to the Sauvie Island Bridge. Follow NW Sauvie Island Rd. (which parallels the Multnomah Channel) north for approximately 2.5 miles. Turn right at the junction with NW Reeder Rd. and continue for approximately 3.1 miles. The parking lot will be on your left.

By Donna Matrazzo

For more information: Oregon Department of Fish and Wildlife: Sauvie Island Wildlife Area, see Resources.

Location
NW Reeder Rd., approx. 5.5 miles from the Sauvie Island Bridge; 3 miles from the junction of NW Sauvie Island Rd. and NW Reeder Rd.

Activities
Birdwatching

Facilities
Toilets
Wheelchair accessibility
Parking
Interpretive information

Fees and Regulations
Parking fees: A parking permit is required. Permits, for the day or all year, are currently available in Oregon at G.I. Joe's, Fred Meyer, Walmart, and Payless stores, as well as the 7-11 in Linnton and the Cracker Barrel Grocery on Sauvie Island.

Hours: 10 A.M. to 4 P.M.
Pets on leash

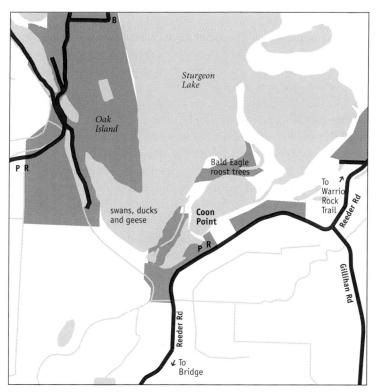

Highlights
During the great migrations of spring and fall, Coon Point's lakefront locale and panoramic vistas make it a prime bird-watching spot and terrific site for a sunset picnic.

Public Transit
Tri-Met #17 to the parking lot beneath the Sauvie Island bridge. From there it's approx. 5.5 miles by bicycle or foot.

Thomas Guide 505

Oak Island Trail

Old oak trees, with their gnarled branches and corrugated trunks, line the trail and shape a wonderful woodland, shelter for a multitude of bird species. Oak Island is no longer an island, but a narrow peninsula jutting into the lakes of the Wildlife Area.

This is a place where naturalists like to "pish"—throwing out a pschee-pschee sound that a lot of birds seem to hear as a distress signal (though no one professes to know how it really works), which lures them out in the open to check out the scene.

Frequently-seen birds include species of sparrows, jays, creepers, kinglets, chickadees, both red-breasted and white-breasted nuthatches, and warblers. Their various songs and sounds overlap and harmonize to fill the air with rich melodies, pierced by the sharp, flirty whistle of red-winged blackbirds. Years ago, you could count on seeing Lewis' woodpeckers on Oak Island, but the starlings and house sparrows seem to have pushed them out and only a single Lewis' was seen two years ago near Bybee-Howell.

From the tree-lined woods, the trail opens up to a wide meadow, and beyond it the waters of Wagonwheel Hole and Steelman Lake, with the thousand-foot Tualatin Mountains in the background. Bald eagles are regularly seen in these oaks in winter, and northern harriers (raptors formerly known as marsh hawks) sweep low over the fields, harrying their prey.

The next long stretch of trail traces the shoreline of Sturgeon Lake. Here great blue herons, sandhill cranes, Canada geese and snow geese, and many species of ducks feed and flourish with the seasons. A solitary bench sits facing the lake and the view beyond—the Cascade Mountains and their snow-capped volcanoes stretching across the horizon.

Location
At the end of Oak Island Rd., nearly 7 miles from the Sauvie Island Bridge.

Activities
Hiking
Canoeing, boating
Fishing

Facilities
Toilets
Parking

Fees and Regulations
Parking fees: A parking permit is required. Permits, for the day or all year, are currently available in Oregon at G.I. Joe's, Fred Meyer, Walmart, and Payless stores, as well as the 7-11 in Linnton and the Cracker Barrel Grocery on Sauvie Island.

Hours: day use only

Seasonal restriction: Oak Island is closed throughout the hunting season, October through late January, and frequently the closure extends to mid-April.

Pets on leash

Access
The flat, grassy trail leads directly from the parking lot. Hiking signs mark the direction of the 2-3/4-mile loop.

How to Get There
Take Hwy. 30 northwest to the Sauvie Island Bridge. Follow NW Sauvie Island Rd. (which parallels the Multnomah Channel) north for approximately 2.5 miles. Turn right at the junction with NW Reeder Rd. and continue about 1.2 miles to Oak Island Rd. Turn left and follow the paved road for three miles to the end of the pavement and the entrance to the Sauvie Island Wildlife Area. Continue on the paved road for half a mile, where you'll come to a four-way junction. Continue straight ahead and at .4 mile you'll come to the trailhead.

By Donna Matrazzo

For more information: Oregon Department of Fish and Wildlife: Sauvie Island Wildlife Area, see Resources.

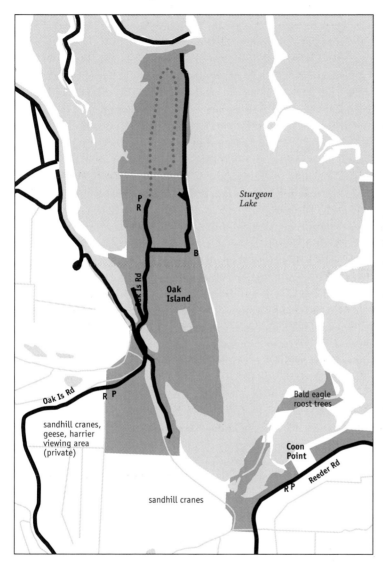

Highlights

A naturalist once said, "If I had one tree I would plant for a diversity of wildlife, it would be oaks." The wooded oak habitat along this trail is resonant with birdsong from dozens of species.

Public Transit

Tri-Met #17 to the parking lot beneath the Sauvie Island Bridge. From there it's approximately 6.7 miles to the trailhead.

Thomas Guide 475/505

Warrior Rock Lighthouse Trail

Location
At the far northeastern end of Sauvie Island, approx. 15 miles from the Sauvie Island Bridge.

Activities
Hiking
Fishing

Facilities
Toilets
Parking

Fees and Regulations
Parking fees: A parking permit is required. Permits, for the day or all year, are currently available in Oregon at G.I. Joe's, Fred Meyer, Walmart, and Payless stores, as well as the 7-11 in Linnton and the Cracker Barrel Grocery on Sauvie Island.

Hours: 10 A.M. to 4 P.M.

Pets on leash

Legend has it that in October 1792, British Lieutenant William Broughton and his crew, as part of a naval expedition led by Captain George Vancouver to explore the Columbia River, became the first white people to set foot on what is now Sauvie Island. As the story goes, 150 warriors of the Multnomah tribe of Chinook Indians paddled up in two dozen canoes to greet them. Indians from another river tribe accompanying Broughton explained his mission, and the islanders welcomed the men, who stayed to trade and slept there that night. Thus, Warrior Rock was named to mark the occasion.

The spot is marked today with the Warrior Rock Lighthouse, a charming outpost from civilization near the northern tip of Sauvie Island. The most interesting way to hike there and back is to follow the forest trail in one direction, and walk along the beach heading the other way. There may seem to be a few spur trails heading inland. Ignore them and take the route that parallels the shore.

Through the woods, black cottonwood trees abound; in summer their white fluff scatters along the path. River views are framed by the trees, glimpses of immense barges and ships piloting up and down the Columbia, sometimes almost silently, followed by a swooshing sound as their wakes wash with force against the eroding banks.

Wild roses, herbs, and blackberries tangle beyond the path. At dusk on clear days, the tangerine orb of a sun glints brilliantly through the trees, while casting "magic hour" coloring on the woods across the river.

Near the lighthouse are the remains of a small house, the roof and walls long ago destroyed by fire, but a stone fireplace and chimney remain, giving testament to a measure of the remote island life of a lighthouse-keeper.

Strolling along the Columbia's shore takes on the personality of the day's weather—sometimes calm waters, shrouded in fog, other days scudding clouds and waves whipped into white-capped breakers. Tracks of raccoons, great blue herons, and shorebirds lace the wide sandy beach.

Access

The trail is a 6-mile round trip over fairly level ground. Options include following a mostly grassy roadbed or walking along the sandy shore of the Columbia River. Cows graze in the area and cow pies spatter the trail. Unlike most of the Sauvie Island Wildlife Area, which is closed during the hunting season (typically October 1 through mid-April), this area remains accessible, although people are hunting there until the end of January.

How to Get There

Take Hwy. 30 northwest to the Sauvie Island Bridge. Follow NW Sauvie Island Rd. (which parallels the Multnomah Channel) northwest for approx. 2.5 miles. Turn right at the junction with NW Reeder Rd. and continue 4.3 miles to its junction with Gillihan Rd. Continue north on NW Reeder Rd.; at 6.1 miles the pavement ends. Follow the unpaved road another 2.3 miles to the parking lot; the trail begins at its northeast corner.

By Donna Matrazzo

For more information: Oregon Department of Fish and Wildlife: Sauvie Island Wildlife Area, see Resources.

Highlights

This sandy shore along the Columbia, with the natural shoreline and woodlands of Ridgefield National Wildlife Area across the river in Washington, must be one of the loveliest beaches in our region. Jutting from craggy rocks near the tip of the island, the charming Warrior Rock Lighthouse offers an enticing locale for a picnic lunch.

Public Transit

Tri-Met #17 to the parking lot beneath the Sauvie Island Bridge. From there it's a 15-mile bicycle ride.

Thomas Guide 415/445

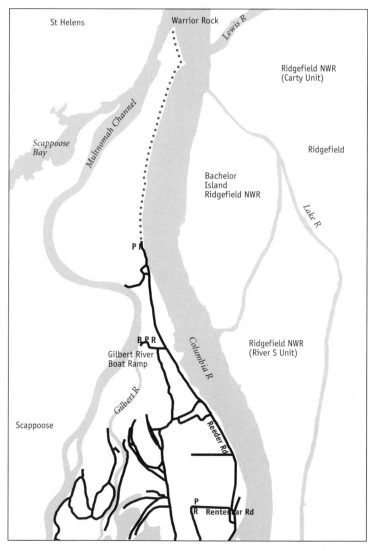

The Columbia River Gorge National Wildlife Refuges

Steigerwald Lake National Wildlife Refuge

Steigerwald Lake National Wildlife Refuge was established to provide partial mitigation for wildlife habitat lost as a result of the construction and operation of the second powerhouse at Bonneville Dam. The approved boundary includes 1,278 acres: 682 for U.S. Army Corps of Engineers mitigation, and an additional 596 proposed for acquisition to provide a buffer from intensive human activity and to allow for wetland enhancement projects and site management. As of 1999, 1,006 acres have been placed under refuge management. The refuge consists of remnant and artificially created wetlands, patches of cottonwood-dominated riparian communities, pastureland, and a remnant stand of Oregon white oak. Gibbons Creek, which supports remnant runs of coho salmon, steelhead, and a variety of native resident species, flows through the refuge.

Franz Lake National Wildlife Refuge

Franz Lake National Wildlife Refuge currently contains more than 550 acres within the approved 649-acre refuge boundary. The refuge provides a variety of habitats including riverine wetlands, blocks of Columbia River riparian communities, old-growth Douglas fir and western red cedar woodlands, open meadows, and numerous springs, seeps, and creeks. Franz Lake and associated wetlands make up about 395 acres, and is one of the few remaining riverine wetland habitats in the Columbia River Gorge. The lake contains healthy stands of wapato, which provides excellent feeding opportunities for wintering tundra swans and other waterfowl. The creeks, springs, and seeps on the refuge have been identified as critical brood areas for coho salmon and other juvenile salmonids. Current management emphasis is on protecting the eroding Columbia River shoreline, wetland enhancement, and protection and enhancement of anadromous and other native fisheries resources.

Pierce National Wildlife Refuge

Pierce National Wildlife Refuge is a 336-acre property that was donated to the U.S. Fish and Wildlife Service by Lena Pierce in 1983. The property was operated as a cattle ranch from 1955 until 1988. A grazing lease was attached to the original donation deed, and grazing was incorporated into the management of the refuge until 1997. Current management focuses on wetland restoration and enhancement, riparian habitat restoration, providing wintering habitat for waterfowl, and the protection and enhancement of anadromous and other native fisheries resources. The refuge provides a variety of habitats including wetlands, blocks of riparian vegetation, Oregon white oak and Douglas fir woodlands, pastures with some native

Location
These three National Wildlife Refuges are located on the Washington side of the Columbia River, within the Columbia River Gorge National Scenic Area. Steigerwald Lake NWR is adjacent to the City of Washougal, Franz Lake NWR is near the town of Skamania, and Pierce NWR is immediately west of the town of North Bonneville. Access to all three refuges is from State Hwy. 14.

Activities
These refuges are currently closed to the public. Comprehensive conservation plans will be developed and implemented for each of the refuges as funding permits. Initial startup funds have been appropriated for an interpretive center at Steigerwald National Wildlife Refuge to serve refuge visitors and provide information about the Columbia River Gorge National Scenic Area. Group tours and other activities are available. Contact the refuge office for additional information, and to find out about tours, events, and volunteer opportunities.

grasses, and numerous creeks, seeps, and springs. Hardy Creek, which bisects the refuge from east to west, supports one of the last remaining runs of chum salmon on the Columbia River, as well as remnant runs of coho, steelhead, and chinook salmon and a variety of non-anadromous native species.

Access

Access is by arrangement with the Refuge Manager. Development of public use facilities will be considered during the development of conservation plans and will be contingent on funding. There are viewing opportunities from outside of the refuge boundaries.

Steigerwald Lake NWR is visible from State Hwy. 14, east of Washougal. A historic marker located at the intersection of Evergreen Hwy. and State Hwy. 14 offers a panoramic view of much of the refuge. In addition, a service road located on a dike between the refuge and Port of Camas-Washougal and the Columbia River serves as a viewing trail. It can be accessed from Steamboat Landing State Park at the intersection of 15th St. and State Hwy. 14.

Franz Lake NWR can be viewed from a scenic overlook near Milepost 31 on State Hwy. 14. The observation platform offers excellent views of the Franz Lake wetland complex and provides opportunities for bird watching, especially tundra swans in the late fall and winter, and other wildlife observation.

Pierce National Wildlife Refuge can be seen from the top of Beacon Rock, looking east up the Columbia River.

How to Get There

Traveling east of Washougal on State Hwy. 14, you will find Steigerwald Lake NWR near Washington's west entrance to the Columbia River Gorge National Scenic Area. Continuing east for about 15 miles, you will find Franz Lake NWR between Mileposts 30 and 32. Pierce NWR is still further east between Beacon Rock State Park and North Bonneville.

By Jeff Holm

For more information: U.S. Fish and Wildlife Service or Ridgefield National Wildlife Refuge Complex, see Resources.

The Columbia River Gorge National Wildlife Refuges are units of the Ridgefield National Wildlife Refuge Complex.

Highlights

These refuges consist of historic Columbia River bottomland. The refuges provide habitat for migrating and wintering waterfowl that travel through the Pacific flyway, serving as resting and wintering areas for tundra swans, Canada geese, and other waterfowl. Seasonal and year-round habitat is also provided for a variety of wildlife including raptors, marsh and shorebirds, riparian woodland songbirds, resident and migratory mammals, reptiles, and amphibians. Coho salmon, steelhead, cutthroat, chum salmon, and native resident fish also occur on the refuges. The best times to view wildlife are in the spring, fall, and winter.

Clark County Road Atlas 5

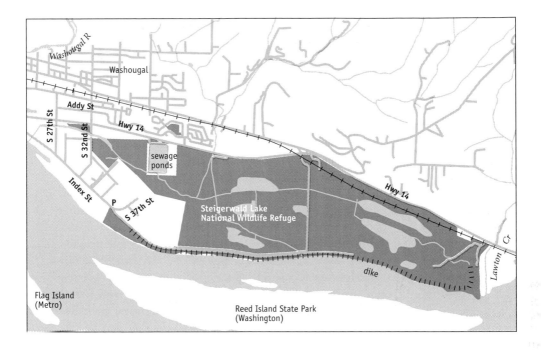

Washougal R
Washougal
Addy St
S 27th St
S 32nd St
Hwy 14
sewage ponds
Index St
P
S 37th St
Steigerwald Lake National Wildlife Refuge
Hwy 14
Lawton Cr
dike
Flag Island (Metro)
Reed Island State Park (Washington)

References

U.S. Department of the Interior. "Columbia River Gorge National Fish Hatcheries and National Wildlife Refuges." U.S. Fish and Wildlife Service.

U.S. Department of the Interior. "Columbia River Gorge, National Fish Hatcheries and National Wildlife Refuges." www.r1.fws.gov/gorgefish/HOME.MAIN.HTM U.S. Fish and Wildlife Service.

Weaver, Ron. *Environmental Assessment, Proposed Acquisition of Steigerwald Lake Property, Clark County, Washington.* Portland, Oregon: Department of the Interior, U.S. Fish and Wildlife Service, Region 1, 1987.

Clark County Marine Park Wetlands

From the overlook, which is near the Water Resource Education Center, you can observe riverside wetlands of the upper wetlands to the east (no paths) and the bank of cottonwoods at the west edge. The 1996 flood came close enough to the Center to shred nerves. You may call ahead to schedule a tour of the nearby Water Reclamation Facility, a state-of-the-art water treatment plant that discharges into the Columbia River. If you are interested in booking a tour for a class or other group call the Education Center.

To view the site, start at the overlook south of the parking area and road. The all-weather view across the broad Columbia is spectacular. Much nearer the overlook you can view aggressively expanding wapato. The wetland below is dynamic, changing seasonally with fluctuating water levels—high during winter months and late spring, lowest in late summer and early fall. The belted kingfisher, usually in a willow to the right, sits patiently waiting to swoop for unwary prey in the nearby waters. High spring levels allow upstream soils, logs, seeds, and debris to be deposited, bringing waterfowl abundant food as they begin to pair off. On most visits, you may be startled by the unexpected squawk of the modern version of a pterodactyl, the great blue heron, erupting from a pond or zeroing in on a landing site. Spring treefrogs persistently serenade you as well.

In springtime the water covers much of the lower floodplain, while at slightly higher elevations clusters of tall willows grow. Higher still, at the edge of the upper floodplain, are tall cottonwoods. Shorter willow and cottonwood rise like grass along the shore and sandbars. The occasional live willow log rafted in at high water may be seen sending stems into the air and odd-looking root systems into the soils. Pushy, invasive reed canarygrass dominates in open areas, but many wildflowers and other grasses fit in where they can.

During the dry summer, established plants fight for space with the new arrivals. The sand isthmus by the Columbia extends and forms a pond below the overlook so that slackening waters flow from the uplands through the sands. This is a great time for great blue herons, kingfishers, osprey, and the like to pick off the trapped fish as the water table inexorably lowers. Plants fill the inevitable waterless void. Flying perpetually here and there are kingfishers, mallards, herons, geese, sparrows, flickers, blackbirds, hawks, chickadees, kinglets, gulls, crows, towhees, doves, robins, woodpeckers, juncos, finches, and cormorants, to name a few. Seasonally, there are mergansers, grebes, swallows, osprey, swans, coots, egrets, and many more casual fly-bys.

Summer is a great time for wildlife trackers as prints of all kinds abound in the exposed mud. Mammals like coyote, fox, muskrat, beaver, mice, voles, and moles have been spotted or have left evidence

Location
North side of the Columbia River in Vancouver, Washington, the Marine Park Wetlands are adjacent to a developed city park (Marine Park), the Water Reclamation Facility, and the Water Resource Education Center, an interpretive site at 4600 SE Columbia Way.

Activities
Hiking
Biking
Canoeing, boating
Fishing

Facilities
Toilets
Wheelchair accessible
Trail paved
Parking
Interpretive center
Interpretive information
    (brochures/maps)
Picnic area
Dock, canoe launch

Fees and Regulations
Parking fees (for boat
    launching)
Pets on leash

of their passing. Of course the cold-blooded types include tree frogs, turtles, snakes, newts, many fish, freshwater clams, snails, worms, and insects.

Across the back parking lot to the east is a wetland that drains water from uplands north of the railroad tracks and SR 14. There is no path across this section but it is full of wildlife year-round if you look carefully. Berms south of the road are cut by culverts to allow the wetland to drain towards the Columbia. Most of this is covered by a mix of second-growth trees and is full of birds and wildflowers. The vegetation along Columbia Way and the sidewalk is urban but becomes natural as soon as you step down to the lower wetlands.

Access
Columbia Way and Columbia Pkwy.

How to Get There
From Portland take I-5 north to Vancouver. Take State Road (SR) 14 exit and head east (toward Camas). Take exit #1 (Columbia Way) and stay in the far right lane. If you come over the I-205 bridge and approach Vancouver from the east on SR 14, take the Columbia Blvd. off-ramp and proceed to Columbia Way. Go south under the railroad bridge and turn left (east) onto SE Columbia Way at the light. Drive east less than 2 miles through a business park, then pass a city park with picnic areas and the Water Reclamation Facility. The wetlands are on the river in front of the Water Resource Education Center at 4600 SE Columbia Way. Drive directly to the Water Center or Marine Park parking areas. Another option is to park just west of the I-5 bridge, near the Port of Vancouver and Doubletree Hotel. Walk east, along the Renaissance Trail, a flat, paved path that extends about 4 miles from the I-5 bridge to east of the wetlands. An overlook allows

Highlights
From the overlook is a dynamic view of the cycle of riverine wetlands: water levels, emergent plants such as wapato or arrowhead, and animal populations. Water level is controlled by dams on the Columbia River and by ocean tides. Where the paved trail swings by the river to the east of the wetlands, you'll find an osprey pair nesting and raising young during the spring and summer. The wetlands shelter a diversity of wildlife. Summer is a great time for tracking animal prints.

Public Transit
C-TRAN #11, Columbia Shores, makes scheduled stops at the overlook.

Clark County Road Atlas 8/9

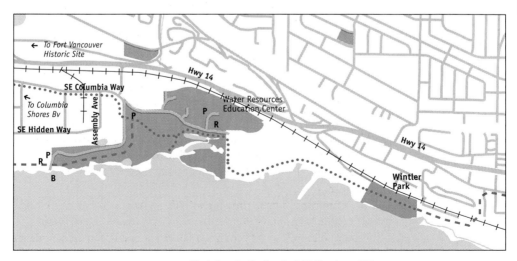

viewing into much of the wetlands and over an inlet leading from the Columbia River. To protect habitat, please stay on the paved areas. The Renaissance Trail will eventually connect the river corridor between I-5 and I-205 bridges.

By Bill Feddeler

For more information: City of Vancouver Water Resources Education Center, see Resources.

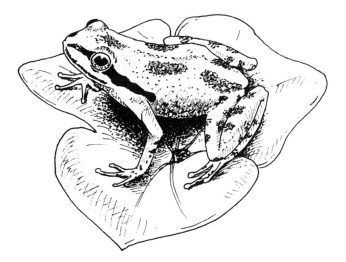

Pussy Willows

Of the several early botanical indicators that spring is drawing near, the willow is one of my favorites. Along with trillium, skunk cabbage, and Indian plum, the "pussy willow's" seemingly overnight appearance lends grace and color to the late winter and early spring scene. Its twigs add bands of bright yellow, orange, or red to our riparian landscape.

Willows are a common and important component of riparian and wetland environments. They are in one of the most widespread genera (*Salix*) of trees and shrubs, with more than 300 species worldwide. We have over 30 species in the Pacific Northwest, eight of which commonly attain tree size. The distinction between tree and shrub can be obscure at times since several of the shrubby species attain tree stature under favorable conditions.

Willow Characteristics
The following are some of the features that distinguish willows from other members of the Willow Family (Salicaceae), although you should be forewarned that field identification of individual species is often difficult, especially in winter and early spring:

- Short-stalked deciduous simple leaves which are longer than they are broad.

- Slender, wiry twigs; leaf buds with single cap-like scale.

- Bark has harmless, quinine-like bitter taste.

- A pair of ear-shaped growths (stipules) at base of leaves on new shoots.

- Leaves and buds alternately arranged on stems.

The familiar "pussy willow" is actually the felty catkins of male and female flowers. The willow is an example of a group that has separate male and female plants (dioecious, Greek for "two dwellings"). In spring, tassel-like catkins on the female plant split open to release numerous tiny seeds covered with tufts of cottony down, which are easily dispersed by wind and water. Germination must occur within 24 hours, since they cannot remain dormant for long periods. This necessitates the dispersal of huge numbers of seeds to ensure that a few land in favorable sites and germinate. In addition to this sexual form of reproduction willows also sprout prolifically from roots, stumps, and cuttings.

How to Know the Willows

Willow identification can be a frustrating experience since it is often necessary to have flower, fruit, and vegetative parts all at the same time. Since all of these parts develop at different times of the year it is sometimes necessary to tag a specimen and return to it several times during the growing season.

Our Common Willows

Exploration of riparian areas and wetlands, and even in some drier upland sites in and around Portland, is likely to yield several species of willow. Four of the most common species in our area that grow to tree and/or large shrub-sized include Pacific willow (*Salix lasiandra*), sandbar or Columbia River willow (*S. fluviatilis*), Sitka willow (*S. sitchensis*), and scouler willow (*S. scouleriana*).

Pacific Willow

This species commonly occurs in stream corridors, along lakeshores, and in other wet sites, preferably in gravelly, sandy soil. It is the most common and easily recognized tree-sized native willow in our area and is the dominant species in Oaks Bottom Wildlife Refuge and Smith and Bybee Lakes. Under favorable conditions it can grow to 60 feet, although 30-foot specimens are the norm. Wart-like glands at the base of the leaf blade; distinctly shiny orange or yellow twigs; and long, pointed leaves (four and a half to five inches), finely toothed along the margins, shiny on the upper surface and whitish below, distinguish this species.

Sandbar Willow

This species will grow to a height of 10 to 20 feet. It typically occurs on sandbars in moist to wet sand and gravel which is overlain with silt, which is retained by its reed-like stems. Newly dredged or filled sites and areas of accretion are its favored environment. This slender-stemmed shrub or small tree has narrow, delicate leaves (one eighth to one quarter of an inch wide) that can be up to 16 times as long as broad. The leaves are light green above and silvery-silky beneath.

Sitka Willow

This species commonly occurs along streams and beaches as well as the borders of meadows and forest clearings. It is a large shrub to small tree (height of 10 to 23 feet), depending on site conditions. The leaves are two to four times as long as they are broad, the margins are smooth and often slightly wavy, and they are dull green above and densely silver-haired below.

Scouler Willow

This tall spindly shrub or multi-stemmed small tree (six to 21 feet) has a wide range of moisture tolerance. It can grow in wet sites such as around wetlands, and along drainage ditches and streams, as well as drier sites on floodplains, forests borders, and sandy beaches and dunes. Branches are brown to yellowish brown and often velvety, while the yellow-green twigs are densely woolly. The leaves (two to four inches long) are typically obovate, being wider at the tip and wedge-shaped at the base, dark green above and densely hairy below. The leaf margins are smooth or have small, gland-tipped teeth, which are often rolled under.

Wildlife Values

Willows provide food and cover throughout the year. The buds and small tender twigs are a staple for birds and mammals such as grouse, deer, rabbit, beaver, and muskrat. Flowers provide an important early spring food supply for honeybees. The willow is also an important bank stabilizer that provides summertime shading of water and contributes significantly to the aquatic ecosystem through leaf fall. One of its chief economic values is its use for erosion control. Cuttings are frequently used in streamside planting efforts in the Portland area and elsewhere in the Northwest.

Native peoples of the Pacific Northwest used willow to make clothing, to smoke fish and game, to start fires, and to create woven containers with the stems and twigs.

By Ralph Thomas Rogers

Vancouver Lake Lowlands

Fruit Valley Road Sewage Ponds and Washington Wildlife Access Area

Activities

Hiking: all (access restricted at all but the parks during hunting season)

Biking: all

Canoeing, boating: Vancouver Lake, Fruit Valley Wildlife Area, Frenchman's Bar, and some areas of the Shillapoo Wildlife Area have boat ramps

Fishing: all with appropriate licenses

Swimming: Vancouver Lake Park (no lifeguards)

Play area and picnic structures at both Vancouver Lake and Frenchman's Bar.

If you have a bicycle, you may want to park at Fruit Valley Park and ride into the Wildlife Access Area. About a quarter of a mile on the left are sewage ponds that are easily visible from the raised dike that runs perpendicular to the road. There is limited parking, but it's possible to put spotting scopes on the grassy dike to scan the ponds for ring-necked duck, lesser scaup, ruddy ducks, shovelers, and bufflehead. At first it's difficult to see the ducks amidst the aeration devices.

Another quarter-mile down the paved road is the entrance to the "Wildlife Access Area." Remember, you need an Access Stewardship Decal if you drive. About a half mile from the entrance on the left is a sizable great blue heron nesting colony in a cottonwood grove just beyond two large Oregon white oaks. The wetlands and pastures to the right are perfect habitat for short-eared owls, and you can frequently see northern harriers cruising low over the fields in search of prey.

Just over one mile from the entrance there is a parking lot, complete with skeet range and bathroom. This area is a hunting area, primarily pheasant and waterfowl (late September through January). Hunters and non-hunters use the area, which is restricted to shotgun and bow hunting. Another .2 mile down the now-gravel road is the Fruit Valley boat ramp. This is a good put-in point for kayaking or canoeing, although it is simply a gravel apron without a dock. To the left of the boat ramp is a trail that provides excellent access to the shores of the south end of Vancouver Lake.

Vancouver Lake Park

There is an excellent viewing point at the junction of Lower River Road and the Reiger Memorial Highway to Vancouver Lake Park at the Flushing Channel, which allows water from the Columbia River into and out of the lake. There is a small grassy overlook and portable toilet here.

In addition to having a huge picnic area, lots of restrooms, and open grass fields, Vancouver Lake Park offers spectacular views of the lake. This is the most consistent place in the Portland metro area to find diving birds in migration, especially in the fall. All six grebes commonly found in Oregon and Washington have been seen on the Lake, although western and pied-billed are the most common in winter. Loons, gulls, and double-crested cormorants frequent the lake as well. Bald eagles can be seen in the cottonwoods surrounding the lake, and at least one active nest is within a mile of the lake. Several great horned owl nests can also be found early in the winter in the trees surrounding the lake.

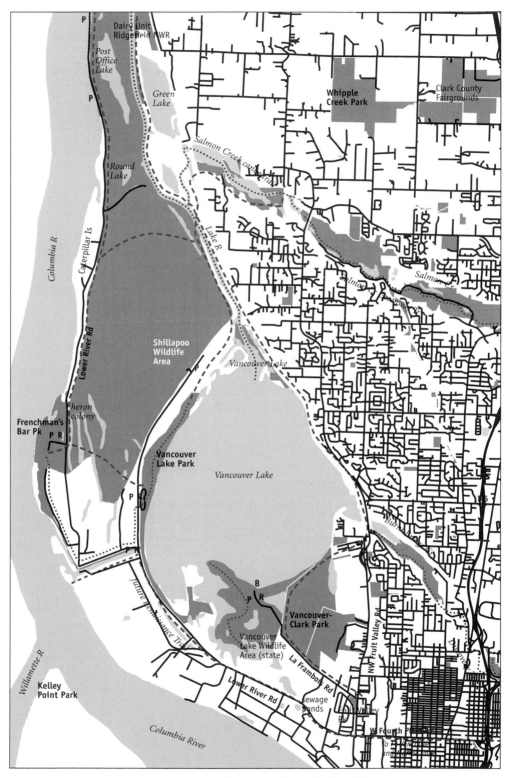

Wildlife viewing is best at Vancouver Lake in fall, winter, and spring, while outdoor activities like swimming and picnicking can be enjoyed during the summer.

If you continue past the park, you can reach the Shillapoo and Vancouver Lake Wildlife Areas, which are maintained by the Washington Department of Fish and Wildlife. Upland game bird and waterfowl hunting occurs in these areas during the winter, but birders can encounter a variety of species on off-hunt days. Short-eared owls are often encountered hunting at dusk north of Vancouver Lake, and a heronry of over 100 nests is an outstanding feature of the Shillapoo Wildlife Area. One parking area allows for access to a side channel of the Columbia River, where diving birds like loons can often be observed.

Frenchman's Bar County Park

Opened in 1998, Frenchman's Bar County Park offers access to the Columbia River as well as a hiking trail through riparian habitat. The fields south of Frenchman's Bar often have flocks of sandhill cranes, swans, and geese in the winter, and the number and proximity of the birds here is often better than at Sauvie Island.

Across Lower River Road from Frenchman's Bar is perhaps the region's largest accessible great blue heron nesting colony. The road is quite busy and parking along it is not advised. It's often better to park at Frenchman's Bar and to use a spotting scope to view the heron colony, which has more than 250 nests. If you use caution, you can stroll across Lower River Road from the park to view the Shillapoo heronry. Look for small flocks of western meadowlarks in the fields.

Bridgeport Dairy Unit

The final stop on Lower River Road is the Bridgeport Dairy Unit of Ridgefield NWR, about 5.5 miles from Frenchman's Bar Park. The road that runs into the refuge allows close viewing of goose and duck flocks; shorebirds are often encountered as well. There are several turnouts en route to the gated dead-end road that provide excellent views of open water and wetland habitat. Some of the best views of tundra swans, Canada geese, and waterfowl can be had from these viewing areas. You can also get great views of the Columbia River as the road skirts along the main channel of the Columbia. Across the river you can see Willow Bar and the Sauvie Island Marina on the Oregon shore. Besides the usual flocks and winter birds, northern shrike is annual, and rarities like gyrfalcon and emperor goose have been found in the past few years.

Facilities

Toilets: all but Ridgefield NWR unit and Fruit Valley Wildlife Area have indoor toilets. These have portable toilets.

Wheelchair accessibility: some paved paths at both parks; handicapped parking there as well.

Parking: at all parks and at several spots along road, especially at Ridgefield NWR (the refuge area is gated and only open dawn to dusk)

Interpretive information at Vancouver Lake Park

Picnic area: larger areas at Vancouver Lake Park (can accommodate groups); smaller ones at Frenchman's Bar

Dock, canoe launch: all, various areas (see above)

Access

Trails at the parks connect to the parking lots, and some are paved. Trails at wildlife areas are more primitive and start at parking areas. There are plans for a trail at the Bridgeport Dairy Unit. Access restricted at the wildlife areas and refuges once hunting season starts.

How to Get There

To Vancouver Lake Wildlife Area, Fruit Valley Road: Take I-5 North from Portland to Exit 1D, Fourth Plain Ave. Head west on W Fourth Plain through Vancouver. About 2 miles from I-5 turn right at the stop sign onto Fruit Valley Rd. and drive north .4 mile to La Frambois Rd., which bounds the north end of Fruit Valley Park. Turn left (west) onto La Frambois, then 1/4 mile on the left are the sewage ponds. Another 1/4 mile west on La Frambois is the entrance to the "Wildlife Access Area."

To Vancouver Lake Park: Follow the directions above but at the stoplight at W Fourth Plain and Fruit Valley Rd. continue straight (west) on Lower River Rd. (SR 501). After about 3.5 miles you can either go left and continue on NW Lower River Rd. to Frenchman's Bar and Ridgefield NWR or continue straight for .6 mile to Vancouver Lake Park.

To Frenchman's Bar Park, Shillapoo Wildlife Area, and Bridgeport Dairy Unit of Ridgefield NWR: Instead of continuing north on NW Reiger Memorial Hwy. to Vancouver Lake Park, turn left, and continue on NW Lower River Rd. Frenchman's Bar Park is 1.5 miles past the junction on the left. The Shillapoo Wildlife Area is another 2.7 miles on the right past Frenchman's Bar. The Bridgeport Dairy Unit of Ridgefield National Wildlife Refuge is at the gate about 5.5 miles further on Lower River Rd.

By Ray Korpi and Mike Houck

For more information: Vancouver-Clark Parks and Recreation, Washington Department of Fish and Wildlife Lands, or Ridgefield National Wildlife Refuge, see Resources.

Fees and Regulations

Vancouver Lake and Frenchman's Bar have parking fees for motorized vehicles from May to September; the areas are free other months. The WDFW Wildlife Areas can be accessed with an Access Stewardship Decal, which costs $10 per year (free with a hunting or fishing license and obtainable where such licenses are sold). Youth groups do not need this permit.

Ridgefield NWR has no fees.

All areas are open daylight hours only; there is a gate across the road at the NWR—be sure to note the closing time before heading in (usually around dusk).

Highlights

Some of the best diving bird viewing in the region is at Frenchman's Bar Park and Vancouver Lake Park. A large heronry is in view across from Frenchman's Bar Park. The auto tour and trails offer close viewing of wintering waterfowl, cranes, raptors, and diving birds.

Clark County Road Atlas 7/15/16/24

Clark County Canoe Trip

Vancouver Lake Lowlands and Ridgefield Wildlife Refuge, and Gee Creek

This canoe trip originates from the Ridgefield Moorage, located at the foot of Mill Street, in Ridgefield, Washington. There are several other places for putting in and the adventurous should discover those and their idiosyncrasies. A map of Clark County will assist in identifying all of the other places to put in. Be prepared to encounter high winds on your trip, which can be a severe threat to even experienced canoeists. It is important to pay attention to tides as well, as they can greatly aid or retard your progress.

After departing from the Ridgefield Moorage, one option is to continue counter-clockwise around Bachelor Island, which involves a three-mile paddle on the open waters of the Columbia River to the upstream end of Bachelor Island, where you can return to the Lake River and the moorage at Ridgefield. Gee Creek is effectively closed due to fluctuating water levels, downed trees, and other obstacles. Portaging would lead to trespass violations. No access is permitted on Gee Creek. This is about a nine-mile loop. Another alternative is to paddle back upstream on Lake River past the boat ramp where you put in and keep paddling south to the mouth of Salmon Creek and paddle up this scenic urban waterway. If you keep going south on Lake River you will wind up in Vancouver Lake, which is fed by both Lake River and Burnt Bridge Creek.

Most of this trip has very calm and slack water except in periods of spring flooding. In high water you may be able to travel across many flooded acres of the Vancouver Lake Lowlands. The Ridgefield Refuge maintains a public access closure from any waterway, allowing waterfowl an undisturbed resting area. Be sure to keep track of where you are going so you will be able to find your way home.

There will be many surprises as great blue heron, a variety of waterfowl, and other wildlife scurry up or out of your wake. Beaver, nutria, weasels, and mink or river otter may be readily seen if you travel quietly. Bald eagles nest in the area and osprey, red-tailed hawks, northern harriers, and American kestrels all frequent the area as well. Most of the land is in public ownership as part of the Ridgefield Wildlife Refuge or Washington State Department of Fish and Wildlife lands. These lands provide resting and wintering grounds for many of the waterfowl in the Vancouver Lake Lowlands and the Sauvie Island Complex. Therefore, remain in your canoe as much as possible to cause the least amount of disturbance when they are in the area.

Your trip will take you past the Lake River site where Lewis and Clark spent a restless night unable to sleep due to the continuous noise of the Canada geese. This was the site of the village of the

Location
Begin at the foot of Mill St. in Ridgefield, Washington at the Ridgefield Moorage

Activities
Canoeing, boating

Facilities
Toilets (at the moorage)
Parking (at the moorage)

Fees and Regulations
Parking fees ($2.00 at the boat ramp, coin-operated machine)

Highlights
The best water access to Bachelor Slough, Lake River, and Vancouver Lake and around the Ridgefield Refuge on water.

Clark County Road Atlas 16/24/25/33/34/42

Cathlapotle, the largest native American settlement on the Lower Columbia River where their large long houses fronted Lake River. Many of the flooded areas on the Ridgefield Refuge were sites for the gathering of wapato, a staple of the Native Americans' diet, along with salmon.

A land visit to the refuge during the spring and early summer to view the large Oregon ash, oak trees, and great abundance of wildflowers in bloom would be worth the extra effort. An abundance of non-water fowl are to be discovered at the Refuge. Take the time to seek out the wapato. The introduced carp have decimated this plant by their wallowing nesting behavior which uproots native wetland vegetation, but some can be discovered if you search diligently.

Have fun, and take your drinking water, flotation devices, adequate maps, and warm clothing. Be sure to let someone know where you are going and when you plan to return. Remember, pay attention to the winds and the tides, either of which can make your trip enjoyable or a chore, especially if you choose to venture into the Columbia River.

Access
Ridgefield Moorage, Ridgefield, Washington

How to Get There
To get to the Ridgefield Marina from Portland take I-5 north to the Ridgefield exit and take NW 269th (Hwy. 501) west into Ridgefield. Turn right on Main Ave. and proceed a short distance to Mill St. and turn left; proceed to the parking area. There is a coin-operated parking tag machine at the top of the boat ramp (8 quarters). A change machine is at the nearby restrooms. *See map on page 355.*

By Don Cannard

For more information: Ridgefield National Wildlife Refuge, Washington Department of Fish and Wildlife, or Vancouver-Clark Parks and Recreation Services, see Resources.

Ridgefield National Wildlife Refuge

Ridgefield: A Bird Haven

The mild, rainy winter climate of the lower Columbia River Valley provides an ideal environment for migrating and wintering waterfowl that travel through the Pacific Flyway west of the Cascade Mountains. The Ridgefield National Wildlife Refuge offers extensive resting and feeding areas for migrating birds on the many sloughs, ponds, and shallow lakes bordering the edges of the lower Columbia River. Each fall, ducks, geese, and swans leave their northern nesting areas and migrate down the Pacific Coast to escape the Alaskan winter. By winter, up to 200,000 waterfowl can be found between Portland, Oregon and the mouth of the Columbia River. The most conspicuous species are mallard, northern shoveler, American wigeon, green-winged teal, northern pintail, Canada geese, and tundra swans.

Over 180 bird species have been identified throughout the various seasons. Sandhill cranes, shorebirds, and a great variety of songbirds stop at the refuge during spring and fall migrations. A few waterfowl and some shorebirds and songbirds remain on the refuge to nest. Year-round residents include mallards, cinnamon teal, great blue herons, and red-tailed hawks. Black-tailed deer are the largest mammal on the refuge. Coyote, fox, raccoon, skunk, beaver, river otter, and brush rabbit are occasionally seen. It is common to see nutria, a rodent native to South America and introduced into the Columbia River basin in the 1930s, burrowing and feeding along dikes and ditch banks.

Dusky Geese and an Alaskan Earthquake Equals a Refuge

A violent earthquake that rocked southern Alaska in 1964 played a role in establishing the refuge. Repeated shock waves lifted the Copper River Delta six feet, changing, in a matter of minutes, the only area where dusky Canada geese had been nesting for centuries. Willow and alder trees invaded the higher, drier land, replacing the marshy meadows that had once been goose-nesting habitat. The resulting shrub thickets provided perfect cover for brown bears and coyotes, allowing them to approach nesting geese unnoticed. The altered habitat and increased predation greatly reduced their ability to successfully hatch and raise their young, resulting in a declining population.

Migratory waterfowl must endure the good and bad years on wintering grounds and summer nesting areas. When either the winter or summer habitat is disrupted, the other becomes much more important. Dusky Canada geese spend the winters along the lower Columbia River and in the Willamette River Valley in Oregon. While wildlife managers were unable to change the geology of the Copper

Location
Refuge entrances are located north and south of the Ridgefield city limits.

Activities
Hiking

Biking: Permitted on public access roads on the River "S" Unit only

Canoeing, boating: Lake River, Bachelor Slough and the Columbia River offer opportunities to boat along the refuge boundaries. Boat launch facilities are available at the Ridgefield Marina in Ridgefield

Fishing: Fishing is permitted during daylight hours from March 1 to September 30 in accordance with Washington state regulations. Areas open to fishing include the Carty Unit and the area adjacent to the bridge crossing Lake River at the entrance of the River "S" Unit. Carp, catfish, crappie, and bluegill sunfish are commonly caught.

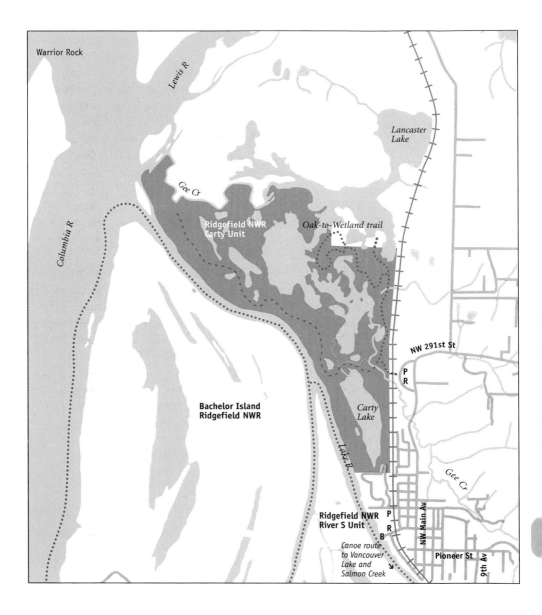

Warrior Rock

Lewis R

Columbia R

Gee Cr

Lancaster
Lake

Ridgefield NWR
Carty Unit

Oak-to-Wetland trail

NW 291st St

P
R

Bachelor Island
Ridgefield NWR

Carty
Lake

Lake R

Gee Cr

Ridgefield NWR
River S Unit

P
R
B

Canoe route
to Vancouver
Lake and
Salmon Creek

NW Main Av

Pioneer St

9th Av

Facilities
Toilets vault and portable
    toilets
Wheelchair accessible: In
    the River "S" Unit, a
    paved trail to an
    observation blind at
    Rest Lake is open
    year-round.
Trail unpaved
Parking

Fees and Regulations
Restricted hours: The
refuge is open for day use
only. Because the spring
and winter periods are
especially stressful times
of the year for migratory
and nesting birds, a
portion of the River "S"
Unit and the Roth Unit are
closed to all public entry
year-round to protect
species from disturbance.
Another portion of the
River "S" Unit is closed to
non-hunter access during
limited-entry waterfowl
hunting days from October
through January. Bachelor
Island is closed to all
public entry now so that it
can be maintained as a
wildlife preserve. Closure
rules may change at any
time, so contact the
refuge office for current
information.

No pets, except for
retrieving waterfowl
when hunting.

River Delta, they could ensure that the geese and other species had secure wintering areas. Public lands were acquired to secure critical winter habitat that was at risk of development to aid in recovering and supporting the dusky geese and numerous other species. Thus, the establishing of the Ridgefield National Wildlife Refuge in 1965, along with three other refuges in the Willamette Valley in Oregon. Unfortunately, much of the unprotected species-rich habitat along the lower Columbia River has continued to shrink due to diking, draining, filling, and development of floodplains and associated wetlands.

Agriculture for the Birds

The 5,150 acres of marshes, grasslands, and woodlands are characterized by two types of refuge management—natural and agricultural. Preservation of the natural Columbia River floodplain is the management objective on the Carty and Roth Units. When snow-melt from the mountains swells the Columbia each spring, these units are flooded until the river level drops again. Basalt outcroppings on the Carty Unit form knolls above the high water level. These knolls are wooded with ash, oak, and Douglas fir and are covered with brilliant wildflowers in the spring. The knolls become extremely dry in summer, in contrast with the lush greenery of surrounding marshes. The Roth Unit is flatter and forested with cottonwood, ash, and willow. Cattle graze on parts of these units to maintain short grass pastures preferred by many waterfowl for loafing and feeding.

The River "S" Unit and Bachelor Island, on the other hand, are protected from flooding by dikes around their perimeters. Pumps provide the proper amount of water to each pond and lake to foster the growth of aquatic waterfowl food plants and to create resting areas for the birds. Grasslands are grazed by cattle, and grass and clover are cut for hay or silage. This leaves behind the short green browse preferred by Canada geese when they arrive in the fall.

With the combination of natural and agricultural environments, waterfowl populations on the refuge have peaked at 30,000 geese and 40,000 ducks. Research is currently being conducted on the refuge to evaluate the effectiveness of various methods for reducing reed canarygrass, a highly invasive non-native species. Results will contribute to knowledge about this widespread, problematic species.

A 2,000-Year-Old City

The mild climate and abundant fish and wildlife made the Ridgefield area attractive for human occupation long before recorded history. It was only recently discovered, after the U.S. Fish and Wildlife Service and Portland State University began exploring the area in 1992, that the refuge contained the site documented in 1806 by Lewis and Clark as one of the largest Chinook Indian villages in the Lower Columbia River.

This prosperous village, known as Cathlapotle, contained 14 large wooden houses, known as long houses, and some 900 inhabitants of the Chinook Nation. Archaeological research at the site has provided a glimpse into the Chinook way of life on the Lower Columbia River. Artifacts and other evidence found on the refuge indicate that Native Americans were living along the banks of the Columbia as early as A.D. 500. Although the site is not accessible to the public, information and an educational resource kit have been developed to share the rich past and fascinating discoveries at Cathlapotle with interested groups and individuals.

Access

There are two public road entrances into the refuge. One leads into the Carty Unit located north of Ridgefied. The second access is into the River "S" Unit located south of Ridgefield.

The Carty unit is open to foot traffic only. There is a two-mile self-guided interpretive trail known as the "Oaks to Wetlands Wildlife Trail." The trail provides opportunities to see many species of wildlife as it follows the shoreline of floodplain wetlands and passes through oak and Douglas fir woodlands and open water habitats. Wildlife viewing includes a variety of bird species from ducks to passerines.

The River "S" Unit includes a four-mile gravel road that makes a loop. It is open year-round for touring by vehicle. Pedestrians are allowed to walk the road, hike along the banks of Bower Slough, or cross over a dike to Campbell Lake from May 1 through September 30 only. During the rest of the year, visitors may leave their vehicles to go to the kiosk and observation blinds.

How to Get There

Take I-5 approximately 14 miles north of Vancouver, Washington to Ridgefield Exit 14. Drive 3 miles west. Refuge entrances are located just north and south of the Ridgefield city limits. Follow signs from town.

By Jennifer Thompson

For more information: Ridgefield National Wildlife Refuge or Cathlapotle/U.S. Fish and Wildlife Service, Cultural Resources Team, see Resources.

References

Donovan, Yvette. Personal communication. U.S. Fish and Wildlife Service. Ridgefield National Wildlife Refuge, Washington. 1999.

Molnar, Darin. Discover Cathlapotle! http://www-adm.pdx.edu/user/anth/cathla/environ.htm. Portland, Oregon: Anthropology Department, Portland State University, 1995.

Highlights

Lake River may be the only river that flows in both directions, reversing direction from its headwaters to its mouth and back again twice a day because of tidal influence.

Cathlapotle, an archaeological site located on the refuge, is one of the largest and most important Chinook towns along the Columbia River.

All seven subspecies of Canada geese found in the Pacific Flyway can be seen at Ridgefield: Taverner's, dusky, western, cackling, lesser, Vancouver, and the endangered Aleutian.

About 2,000 tundra swans that spend their summers in northern Alaska and Canada can be observed roosting from December through March as they overwinter in the area.

Over 800 sandhill cranes have been observed during the fall as they migrate between their summer and winter ranges.

Endangered species that can be found on the refuge include bald eagles, peregrine falcons, Aleutian Canada geese, and the plant *Howellia aquatilis*.

Clark County Road Atlas 33/34/42

Parks, Virginia. U.S. Department of the Interior. *From Cathlapotle to the Classroom: A Multidisciplinary Hands-On Resource Kit* (fact sheet) and personal communication. Sherwood, Oregon: U.S. Fish and Wildlife Service, Region 1 Cultural Resources Team, Undated.

U.S. Department of the Interior. "Ridgefield National Wildlife Refuge Washington." Ridgefield, Washington: U.S. Fish and Wildlife Service, 1992.

Wille, Steve. Personal Communication. Portland, Oregon: U.S. Fish and Wildlife Service, Oregon State Office, 1999.

A Flock by Any Other Name

A flock by any other name can be hard to remember. What bird, for example, gathers to form a "watch?" Or how do you refer to a flock of wigeon? Many names that we associate with the flocks of particular species evoke a sense of the bird—a "whiteness" of swan or a "flight" of doves—but others, such as a "judgement" of crows or a "siege" of heron, seem instead to suggest some intriguing yet forgotten story.

At least 20 different names distinguish the groupings of various species. And to make matters worse, the flocks of certain birds are named differently depending on whether they are on the ground or in flight. Geese afoot are a "gaggle," but in the air they're a "skein."

Whatever name we give to its socializing, it is a rare bird indeed that doesn't exhibit some flocking behavior. Flocking provides protection, food, and companionship to the individual and helps ensure continuation of the species.

For small birds, flocking decreases their vulnerability to birds of prey. Predators can easily "stoop" a single quarry in the air but cannot pick out a target from a moving mass of birds. Starlings, for instance, quickly close ranks against an attack from a hawk or falcon. And to confuse the predator, they fly in a constantly shifting, rolling motion, with members at the rear of the pack surging up and over the leaders, then slowing to be overtaken themselves by others in the group.

The cooperative effort of individuals in a flock improves the group's ability to find food. Flocks of evening grosbeak and cedar waxwing cover wide-ranging areas of dispersing scouting parties in search of food. When a spotter from one of the flocks discovers an abundant food supply, the group quickly settles in the area for a few days or weeks and feeds until the food resources are exhausted. The flock then sends out more searchers and soon moves on to newer feeding grounds.

Flocks of bushtit, red-winged blackbird, and golden-crowned kinglet function in a similar manner, although these species tend to settle in one area for longer periods of time.

Individual species flock at different times of the year. Certain birds, such as herons, join together during the nesting season and remain solitary during the rest of the year. But usually the opposite pattern prevails and flocking occurs most frequently outside of the nesting period.

Crows, for example, begin gathering in feeding locations at the end of their nesting season and establish small roosts for shelter at night. Later in the year, as migrant birds arrive from other areas, the size of some crow roosts grows quite large. During the fall, you commonly see flocks of crows flying from feeding areas in the Willamette Valley to their roosts in the mountains as much as 60 miles away.

The population of many other species, especially waterfowl, swells during the migratory season. As a major stop-off point in the Pacific Flyway, Sauvie Island, Ridgefield, and the marshes and rivers throughout the area provide refuge for large numbers of geese, ducks, coots, and shorebirds.

Different birds flock for varying lengths of time. Because they gain less from banding together, birds of prey generally remain alone for longer periods. Other birds, though, are highly dependent on the flock. Some theories suggest that the passenger pigeon's extinction resulted in part from the bird's heavy dependence on its established colonies, which were greatly disrupted by hunters in the 1800s.

The old proverb "birds of a feather flock together" is true enough, but it doesn't tell the whole story. Mixed flocks of birds are also common, especially for purposes of feeding.

Flocks of sparrows tend to be "heterospecific"—that is, made up of individuals from several species. You can often find pine siskin joined with American goldfinch or red crossbills foraging for food in pine cone-laden trees. And you usually find mixed groups of gulls—glacous-winged, herring, and Thayer's—feeding in the city parks and local landfills.

During the late fall and winter, forests may appear at first devoid of birdlife, but as you walk the trails, you will eventually come across noisily feeding mixed flocks of downy woodpeckers, nuthatches, kinglets, and chickadees.

Fall is a good time of the year to observe flocking behavior because of both the decreased nesting activity of most species and the influx of migratory birds that pass through or winter in the Portland area.

By Thomas E. Hanrahan

Sandy River Watershed

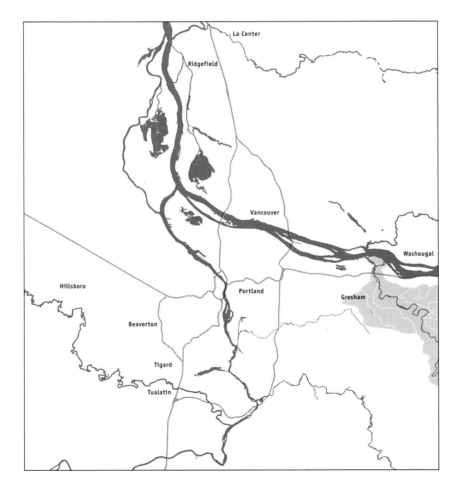

Sandy River Watershed

The Sandy River and its tributaries gather water from over 500 square miles as the Sandy cascades over 50 miles from its origins at 6,000-foot Reid Glacier on Mt. Hood to near sea level at its confluence with the Columbia River near Troutdale.

Its larger tributary watersheds include the Ziz Zag, Bull Run, Little Sandy, and Salmon Rivers. More than 90 tributary streams like Gordon, Ramona, Whiskey, Badger, Otter, Bow and Arrow, Tumbling, and Arrahwanna contribute their waters to the Sandy.

Below the Marmot Dam, where the Sandy is joined by the Bull Run River at Dodge Park, the Sandy flows through the Sandy River Gorge with its rugged, high bluffs, deep-green pools, and rapids. By the time the Sandy reaches The Sandy River Nature Conservancy Preserve, Indian John Island, and Oxbow Regional Park, the river has begun to meander along its lower gradient run to the Columbia where it drops much of its sediment load onto the 1,400-acre Sandy River Delta. It was probably the accumulated sands at the Sandy's mouth that prompted the Lewis and Clark expedition to name it "Quicksand River" when they stopped there on November 3, 1805; they noted that the local native Americans called it "Ye-ki-oo."

The Sandy's abundant riffles, pools, side channels, and smaller tributaries are home to an amazing array of native fish including Pacific and western brook lamprey, steelhead, rainbow trout, coho salmon, spring and fall chinook salmon, cutthroat trout, mountain whitefish, redside shiner, white sturgeon, and smelt. Mammalian inhabitants include Roosevelt elk, black-tailed deer, cougar, lynx, bobcat, wolverine, and black bear.

One of the most significant human uses of the Sandy River is for drinking water. The City of Portland was successful in persuading President Benjamin Harrison to establish a 139,520-acre Bull Run Reserve in 1892. Water was diverted to Portland from a site that is now occupied by the city's Headworks Dam via a large conduit on January 1, 1895. In 1911 a second conduit was added to carry water to Portland. A succession of projects including a check dam at Bull Run Lake in 1915, the Headworks Dam in 1922, and construction of the 200-foot high Ben Morrow Dam (Bull Run Dam No. 1) means that Portland now has storage capacity of 17 billion gallons of drinking water. One negative consequence of these actions is that at times the Bull Run River literally runs dry. Recent listings of steelhead and salmon as "Threatened" under the Endangered Species Act have led the City of Portland to propose altering its management of the Bull Run system to ensure adequate river in the Bull Run at all times of the year and removing a dam on the Little Sandy River to assist in recovering salmonids throughout the Sandy River system.

From Sandy River Basin Watershed Council, Phase I Watershed Assessment, November 15, 1999.

Oxbow Regional Park

Location
3010 SE Oxbow Pkwy.
8 miles east of Gresham

Activities
Horseback riding
Hiking
Biking
Canoeing, boating
Fishing
Camping
Swimming
Picnicking
Natural history/
  environmental education
  programs

Facilities
Toilets

Wheelchair accessibility:
  The boat ramp, fishing
  platform, and picnic
  shelters are wheelchair-
  accessible. The restroom
  at the top of the boat
  ramp area is accessible,
  as is the paved portion
  of trail going upstream
  from the boat ramp for a
  short distance.
Parking: numerous
  pullouts are located
  along the road
  throughout the park
Interpretive center:
  planned for the future
Interpretive information
  available at the park
  office
Year-round public
  campground

Oxbow Regional Park is a 1,200-acre park and wildlife area in the heart of the Sandy River Gorge, 20 miles east of Portland. One of the "crown jewels" of the natural areas in our region, Oxbow features beautiful scenery, an old-growth forest, access to the Sandy River (part of the National Wild and Scenic River system), plentiful habitat for fish and wildlife, and a variety of recreational opportunities.

As visitors descend Oxbow Parkway, they are greeted by the sight of the Sandy River winding along the bottom of a steep forested canyon. The serpentine shape of the river is called an "oxbow" and gives the park its name. Most people come to Oxbow for the scenery, but it is well worth the effort to explore a little deeper. Those in search of solitude or wildlife viewing can always find quiet places along the miles of trails that begin just a few steps away from the busy picnic areas flanking the park road. Camping, hiking, and canoeing are great ways to explore the area. There is much to discover here, but not to be missed are the ancient forest, the annual return of the salmon, and the chance to observe an abundant array of wildlife.

Not long ago, in the attic of the Oxbow Park offices, a forgotten stash of 1970s-era polyester blue T-shirts was re-discovered. The shirts sport a picture of an osprey and the words "Oxbow Park . . . More than just another pretty place." The message is perhaps even more relevant today. Large pieces of intact habitat like Oxbow, linked to other protected lands along the Sandy River Gorge, are essential pieces in the bigger picture of natural areas and wildlife corridors in our fast-growing region.

The 160-acre lowland ancient forest at Oxbow is the largest accessible area of old-growth near Portland. The narrow footpaths meander through a peaceful cathedral-like forest where many of the giant Douglas firs are 700 to 800 years old. The trees are blanketed with moss and lichens, with an understory of ferns (sword, bracken, lady, maidenhair, deer, wood, and licorice-ferns can all be found), salal, Oregon grape, red huckleberry, oxalis, and a variety of wildflowers. Tiny winter wrens sing from the undergrowth, and nurse logs host delicate gardens of plants and hemlock seedlings. When the fall rains start, several species of mushrooms and salamanders poke their heads out from under the leaves on the forest floor. Snags (dead standing trees) are an integral part of the old-growth forest ecosystem and provide homes for insects, birds, and mammals. Check them for the holes created by the five species of woodpeckers that are common at Oxbow, including the impressive, crow-sized pileated woodpecker. Northern flying squirrels, another cavity-nester, have been sighted here too. Adventuresome types may search out the small, hidden "Dismal Swamp" wetland, home to red-legged and Pacific chorus frogs. The ancient forest is worth a visit at any time of year. A park map is useful here, as the trails criss-cross both sides of the road; most of the largest trees are on the "uphill" side.

Salmon are another reason to visit Oxbow. The Sandy River supports several seasonal runs of coho, chinook, and steelhead, and many other native fish whose lives are intricately tied to the health of the surrounding forest and watershed. The return of wild chinook salmon to their spawning grounds is a must-see event for anyone who lives in or visits the Pacific Northwest. "Fish-watching" may not immediately appeal to those who prefer binoculars or mountain bikes to fishing rods, but don't be fooled. At about three feet long and weighing in at up to 40 pounds, these salmon are an impressive sight, and their spawning ritual is fascinating.

The fall chinook salmon, the run that is most easily observable at Oxbow, can be seen from late September through early November. Guided walks are offered by the Oxbow naturalists on October weekends. The annual Salmon Festival is held the second weekend in October, and celebrates the salmon's return with music, educational displays, an art show, children's activities, and of course, salmon viewing. Viewing conditions vary with the weather, and binoculars and polarized sunglasses will help. Although the spawning locations can change, the best viewing areas for the past several years have been the riffles at Picnic Area D (overlooking the railing) and near the Boat Ramp (follow the trail upstream from the Boat Ramp to two overlooks).

Those seeking other "watchable wildlife" opportunities will find much to enjoy at Oxbow. Birders will find plenty of species typical of riparian areas and westside coniferous forests. One good bet is the Floodplain Trail, which loops through a cottonwood stand heavily used by songbirds, and connects with a spur trail leading out to a vantage overlooking the river. In the ancient forest, one of the best places to look is along the trails on the "uphill" side of the road, particularly where some of the rocky outcroppings break up the forest canopy (across the road from the pumphouse). Listen for the flute-like, spiraling song of Swainson's thrushes in any part of the forest in the summer. Raptor buffs will enjoy the many osprey, and can walk down to the river on the trail near picnic area A to scan the treeline for the pair that return each spring to their impressive nest in a Douglas fir snag. Great blue herons, Canada geese, and common mergansers frequent the river as well.

For those in search of wildlife of the four-legged sort, tracks and signs are abundant, and a little patience and good timing (early morning and dusk) can be well rewarded with sightings. Graceful Columbia black-tailed deer are abundant throughout the park, especially near the campground and in the ancient forest. The deer are accustomed to people, allowing for up-close views. A herd of

Picnic areas several uncovered, individual sites throughout the park, plus large covered shelters available by reservation

Boat ramp (paved)

Fees and Regulations
Entrance fees: $3 per car, $6 per bus
Hours: 6:30 A.M. to legal sunset
No pets
Camping fee: $10 per night on a first-come, First-served basis.

Highlights
One of the "crown jewels" of the area, beautiful setting, the scenic Sandy River, hiking trails in an old-growth forest, wildlife watching and recreational opportunities, and the annual Salmon Festival. Scan the riverbanks for deer, river otter, beaver, osprey, and great blue herons.

A variety of natural history programs are offered, including animal tracking in one of the best tracking locations in the Northwest.

Public Transit
No public transit reaches the site. It is possible for cyclists to take MAX to Gresham and bike the remainder of the route.

Thomas Guide 630

Roosevelt elk also live in the Sandy River Gorge, but are harder to spot. They use the area around the Floodplain trail in the early winter, where their tracks, scat, and antler-rubs on trees are easy to find. Hike up to the Elk Meadow on Alder Ridge to look for both deer and elk, particularly in winter. Red foxes den in the park, and visitors in late May and early June are sometimes treated to the sight of brazen young fox kits frolicking in the sunshine. Also watch for brush rabbits along the edge of the woods, and scan the riverbanks for mink, river otter, beaver, and the occasional shy black bear.

One of the best ways to learn more about the ecology and wildlife of Oxbow is to join one of the park's many natural history programs and classes. Oxbow is particularly well-known for its animal-tracking classes, since the abundance of animals—and sandy ground—make for some of the best tracking conditions in the Northwest. Oxbow Park classes are listed in the Metro *GreenScene* calendar.

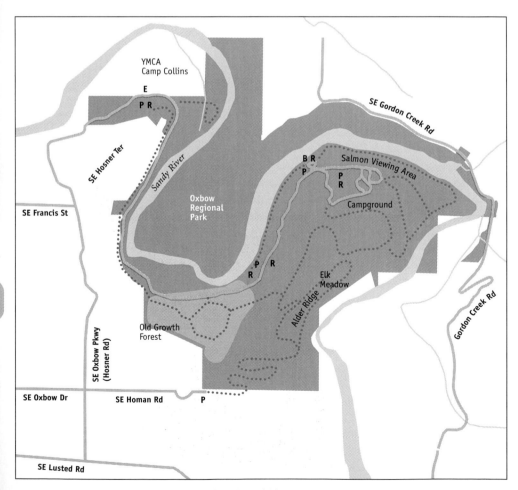

Access
Fifteen miles of trails allow visitors to walk along the river (easiest), through upland forest (easy to moderate), and up to Alder Ridge (more difficult). Several loops are possible, and there are many places to park to access the trails. See park map for information on equestrian and bike trails. Oxbow Park is open year-round.

How to Get There
From Portland, take I-84 to Troutdale exit 17. Go past the truck stops to the light. Turn right on 257th, and go 3.5 miles to SE Division St. Turn left onto Division. Follow the signs 8 miles and turn left, down to the park.

By Elisabeth Neely

For more information: Oxbow Regional Park see Resources

The Return of the Oncorhynchus

*O*ncorhynchus. It's not a word you read much in the press. Yet, it is often there drifting beneath the text. Sometimes it's invisible and other times it's disguised by its abbreviation "*O.*"

Oncorhynchus is the genus, or first part of the scientific name, of a closely related group of fish that have long been important to the Pacific Northwest. These include the chinook salmon (*O. tshawytscha*), coho salmon (*O. kisutch*), sockeye salmon (*O. nerka*), chum salmon (*O. keta*), pink salmon (*O. gorbuscha*), steelhead trout (*O. mykiss*), and cutthroat trout (*O. clarki*). These species relate to one another biologically, environmentally, and increasingly politically.

Biological Characteristics

Virtually all the *Oncorhynchus* species are anadromous—they are spawned in fresh water rivers, migrate to the sea, and return to their original freshwater breeding grounds to spawn as adults. In some cases the entire species is anadromous, as with the chinook salmon, and in other cases, such as the cutthroat trout, only some members of the species make the migration, while others remain in their fresh water environment.

Between the time a sea-run salmon or trout leaves and returns to its spawning ground, it goes through tremendous biological changes. As it passes from fresh to salt water, it undergoes a process called smoltification. Its kidneys, gills, and blood chemistry all transform to accommodate the radical change in environment.

Its return journey involves equally major biological changes. Once it reaches fresh water, the salmon and trout stop eating. They live off the oils they've stored in their bodies and, as these are depleted, take nourishment from their deteriorating internal organs. Often the fish's color gradually changes from silver to mottled brown, and its skin is invaded by a white fungus.

Environmental Dependencies

Because of their sea-going nature, the *Oncorhynchus* species share many environmental dependencies. These environmental dependencies can be summarized by three general requirements: permanent spawning grounds; free river access from their spawning grounds to the sea (both for their outbound and inbound journeys); and an abundant and predictable food supply at sea.

Although the exact spawning ground characteristics required by each species vary somewhat, they all require shallow, free-flowing rivers and streams to provide spawning habitat. Most of the species require a gravel bed in which to build their nest, called a redd. The female chinook salmon, for example, builds her redd by lying on her side and vigorously flipping her tail, creating a depression in the loose gravel. Where larger rocks are exposed, the female pushes them out of the way, often with such force she is left injured and bleeding.

While the redd is being built, the male chinook fends off competing males and other intruders. When the redd is completed, the male and female salmon swim over the nest and simultaneously release their milt and eggs. The river current mixes the two and begins to cover the redd with gravel as the eggs sink to the bottom. Each redd holds thousands of fertilized eggs. Clear, free-running water is needed in order to maintain a relatively constant water temperature. The water must stay between 45° and 55° F. Instead of "hatching," each immature fish grows out of its yolk sac while remaining in its gravel-covered nest. Once its yolk sac is depleted, the young fish emerges from its redd as a swim-up fry.

At first, fry stay in their spawning grounds, where they feed on insects and larvae. Sheltered pools created by fallen trees and boulders are essential to the fry, allowing them to grow in preparation for their migration to the ocean. These sheltered areas, however, do not completely protect the fry from their position in the food chain. The fry are generally food to heron, kingfishers, mergansers, and other salmon and trout.

To support the young fry, the spawning grounds must be rich in nutrients and oxygen. Rivers by themselves are sterile. The nutrients they carry are fed to them by their banks. Healthy banks must be covered by a variety of vegetation, which in turn fosters the growth of insects. Nutrients and insects enter the water from the banks. An underabundance of nutrients in the water can lead to depletion of the population due to inadequate food resources, but an overabundance of nutrients reduces the oxygen content in the water and also leads to depleted populations. The right balance is required and can be achieved only by proper bank management and water flow.

During migration to and from the ocean, the *Oncorhynchus* require free river access for the entire length of their journey. On their outbound trip, the young fish still require food and sheltered places in which to safely rest. On their return trip, the mature adult fish no longer require food, but do require sheltered areas in which to rest. The key arterials in the Portland metropolitan area are the Columbia, Willamette, Sandy and Clackamas Rivers. These provide passage to the hundreds of creeks and streams that support populations of *Oncorhynchus*.

While at sea, *Oncorhynchus* requires an abundant and predictable food supply. We know little about its migration patterns at sea and even less about its homing instinct. Migration patterns are dictated by a combination of currents and temperature patterns effected by events such as El Niño and La Niña. The timing of return for the species is a mystery. Chinook salmon, for example, spawned at the same time and location do not all return in the same year. This enhances the genetic diversity of the breeding ground, but the mechanism that causes this variation in behavior is unknown.

Local spawning areas for chinook salmon include the Sandy and Clackamas Rivers. Oxbow Park has a salmon festival each October and offers guided salmon walks to view the spawning grounds along its segment of the Sandy River. Coho salmon spawn in the Sandy and Clackamas Rivers and in Johnson Creek. Winter steelhead maintain spawning grounds in Johnson Creek and Tryon Creek as well as in the Clackamas River and its tributaries. Sea-run cutthroat spawn in the Sandy and Clackamas Rivers, while resident cutthroat spawn in many local streams including Willow, Johnson, Tryon, and Fanno Creeks.

Political and Economic Impact of Listings

In order to ensure that their environmental requirements are met, a growing number of *Oncorhynchus* species are being listed as Threatened or Endangered under the federal Endangered Species Act. Endangered species now include the sea-run cutthroat and Umpqua cutthroat. Threatened species in a variety of locations include chinook, sockeye, chum, and steelhead. The effects of these listings are potentially far-reaching. The major areas of impact will be in controlling urban stormwater runoff, controlling agricultural and timberland runoff, preserving and restoring instream and riparian habitat, and managing access and water quality at dam sites.

For the Portland metropolitan area in particular, the effects of managing urban runoff will depend on the extent to which we attempt to change our current practices. To control the quality of water entering our streams requires limits on the use of lawn and garden chemicals and an effort to control oils and other chemicals that enter the system from our roads. To control the quantity of runoff requires an extensive system of wetlands, sumps, underground faults, and catch basins, much of which do not currently exist. To further control both the quality and quantity of water entering the system requires that limits be placed on construction within as much as 200 feet on both sides of streams and rivers. Discussions about how to make these changes and how to structure the relationship between Metro and local planning authorities are ongoing.

To manage agricultural and timberland runoff, greater restrictions need to be placed on the use of pesticides and runoff from manure, and greater buffers need to be placed on harvesting timber from stream banks.

Many factors affect our ability to control access and water quality at dam sites. By their nature, dams impede the movement of water and fish. Attempts to provide access around the dams, through portals and sometimes even barging the fish, have generally proven unsuccessful. Water quality is another tricky dimension to the problem. As water flow over a dam is slowed, water temperature behind the dam increases because of the decreased flow and increased surface area of the water backed up behind the dam. As water flow over a dam increases, more nitrogen is introduced into the water, decreasing its quality downstream.

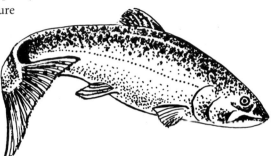

As a result, the upstream water temperature and downstream water quality needed by the migrating salmon and trout often cannot be met by water flow regulation at a dam site.

Perhaps most controversial of all proposals for dam management is the recent call to breach dams on the Snake River in order to ensure the fish safe passage. Studies continue to be conducted by the Army Corps of Engineers to determine whether technological solutions to the problems of access and water quality can be found. In the absence of such solutions, however, dam breaching is the only scientifically viable alternative.

Salmon and trout have long been symbols of the Pacific Northwest. To Native Americans they have always been symbols of nature's bounty. To early European settlers they became symbols of industry and commerce. Today they are symbols of our heritage and environment. What symbols they become in the future will depend on our success in ensuring their survival.

By Thomas E. Hanrahan

Trees, Winter Strategies

Wintertime is difficult for flora and fauna, but unlike animals, plants are less concerned with freezing than with drying up. Plants draw an astonishing amount of water from the soil—up to 300 gallons a day in some trees. Most of that water, however, is not retained in the tree, but discharged directly into the atmosphere—transpired—by the leaves.

Meanwhile in winter, roots have great difficulty extracting water from the cold soil, so if transpiration were not controlled, trees would discharge more water than they took in, risking dehydration and death. To deal with this problem, conifers and flowering trees have each developed a characteristic strategy.

Coniferous Strategies

Conifers were faced partway through their evolutionary history with adapting to a major, and unpleasant, climatic change to cold, dry glacial conditions. They were able to adapt by developing a number of features characteristic of drought-tolerant plants around the world, most obviously in their leaves.

The leaves or needles of conifers have an inner coating of resin, not found in flowering trees; they also have a much heavier outer coating of wax. This "weatherproofing" provides sufficient control of transpiration to allow the leaves to remain on the tree—ready to photosynthesize all year long.

Thus protected, conifers can live in extreme conditions—near the Arctic Circle and close to the tops of the tallest mountains. Compared to existence in these forbidding places, life in the maritime Northwest is pretty cushy, which no doubt explains why our region is home to the biggest trees and the most spectacular coniferous forests in the world.

Deciduous Strategies

Flowering trees have evolved a more complicated method of coping with winter. Unlike conifers, flowering plants are believed to have accomplished much of their development in the tropics where they evolved the deciduous habit—the practice of dropping their leaves—in order to combat periods of drought.

During adverse conditions, the "separation layer" at the base of each deciduous leaf seals it off from the tree, causing it to fall, halting transpiration for the year. This trick, developed to combat drought, enabled flowering trees to survive hard winters and invade the temperate zone, bringing to it the brilliant fall colors that accompany autumn leaf drop in such species as big-leaf and vine maple.

Actually, the deciduous habit, while characteristic of flowering trees, can also be found in a few conifers. The most common deciduous conifer in Oregon is the western larch, typically found east of the Cascades. But more familiar to many of us are the deciduous dawn redwoods found all over Portland, including the parking lot at the Audubon Society of Portland.

Evergreens can be found among the flowering trees as well, and not just in the tropics. The leathery-leafed Heath Family, truly a northern assemblage, has produced a lot of evergreen members including rhododendron and a striking evergreen tree, the Pacific madrone.

Which of these strategies proves most successful probably depends on what climatic surprises are in store for us. But for the moment, it is enough simply to enjoy the rich assemblage of coniferous and flowering trees that have been able to make their home in temperate North America.

By Bob Wilson

Clark County Watersheds

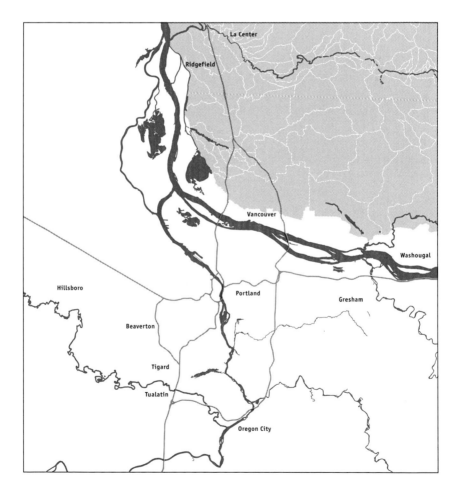

Clark County Watersheds and Trails

Burnt Bridge Creek, Salmon Creek Greenway, Lacamas Lake, East Fork of the Lewis River, and Vancouver Lake Lowlands form the networks of green in Vancouver and Clark County, Washington. These watersheds, along with an ever-expanding trail system, form Clark County's green infrastructure.

In addition to the watersheds and Greenspaces featured in this chapter, as with the 40-Mile Loop on the Oregon side of the Columbia, there is an emerging, inter-connected trail system on the Washington side of the river. The Chinook Trail aims to connect both Oregon and Washington urban areas with the Columbia Gorge Scenic Area. The Waterfront Renaissance Trail, much of it already in place between Fort Vancouver National Historic Site and the Water Resources Education Center to the east, will one day extend from the Vancouver Lake Lowlands in the west all the way to Wintler Park, the I-205 bicycle path, and Camas to the east. The Discovery Trail and Ellen Davis Trail connect inner-city neighborhoods from the confluence of Burnt Bridge Creek at Vancouver Lake east to Fourth Plain, with expansions proposed to Lacamas Lake and north to Meadowbrook and Beaver Marsh natural areas.

Taken together with the regional trail system in the Portland metropolitan region, Clark County's pedestrian trail network will soon provide excellent access to most of the region's significant Greenspaces and parks.

Adapted from "Exploring Salmon Creek;" Clark County Water Quality Division

Beaver Marsh Nature Preserve

The Beaver Marsh represents one of the last remaining transitional wooded wetlands of the Burnt Creek watershed. Virtually all the other urban wetland areas have been ditched and cleared for agriculture or other uses. The marsh is a 31-acre oasis north of the Oakbrook neighborhood residential area. The marsh is bordered on the west by the Royal Oaks golf course, I-205 to the east, and State Road 500 to the north. Prior to the construction of the freeways, the wetland thrived with beaver that dammed the creek to form a large pond. Today, however, sediment has filled the pond, which has resulted in a lovely meandering stream. On rare occasions a beaver will still pass through and bring down a tree.

The land was acquired by the Burnt Bridge Creek Utility District to protect the creek and the aquatic life as well as to rehabilitate Vancouver Lake. The land is now owned by the city of Vancouver and is managed by the Surface Water Department, which is responsible for quality monitoring and protection.

West of the creek, within the preserve, is found a very marshy area which represents a significant aquifer recharge system. It is impassable during the rainy season.

A four-foot wide gravel-based trail makes a delightful loop through the upland Douglas fir forest. A few yards from the entrance on NE 98th Avenue, the trail crosses Burnt Bridge Creek by a 120-foot serpentine wooden bridge which allows year-round crossing. The trail winds through the forest, affording glimpses and access to the creek at several points along the way. An excellent panorama of the marsh is obtained close to I-205 where the creek is again crossed. Just before the crossing, next to the freeway fence, is a very large anthill which has been active for 15 years or more. The forest floor in April is known for its abundant trillium; less common are false Solomon's-seal, *Tellima*, and tiger lilies. Hazelnut, ocean-spray, Oregon grape, salmonberry, serviceberry, vine maple, and alder are common. Birds observed are ducks, red-tailed hawks, scrub and Steller's jays, belted kingfisher, chickadees, kinglets, bushtits, spotted towhees, song sparrow, and short-eared owls. Owl pellets are a common finding beneath the trees.

Access

A 4-foot gravel-based path makes a loop through Douglas fir forest. A few yards from the entrance at the end of 98th the trail crosses Burnt Bridge Creek on a 120-foot, lovely curved bridge which allows year-round access, even when Burnt Bridge Creek is swollen with heavy winter rains.

Location
Near Vancouver, WA. Entrance is at NE 98th which dead-ends at the trailhead.

Activities
Hiking
Biking

Facilities
Trail unpaved
Parking (limited)

Fees and Regulations
Pets on leash

Highlights
A 31-acre oasis in the midst of development. One of the last remaining transitional wooded wetlands of the Burnt Creek watershed. There is a large anthill which has been active for 15 years or more. The forest floor in April is known for its abundant trillium. Look for owl pellets beneath the trees.

Public Transit
Take C-TRAN #30 from downtown Vancouver, Washington to NE 98th and Burton Rd.; from there, it is a five-block walk north on 98th.

Clark County Road Atlas 9/18.

How to Get There

Exit Mill Plain Blvd. from I-5 or I-205; travel west on Mill Plain from I-205 or east from I-5 to NE 97th Ave. Drive north on 97th Ave. to Burton Rd. and continue north on 98th Ave. across Burton for about .7 mile to the dead-end where the trail begins. Limited parking and no restrooms.

By Paul Clare

For more information: Vancouver-Clark Parks and Recreation Services, see Resources.

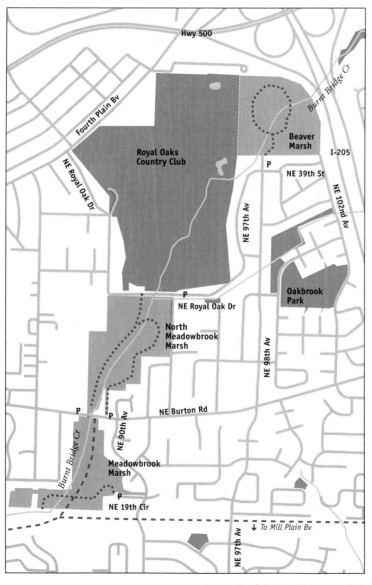

Meadowbrook Marsh and North Meadowbrook Marsh

Location
South and north of Burton
Rd. between 87th Ave. and
90th Ave., Clark County,
Washington.

Activities
Hiking

Facilities
Trail unpaved

Fees and Regulations
Pets on leash

Highlights
Wetlands, natural
forest, trilliums, owls,
a magnificent grove of
Oregon ash.

Public Transit
Take C-TRAN Burton Rd.
#30 from the transit mall;
exit at NE 98th, and
walk five blocks north
to dead-end.

Clark County Road Atlas 9

Meadowbrook Marsh is a two-acre L-shaped greenway on Burnt Bridge Creek. In 1991 Burnt Bridge Utility District constructed the largest mitigation project in the city, creating two large ponds to slow down the creek flow as a part of an overall effort to protect the creek and aquatic life as well as to rehabilitate Vancouver Lake.

The ponds are home to a variety of ducks and some geese. At the south end are cattails, skunk cabbage, sedges, and bulrushes. The cattails favor an abundance of red-winged blackbirds. Swallows sweep across the ponds in search of insects throughout the spring and summer months. Vegetation includes serviceberry, native cherry, and ash. A fine grove of 19 Oregon white oaks borders the area to the southwest. School groups have planted numerous trees and shrubs, not all of which have flourished. Heron and ducks frequent the rushes at the lower end of the marsh.

North Meadowbrook, a continuation of the Meadowbrook greenway, lies to the north of Burton Road. It opens up into a splendid grassy area after following a corridor next to the creek for one eighth of a mile. An unimproved trail follows the creek to Royal Oaks Drive, a private road at the southern edge of Royal Oaks golf course.

Burnt Bridge Creek meanders through this large, 22-acre greenway, which has some trees along the creek. A notable feature of the landscape is a magnificent grove of Oregon white oak at the northwest corner of the area. Beneath the oak is a heavy understory of young oak, serviceberry, ash, cherry, and willow. The familiar call of the belted kingfisher can often be heard as they regularly patrol Burnt Bridge Creek and Peterson Creek, which feeds Burnt Bridge from the east. Red-tailed hawks patrol the open area. Mourning doves, chickadees, and towhees can also be heard. The creek still has a reasonably good gravel base which could support coho salmon in time as restoration continues. Cutthroat trout are found as far up as 112th Avenue.

Access

From 19th Circle off 90th Ave., south of Burton Rd. You can walk north to view the two ponds, one of which has an island. You can walk along Burnt Bridge Creek to Andresen Rd., which eventually will be part of the Discovery Trail from Vancouver Lake. A new bridge is planned for NE 8th Ave.

From Royal Oak Drive, parking is very limited and there are no restrooms. Walk around the gated fence which blocks the private road. Proceed about 50 feet and take the path on the right through a fence that takes you to the greenway.

By foot, North Meadowbrook can be accessed from the south from the locked service road just west of the bridge on Burton Rd. There is limited parking at gravel turnouts on both sides of Burton Rd.

How to Get There

The marsh is reached by taking Mill Plain Road off I-205. Head west on Mill Plain and take Andresen north to E 18th St. Continue east on 18th to Burton Rd. and drive east on Burton to NE 90th Ave. Turn right (south) onto 90th and continue to 19th circle; turn right to the dead-end, which is Meadowbrook Marsh.

To reach the greenway from the north, via Burton Rd., take NE 86th north (toward Fourth Plain Ave.). Turn right (east) onto 33rd St. and go one long block. Turn right on Royal Oak Dr. and continue to the end of the road. *See map on page 379.*

By Paul Clare

For more information: Vancouver-Clark Parks and Recreation Services or Clark County Water Quality Division, see Resources.

Discovery Trail

Stewart's Glen. This section of the trail is heavily used by hikers, joggers, bicyclists, and people walking dogs. Burnt Bridge Creek is ponded by road and railroad fills just above its entrance into Vancouver Lake. The pond is about 660 feet wide and one third of a mile long. An extensive reed canarygrass wetland extends another 1,500 feet, with the creek meandering through it. In winter, the pond and wetlands host a number of ducks, including mallards (which also nest here), northern pintail, northern shoveler, gadwall, and American wigeon. Double-

Location

Vancouver, WA. The Stewart's Glen portion of the trail runs from Fruit Valley Rd. and Bernie Dr. to Hazel Dell Ave. The other portion goes from Leverich Way to Nicholson Rd.

Activities

Hiking
Biking
Fishing
Roller-blading

Facilities

Toilets
Wheelchair accessibility
Trail paved
Parking

Fees and Regulations

Hours: 5 A.M. to 10 P.M.
Pets on leash
No motorized vehicles

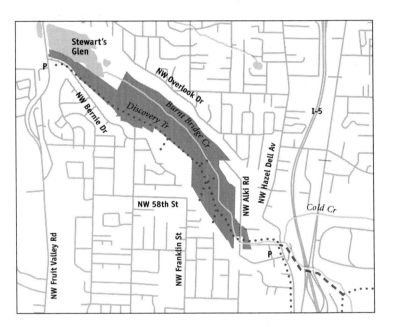

crested cormorants and great blue herons may be seen fishing year-round. Bald eagles occasionally fly by and an osprey recently nested on the trestle. A pair of red-tailed hawks nests in the area. Early morning and late evening, large numbers of crows fly overhead, coming and going from a roost in Vancouver Lake. All the songbirds normally found in these habitat types are present. Common species are bushtits, jays, chickadees, kinglets, woodpeckers, thrushes, sparrows, wrens, spotted towhees, swallows, and warblers.

Stewart's Glen is also home to a variety of animals including deer, coyotes, cottontail rabbit, raccoon, opossum, moles, voles, mice, and feral cats.

The floodplain in the lower 3,000 feet is bordered by steep slopes 80 to 130 feet high. A railroad spur runs on the north slope, while the south slope is heavily wooded. Houses rim the slopes, but are only visible on the north side. Discovery Trail runs about one-fourth of the way up the south slope, following a sewer line. The south slope is a typical West Cascade lowland mixed forest with Douglas fir, red alder, big-leaf maple, western red cedar, and bitter cherry as canopy trees on the uphill side of the trail. Oregon oak and Oregon ash are the dominant trees below the trail. Common understory trees are hazelnut, Indian plum, ocean-spray, elderberry, salal and Oregon grape. Prominent forbes include sword-fern, vanillaleaf, fringecup, waterleaf, fawn lily, trillium, *Vancouveria*, and mosses. Invasive exotics are English ivy, Scot's broom, and Himalayan blackberry. Oregon oaks start appearing in the creek side of the trail at about a quarter of a mile. There is a bench in the vicinity for resting. Marsh wrens and Virginia rails can be heard from an open area between the trail and wetlands at about half a mile. A little further on, a trail to the right leads up to Bernie Drive.

There are numerous other paths leading off both sides of the trail which go down to the wetlands or up into the woods. For the next quarter-mile, the trail goes through a mature Douglas fir forest on both sides, then drops down into a wide meadow, crossing the meadow and continuing along the creek, where you can find another

Highlights
Discovery Trail follows Burnt Bridge Creek. The trail is located in the creek basin or on the south slopes which, for the most part, are heavily wooded with native vegetation. Because of the height of the slopes the trail is effectively insulated from urban residential development and provides a natural area in the midst of the city. The diverse habitat—open water, wetlands, mature forest, shrub, and meadows—provides numerous birding opportunities. The Stewart's Glen portion is included in the annual Sauvie Island Christmas Bird Count.

Public Transit
Stewart's Glen: C-TRAN #2 from Vancouver. *Leverich-Nicholson*: C-TRAN #25 on St. Johns Rd. C-TRAN #4 stops at Bagley Downs Community Center.

Clark County Road Atlas 8/16/17.

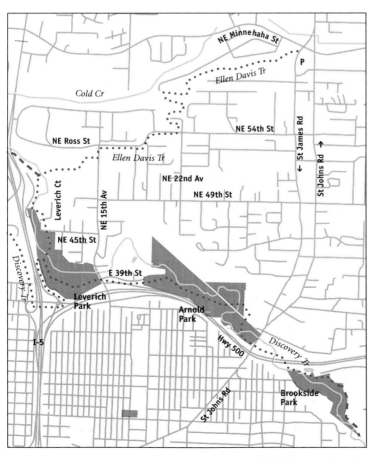

bench to rest. You will pass an old pear orchard and find another bench for convenience about half a mile down the trail. A little more than a mile along, the trail crosses the creek and Alki Road just beyond that. The trail continues along the creek to Hazel Dell Avenue, crossing a private drive. There are houses on either side. When I-5 is widened (sometime soon), provision will be made for pedestrian access across I-5 to Leverich Park.

Leverich Park-Nicholson Road. This section of the trail is newer and use is lower. The trail starts at the southeast corner of the parking lot and goes through Leverich Park, crossing the creek at least once, depending on which path is taken. Vegetation is manicured native for the most part, with cottonwood, willow, and ninebark found along the creek. In about half a mile, the trail crosses 15th Avenue. Cross in the crosswalk and go east on 41st Court (the trail runs more or less parallel to SR500) until you reach the end of 41st Court, where the trail enters Arnold Park. This portion of the trail is approximately a mile long and is relatively open and flat except where it goes up to St. Johns Road. Here, the flood plain is relatively wide where the dominant species is Scot's broom. The creek was moved north when SR500 was built and the cutoff portion of the creek south of the trail has standing water-runoff from SR500 and the neighborhood. Native trees and shrubs have been planted along this section. Where the trail nears the power lines, evidence of dirt bike activity can be seen. Look for an old orchard at about half a mile in, with a bench a little further on. The trail reaches St. Johns Road about 300 feet from the intersection with SR500. Cross at the light, where you will find the last section of the trail at that corner crosses under SR500. This portion of the trail is at the north edge of Brookside Park, which is very pleasant except for the traffic noise. The trail rises again to end up on Nicholson Road.

Access

Stewart's Glen: 1.5 miles. 10–12-foot asphalt path. Some ups and downs, but an easy trail. There is a small graveled parking lot (10–12 cars) at the corner of Fruit Valley Rd. and Bernie Dr. On-street parking on Bernie Dr.

Leverich Park to Nicholson Rd.: 2.0 miles. 10–12-foot asphalt path, on street in places. Rises up to road crossings, easy. Large parking lot on Leverich Way, just north of the main entrance to the park. Nicholson Rd. has limited parking on the shoulder a few hundred feet east of the trailhead. Additional parking available at Bagley Downs Community Center, east of Falk Rd. on Plomondon, about 1/2 mile away.

How to Get There

Stewart's Glen Access Point: From the south, exit I-5 at 39th St. Turn left on 39th, go west to Lincoln Ave., and turn right. Take Lincoln to Bernie Dr. and turn left. Follow Bernie Dr. to parking lot at Fruit Valley Rd. From north, exit I-5 at 78th St.; turn right and take 78th to Fruit Valley Rd., then turn left to Bernie Dr. and the parking lot.

Leverich-Nicholson Access Point: From north or south, exit I-5 at 39th Ave. and turn right (east). Turn left just before going under SR500 overpass, to Leverich Way. Keep to left. Parking lot is third entrance to right.

Nicholson Rd. Access Point: From SR500 turn south on Falk Rd.; Nicholson is first road to the right.

By Nancy Ellifrit

For more information: Vancouver-Clark Parks and Recreation Services, see Resources.

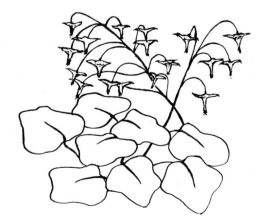

Ellen Davis Trail

Location
St. James Rd. and NE
Minnehaha St., Vancouver,
Washington

Activities
Hiking
Biking
Birdwatching

Facilities
Trail unpaved
Parking

Fees and Regulations
Open dawn to dusk
Pets on leash

Highlights
An abundance of plant and
animal diversity, including
butterflies, spring wild-
flowers, unusual plants,
lichens, and mushrooms.
Remnant farm plantings
including fruit trees, flowering locusts, daffodils.
Red cedar forest and
Friendship Bridge over
Burnt Bridge Creek.

Public Transit
C-TRAN available from
downtown Vancouver to
BPA-J.D. Ross Park and
Ride and St. James at
Minnehaha St.

Clark County Road Atlas 17

This 2.6-mile urban dirt and graveled trail connects Leverich Park and Discovery Trail to the southwest to the Minnehaha community to the north, at St. James Boulevard. The trail's namesake, Ellen Davis, was a resident of Minnehaha and a charter member of the Minnehaha Garden Club, the 50-year-old Minnehaha Social Club, and the Vancouver Audubon Society. Up until a few short years ago, Ellen accompanied the local hiking club, the "Ptarmigans," on hiking, back-packing, and rafting trips into the wilderness areas of the Northwest. This more than 90-year-old grandmother served as a beacon for those wishing not to grow old in mind and spirit.

The trail traverses a variety of environments from stark looking storage yards to forest. The southern end begins at Leverich Park, where it follows Burnt Bridge Creek to the Friendship Bridge. The all-wood Japanese-style bridge was constructed by Shin Etsu Handotai (SEH) America.

At this point, the trail enters an area which was once the propagation gardens of the J.D. Ross Complex, dating back to the early 1950s. Many plants were started here that ended up as plantings around some of the northwest power substations, such as the J.D. Ross Complex and Bonneville Dam. Remnant plantings of birch, locust, cypress, and a variety of ground covers can still be seen here. This also was the site of a farm that occupied the area prior to the construction of the complex. Seedling fruit trees and wild grape serve as living evidence of this earlier land use. The fruit from these provides abundant food and cover for native bird populations of cedar waxwings, song sparrows, house and purple finches, American robins, spotted towhees, and the ubiquitous European starling. Northern flickers and hairy and downy woodpeckers can also be seen here. Bullock's orioles and western tanagers frequent the stately Douglas fir and Oregon ash along Burnt Bridge Creek.

Early spring treats the hiker to the fragrance of the flowering locusts and violas, both remnants of the earlier gardens. Western yew trees can be viewed here and daffodils of past plantings are a sur-prise sight.

Nettles beneath the locust trees provide a great food source for the larvae of the Milbert's tortoiseshell butterfly, which can also be found here. Wild mustard affords the Sara orange tip butterfly with the food source necessary for its survival. Sara orange tip is used for the symbol on the stylized patch for the Ellen Davis Trail. In July and August of most years, a wide variety of other butterflies can be seen in this rather wild meadow-like setting. A short loop in the trail at this point provides variety on the return trip.

Up a very steep grade you enter the J.D. Ross Complex itself. This complex serves as the hub of the Northwest power grid for the

Bonneville Power Distribution System. Some excellent and dramatic photo opportunities of the towers supporting electrical cables exist here. The substation with its expanse of lawns its another picture-perfect opportunity.

You will travel through the complex along the trail adjacent to Ross Street, which becomes 54th Street. At 22nd Avenue, turn north and proceed a short distance along a narrow road, where you will approach nine tight switch-backs. You will get your workout on this stretch. Immediately, you will enter a mixed deciduous-coniferous forest. Watch carefully, for there have been frequent sightings of a sharp-shinned hawk here. You can also spot a variety of small birds such as chestnut-backed and black-capped chickadees, golden-crowned and ruby-crowned kinglets, and winter and Bewick's wrens. Spotted towhees and dark-eyed juncos also frequent the area. Swainson's, hermit, and varied thrushes and American robins are to be expected as well in early spring, along with an abundance of several species of violets, including *Viola glabella* and *V. sempervirens,* that present an array of yellow, white, and purple.

Following an exposed and steep ascent under some power lines (before you damn them, keep in mind that these bring inexpensive power from throughout the northwest grid system), you are in for a surprise as you enter a thick forest. The trail splits just inside the forest. This allows for another interesting return route. This mixed forest of Douglas fir, wild cherry, and occasional big-leaf maple is frequently sprinkled with large western red cedars. Some of these trees have been made into dramatic candelabra shapes as a result of their tops being broken in the big ice storm of 1948. In one area you will walk through a full grove of over a dozen of these splendid remnants of what was an ancient forest. How fortunate we are that the Bonneville Power Administration chose to hold back their fences and provide the community with such a splendid buffer to their complex.

In this area, three plants are a treat to see: inside-out-flower; sweet-after-death or vanillaleaf; and carpets of *Geranium robertianum.* There are also patches of wild ginger—be sure to seek out its tri-tendriled, orange-colored blossom, which hugs the ground in the spring. Also, hordes of trillium, red and white baneberry, and western and starry Solomon-plume bloom here. For the ever-searching botanist, there is the European escapee, *Epipactis helleborine* (Helleborine), that has been seen only on Vancouver Island and in Montana, according to C. Leo Hitchcock and Arthur Cronquist in *Flora of the Pacific Northwest.*

In the fall and spring a great variety of mushrooms and lichens are in evidence, such as the diminutive bird's nest fungi and a variety of *Cladonia,* better known as British soldier lichen. A variety of slime

For the ever-searching botanist, there is the European escapee, Epipactis helleborine that has been seen only on Vancouver Island and in Montana, according to C. Leo Hitchcock and Arthur Cronquist in Flora of the Pacific Northwest.

molds round out an astounding diversity of plant and animal life that occurs in this natural setting. Proceeding on, you will arrive at St. James Boulevard Ellen Davis Trailhead.

Access
Two access points: On the west side of St. James Rd., just south of NE Minnehaha St., or to the south at the end of Leverich Pkwy., off NE 45th St. A gravel path connects Discovery Trail and Leverich Park with the Ellen Davis Trail trailhead. A diversity of terrain, including some steep climbs and switchbacks—a good workout.

How to Get There
Take I-5 to 39th St., then go east to NE 15th. Go north on 15th to 45th, then west to Leverich Pkwy. At the dead-end cul-de-sac on the west side of Burnt Bridge Creek there is a trailhead. If you want to access the trail from the north, exit at Hazel Dell onto NE 78th; take 78th east to St. Johns and drive south on St. Johns to St. James Rd. (one-way south), which branches south and crosses NE Minnehaha. The trailhead is just south of Minnehaha St. on St. James on the right. *See map on page 383.*

By Don Cannard

For more information: Vancouver-Clark Parks and Recreation Services, see Resources.

Salmon Creek Greenway, Salmon Creek Park

The Salmon Creek Greenway is 850 acres of varying terrain, including forest, creeks, meadows, and ponds. Planning for Salmon Creek Park at the Klineline Ponds began in the 1960s and culminated in the park's opening in 1976. Land acquisition funds for the Greenway Trail came from a number of sources after much planning by county, state, and federal agencies. The three-mile paved Salmon Creek Trail opened in 1996.

There are steep slopes on the edge of the basin with upland forest, dominated by Douglas fir, big-leaf maple, red alder, Oregon white oak, and smaller numbers of western red cedar. The lower slopes are dominated by big-leaf maple with a canopy of cherry, elderberry, buckthorn, vine maple, and apple trees. There is a dense understory of Indian peach or plum, various species of blackberry, Oregon grape, ninebark, roses, and snowberry. Black cottonwood is in the riparian area for the first mile of the trail, along with Pacific willow and alder. The lower mile of the riparian area trees is dominated by the willow. Large areas of the last two miles are covered with reed canarygrass.

The stream portion of the area is composed of two habitat sub-types: a free-flowing stream that responds to rainfall cycles controlled by channels and over-flow channels, functioning as a normal meandering stream; and the Columbia River backwater which is under tidal influence.

The streams attract frogs, salamanders, and snakes that feed on insects, and in turn attract predators such as mink, raccoon, weasel, river otter, muskrats, nutria, and coyote. Watch for signs of beaver, which have cut down some of the willow and alder. Deer are also present, and you may see rabbits scampering near their blackberry thickets, especially early in the morning during the summer.

There are some small ponds, one of which is about a mile down the trail, and another at about 2.25 miles, that have waterfowl throughout the year. By autumn, these ponds are nearly dry and covered by duckweed. A frequent visitor at the ponds is the great blue heron.

The upper park area features Klineline Pond, which was once a gravel pit and now has clean spring-fed water for swimming in the summer. The pond is stocked with trout, and is a popular fishing spot for everyone including cormorants, heron, and mergansers. The adjacent area has many picnic tables in a grassy setting along with the rest rooms. On the trail at .5 mile, large dead cottonwood trees offer good bird spotting, where you can see osprey, kingfisher, crows, and northern flickers.

There are benches farther down the trail close to the stream that allow one to rest, listen to the water, and enjoy the view. Just beyond this point, the trail enters a broad area of tall reed canarygrass, a favorite nesting area for the beautiful common yellowthroat in the

Location
Salmon Creek Park, Klineline Ponds, and Salmon Creek Sports Complex, NE 117th St. at east end and NW Seward Rd. at the Felida Bridge, west end, Clark County, WA.

Activities
Hiking
Canoeing, boating
Fishing

Facilities
Toilets
Paved trail
Parking

Fees and Regulations
Entrance fees: $2, seasonal
Open dawn to dusk
Pets on leash

Highlights
A scenic natural area providing outstanding habitat for wildlife with many waterfowl in the winter months, and a nesting area for many species of birds in the summer months. Klineline Pond, once a gravel pit, has clean spring-fed water for swimming in the summer. The pond is stocked with trout, and is a popular fishing spot.

summer months. At 1.6 mile there is a quarter-mile spur trail looking over the steep hillside where you can catch a springtime display of sessile trillium (*Trillium chloropetalum*) among the sword-fern. At a short distance, the Cougar Creek trail goes off to 119th Street. Parts of this trail are not paved, but it is usually an easy walk (except for some areas farther upstream where flooding brings down sand on the trail). Cougar Creek cuts down deeply into rock near its juncture with Salmon Creek. The upper portion of this trail has skunk cabbage blooming in the spring.

A bridge crosses Cougar Creek on the Salmon Creek Trail and just beyond is another bench that affords an open view of a bend in the stream—a favorite spot for kingfishers in nearby trees. In the winter months, many mallard, northern pintail, and wigeon, and smaller numbers of northern shoveler, teal, and ring-necked ducks feed in the

Public Transit
C-TRAN #6 for the east upper Park area; C-TRAN #21 for the west lower end.

Clark County Road Atlas 17/25/26

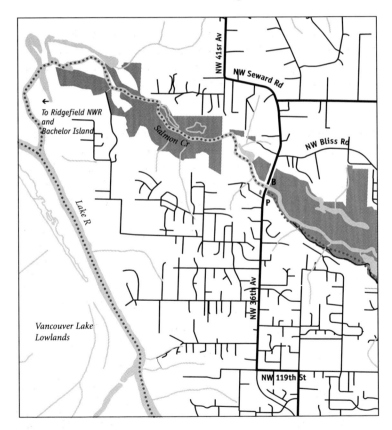

marsh and ponds. Wood ducks are also present but are usually more difficult to see from the trail. Canada geese and tundra swans are often on the far side of the creek on the lower reaches. The silhouette of the white swans in flight against the backdrop of the trees is a most beautiful sight. The shrubs and trees along the trail often have flocks of golden-crowned and ruby-crowned kinglets, bushtits, black-capped chickadees, and dark-eyed juncos. During the summer months, small numbers of mallards and wood ducks remain.

The trail near the 2-mile mark has a steep bank that provides nesting for kingfishers and northern rough-winged swallows. Near the 2.25-mile mark is a bench overlooking a large pond that is a good spot to watch many swallows catching their prey low over the water. Some black-headed grosbeaks often are singing their melodious call in this area. Red-winged blackbirds sing near their nests near the 2.5-mile mark and robins flock in to feed when the cherries are ripe. Just beyond the 2.75-mile mark is a stunning view looking upstream on the main channel, framed by willows to the side. On a clear day, one gets a view of Mt. Hood in the background. This view is very striking late in the afternoon with the soft light on the mountain—a Kodak moment!

Access
Access to the upper Salmon Creek Greenway trail is at the Salmon Creek Park entrance off NE 117th St. at the east end and at the Salmon Creek Sports Complex, another .3 mile to the west on 117th. Access to the west from the Felida Bridge, NW Seward.

How to Get There
Upper Trail: from the south, take I-5 to the 134th St. exit. Then head east a short distance to Hwy. 99 and turn south to NE 117th St. Turn right (west) and enter the park just past the I-5 overpass. The distance from where you originally exited I-5 at 134th is 1.2 mile. If you pass the park entrance and drive another .3 mile west on 117th St. to the

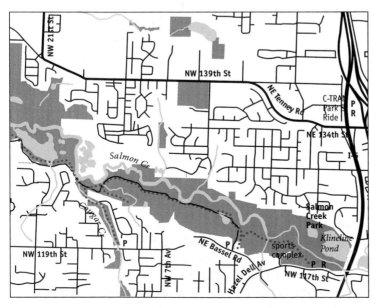

Salmon Creek Sports Complex, there is another trail access. Both entrances are on the right side (north) of 117th. If you continue on 117th for a short distance and take Bassel Rd. to the west, there is a Salmon Creek Greenway trailhead on the north side of Bassel.

Middle Trail: There is also access along Cougar Creek, a tributary which flows into Salmon Creek from the south at NW 119th St. This access can be reached from the west by taking 119th east off NW 36th south of the Felida Bridge or from the east by taking 117th west to 114th and jogging north on NW 7th to 119th, and heading west on 119th to the trailhead.

Lower Trail: Take 134th St. exit off I-5 and drive west. 134th turns into Tenny Rd. and then NE 139th, and eventually becomes NW Bliss just before meeting NW Seward at a T-intersection. Turn left (south) and park at the Salmon Creek bridge. The trailhead is on the southeast corner of the bridge. There is also a canoe launch on the east side of the bridge. There are steps down to Salmon Creek north of the Greenway Trail.

By Galen Schoenthal

For more information: Vancouver-Clark Parks and Recreation Services, see Resources.

Spider Slayers and Caterpillar Killers

Chivalry is not dead! There are tiny knights in shining armor thriving in your garden, riding not on white steeds, but on crystal wings! These fearless warriors wield venomous swords and joust serpentine caterpillars and spider dragons. Some even build castles that rival King Arthur's! Ironically, the damsels do all the work.

There are many kinds of predatory, solitary wasps, but some of the most fascinating species are those that duel with spiders and caterpillars.

Spider Wasps

The spider wasps of the family Pompilidae are high-strung hunters of field and forest. With flickering wings and quivering antennae, they nervously seek their spider prey. One local species, *Chirodamus pyrrhomelas*, stands out, being large and velvety black with bright orange wings. *Priocnemis oregona* is smaller and black, with a red abdomen and smoky wings. Both species prey on folding-door tarantulas, a kind of trapdoor spider common in woodlands.

The female wasp paralyzes her victim by stinging a nerve center. She then drags it laboriously to a burrow or cavity she has already prepared. She lays an egg on the spider and the emerging larva eagerly consumes its meal. When mature it pupates, emerging the following spring as an adult.

Mud Daubers

The mud daubers are the expert masons of the insect world. They are members of the very large family Sphecidae.

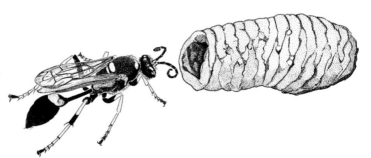

The common black-and-yellow mud dauber, *Sceliphron cae-mentarium*, stocks its mud "crypt" with paralyzed spiders of all kinds. Once the cavity is filled to the brim, the female lays an egg on the last victim and seals the cell. The larva that hatches feasts on the living "corpses" and finally pupates, emerging later as a sleek black-and-yellow adult.

Many other wasps use the abandoned nests, including the blue mud dauber, *Chalybion californicum*. It locates a nest of its cousin's, cleans it out, and harvests its own spiders. How's that for urban renewal?

Keyhole Mud Wasps

The so-called "keyhole" wasps may also rent mud dauber nests. They, too, belong to the family Sphecidae. These small wasps usually nest in nail holes, the hollow pith of plant twigs, or in old beetle borings in logs and stumps. They divide such tunnels with mud partitions, stockpiling spiders in each cell as food for their offspring. In the genus *Trypoxylon*, subgenus *Trypargilum*, the liberated males share in such housekeeping duties as cleaning out the nest hole, storing prey collected by the female, and chasing away the parasites and predators that plague all wasps.

Thread-waisted Wasps

The thread-waisted wasps are caterpillar hunters. Each female excavates a burrow and seals the entrance before going hunting. How she ever finds it again remains a

mystery, but she probably uses landmarks to orient herself. After entombing her paralyzed caterpillar provisions, and placing an egg in the dungeon, she buries the entrance once again, taking care to firmly plug the tunnel. In some species, the female even picks up a pebble in her jaws and tamps down the loose soil. Whether this demonstrates the use of a tool is still open to debate, but she erases her tracks so thoroughly, it would put a human criminal to shame!

Ammophila kennedyi is the only thread-waisted wasp the author has seen in Portland. It occurs in Oaks Bottom and on Kelly Butte.

Potter Wasps

The potter wasps are related to yellowjackets, but unlike their cousins, they construct marble-sized nests of mud, not paper. Inside each tiny, graceful urn, a single wasp larva develops, feeding on paralyzed caterpillars stored by its mother. The nests are well hidden in sheltered crevices. Our common species is *Eumenes crucifera*.

Home Made Wasp Nest Boxes

With little effort, you can make comfortable "apartments" for these cavity-nesters. Pieces of bamboo, cut into six-inch sticks with one end sealed off, accommodate wasps nicely, provided the diameter does not exceed about one quarter of an inch. Bundling a few of these straws together and placing them in sheltered spots, such as under the eaves of houses, will allow you to view any activity without disturbing the insects (or vice versa)! Holes drilled in sticks of straight-grained pine will also suffice.

All adult wasps fuel their energetic activities with nectar, and they are easily observed as they visit the flowers of poison hemlock (*Conium*), Queen Anne's lace (*Daucus*), and snowberry (*Symphoricarpos*).

Oaks Bottom, Kelly Butte, and Oregon Episcopal School Marsh are hot spots, but wherever the urban naturalist goes, he or she is sure to find adventure in exploring the insect realm. Happy wasp watching!

By Eric R. Eaton

Whipple Creek Park

The original 239 acres of Whipple Creek Park were officially dedicated to Clark County in 1968. Since then, the total acreage has increased to about 375 acres, making the park one of the largest undeveloped open spaces in the county. It is currently maintained by Vancouver-Clark County Parks and Recreation Services.

Whipple Creek Park has three distinct habitats: about 100 acres are hayfield and open pasture; about 150 acres are shrub/scrub with some trees; and about 125 acres are dense second growth forest. With the exception of the hayfield, most of the habitats are relatively undisturbed, allowing you to view the interacting plant communities.

The park has five small brushy perennial streams meandering through it. One, the park's namesake Whipple Creek, is located on the south side of the property; the other four are unnamed.

The wide diversity of terrain and vegetation allows for a wide diversity of wildlife. You will find many birds including pileated woodpeckers, common flickers, sapsuckers, robins, varied thrushes, nuthatches, wrens, Steller's jays, and scrub jays. Red-tailed hawks may also be seen, sometimes feasting on mice they have caught in the open fields. The park is home to black-tailed deer, coyotes, raccoons, opossums, and squirrels, too.

Under the evergreen canopy, a carpet of salal, Oregon grape, and sword-fern is punctuated by taller vine maple, hazelnut, Indian plum, Pacific dogwood, and an occasional English holly.

In late March and early April, you will find an abundant display of western trilliums alongside the muddy trails. Also look for an abundance of bleeding heart, yellow wood violet, Robert geranium, Oregon

Location
About 1.5 miles west of the Clark County Fairgrounds on NW 21st Ave.

Activities
Horseback riding
Hiking
Biking

Facilities
Parking

Fees and Regulations
Restricted hours
Pets on leash

Highlights
The park's most impressive feature is the large expanse of second growth forest. The 130–150 year old forest is a mixture of co-dominant Douglas fir and grand fir, with some western red cedar, pacific yew, and western hemlock. The trees average about 20 to 24 inches in diameter, with a few larger ones approaching 30 inches in diameter. In autumn, a stunning display of big-leaf maple and red alder.

Clark County Road Atlas 25

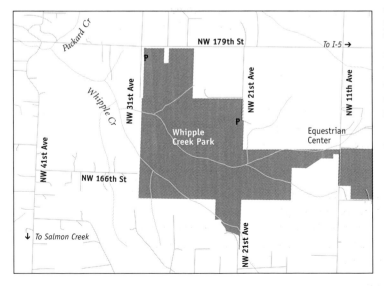

oxalis, Pacific waterleaf, wild ginger, oxeye daisy, Canadian and bull thistle, buttercup, and Queen Anne's lace.

A significant break in the evergreen canopy occurs where a three- to five-acre grove of big-leaf maple and red alder grows. In autumn, the maple leaves turn to a brilliant shade of yellow, making a stunning display of color against the evergreen backdrop and a blue October sky.

An unmapped network of semi-primitive trails winds throughout the park. They are often used by horses from Whipple Creek Riding Center located on the east side of the park. Most of the trails are rough and muddy even in the summer. Two sections have been improved with gravel and waterbars for drainage.

The trail leads you back into the forest and eventually to the south side of the park where an old stone building and stone bridge stand. A closer look reveals a refurbished waterwheel beside the building. You will also find an old dam that once held a pond.

Follow the rough trail up the hill and it will eventually take you back to the north side of the park, where you cross a small footbridge over a stream. Then follow the gravel trail uphill to your starting point.

Access
Access to Whipple Creek Park is somewhat limited because of the surrounding private property, its brushy borders, and the fact that it has only four designated entrances. The easiest access is located off NW 179th St. 1.5 miles west of Clark County Fairgrounds. Turn onto NW 21st Ave., a short dead-end road, and follow it to a gravel parking lot. Then walk south along the field edge to an unmarked trailhead and start exploring!

How to Get There
Take the 179th St. exit from I-5 and proceed left (west) on 179th to NW 21st Ave. Turn left (south) on NW 21st.

By Roger Anderson

For more information: Vancouver-Clark Parks and Recreation Services, see Resources.

Lacamas Lake Park

Lacamas Lake Park on Round Lake has been a popular site since it was donated to Clark County by Crown Zellerbach. The park is now maintained by the Vancouver-Clark Park and Recreation Department. Fishing is a popular activity, and the lake offers excellent fishing for trout, bass, bluegill, and perch.

South of the lake, below the dam, Lacamas Creek becomes a rushing stream cascading across a unique rock formation called "Pot Holes." Huge old-growth trees set off a wilderness area where a nest of osprey, along with other native birds, attracts bird watchers. Wildflowers abound, including the camas lily, which blooms in mid-April. Hiking trails cover the 312 acres, providing a ringside view of the natural habitat with its wide variety of wildlife. These hiking trails are also popular with cyclists. They, too, enjoy the challenges of the lava flow areas, the steep slopes, and the beauty of the lush ferns and other riparian vegetation of Lacamas Creek.

Vancouver Audubon uses this park each summer for a day camp site. Here is a list of favorite wildlife sightings: black-tailed deer, pileated woodpeckers, cedar waxwings, red-breasted nuthatch, turkey vultures, green heron, osprey, bald eagle, grouse, and western swallowtails. There are also many insects, including aquatic ones. Lacamas Creek is an excellent source for caddis fly larvae, crayfish, and other aquatic species.

Lacamas Lake Park is a great place to recreate and/or commune with nature because of the diverse habitats—geologic features including waterfalls, and the miles of trails. Watch out for poison oak on the lava fields in summer.

Access

Round Lake is located at the southern tip of Lacamas Lake and is fed by Lacamas Creek. The north section of the park is the most developed. Here a trail encircles Round Lake. Close to the lake are a covered picnic shelter, a restroom, and a play center. A launch area is provided for canoes or rowboats near the restroom area.

The trails at the park entrance and around the restroom area are asphalt, and therefore wheelchair accessible. The trails on the south side of the lake are very steep and wide. Trails over the Camas Lily fields are moderately steep and narrow. Through the center of the park, trails were turned into fire roads, and are covered with gravel with a moderate elevation gain.

Location
The northwest side of Camas, Washington, at the intersection of Everett Rd. and 1st St.

Activities
Hiking
Biking
Canoeing, boating
Fishing
Birdwatching
Picnicking

Facilities
Toilets
Picnic area

Fees and Regulations
Pets on leash

Highlights
Unique lava formations, waterfalls, a spring display of camas lilies in April and May.

Clark County Road
  Atlas 3/12

How to Get There

Head east from Vancouver, Washington on Hwy. 14 to Camas. Take Exit 12. Continue east on 6th to Garfield. Turn left. At the top of the hill, turn left on 14th, then right on Everett. Continue on Everett to just before the bridge. Parking is on the right side of the road.

By Carol Peterson

For more information: Vancouver-Clark Parks and Recreation Services, see Resources.

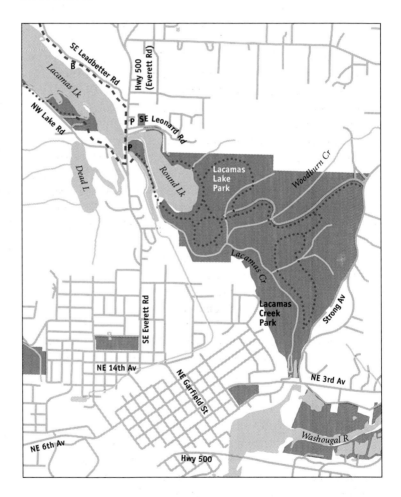

La Center Bottoms

The La Center Bottoms wildlife preserve is part of a habitat and open space system that covers over 1,200 acres on the lower East Fork Lewis River. The East Fork Lewis is Clark County's largest free-flowing stream. Rising in the Cascade Mountains near Cougar Rock, the East Fork flows for 43 miles through Skamania and Clark Counties and empties into the Columbia River on the north side of the Ridgefield National Wildlife Refuge. The La Center Bottoms is located on the lower end of the East Fork, where the basin expands into a broad floodplain and the river has slower-moving, tidally influenced flows.

The preserve itself covers 125 acres, and is one of three state-designated "Watchable Wildlife" sites in Clark County. The property includes 3,500 feet of shoreline on the East Fork Lewis, and Brezee Creek, a year-round tributary, cuts through the northeast corner of the preserve. The La Center Bottoms features a variety of habitat types, including emergent wetlands, flood plain/meadow, open ponds, and forested uplands. The expansive bottom lands, which dominate the site, attract a wide variety of migratory waterfowl and other wildlife, including Canada geese, wigeon, pintail, mallard, cinnamon teal, tundra swan, wood duck, bufflehead, bald eagle, osprey, and great blue heron. The East Fork and its associated tributaries, side channels, and wetlands are also critical to the support of federally listed salmon and steelhead runs. Anadromous fish populations include summer and winter steelhead, chinook, coho, and sea-run cutthroat trout. Historically, the East Fork also supported chum.

The La Center Bottoms provides an outdoor education and public access hub for the greenway system. A pedestrian trail borders the west edge of the preserve; two viewing blinds overlook the bottomlands and the extended greenway system. The La Center School system uses the bottomlands throughout the year as an outdoor education classroom. The city of La Center borders the preserve to the north and provides restaurants, groceries, and other services.

Access

A short trail (2/3 mile) extends along a dike bordering the East Fork Lewis River. The trail crosses Brezee Creek, a small tributary with year-round flows, and provides access to two wildlife viewing blinds on the edge of the La Center Bottoms wildlife preserve. Trail contours are mostly flat, and the trail is paved to Brezee Creek.

Location
East Fork Lewis River immediately upstream of La Center Bridge, Clark County, Washington.

Activities
Hiking

Facilities
Wheelchair accessible
Paved and unpaved trail
Parking

Fees and Regulations
Hours: 7 A.M. to dusk

Highlights
The La Center Bottoms is one of three state-designated "Watchable Wildlife" sites in Clark County. The site is heavily used by migratory waterfowl, with best viewing November through March.

Public Transit
C-TRAN from Salmon Creek Park and Ride to La Center. Monday-Friday: 3 times A.M/ 3 times P.M.

Contact C-TRAN Customer Service: 360-695-0123

Clark County Road Atlas 44

How to Get There

Take exit #16 (319th St.) from I-5 and turn east on La Center Rd. Drive approximately 1.5 miles and take the first right after crossing the La Center Rd. Bridge. A gravel parking area is located immediately adjacent to the trailhead.

By Bill Dygert

For more information: Vancouver-Clark Parks and Recreation Department, see Resources.

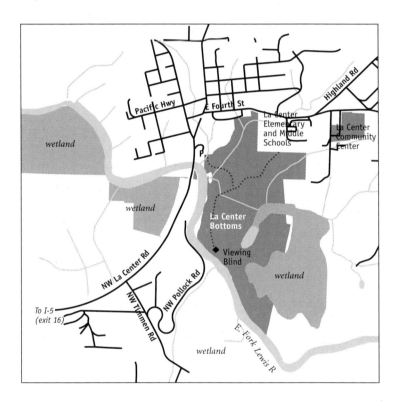

Wild Calendar

January

Abundant wintering **waterfowl**.

Watch for **tundra swans**, sandhill cranes, double-crested cormorants on Sauvie Island, Ridgefield, Columbia Slough.

Bald eagle numbers peak in mid-January at their winter roosts.

Winter night **sky** illuminated with constellations.

Audubon **Bald Eagle** Watches at Sauvie Island.

Good time for identifying **lichens** and mosses when deciduous trees are bare.

Anna's hummingbirds energetic. Flashy males hawk for insects, pose, and sing on territorial perches.

Great blue herons enjoy last opportunity for quiet and solitude before courtship commences.

February

Spring arrives! Imbolc, Celtic celebration of spring.

February 2nd, Groundhog Day.

Wetlands still teeming with wintering **swans**, geese, ducks.

Pussy willows appear.

Shining brilliantly in the winter sky is the giant red star **Betelgeuse** found in the constellation Orion.

Indian plum begins to leaf out.

Western **hazelnut** flaunting long yellow catkins.

Pacific **tree frogs** begin calling.

Frog egg masses in ponds.

Smelt should be running in the Sandy River.

Great-horned owls, **hawks**, and eagles begin nesting.

Pine siskins create a din in the Park Blocks downtown.

Earthworms on the move.

Robins and common **bushtits** flock.

Bewick's and **winter wrens** stake out territories.

Rough-skinned newts breeding and producing eggs in ponds.

Starlings congregate on the Broadway Bridge.

Great blue herons begin breeding season, exhibiting courtship.

March

Hibernating adult mourning cloak and other **anglewing butterflies** wake up and flutter on warm, sunny days.

Ferns unfurl.

Early **wildflowers** appear in woodlands—wood violet, wild ginger, bleeding heart, fringecup, false Solomon's seal, sweet coltsfoot.

Northern Flickers and downy **woodpeckers** drumming on trees, houses, and downspouts.

Most major stars and constellations of the **winter sky** slide into the west.

Testosterone-crazed **robins** crash into windows attacking their own reflection.

Red-winged **blackbirds** and American robins setting up territories.

Peregrine falcons begin nesting on the Fremont bridge.

Native **amphibians** active and breeding.

March 21st, the **Vernal Equinox**.

Garter snakes emerge to bask in the sun.

Swallows begin to arrive: first the tree, then violet-green, cliff, rough-winged, and barn.

Rufous hummingbirds appear, attracted to blooming red-flowering currant.

Big songs from little birds—varied thrushes and **ruby-crowned kinglets** burst into song.

Skunk cabbage brilliantly blooming in wetlands. **Oregon grape** blossoms.

Moss **sporophytes** erupt.

Indian plum blooms, discreetly segregating male and female blossoms on separate plants.

Douglas' **squirrels**, Townsend's chipmunks, California ground squirrels breeding.

Trilliums begin to flower.

Banana slugs on the move.

Sweet smell of spring as the oily resin of **cottonwood** buds permeates the air.

Waterfowl migration heads north.

Great blue heron nests complete.

April

Peregrine falcons laying eggs.

Trilliums profuse in forests.

Dogwood and salmonberry in bloom; **spring chinook** return.

Bird activity in full swing. Territorial establishment, spring **migrants** passing through.

Resident **winter wrens**, brown creepers, common bushtits, American robins are singing, breeding, and producing eggs.

Shorebirds begin heading north.

The stars of the **constellation Leo** shine brightly to the east and southeast of the city.

Red **elderberry** in bloom.

Pacific **jumping mice** emerge.

Turtles bask in warm, sunny spots.

Moles and **pocket gophers** clean house. Lots of fresh dirt mounds in yards and fields.

Tryon Creek State Park **Trillium Festival.**

Camas blooming.

Solitary **orchard mason bees** visit early-blooming trees and flowers.

Wildflowers galore.

Opossum and raccoon **road-kill** soars as males wander hunting for mates.

Maples flowering. Tree **squirrels** and chipmunks chow down on buds.

Swallows on wing, exploring neighborhoods for nesting sites

Great blue heron laying eggs.

May

Yellowjackets and paper wasps scouting for likely nesting sites.

Peak **spring bird migration.** Western tanagers, black-headed grosbeaks, and warblers highlight woods and forests.

Songbirds feverishly happy.

Tualatin River National Wildlife Refuge **Migratory Bird Festival.**

Evening grosbeaks gather in downtown Park Block elm trees.

The **Big Dipper** appears in the northern sky.

Conifers display new greenery.

Purple martins are back.

Early clutches of **mallards**, Canada geese, hatch.

Bullfrogs breeding; native amphibians nearly finished breeding.

Morel **mushrooms** poking out.

Reptiles alert.

Most **native mammals** will have given birth by now, but young still tucked away.

Great blue heron frenetically feeding young.

June

Great Blue Heron Week, 1st week in June

A great time for **insects**. Aquatic insects, spittle bugs, and butterflies abundant.

Evening grosbeaks, fox sparrows, and golden-crowned sparrows depart for higher elevation breeding grounds.

Rough-skinned **newts** hanging out in ponds.

June 21st, **summer solstice**, the longest day as the sun reaches its highest point in the sky.

Young of Townsend's **chipmunks**, Douglas' squirrels, California ground squirrels come out of hiding.

Blacktail **deer** drop fawns.

Tree frog **tadpoles** under metamorphosis.

Baby birds! Leave them alone, their mothers will take care of them.

Swifts nesting in fireplace chimneys.

Red **huckleberries** and wild strawberries ripe.

Great blue heron young are noisy "branchers."

July

Allergy season. Abundant **pollen** adrift in the air.

Cottonwood seeds fill the air.

By 4th of July young **swifts** clambering in chimneys, some falling into fireplaces.

Tent caterpillars mass in trees.

Antares, another red **giant star** appears in the night sky.

Big, black and white banded alder borer **beetles** create spectacle as they swarm to fresh paint in downtown Portland.

Fireweed, foxgloves, blue elderberry in bloom.

Excellent **dragonfly**-damselfly watching through August.

Great blue heron young leave nests.

Columbia Slough Small Craft Regatta.

August

Young-of-the-year **raccoons** trail behind their mothers.

Camas **pocket gopher** young leave home.

Townsend's **chipmunks** feverishly gathering and storing food.

The annual Perseid **meteor shower** bedazzles, second week in August.

Barn swallows fledge first clutch and lay eggs for second. Other swallows' young fledged.

Young scrub and Steller's **jays** fledged and marauding neighborhoods.

The melodious ascending scale of **Swainson's thrush** song prevalent, especially along river bottom cottonwood forests.

Cicadas and **katydids** buzzing.

Band-winged **grasshoppers** hopping in fields, vacant lots, roads.

First signs of fall bird **migration**.

Vaux's **swifts** begin to roost in local chimneys.

Some **ponds** dry up. Rivers low.

Annoying surplus of **mosquitoes**.

Yellowjackets become aggressive, sometimes stinging with seemingly no provocation.

Blue and **red elderberry**, blue huckleberry, Oregon grape, big-leaf maple bearing fruit.

Douglas' squirrels begin cutting Douglas fir cones in late August and continue through early autumn.

Blackberries ripe. Fruits, **berries**, nuts at their peak. (Sullivan's Gulch Blackberry Festival.)

Blacktail fawns' spots begin to fade.

Yellowjacket nests humming with activity, then disintegrate as males, new queens, and the founding queen all desert the colony, leaving the workers with no direction.

Great blue heron young and adults disperse from nest sites.

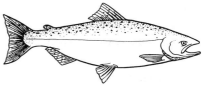

September

Big-leaf maples begin to lose leaves, some of which catch on strands of spider silk giving a **"hanging leaf"** phenomenon.

Orb-weaving **spiders** are everywhere. Webs dominate fields, gardens, and woods aggravating hikers, disturbing city folk.

Male **folding-door spiders** wander in search of mates, falling into window wells and swimming pools en route.

September 23rd, the first day of fall.

Clear skies, shorter days, bring excellent **star gazing** as summer stars linger in the evening sky.

Roosting **Vaux's swifts** congregate en masse at Wallace Park's Chapman Elementary School chimney.

Fall chinook **salmon** return to spawn.

Throngs of **swallows** gather in huge flocks anticipating migration.

Shorebirds and migratory waterfowl begin to return.

Annual Oregon Historical Society **"Wintering In"** at Sauvie Island's Bybee-Howell Territorial Park.

Big-leaf maple **"helicopters"** take flight.

Annual Audubon Society of Portland **Swift Watch** at Wallace Park.

Second litters of Townsend's chipmunks and **Douglas' squirrels** emerge.

Blacktail **fawns** have lost their spots.

Winged reproductives of dampwood **termites** demonstrate mating flights.

Poison oak turning color, at its prettiest. Don't touch!

Great blue heron dispersed along rivers and streams.

October

Conifer **pollen** prolific, dusting cars and outdoor areas in yellow.

Some species of **ladybird beetles** amass in grass clumps, and furrows of tree bark, to hibernate.

Colorful **autumn displays** of big-leaf, vine, and other maples, oaks.

Annual **Salmon Festival** at Oxbow Regional Park.

Monarch butterflies migrating.

Mushrooms materialize as if by magic following autumn rains.

Rough-skinned **newts** abandon ponds and may be seen wandering during and right after rainy days.

Cedar **waxwings** gorge on fermented berries, become inebriated, and plow into windows.

Nightcrawlers and other **earthworms** on the move. Rains stimulate earthworms and moles to become active again, resulting in more fresh mounds.

Pacific **jumping mice** enter hibernation.

Most **stars** begin to dim, lost in the city light glare.

Most **rufous hummers** gone. Anna's reappear to overwinter.

Fall bird migration in earnest. Waterfowl numbers swell. Varied **thrushes** return from mountain nesting grounds. Dark-eyed **juncos** reappear at low-elevation feeders.

Sandhill cranes return to Sauvie Island.

Woollybear caterpillars show their stripes. Will it be a long, cold winter?

Great blue herons just hanging out.

November and December

Rough-legged hawks return to Sauvie Island fields from their arctic nesting grounds.

Male winter **moths** flutter at porch lights. Females are wingless.

Feeder activity dominated by resident black-capped and chestnut-backed **chickadees**, house finches, song sparrows, spotted towhees, pine siskins, and American **goldfinches**.

Annual Audubon Society of Portland's Wild Arts Festival, near Thanksgiving.

Brilliant fireballs light up the sky as the annual Leonid **meteor shower** performs, mid-November.

Waterfowl are back in force.

December skies are rich in stars and clusters when you can sort through the clouds.

You might see the Geminid meteor shower mid-December.

Douglas' squirrels continue activity, but Townsend's chipmunks' prefer their burrows, presumably dining on stores of seeds.

December 21st, **winter begins**.

Audubon Society Christmas bird counts one week either side of Christmas

Great blue herons hunkering down.

Mosses at their best.

Drip, drip, drip.

The editors would like to thank Richard B. Forbes, Robert Michael Pyle, Eric Eaton, James Davis, Connie Levesque, Bob Wilson, Harry Nehls, Ralph Rogers, and Bob Duke for helping them compile the calendar.

Afterword: Protecting Urban Greenspaces

" . . . the belief that the city is an entity apart from nature and even
antithetical to it has dominated the way in which the city is perceived and
continues to affect how it is built. This attitude has aggravated and even
created many of the city's environmental problems. The city, the suburbs,
and the countryside must be viewed as a single, evolving system within
nature . . . Nature in the city must be cultivated, like a garden, rather than
ignored or subdued."
—Anne Whiston Spirn,
The Granite Garden: Urban Nature and Human Design, 1984

We wrote *Wild in the City* because we wanted to celebrate the wild where we live, in
our backyards. Now that you have explored our region's Greenspaces, consider that
virtually none of these wild places would exist without committed citizens working
diligently with their neighborhood association, park planners, and elected officials to
protect and restore them. We are fortunate in the Portland-Vancouver metropolitan
region to have the only directly elected regional government in the United States—
Metro.

Working with all 24 cities and three counties in the region, Metro has the ability to
look beyond political boundaries and to put in place watershed-based natural area
protections. While the New Urbanism and Smart Growth movements are sweeping
the nation, promoting walkable, well-designed communities, there is much work
to be done to also make our communities ecologically sustainable. The Portland
metropolitan region is just beginning, through Metro's 2040 program, to plan
the region as if it were a unique ecosystem integrating the built and natural
environment. We hope that *Wild in the City* will inspire and encourage you to
get involved in protecting and restoring your own favorite greenspaces.

For those of you who live in the Portland-Vancouver region, the Audubon Society
of Portland's *Urban Natural Resource Directory* lists every citizen group, agency, and
park provider working on Greenspace issues. There are also many sources in the
directory at the back of this book where you can find a group that may be working
on your favorite wild place.

—*Mike Houck & M.J. Cody*

The Essential Nature Library

For the Portland metropolitan region and nearby areas

American Bird Conservancy. *All the Birds of North America.* New York: HarperCollins, 1997. (the newest field guide, except for the National Geographic 3rd edition; popular with beginners; great habitat scenes)

Arno, Stephen F.; illus. Ramona Hammerly. *Northwest Trees.* Seattle: The Mountaineers, 1977. (the most information on local trees, awesome pen and ink drawings)

Arora, David. *All that the Rain Promises and More . . . A Hip Pocket Guide to Western Mushrooms.* Berkeley: Ten Speed Press, 1991. (the best beginning mushroom book)

Audubon Society of Portland. *The Warbler,* monthly publication of the Society listing field tours, natural history classes, and other events.

Audubon Society of Portland. *Urban Natural Resources Directory,* a comprehensive listing of environmental issues, including "Who Ya Gonna Call?", a citizen guide to becoming involved in conservation issues. Also lists all non-profit groups, stream and watershed councils, and agencies and parks involved in urban natural resource issues.

Brown, Herbert, and Bruce Bury. et al. *Reptiles of Washington and Oregon.* Seattle: Seattle Audubon Society, 1995. (great for all levels, super photos)

Brown, Tom, and Brandt Morgan. *Tom Brown's Field Guide to Nature Observation and Animal Tracking.* New York: Berkley Books, 1988. (the best start for this topic)

Burt, William H., and Richard P. Grossenheider. *A Field Guide to the Mammals,* 3rd. Ed. A "Peterson Series" guide. Boston: Houghton Mifflin, 1980.

Cassidy, James, ed. *Book of North American Birds.* Pleasantville, NY: Reader's Digest, 1990.

Corkran, Charlotte, and Chris Thoms. *Amphibians of Oregon, Washington and British Columbia.* Edmonton, AB: Lone Pine, 1996. (comprehensive for a large area)

Davis, James L. *Seasonal Guide to the Natural Year: Oregon, Washington, British Columbia.* Golden, CO: Fulcrum Press, 1996. (single most comprehensive book on wildlife watching for the region)

Duda, Mark. *Watching Wildlife.* Helena, MT: Falcon Press, 1995. (covers all the basics of how to find, watch, and photograph wildlife)

Evanich, Joseph E., Jr. *The Birder's Guide to Oregon.* Portland, OR: Portland Audubon Society, 1990. (where to find the birds in the whole state)

Feltwell, John, and Brian Hargreaves, Illus. *Butterflies of North America.* American Nature Guides series. New York: Smithmark, 1992.

Harper, Alice B. *The Banana Slug.* Aptos, CA: Bay Leaves Press, 1988. (booklet)

Hartson, Tamara. *Squirrels of the West.* Edmonton, AB: Lone Pine, 1999.

Hitchcock, C. Leo, and Arthur Cronquist. *Flora of the Pacific Northwest: An Illustrated Manual.* Seattle and London. University of Washington Press, 1973.

Houle, Marcy C. *One City's Wilderness: Portland's Forest Park,* 2nd ed. Portland: Oregon Historical Society Press, 1995. (natural history and hiking guide)

Jolley, Russ. *Wildflowers of the Columbia Gorge.* Portland: Oregon Historical Society Press, 1988. (many of the flowers covered are found in the Portland region)

Jones, Philip N. *Canoe and Kayak Routes of Northwest Oregon.* Seattle: The Mountaineers, 1997.

Kaufman, Kenn. *Lives of North American Birds*. Boston: Houghton Mifflin, 1996. (a wonderful mini-encyclopedia with great information on habitat, diet, nesting, behavior, conservation, etc. for every species of bird in North America)

Kozloff, Eugene N. *Plants and Animals of the Pacific Northwest*. Seattle: University of Washington Press, 1976. (might be a bit technical for some beginners)

Kress, Stephen W. *Bird Life: A Guide to the Behavior and Biology of Birds, a Golden Guide*. Racine, WI: Western, 1991. (one of those awesome little Golden Guides with all the basics for beginners, adults or kids)

Larrison, Earl J. *Mammals of the Northwest*. Seattle: Seattle Audubon Society, 1976.

Leonard, W. P., et al. *Amphibians of Washington and Oregon*. Seattle: Seattle Audubon Society, 1993. (awesome photos)

Levi, Herbert and Lorna. *Spiders and Their Kin, a Golden Guide*. Racine, WI: Western, 1968. (the only good book for average folks on identifying arachnids)

Maser, Chris. *Mammals of the Pacific Northwest: from the Coast to the High Cascades*. Corvallis: Oregon State University Press, 1998. (comprehensive natural history)

Mathews, Daniel. *Cascade-Olympic Natural History*, 2nd ed. Portland: Raven Editions/Portland Audubon Society, 1999. (complete natural history guide for our mountains in one small book, much applies to the Portland area)

McGavin, George C., and Richard Lewington, Illus. *Insects*. American Nature Guides Series. New York: Smithmark, 1992. (good drawings of a good selection of common insects)

Metro. *GreenScene*, quarterly listing of natural history tours, classes, and events throughout the Portland-Vancouver region, published by Metro's Regional Parks and Greenspaces program.

Mitchell, Robert, and Herbert Zim. *Butterflies and Moths, a Golden Guide*. Racine, WI: Western, 1964. (great for all beginners, about the only book with moths)

Murie, Olaus J. *A Field Guide to Animal Tracks*. A "Peterson Series" guide. Boston: Houghton Mifflin, 1954. (this great classic is still very useful)

National Geographic Society. *Field Guide to the Birds of North America*, 3rd. ed. Washington, DC: National Geographic Society, 1999. (too much for beginners but a favorite of advanced birders)

Nehls, Harry B. *Familiar Birds of the Northwest*, 3rd ed. Portland: Portland Audubon Society, 1989. ("personal" and local information on our birds)

Niehaus, Theodore, and Charles Ripper. *A Field Guide to Pacific States Wildflowers*. A "Peterson Series" guide. Boston: Houghton Mifflin, 1976. (covers a huge area so many local species are missing, but very easy to use and great for identifying families and genera)

Norse, Elliott. *Ancient Forests of the Pacific Northwest*. Washington, DC: Island Press, 1990.

Paulsen, Dennis. *Dragonflies of Washington*. Seattle: Seattle Audubon Society, 1999.

Peterson, Roger T. *A Field Guide to Western Birds*, 3rd. ed. A "Peterson Series" guide. Boston: Houghton Mifflin Co., 1990. (still the best all-around bird identification guide)

Pojar, Jim, and Andy MacKinnon. *Plants of the Pacific Northwest Coast*. Edmonton: Lone Pine, 1994. (excellent and the only plant book to include trees, shrubs, flowers, mosses, and lichens in one volume)

Pyle, Robert Michael. *The Butterflies of Cascadia: A Guide to All the Species of the Pacific Northwest*. Seattle: Seattle Audubon Society, 2000.

Reid, George K. *Pond Life, a Golden Guide*. Racine, WI: Western, 1987. (another one of those great little Golden Guides that has the most common animals and plants beginners will find)

Saling, Ann. *The Great Northwest Nature Factbook*. Seattle: Alaska Northwest Books, 1991. (amazing "factoids" about animals, plants, and geology)

Schwartz, Susan. *Nature in the Northwest.* Englewood Cliffs: Prentice-Hall, 1983. (good introduction to the natural history of the region)

Scott, Douglas. *Heritage from the Wild: Familiar Land and Sea Mammals of the Northwest.* Bozeman, MT: Northwest Panorama, 1985.

Sheldon, Ian. *Animal Tracks of Washington and Oregon.* Edmonton: Lone Pine, 1997. (very handy pocket-sized guide)

Steelquist, Robert. *Field Guide to the Pacific Salmon.* Seattle: Sasquatch, 1992.

Stokes, Donald. *A Guide to Bird Behavior, Vol. 1* (1979) and Donald and Lillian Stokes, *A Guide to Bird Behavior, Vols. 2 and 3* (1983 and 1989). Boston: Little, Brown. (outstanding books with fascinating details of common birds' behavior)

Stokes, Donald. *A Guide to Observing Insect Lives.* Boston: Little, Brown, 1983. (get the real inside story on the amazing lives of some of our most common insects)

Stokes, Donald and Lillian. *Stokes Beginner's Guide to Birds, Western Region.* Boston: Little, Brown, 1996. (absolutely the best *beginner's* bird guide, all photographs)

Teale, Edwin W. *The Strange Lives of Familiar Insects.* New York: Dodd, Mead, 1962. (one of the great American "bug classics")

Terres, John K. *The Audubon Society Encyclopedia of North American Birds.* New York, Alfred Knopf, 1980. (huge, comprehensive home reference book)

Tualatin Riverkeepers. *Tualatin Riverkeepers' Guide to Wildlife Viewing in the Tualatin Basin.* Sherwood, OR: Tualatin Riverkeepers, 2000.

Tuttle, Merlin. *America's Neighborhood Bats.* Austin: University of Texas Press, 1988.

Wahl, Terence, and Dennis Paulson. *A Guide to Bird Finding in Washington.* Bellingham, WA: T. R. Wahl, 1991.

Whitaker, John. *The Audubon Society Field Guide to North American Mammals.* New York: Alfred Knopf, 1980. (all photographs, lots of great information)

Whitney, Stephen. *A Sierra Club Naturalist's Guide to the Pacific Northwest.* San Francisco: Sierra Club Books, 1989. (good introduction to the main habitats)

Whittlesey, Rhoda. *Familiar Friends: Northwest Plants.* Portland: Rose Press, 1985. (lots of interesting tidbits on our most common local plants)

Yuskavitch, James. *Oregon Wildlife Viewing Guide.* Helena, MT: Falcon Press, 1994.

Zim, Herbert, and Clarence Cottam. *Insects, a Golden Guide.* Racine, WI: Western, 1987. (a great way to get started on those bugs)

Zim, Herbert, and Donald Hoffmeister. *Mammals, a Golden Guide.* Racine, WI: Western, 1987. (yet another Golden Guide with all the basics that is very easy to use)

Zim, Herbert, and Hurst Shoemaker. *Fishes, a Golden Guide.* Racine, WI: Western, 1987. (where would we be without Golden Guides?)

Editor's Note: This bibliography was compiled by James Davis based on research for his book *Seasonal Guide to the Natural Year: Oregon, Washington, British Columbia.* These are the most helpful books for identifying the plants and animals in our area and learning about their natural history. They were selected because they are the most relevant to the greater Portland metropolitan area but they all cover a greater range and are useful for much of the Northwest. Other references were added by contributors to *Wild In The City.*

Checklist of Portland Area Birds

By Harry B. Nehls

Range

Portland metropolitan area, including Forest Grove, Sauvie Island, Ridgefield National Wildlife Refuge, Vancouver and Washougal, Washington, the Sandy River Delta, south to Canby and Wilsonville.

Seasons

Sp March through May
S June and July
F August through October
W November through February

Status

c **Common:** seldom missed in proper habitat

u **Uncommon:** usually present in proper habitat but may not always be seen; may be present in low numbers.

r **Rare:** only a few individuals seen in a year; may be some years with no sightings. May be local in distribution.

ca **Casual:** Seldom seen. May be out of range birds, or birds present in very low numbers.

n Nests in Portland area.

Species	Sp	S	F	W
Loons and Grebes				
Red-throated Loon	r	–	r	r
Pacific Loon	r	–	ca	r
Common Loon	r	r	r	r
Pied-billed Grebe	u	u	u	u	n
Horned Grebe	r	–	r	r
Red-necked Grebe	ca	–	–	ca
Eared Grebe	r	–	r	r
Western Grebe	u	–	r	u
Clark's Grebe	ca	–	ca	ca
Pelicans and Cormorants				
American White Pelican	ca	ca	ca	ca

Species	Sp	S	F	W
Brown Pelican	–	–	ca	ca
Double-crested Cormorant	c	r	c	c
Bitterns, Herons, and Ibises				
American Bittern	u	u	u	r	n
Great Blue Heron	c	c	c	c	n
Great Egret	u	r	u	u	n
Snowy Egret	–	–	ca	–
Cattle Egret	r	–	r	r
Green Heron	u	u	u	r	n
Black-crowned Night-Heron	r	ca	r	u
White-faced Ibis	r	–	ca	ca
New World Vultures				
Turkey Vulture	u	u	u	–	n
Ducks, Geese, and Swans				
Greater White-fronted Goose	u	–	u	r
Emperor Goose	ca	–	–	ca
Snow Goose	u	–	u	r
Ross's Goose	r	–	ca	ca
Canada Goose	c	c	c	c	n
Brant	r	–	r	r
Trumpeter Swan	r	–	–	r
Tundra Swan	u	–	r	c
Wood Duck	u	u	u	u	n
Gadwall	u	r	u	u
Eurasian Wigeon	u	–	u	u
American Wigeon	c	r	c	c
Mallard	c	c	c	c	n
Blue-winged Teal	u	u	u	ca	n
Cinnamon Teal	u	c	u	r	n
Northern Shoveler	c	r	c	c	n
Northern Pintail	c	ca	c	c
Green-winged Teal	c	r	c	c
Canvasback	u	–	r	u
Redhead	r	–	r	r
Ring-necked Duck	c	r	c	c
Tufted Duck	ca	–	ca	ca
Greater Scaup	r	–	r	r
Lesser Scaup	c	r	u	c
Harlequin Duck	ca	–	–	–
Surf Scoter	ca	–	r	ca

Species	Sp	S	F	W	
White-winged Scoter	–	–	ca	ca	
Long-tailed Duck	–	–	–	ca	
Bufflehead	c	r	u	c	
Common Goldeneye	u	–	r	u	
Barrow's Goldeneye	–	–	ca	ca	
Hooded Merganser	u	u	u	u	n
Common Merganser	c	r	u	c	
Red-breasted Merganser	ca	–	ca	r	
Ruddy Duck	u	r	u	u	n
Hawks, Eagles, and Falcons					
Osprey	u	u	u	ca	n
White-tailed Kite	ca	ca	ca	ca	
Bald Eagle	u	u	u	u	n
Northern Harrier	u	u	u	u	n
Sharp-shinned Hawk	u	r	u	u	n
Cooper's Hawk	u	r	u	u	n
Northern Goshawk	ca	–	ca	r	
Red-shouldered Hawk	ca	–	ca	ca	
Swainson's Hawk	ca	–	ca	–	
Red-tailed Hawk	c	c	c	c	n
Ferruginous Hawk	ca	–	ca	ca	
Rough-legged Hawk	u	–	r	u	
Golden Eagle	ca	–	ca	ca	
American Kestrel	c	c	c	c	n
Merlin	r	–	r	r	
Gyrfalcon	ca	–	ca	ca	
Peregrine Falcon	u	u	u	u	n
Prairie Falcon	–	–	ca	ca	
Pheasants, Grouse, and Quail					
Ring-necked Pheasant	u	u	u	u	n
Ruffed Grouse	r	r	r	r	n
California Quail	u	u	u	u	n
Rails, Coots, and Cranes					
Virginia Rail	u	u	u	u	n
Sora	u	u	u	u	n
American Coot	c	u	c	c	n
Sandhill Crane	c	ca	c	c	
Shorebirds					
Black-bellied Plover	r	–	u	ca	
American Golden-Plover	–	–	r	–	
Pacific-Golden-Plover	–	–	–	ca	
Semipalmated Plover	r	r	u	–	
Killdeer	c	c	c	c	n
Black-necked Stilt	r	–	ca	–	
American Avocet	r	–	r	–	
Greater Yellowlegs	u	r	u	r	

Species	Sp	S	F	W	
Lesser Yellowlegs	u	r	u	–	
Solitary Sandpiper	r	–	r	–	
Willet	ca	–	–	–	
Spotted Sandpiper	u	u	u	r	n
Whimbrel	ca	–	ca	–	
Long-billed Curlew	ca	–	ca	–	
Marbled Godwit	ca	–	ca	–	
Ruddy Turnstone	–	–	ca	–	
Black Turnstone	ca	–	ca	–	
Sanderling	ca	–	r	ca	
Semipalmated Sandpiper	ca	ca	r	–	
Western Sandpiper	c	c	c	r	
Least Sandpiper	c	c	c	u	
Baird's Sandpiper	ca	ca	r	–	
Pectoral Sandpiper	–	r	u	–	
Sharp-tailed Sandpiper	–	–	ca	–	
Dunlin	c	–	r	c	
Stilt Sandpiper	–	–	r	–	
Buff-breasted Sandpiper	–	–	ca	–	
Ruff	–	ca	ca	–	
Short-billed Dowitcher	r	ca	r	–	
Long-billed Dowitcher	c	r	c	u	
Common Snipe	u	r	u	u	n
Wilson's Phalarope	r	r	r	–	
Red-necked Phalarope	u	–	u	–	
Red Phalarope	–	ca	ca	ca	
Gulls and Terns					
Franklin's Gull	ca	–	r	ca	
Bonaparte's Gull	r	r	r	r	
Heermann's Gull	–	–	ca	–	
Mew Gull	c	r	c	c	
Ring-billed Gull	c	u	c	c	
California Gull	c	u	c	c	
Herring Gull	c	–	u	c	
Thayer's Gull	c	–	r	c	
Slaty-backed Gull	r	–	–	r	
Western Gull	r	–	r	r	
Glaucous-winged Gull	c	r	c	c	n
Glaucous Gull	r	–	–	r	
Sabine's Gull	–	–	ca	–	
Black-legged Kittiwake	ca	–	ca	–	
Caspian Tern	u	u	u	–	
Common Tern	–	–	r	–	
Arctic Tern	–	ca	ca	–	
Forster's Tern	ca	ca	ca	–	
Least Tern	ca	–	–	–	

Species	Sp	S	F	W	
Black Tern	ca	–	–	–	
Pigeons, Doves, Parrots, and Cuckoos					
Rock Dove	c	c	c	c	n
Band-tailed Pigeon	c	c	c	u	n
Mourning Dove	c	c	c	u	n
Monk Parakeet	u	u		u	n
Yellow-billed Cuckoo	–	–	ca	–	
Owls					
Barn Owl	u	u	u	u	n
Western Screech-Owl	u	u	u	u	n
Great Horned Owl	u	u	u	u	n
Snowy Owl	ca	–	–	ca	
Northern Pygmy-Owl	u	r	u	u	n
Barred Owl	ca	ca	ca	ca	
Long-eared Owl	ca	ca	ca	ca	
Short-eared Owl	r	–	–	r	
Northern Saw-whet Owl	u	u	u	u	n
Nighthawks and Swifts					
Common Nighthawk	ca	u	u	–	n
Common Poorwill	ca	–	–	–	
Black Swift	ca	ca	ca	–	
Vaux's Swift	c	c	c	–	n
White-throated Swift	ca	–	–	–	
Hummingbirds					
Black-chinned Hummingbird	ca	ca	–	–	
Anna's Hummingbird	u	u	u	u	n
Costa's Hummingbird	ca	ca	ca	ca	
Calliope Hummingbird	ca	–	–	–	
Rufous Hummingbird	c	c	u	ca	n
Kingfishers					
Belted Kingfisher	u	u	u	u	n
Woodpeckers					
Lewis's Woodpecker	ca	–	ca	ca	
Acorn Woodpecker	u	u	u	u	n
Red-breasted Sapsucker	u	u	u	u	n
Downy Woodpecker	c	c	c	c	n
Hairy Woodpecker	u	u	u	u	n
Northern Flicker	c	c	c	c	n
Pileated Woodpecker	u	u	u	u	n
Flycatchers					
Olive-sided Flycatcher	r	r	r	–	n
Western Wood-Pewee	u	u	u	–	n
Willow Flycatcher	u	u	u	–	n
Least Flycatcher	–	ca	ca	–	n
Hammond's Flycatcher	u	u	u	–	n
Dusky Flycatcher	ca	–	ca	–	

Species	Sp	S	F	W	
Pacific-slope Flycatcher	u	u	u	–	n
Black Phoebe	–	–	–	ca	
Say's Phoebe	r	–	–	ca	
Vermilion Flycatcher	–	–	–	ca	
Ash-throated Flycatcher	ca	ca	ca	–	
Tropical Kingbird	–	–	–	ca	
Western Kingbird	r	ca	ca	–	n
Eastern Kingbird	ca	ca	ca	–	n
Shrikes					
Loggerhead Shrike	ca	–	–	ca	
Northern Shrike	r	–	ca	r	
Vireos					
Cassin's Vireo	r	r	r	–	n
Hutton's Vireo	r	r	r	r	n
Warbling Vireo	u	u	u	–	n
Red-eyed Vireo	ca	r	r	–	n
Jays and Crows					
Gray Jay	ca	–	–	ca	
Steller's Jay	c	c	c	c	n
Blue Jay	ca	–	–	ca	
Western Scrub-Jay	c	c	c	c	n
Black-billed Magpie	ca	–	ca	ca	
American Crow	c	c	c	c	n
Common Raven	ca	–	ca	ca	
Larks					
Horned Lark	–	–	ca	ca	
Swallows					
Purple Martin	u	u	u	–	n
Tree Swallow	c	c	c	u	n
Violet-green Swallow	c	c	c	u	n
Northern Rough-winged Swallow	c	c	c	–	n
Bank Swallow	–	–	ca	–	
Cliff Swallow	c	c	c	–	n
Barn Swallow	c	c	c	r	n
Chickadees, Nuthatches, and Creepers					
Black-capped Chickadee	c	c	c	c	n
Mountain Chickadee	ca	ca	ca	ca	
Chestnut-backed Chickadee	c	c	c	c	n
Bushtit	c	c	c	c	n
Red-breasted Nuthatch	c	c	c	c	n
White-breasted Nuthatch	u	u	u	u	n
Brown Creeper	u	u	u	u	n
Wrens					
Rock Wren	ca	–	–	–	
Bewick's Wren	u	u	u	u	n

Species	Sp	S	F	W	
House Wren	c	c	c	–	n
Winter Wren	u	r	u	u	n
Marsh Wren	c	c	c	u	n
Dippers					
American Dipper	ca	–	–	r	
Kinglets					
Golden-crowned Kinglet	c	c	c	c	n
Ruby-crowned Kinglet	c	–	c	c	
Thrushes					
Western Bluebird	r	r	r	r	n
Mountain Bluebird	ca	–	–	ca	
Townsend's Solitaire	r	–	r	r	
Swainson's Thrush	u	c	c	–	n
Hermit Thrush	u	–	ca	u	
American Robin	c	c	c	c	n
Varied Thrush	c	r	u	c	
Thrashers					
Northern Mockingbird	ca	–	ca	ca	
Sage Thrasher	ca	–	–		
Brown Thrasher	ca	ca	–	ca	
Starlings, Pipits, and Waxwings					
European Starling	c	c	c	c	n
American Pipit	c	–	c	r	
Bohemian Waxwing	ca	–	–	ca	
Cedar Waxwing	u	u	u	u	n
Warblers					
Tennessee Warbler	ca	–	–	ca	
Orange-crowned Warbler	c	c	u	r	n
Nashville Warbler	u	–	ca	–	
Yellow Warbler	u	u	u	ca	n
Yellow-rumped Warbler	c	r	u	u	
Black-throated Gray Warbler	c	u	u	ca	n
Townsend's Warbler	c	r	u	r	
Hermit Warbler	r	–	–	ca	
Palm Warbler	ca	–	–	ca	
Black-and-white Warbler	ca	ca	ca	ca	
MacGillivray's Warbler	u	r	r	–	n
Common Yellowthroat	c	c	c	r	n
Wilson's Warbler	c	c	u	–	n
Yellow-breasted Chat	r	r	–	–	n
Tanagers					
Western Tanager	c	u	u	–	n
Sparrows					
Spotted Towhee	c	c	c	c	n
American Tree Sparrow	ca	–	–	ca	
Chipping Sparrow	u	u	r	ca	n

Species	Sp	S	F	W	
Clay-colored Sparrow	ca	–	ca	ca	
Brewer's Sparrow	ca	–	–	–	
Vesper Sparrow	ca	ca	ca	ca	
Lark Sparrow	ca	–	ca	–	
Black-throated Sparrow	ca	–	–	–	
Sage Sparrow	ca	–	–	ca	
Lark Bunting	ca	–	–	–	
Savannah Sparrow	c	c	c	r	n
Fox Sparrow	u	–	u	u	
Song Sparrow	c	c	c	c	n
Lincoln's Sparrow	u	–	u	u	
Swamp Sparrow	r	–	ca	r	
White-throated Sparrow	u	–	r	u	
Harris's Sparrow	r	–	–	r	
White-crowned Sparrow	u	u	u	u	n
Golden-crowned Sparrow	c	r	c	c	
Dark-eyed Junco	c	u	c	c	n
Lapland Longspur	–	–	ca	ca	
Snow Bunting	–	–	–	ca	
Grosbeaks					
Black-headed Grosbeak	c	c	u	–	n
Lazuli Bunting	u	u	–	–	n
Blackbirds					
Red-winged Blackbird	c	c	c	c	n
Tricolored Blackbird	r	r	–	–	n
Western Meadowlark	u	r	u	u	n
Yellow-headed Blackbird	u	u	u	ca	n
Rusty Blackbird	–	–	–	ca	
Brewer's Blackbird	c	c	c	c	n
Brown-headed Cowbird	c	c	c	r	n
Bullock's Oriole	c	c	u	–	n
Finches					
Brambling	ca	–	–	ca	
Purple Finch	r	r	r	r	n
House Finch	c	c	c	c	n
Red Crossbill	r	r	r	r	n
Common Redpoll	ca	–	ca	ca	
Pine Siskin	u	u	u	u	n
Lesser Goldfinch	r	r	r	r	n
American Goldfinch	u	u	c	u	n
Evening Grosbeak	c	u	u	u	n
Old World Sparrows					
House Sparrow	c	c	c	c	n

Resources

Audubon Society of Portland
5151 NW Cornell Rd.
Portland, OR 97210
503-292-6855
Nature Store: 503-292-9453
Web: www.audubonportland.org

Blue and Fairview Lake Land Trust
PO Box 367
Fairview, OR 97024
503-667-0879

Blue Lake Regional Park
20500 NE Marine Dr.
Troutdale, OR 97024
503-665-4995
Web: www.metro-region.org/parks/
    parkfacils.html

Cathlapotle
U.S. Fish and Wildlife Service, Cultural Resources Team
20555 SW Gerda Ln.
Sherwood, OR 97140
503-625-4377

Cedar Mill Creek Watershed Watch
1405 NE Broadway
Portland, OR 97232
503-288-9338

Chinook Trail Association
PO Box 997
Vancouver, WA 98666-0997
Web: www.chinooktrail.org
E-mail: cta@pacifier.com

Clackamas County Parks Department
9101 SE Sunnybrook Blvd.
Clackamas, OR 97015
503-353-4415
Web: www.co.clackamas.or.us/dtd/parks/
    htmls/park.html

Columbia Slough Watershed Council
7040 NE 47th Ave.
Portland, OR 97218
503-281-1132

Crystal Springs Rhododendron Garden
PO Box 86424
Portland, OR 97286
503-771-8386
Web: www.parks.ci.portland.or.us/Parks/
    CrysSpringRhodGar.htm

Fans of Fanno Creek
PO Box 25835
Portland, OR 97225-0835

Friends of Jackson Bottom
PO Box 114
Hillsboro, OR 97123

Friends of Marquam Nature Park
PO Box 8932
Portland, OR 97207

Friends of Mt. Scott and Kellogg Creeks
PO Box 22373
Milwaukie, OR 97269

Friends of the Peninsula Crossing Trail
503-289-9475

Friends of Powell Butte
503-972-7714

Friends of Smith and Bybee Lakes
PO Box 83862
Portland, OR 97203
503-283-1145

Friends of Tryon Creek State Park
11321 SW Terwilliger Blvd.
Portland, OR 97219
503-636-4398

Friends of the Tualatin River National Wildlife Refuge
PO Box 1306
Sherwood, OR 97140
503-625-1205

Gresham Parks
1333 NW Eastman Pkwy.
Gresham, OR 97030-3825
503-618-2485
Web: www.ci.gresham.or.us/departments/
    des/parksandrec/

Hoyt Arboretum
4000 SW Fairview Blvd.
Portland, OR 97221
503-228-8733
Web: www.parks.ci.portland.or.us/Parks/
 HoytArboretum.htm

Hoyt Arboretum Friends Foundation
4000 SW Fairview Blvd.
Portland, OR 97221
503-228-8733

Jackson Bottom Wetland Preserve
2600 SW Hillsboro Hwy.
Hillsboro, OR 97123
503-681-6206
Fax: 503-681-6277
Web: www.jacksonbottom.org

John Inskeep Environmental Learning Center
19600 S Molalla Ave.
Oregon City, OR 97045
503-657-6958, ext. 2351
Fax: 503-650-6669
Web: depts.clackamas.cc.or.us/elc/index.htm

Lake Oswego Parks and Recreation
380 A Avenue
PO Box 369
Lake Oswego, OR 97034
503-636-9673
Web: www.ci.oswego.or.us/PARKSREC/
 geninfo.htm

Metro Regional Environmental Management: St. Johns Landfill Section
503-286-9615

Metro Regional Parks and Greenspaces
600 NE Grand Ave.
Portland, OR 97232
503-797-1850
Fax: 503-797-1849
Web: www.metro-region.org

Multnomah County Drainage District #1
503-281-5675

The Nature Conservancy of Oregon
821 SE 14th Ave.
Portland, OR 97214
503-230-1221
Web: www.tnc.org/oregon/oregon.htm

North Clackamas Park District
11022 SE 37th
Milwaukie, OR 97222
503-794-8002
Fax: 503-794-8005
Web: ncprd.co.clackamas.or.us/
 ncprd.index.html

Oregon Department of Fish and Wildlife Sauvie Island Wildlife Area
503-621-3488

Oregon Episcopal School
6300 SW Nicol Rd.
Portland, OR 97223
503-246-7771

Oregon State Parks and Recreation: Champoeg State Park
503-678-1251

Oregon State Parks and Recreation: Tryon Creek State Park
11321 SW Terwilliger Blvd.
Portland, OR 97219
503-636-9886
Fax: 503-636-5318
Web: www.ohwy.com/or/t/tryoncrk.HTM

Oxbow Regional Park
3010 SE Oxbow Pkwy.
Gresham, OR 97080-8916
503-663-4708
Park Naturalist: 503-797-1899

Pittock Mansion Acres
3229 NW Pittock Dr.
Portland, OR 97210
503-823-3624
Web: www.parks.ci.portland.or.us/Parks/
 PittockManAcres.htm

Portland Bureau of Environmental Services
1120 SW 5th Ave.
Portland, OR 97204
503-823-7740
Fax: 503-823-5344
Web: www.enviro.ci.portland.or.us

Portland Bureau of Parks and Recreation
1120 SW 5th Ave.
Portland, OR 97204
503-823-2223
Fax: 503-823-6007
Web: www.parks.ci.portland.or.us
Or: www.portlandparks.org

Reed College
3203 SE Woodstock Blvd.
Portland, OR 97202-8199
503-771-1112

Ridgefield National Wildlife Refuge Complex
301 N 3rd Ave.
PO Box 457
Ridgefield, WA 98462
360-887-4106
Fax: 360-887-4109

Three Rivers Land Conservancy
PO Box 1116
Lake Oswego, OR 97035
503-699-9825
Fax: 503-699-9827
Web: www.trlc.org
E-mail: trlc@teleport.com

Tigard Parks Department
13125 SW Hall Blvd.
Tigard, OR 97223
503-639-4171
Fax: 503-684-7297
Web: www.ci.tigard.or.us/PARKS/PARKS.HTM

Tualatin Hills Nature Park Interpretive Center
15655 SW Millikan Blvd.
Beaverton, OR 97006
503-644-5595
Fax: 503-641-7761
Web: www.thprd.org
E-mail: nature1@thprd.com

Tualatin Hills Park and Recreation District
15707 SW Walker Rd.
Beaverton, OR 97006
503-645-6433
Fax: 503-690-9649
Web: www.thprd.org
E-mail: nature@thprd.org

Tualatin Parks Department
8515 SW Tualatin Rd.
Tualatin, OR 97062
503-692-2000,ext. 932
Web: www.ci.tualatin.or.us

Tualatin River National Wildlife Refuge
16340 SW Beef Bend Rd.
Sherwood, OR 97140-8306
503-590-5811

Tualatin Riverkeepers
16340 SW Beef Bend Rd.
Sherwood, OR 97140-8306
503-590-5813

U.S. Fish and Wildlife Service
36062 SR 14
Stevenson, WA 98648
509-427-4723
Fax: 509-427-4707
Web: www.r1.fws.gov/gorgefish/
    HOME.MAIN.HTM

**U.S. Forest Service,
Mt. St. Helens Monument District**
42218 NE Yale Bridge Rd.
Amboy, WA 98601-9715
360-247-3900

Urban Bounty Farm
503-282-4245

Vancouver-Clark Parks and Recreation Services
PO Box 1995
Vancouver, WA 98668-1995
360-696-8171
Fax: 360-696-8009
Web: www.ci.vancouver.wa.us/vanparks/
    parks.htm

Vancouver Water Resources Education Center
4600 SE Columbia Way
PO Box 1995
Vancouver, WA 98668-1995
360-696-8478
Fax: 360-693-8878
Web: www.ci.vancouver.wa.us

Washington Department of Fish and Wildlife
2108 Grand Blvd.
Vancouver, WA 98661
360-696-6211
Web: www.wa.gov/wdfw

Washington Department of Natural Resources
PO Box 280
Castle Rock, WA 98611
360-577-2025

West Linn Parks Department
22500 Salamo Rd.
West Linn, OR 97068
503-557-4700

The Wetlands Conservancy
5485 SW Nyberg Ln.
Tualatin, OR 97062
503-691-1394
E-mail: wetlands@teleport.com

About the Contributors

Roger Anderson is a long-time employee of Vancouver-Clark Parks and Recreation Services and a board member of the Chinook Trail Association.

Elayne Barclay is an artist and naturalist in the Portland area. She was formerly a naturalist with Tualatin Hills Park and Recreation District.

Diana Bradshaw dabbles in all sorts of things. She is an illustrator and graphic designer who enjoys birdwatching and natural history.

Eric Brattain is an educator with Forest Grove School District and an Ed. D candidate in curriculum and instruction, with emphasis on community and environmental renewal, at Portland State University. He is the coordinator for the Friends of Fern Hill Wetlands.

Don Cannard is the co-founder of Chinook Trail Association and a long-time Vancouver Audubon member.

Ron Carley is a native Oregonian who grew up thriving on what Robert Michael Pyle refers to as "hand-me-down habitats." He is the Urban Conservationist for the Audubon Society of Portland, where he has worked for the last eight years.

Virginia Church is an artist and long-time contributor to the *Urban Naturalist.*

Paul Clare is a long-time Clark County Washington preservationist.

M.J. Cody was an art director and television writer who is currently the editor of *Best Places to Stay/Pacific Northwest,* and writes a travel column in the Sunday *Oregonian.*

Robin Cody is the Portland author of *Ricochet River,* a novel, and *Voyage of a Summer Sun,* exploring the Columbia River at water level.

Jayne Cronlund is the executive director of Three Rivers Land Conservancy.

Victoria Crowe works for the Audubon Society of Portland and makes art—from fledgling shapes to avian landscapes.

James L. Davis is a Metro Parks Naturalist and author of the *Seasonal Guide to the Natural Year: Oregon, Washington, British Columbia.*

Peter DeChant is a Field Development Specialist with Valent BioSciences Corporation. Since 1997, Peter has been working to increase the global utility of naturally occurring microbial agents for mosquito control.

Bob Duke is a "Special Science Writer" for the Oregonian.

Bill Dygert is a park and natural resources consultant who specializes in community-based planning, grant writing, and project management. He is a principal in the Vancouver-based firm of Dygert and Simpson.

Eric R. Eaton is an entomologist, researcher, writer, and illustrator.

Kris Elkin is a graphic designer, illustrator, and artist.

Nancy Ellifrit is a retired U.S. Fish and Wildlife biologist, environmentalist, and member of Vancouver Audubon Society.

Bill Feddeler is a retired science educator and volunteer for the Sierra Club, Vancouver Audubon Society, City of Vancouver Water Resources Education Center, the Environmental Information Cooperative at Washington State University, and Habitat Partners, a non-profit group in Vancouver, Washington.

Richard Forbes is Professor of Biology at Portland State University, where he teaches classes in mammalogy, ornithology, herpetology, vertebrate zoology, and Principles of Biology. He has studied the ecology and natural history of terrestrial vertebrates in Oregon for more than 30 years.

Christie Galen is an ecologist who has lived in the Northwest all her life.

Marshall Gannett is a professional geologist, living in Portland, who specializes in regional groundwater hydrology.

Martha Gannett is a graphic designer, and long-time Audubon Society of Portland volunteer.

Bruce Godfrey is a resident of Cedar Mill Creek watershed and is a member of the Cedar Mill Creek Watershed Watch grassroots organization.

Tom Hanrahan is a frequent contributor to Portland Audubon Society publications.

Evelyn Hicks is a Portland illustrator who has done work for both the *Urban Naturalist* and for the Oregon Historical Society Press.

Jeff Holm is Refuge Manager, U.S. Fish and Wildlife Service, Columbia River Gorge National Wildlife Refuges.

Mike Houck has been Audubon Society of Portland's Urban Naturalist since 1982, when the Society initiated its Urban Naturalist Program.

Lynn Kitagawa is a Medical Illustrator at the VA Medical Center, and faculty member at the Pacific Northwest College of Art.

Ray Korpi is an instructor of English at Clark College and President of Oregon Field Ornithologists. He has recently completed his doctoral dissertation on the history and evolution of bird field guides.

John LeCavalier was president of Fans of Fanno Creek and taught biology at Oregon Episcopal School for several years. He is currently the executive director at the John Inskeep Environmental Learning Center at Clackamas Community College.

Deborah Lev, formerly the Natural Resources Coordinator for the City of Lake Oswego, works for the City of Portland Park Bureau.

Connie Levesque is a freelance writer and long-time Audubon Society of Portland volunteer. She lives in Southwest Portland with her husband and angora rabbit.

Mitch Luckett is the Sanctuaries Director for the Audubon Society of Portland.

David B. Marshall is a consulting wildlife biologist.

Donna Matrazzo is a scriptwriter who specializes in nature films.

Tom McAllister is a writer-lecturer who has spent a lifetime covering the Pacific Northwest outdoor scene. He was the outdoor editor of the *Oregon Journal* and the *Oregonian* daily newspapers for 39 years. He has been a member of the Audubon Society of Portland since 1939.

Bruce McCullough lives on a farm near Eagle Creek.

Holly Michael is the wildlife diversity biologist for the North Willamette District of the Oregon Department of Fish and Wildlife, Northwest region. Her life-long interests include hummingbirds, Native American history, and the Lewis and Clark Corps of Discovery.

Karen Murray grew up in Portland and is currently a biologist for the Oregon Department of Fish and Wildlife, with hopes of getting into the field of conservation biology and going to graduate school soon. Her senior thesis at Vassar College was on Portland's 40-Mile Loop.

Mary Rose Navarro has been engaging citizens in environmental issues for over six years, as planting coordinator for Friends of Trees, as Urban Forestry Coordinator for Portland Parks and Recreation, and as Public Involvement Coordinator for Portland Parks and Recreation's 2020 Vision Plan.

Elisabeth Neely is the naturalist at Oxbow Regional Park, where she enjoys leading natural history programs, tracking foxes, and searching for salamanders.

Harry B. Nehls is the Field Notes editor for the Audubon Society of Portland newsletter, the "Audubon Warbler," and is the secretary of the Oregon Bird Records Committee. He is also the author of *Familiar Birds of the Northwest*.

Carol Peterson is the education specialist for Vancouver Audubon Society. She is an educator and naturalist for programs facilitating environmental workshops for adults.

Nancy Pollot is a naturalist who works as an information and education specialist at U.S. Fish and Wildlife Service.

Joe Poracsky is Professor of Geography at Portland State University and Chair of Portland's Urban Forestry Commission.

Robert Michael Pyle has written *Wintergreen, The Thunder Tree, Where Bigfoot Walks, Chasing Monarchs*, and a flight of butterfly books.

Florence Riddle is a retired English professor and a longtime contributor to the *Urban Naturalist.*

Ralph Thomas Rogers is the Regional Wetland Ecologist at the Environmental Protection Agency, Region 10, and an avid odonate watcher.

Bob Sallinger is Director of the Audubon Society of Portland Wildlife Care Center and Portland Peregrine Watch Coordinator.

Galen Schoenthal is an outdoorsman and past president of the Vancouver Audubon Society, and is active in nature conservancy. He works with Clark County Parks installing and maintaining wood duck nest boxes.

Ethan Seltzer is the Director of the Institute of Portland Metropolitan Studies at Portland State University, and a resident of Northeast Portland.

Lynn Sharp is an ecologist whose work in the Portland area includes participation in the Metro Greenspaces inventory, performing landscape ecology work in the West Hills, and acting as a Regional Advisory Board member for the North Clackamas Park and Recreation District.

Kathy Shinn is the regional outreach specialist for Oregon Department of Fish and Wildlife, working most recently as an information and education specialist in the Northwest Region Office in Clackamas. She is a member of the Audubon Society of Portland and was on the Board of Directors and Chair of the Education Committee in the 1980s.

Mary Anne Sohlstrom is a life-long birder, secretary of the Oregon Field Ornithologists, and the office manager for The Wetlands Conservancy, an Oregon Land Trust dedicated to preserving wetlands.

Kim Stafford is the Director of the Northwest Writing Institute at Lewis and Clark College, and the author of several works, including *A Thousand Friends of Rain: New and Selected Poems* and *Having Everything Right,* a selection of essays.

Jennifer Thompson is the Metropolitan Greenspaces Program Biologist for U.S. Fish and Wildlife Service.

Pat Willis is the Executive Director of Jackson Bottoms Wetlands Preserve and has been active in environmental education in Oregon for 20 years.

Bob Wilson retains his fascination for the connection between the human and the wild, after 20 years of birding, botanizing, and beating around the urban bush. He is also an Audubon Society of Portland staff member.

Dawn Wilson takes time off from raising her daughter by walking and sketching in Portland's urban greenspaces.

Sharon Wood Wortman is the author of *The Portland Bridge Book* (2nd ed., Oregon Historical Society Press, 2001), and has led urban bridge walks for Portland Parks and Outdoor Recreation since 1991.

Roger Yerke is Manager of Education Programs at the Oregon Zoo. In his free time he takes busman's holidays in Northwest natural areas.

We welcome inquiries and invite readers to share additional information about natural sites in the Portland metropolitan area. Please contact us online in care of the Oregon Historical Society Press at orhist@ohs.org citing Wild in the City *in the subject line.*

Illustration Credits

Elayne Barclay, *pages* 54, 102, 122, 264, 277, 333

Diana Bradshaw, *pages* 74, 110, 125, 128, 228, 243, 249, 285, 292, 301, 302, 303, 315, 330, 369, 370, 371, 381

Virginia Church, *pages* 32, 57, 73, 85, 105, 187, 195, 258, 311, 338, 360, 367

Victoria Crowe, *pages* 131, 144, 147, 148, 151, 168, 235

Eric Eaton, *pages* 77, 164, 192, 193, 216, 217, 218, 267, 393, 394

Kris Elkin, *pages* 120, 199, 200, 320

Martha Gannett, *pages* 140, 278

Evelyn Hicks, *pages* cover, ii, 79, 287, 344

Lynn Kitigawa *pages* 237, 305, 306, 345, 346, 347, 358, 401, 402, 403, 404, 405, 406

Dawn Wilson *pages* 51, 178, 189, 190, 373

Index

Salamanders, 57, 158, 159, 207, 232, 236–37, 273, 364, 389

Salix Park, 177, 183–84

Salmon and Trout, 11, 48, 49, 88, 125, 158, 178, 183, 203, 211, 224, 231, 232, 269, 273, 339–40, 353, 363, 364–67, 368–71, 380, 389, 397, 399

Salmon Creek, 104, 105, 352, 377, 389–92

Salmon Creek Park, 166, 389–92

Salmon Festival, 365

Salmon River, 363

Sandy River, 11, 17, 104, 231, 250, 257, 363–73

Sandy River Gorge, 103, 128, 129, 249, 363–67

Sandy River Gorge Trail, 100

Sandy River Mudstone, 19

Sandy River Nature Conservancy Preserve, 363

Saum Creek, 198

Sauvie Island, 10, 12, 20, 77, 87, 117, 144, 148, 166, 303, 304, 314, 323–37, 350, 352, 360, 383

Sauvie Island Bald Eagle Count, 329

Sauvie Island Bridge, 326, 328, 332, 334, 336

Sauvie Island Wildlife Area, 323, 325, 332–37

Schieffelin, Eugene, 139

Schofield, W.B., 129

Scott, Mt., 8, 19, 63, 104, 107

Scouter's Mountain, 63, 104

Seeds, 167–69, 261, 345–46

Sellwood Bridge, 67, 73, 103, 249

Sellwood-Moreland Improvement League (SMILE), 66, 71

Sellwood Pioneer Church, 66

Sellwood Riverfront Park, 66–67, 68, 88

Seltzer, Ethan, 12, 79

Sewers and sewage treatment, 36–37, 159–60, 161–63, 173, 183, 212, 224, 318–19, 348

Sharp, Lynn, 101

Shillapoo Wildlife Area, 348–51

Simon, Leo, 7

Sjulin, Jim, 71

Skamania, 339–41, 399

Slugs, 108, 121–23, 172

Smith and Bybee Lakes, 9, 76, 78, 104, 298, 303, 309–11, 316, 318, 346

South Park Blocks (downtown Portland), 93–96

Southwest Park (Gresham), 282

Spiders, 53, 185–88, 393–94

Springbrook Creek, 48

Springbrook Park, 48

Spring Park, 61–62

Springwater Corridor Trail, 37, 66, 70, 73, 99, 101, 103, 104, 105, 241, 242, 244, 246, 251, 253, 255, 258, 261, 263, 269, 282

Squirrels, 10, 93, 147–51, 171, 172, 176, 177, 209, 232, 328, 364, 395

Stafford (city), 40

Stafford, Kim, 22–23, 24–25

Stafford, William, 78

Starlings, 10, 81, 133, 134, 139–42, 359

Steamboat Landing State Park, 340

Steel Bridge, 132, 135

Steelhead, see Salmon and Trout

Steelman Lake, 325, 334

Steigerwald Lake National Wildlife Refuge, 339–41

St. Helens, Mt., 12, 108, 162, 255, 325, 332

St. Johns Bridge, 103, 104, 136, 143, 152

St. Johns Landfill, 306, 309, 316–17

St. Mary's Woods, 205

Stout, Rex, 142

Strauss, Joseph, 134

Sturgeon Lake, 325, 332, 334

Sucker Lake, see Oswego Lake

Summer Creek, 211, 212, 224

Summerlake Park, 212, 224–25

Surface Water Department (Vancouver), 378–79

Swan Island, 8, 35, 36

Swede Hill, 19

Sylvan Creek, 211

Sylvania, Mt., 19, 48, 257

Tabor, Mt., 5, 7, 12, 19, 20, 107, 128, 153–54, 257

Talbert, Mt., 63

Telfer, William H., 8 (photo)

Terres, John, 141

Threatened Species, see Endangered Species

Three Rivers Land Conservancy, 56–57

Tideman Johnson Park, 269–70

Tigard, 157, 194, 211, 212

Tigard Parks Department, 215, 225, 226–27

Toe Island, 81, 88–92

Tolan, Terry L., 20

Tom McCall Waterfront Park, 6, 12, 132, 133, 135, 146

Tonquin Scablands, 19, 203

Tracking animals, 286, 312–13, 343, 365–66

Tracking Club, 313

Trillium, 11, 21, 44, 46, 47, 51–52, 58, 62, 207, 209, 232, 271, 345, 378, 380, 383, 387, 390, 395

Trimble, D.E., 20

Trout, see Salmon and Trout

Troutdale, 99, 103, 104, 363

Troutdale Formation, 19, 257

Trust for Public Land, 152

Tryon Creek, 48–53, 370

Tryon Creek State Park, 6, 23, 47, 48, 49–50, 53, 55, 100, 101, 123, 250, 326

Tualatin Community Park, 157, 194

Tualatin Country Club, 194, 226

Tualatin Hills Nature Park, 180, 205–08, 228, 250

Tualatin Hills Park and Recreation District, 104, 170–71, 172, 174, 175–76, 177, 179–80, 184, 208, 210, 212, 215, 219–21, 313

Tualatin Mountains, 16, 17, 177, 211, 326, 332, 334; see also West Hills

Tualatin Parks Department, 197, 198

Wild in the City uses Minion typeface for the text and ITC Officina Sans for the display face. Minion was designed by Robert Slimbach for Adobe in 1990 and is inspired by classical, oldstyle typefaces of the late Renaissance, a period of elegant, beautiful, and highly readable type designs. ITC Officina was designed by Erik Spiekermann in 1990.

This book is "elegant, beautiful, and highly readable" not simply because of the work of the book's authors and illustrators. The production of this book was accomplished with the expertise and assistance of the following people.

Editorial and production oversight:	Adair Law
Editing and indexing:	Amy Stephenson
Design and layout:	Martha Gannett Design
Typography:	William H. Brunson, Typography Services
Cover illustration:	Evelyn Hicks
Maps:	Rafael Gutierrez, Martha Gannett
Printing:	Edwards Brothers, Inc., Ann Arbor, Michigan
Production assistance:	Bob Smith, BookPrinters Network

Praise for Wild in the City

" …a must have for anyone even remotely interested in signs of wildlife amid Portland's concrete canyons and manicured lawns.

Every schoolteacher should be supplied one for field trips.

Every car should be sold with one in its glove compartment.

Tuck one into every hotel room drawer next to the Gideon Bible.

Front to back there's something in this book for everyone — a trip to take, a thought to spark a memory, a term to explain." *The Oregonian*

"*Wild in the City* is, simply, great….History, geology, botany, entomology, and nearly every other science relevant to the study of the natural world and of human impacts upon it find their way into these pages….If you live in Portland, you need to get this book. If you live farther away, and want some inspiration for creating a local natural-places guide, this is the genre at its best." Eugene, *Talking Leaves*

"This book will make most readers realize just how lucky they are to live in the Pacific Northwest." Salem *Statesman Journal*

"From canoe paddles to hikes; from wetlands to ancient forests, the book encompasses the entire naturescape of the Portland-Vancouver area and is a marvelous read.

Immense in scope, the book is rich in texture because of the voices and drawings of its 60 contributors." *Daily Astorian*

"*Wild in the City* is a must for people who have only a few hours or a weekend and the urge to get out — on foot, bike, canoe or kayak. The essays and the information on everyday creatures make it acceptable reading from armchair or while watching a backyard bird feeder." Gresham *Outlook*

"[A] fascinating guide to the wild things all around us….Portland is lucky to have such a guide; every city should have one." *Northwest Palate*

"If you're someone who wants to learn more about the unspoiled natural areas that make the Portland area one of the country's most livable, then you'll want to check out *Wild in the City*." *Lake Oswego Review*

"*Wild in the City* takes readers on a delightful trip through some of the most accessible and unique natural spots in the area." Vancouver *Columbian*.